Invitation to Struggle

D1387568

Invitation to Struggle
Congress, the President, and Foreign Policy
FOURTH EDITION

Cecil V. Crabb, Jr.
Louisiana State University

Pat M. Holt
Former Staff Director,
Senate Foreign Relations Committee

A Division of Congressional Quarterly Inc.
Washington, D.C.

Copyright © 1992 Congressional Quarterly Inc.
1414 22nd Street, N.W., Washington, D.C. 20037

All rights reserved. No part of this publication may be reproduced or transmitted in any form or by any means, electronic or mechanical, including photocopy, recording, or any information storage and retrieval system, without permission in writing from the publisher.

Printed in the United States of America

Cover design: Rich Pottern

Library of Congress Cataloging-in-Publication Data

Crabb, Cecil Van Meter, 1924-
    Invitation to struggle: Congress, the president, and foreign
policy / Cecil V. Crabb, Jr., Pat M. Holt. — 4th ed.
        p.   cm.
    Includes bibliographical references and index.
    ISBN 0-87187-622-1
    1. Presidents—United States. 2. United States. Congress.
3. United States—Foreign relations—1945-   I. Holt, Pat M.
II. Title.
JK573   1991   91-30459
320.4'04'0973--dc20   CIP

CONTENTS

PART III Conclusion   **261**

PREFACE

*The Constitution ... is an invitation to struggle
for the privilege of directing American foreign policy.*

—Edward S. Corwin
The President: Office and Powers

As the United States enters its third century under the Constitution, this quotation by one of the nation's most eminent constitutional authorities remains applicable to the nation's foreign policy process. The "struggle" identified by Corwin is one of the genuinely unique features of the American system of government, and nowhere are its effects more influential than in the sphere of foreign relations.

The contest between the White House and Congress for a dominant position in the conduct of foreign affairs is one of the constants in the nation's history. At the end of the eighteenth century, President George Washington complained about what he viewed as Senate obstructionism in dealing with the proposed Jay Treaty with England. By contrast, some legislators were convinced that "His Majesty" (as Washington was sometimes described by his critics) was attempting to exclude legislators from meaningful participation in an important diplomatic undertaking. More than a century later, the struggle was exemplified by the conflict between President Woodrow Wilson, who advocated American membership in the League of Nations, and his opponents in the Senate. Wilson's diplomatic defeat over the Treaty of Versailles following World War I had damaging consequences for the United States and the rest of the world.

The credibility of the administration of President Lyndon B. Johnson was ultimately destroyed, in no small measure because of mounting opposition in Congress to U.S. participation in the Vietnam War. Inevitably, perhaps, the period after this war was an era of unprecedented legislative activism in foreign policy. Many legislators believed, correctly or not, that among the "lessons of Vietnam" was the necessity for Congress to assert its prerogatives more decisively in foreign affairs. During the 1970s, presidents Nixon, Ford, and Carter repeatedly complained about congressional efforts to limit their diplomatic freedom of action.

The Reagan White House encountered a continuation of this trend. In its efforts, for example, to develop the MX missile system, the B-1 bomber, and the Strategic Defense Initiative (popularly called "Star Wars"), the administration sometimes encountered deep-seated and decisive legislative opposition. Congressional viewpoints were also influential in shaping American policy toward the Middle East and Central America. In the Iran-contra affair during President Reagan's second term, legislators played a key role in investigating the affair, in giving it wide publicity, and in trying to prevent comparable episodes in future administrations.

During its early months in office, the Bush administration enjoyed a relatively high level of cooperation between the White House and Congress in dealing with foreign policy problems. Toward two diplomatic issues especially—the new era in relations between the United States and the Soviet Union and the crisis in the Persian Gulf— legislators overwhelmingly supported the administration's diplomatic and military moves and cooperated with executive officials to achieve American objectives abroad. A major reason was that, as public opinion polls indicated, President Bush's foreign policy enjoyed widespread popular support.

Evidence from the diplomatic record of the United States since World War II, however, leaves little doubt that the nation's foreign policy process continues to reflect an invitation to struggle between the president and Congress. To date, efforts to attenuate or eliminate the problem have been at best only partially successful. This struggle will remain a feature of the American foreign policy process for an indefinite period of time, with sometimes momentous consequences for the nation's diplomatic efforts. Post-World War II experience also clearly indicates that the severity of the problem is likely to vary from one period to another, depending in no small measure upon the incumbent administration's record in achieving its foreign policy objectives. As President Bush discovered during the early months of his administration, for example, Congress shows little disposition to contest the president's diplomatic leadership as long as the White House is enjoying evident success in achieving the nation's goals abroad. By contrast, the Johnson, Nixon, Carter, and Reagan administrations sometimes experienced a sharp decline in executive-legislative cooperation when dramatic military or diplomatic reverses occurred overseas.

Following the pattern established in earlier editions, this fourth edition of *Invitation to Struggle* was written primarily with two groups of readers in mind. For those interested chiefly in substantive problems in recent American diplomacy, the study provides insight into a number of such instances, especially those confronting the United States since the Vietnam War. For readers whose interest is centered on the foreign policy process of the United States, the study supplies a succinct and contemporary analysis of that subject. The extensive reading list at the end of the book should prove useful to readers wishing to undertake more thorough research and reading on selected aspects of the nation's foreign policy.

The fourth edition contains nine chapters. Three provide general and theoretical discussions, while six consist of case studies illustrating various aspects of presidential and congressional powers in the foreign policy field.

Chapter 1 provides the reader with a broad discussion of the roles of the president, the State Department, and other influential members of the executive bureaucracy in the formulation and administration of foreign policy. The basic focus of this chapter is the dominant position maintained by the chief executive in the decision-making process.

In Chapter 2 we analyze the constitutional and historical powers and responsibilities of Congress in foreign affairs. The chapter focuses on the impact of the Vietnam conflict in motivating Congress to assert its powers more forcefully in the sphere of external policy. The congressional assertiveness observed in foreign relations since the Vietnam War can be best understood within a broad historical and constitutional context.

The first case study (Chapter 3) deals with the effort by the United States and the Soviet Union to arrive at durable arms-control agreements. This effort was given a new impetus by the fundamental change in Soviet-American relations witnessed during the Gorbachev era. The issue highlights the prerogatives of the president and the Senate—and, indirectly at least, of Congress as a whole—in the treaty-making process, including the reaching and implementing of executive agreements between the United States and other nations. The chapter also deals with a new and important issue in executive-legislative relations: the roles of the president and the Senate in *interpreting* treaties and less formal international agreements.

Chapter 4 examines American foreign policy toward the Middle East. Specifically, it focuses upon America's historic, strategic, and economic interests in the region; upon the Zionist movement and the creation of the State of Israel; the continuing Arab-Israeli conflict; the provision of U.S. military equipment to Saudi Arabia and Jordan; and the Persian Gulf crisis that erupted in 1990 when Iraqi forces invaded oil-rich Kuwait. The case study is especially useful in calling attention to two major problems confronting the foreign policy process in the United States. One of these is the impact of lobbying, and of public opinion generally, on the diplomatic decision-making process.

The other of these, the subject of Chapter 5, is the role of the armed forces in achieving the nation's diplomatic objectives—a recurrent and still controversial topic. As the evidence presented in the chapter indicates, the American people and their leaders remain uncertain about when, why, and where armed force should be employed to achieve national policy goals. As much as any single issue since World War II, this twofold question—whether armed force ought to be applied overseas and who ought to make the decision—epitomizes the invitation to struggle between the White House and Capitol Hill in the foreign policy process.

Another difficult and recurrent problem for the American democracy, the proper role of agencies that make up the intelligence community within the U.S. government, is examined in Chapter 6. To date, neither executive nor legislative officials have been able to formulate and impose effective control upon intelligence agencies, thereby ensuring that their operations in fact serve the national interest. Many of the reasons for this failure are identified in the case study.

A case study focusing upon the roles of the president and Congress in foreign economic policy is provided in Chapter 7. While the main topic of the chapter is American trade policy, the discussion makes clear that this subject can be meaningfully understood and discussed only in the larger context of internal economic policies and developments. This case study clearly illustrates the growing interrelationship between domestic and foreign policy within the American democracy.

In the fourth edition, a new chapter has been added dealing with an important dimension of American foreign policy in the recent period: Washington's efforts to promote and protect human rights abroad. This goal was especially identified with the Carter administration, and it has elicited a good deal of congressional interest and activity. As much as any other single issue in the nation's recent diplomacy, the problem of human rights has been one in which Congress has left its mark upon external policy. The major consequences of that fact are examined in the case study.

As in earlier editions, the final chapter offers an assessment about the nature and implications of the invitation to struggle in regard to the foreign policy of the United States today and in the years ahead. As already emphasized, a major premise of this study is that rivalry between the executive and legislative branches for primacy in the field of external policy will almost certainly continue to be a prominent feature of American diplomacy. At times, that struggle will no doubt become intense, posing a real threat to the unity and effectiveness of the nation's diplomatic efforts. Yet experience in the post-Vietnam War era also offers valid reasons for believing that at other times a high degree of collaboration between the White House and Congress can be achieved and maintained in the foreign policy field. Officials in both branches of the government appear to be aware of a twofold reality. One is that unrestricted conflict between the president and Congress can seriously impair the nation's diplomatic efforts. The other is that the executive and legislative branches each have something positive to contribute to the foreign policy process. Alone, neither branch is really able to manage or control that process in a manner that promotes the national interest. Washington's diplomatic efforts are clearly enhanced, therefore, under conditions that allow these respective contributions to be made without undue hindrance.

Chapters 1, 2, 4, and 9 of the fourth edition were written by Cecil V. Crabb, Jr. Chapters 3, 5, 6, 7, and 8 were written by Pat M. Holt. As always, the authors are greatly indebted to many individuals who have contributed directly and indirectly to this revision. Their assistance has been invaluable and is gratefully acknowledged.

The comments, suggestions, and criticisms received by the authors from students, faculty members, government officials, and interested citizens have been extremely useful and have been reflected in changes incorporated in this edition. In particular we thank William Lewis and Theodore McNelly for their critiques of the manuscript. The staff of CQ Press has provided indispensable advice and guidance at every stage. Specifically, the authors wish to thank the director of the CQ Book Department, Dave Tarr; the managing editor, Nancy Lammers; the copyeditor, Nola Healy Lynch; and our production editor, Jerry Orvedahl.

While acknowledging the essential contributions of others, the authors accept sole responsibility for any errors of fact or judgment that may be found in these pages.

Cecil V. Crabb, Jr.
Pat M. Holt

The Process of
Foreign Policy Making

A unique feature of the governmental system of the United States is that its powers are divided among separate executive, legislative, and judicial branches. From the perspective of constitutional theory, these are often described as equal and coordinate branches of the government. In practice, however, their powers and influences are not equal, especially in the foreign policy sphere. The purpose of Part I of this study is to provide a context within which congressional efforts to play a more influential role can be understood.

Throughout American history, the judiciary has largely been content to play a passive role in the foreign policy process. When the Supreme Court has concerned itself with foreign policy questions (which it does rarely), it has nearly always taken one of two positions: either it has declared foreign policy issues to be political questions that are not susceptible of resolution by the judicial system,[1] or it has forcefully upheld the exercise of executive power.[2] Over the years, a series of Supreme Court decisions has thus reinforced the claims of successive presidents that in foreign affairs the chief executive is the dominant organ of government.[3]

Both the diplomatic experience of the United States and certain provisions of the Constitution therefore dictate that we begin our inquiry into the making of foreign policy by focusing upon the role of the executive branch. Although recent years have witnessed a new congressional assertiveness in foreign relations, the fact remains that the president is still in charge of American foreign policy. For the most part, Congress's powers are limited to telling the White House what it cannot do beyond the country's borders. The power to decide what the

United States will undertake in its relations with other countries and in carrying out specific programs, such as arms control or the promotion of democracy abroad or military intervention in the Persian Gulf region, continues to reside with the chief executive. As we shall see in Chapter 1, an incumbent president has at his disposal a variety of instruments that create an unequaled position for influencing the diplomatic policies of the United States. More than at any other time in American history, perhaps, the nation's influence abroad now depends upon presidential decisions—including, of course, decisions about whether to work collaboratively with Congress in the foreign policy process.

In the American constitutional system, Congress is also assigned a number of responsibilities that impinge directly and indirectly upon foreign affairs. Despite the opinion expressed by many legislators in recent years that their views have been ignored by the White House, the U.S. Congress has more power to influence foreign affairs than any other national legislature in the world. In addition to its constitutional prerogatives, Congress has acquired over the course of two hundred years extraconstitutional powers and informal techniques for affecting the course of foreign relations. One tendency since World War II—the erosion of the distinction between domestic and foreign affairs—has significantly enhanced the influence of Congress. Chapter 2 provides a discussion of the formal and informal prerogatives of Congress in the foreign policy field, and it identifies and analyzes the forces that have produced the new congressional militancy in external affairs.

Notes

1. In 1855, a federal judge ruled that the interpretation of a treaty was a "political question" and thus was not among the powers that were "confided by the people to the judiciary ... but to the executive and legislative departments of our government." *Taylor v. Morton,* 23 F. Cas. 784 (C.C.D. Mass. 1855) (No. 13,799). See also an earlier case, *Foster v. Neilson,* 2 Pet. 253 (1829).
2. Two landmark decisions affirming the president's prerogatives in foreign relations were the *Prize Cases,* 67 U.S. (2 Black) 635 (1863), and *United States v. Curtiss-Wright Export Corp.,* 299 U.S. 304 (1936). Several decisions during the late 1970s and early 1980s sustained that position. In *Edwards v. Carter,* 436 U.S. 907 (1978), the Supreme Court upheld the right of the president to dispose, through the treaty process (thus requiring the consent of the Senate), of property belonging to the United States, as provided for in the Panama Canal treaties that had recently been negotiated by the Carter administration. In another case, growing out of the Iranian hostage crisis of 1979-1980, the Court upheld the president's authority over several billion dollars of Iranian assets, which had been frozen after the hostages were seized. In *Dames and Moore v. Regan,* 453 U.S. 654 (1981), the Court stated that in the foreign policy field Congress had accorded the chief executive more freedom to settle claims with foreign countries than was the case in

domestic affairs. In *Agee v. Haig*, 453 U.S. 280 (1981), the Supreme Court upheld the right of the executive branch to deny a passport to a former employee of the Central Intelligence Agency whose writings were viewed as endangering the lives of current CIA agents and as detrimental to national security.

The Supreme Court has not yet ruled on the constitutionality of the War Powers Resolution of 1973, which sought to limit the president's power to use the armed forces abroad without the consent of Congress. During the Persian Gulf crisis of 1987, several legislators sought to get a federal court to rule that the Reagan administration had not complied with the resolution, but they were not successful. For more detailed discussions of and commentary on these cases, see Warren Christopher, "Ceasefire between the Branches: A Compact in Foreign Affairs," *Foreign Affairs* 60 (Summer 1982): 990-995.

3. The concept of the imperial presidency, which has come into wide currency since the Vietnam War and Watergate crises, is actually a variation on a very old theme in American history: pervasive apprehension about the abuse of executive power. This fear strongly colored the attitudes of those who wrote both the federal and the early state constitutions, in which the powers of the chief executives were severely limited. In the context of the Vietnam and Watergate experiences, the idea of the imperial presidency suggests a president who routinely infringes upon the constitutional authority of the legislative and judicial branches; who believes the presidency to be above the law, particularly in the conduct of foreign relations; who manipulates and deceives Congress and the American people in order to accomplish domestic and foreign policy objectives; and who surrounds the operations of the executive branch with a wall of secrecy. As a leading student of the presidency has asserted, this conception of the presidential office implies a "radical transformation" in the American system of government, which is founded upon the doctrine of separation of powers. Arthur M. Schlesinger, Jr., *The Imperial Presidency* (Boston: Houghton Mifflin, 1973), viii. This study provides a detailed analysis of the emergence of the imperial presidency during two hundred years of U.S. history.

Yet it must also be emphasized that—especially since the administration of President Franklin D. Roosevelt—the American people have fundamentally accepted the idea of a strong or forceful president who takes the lead in meeting internal and external challenges energetically and successfully. Perhaps even more today than in the 1930s, citizens look to the White House, rather than to Congress or the courts, for the dynamic leadership required to solve urgent national problems.

Insofar as it is regarded as constitutionally and ethically objectionable, therefore, the imperial presidency has two specific connotations: behavior by the chief executive and his subordinates that is patently illegal or of questionable constitutional validity; and the failure of the chief executive to achieve his major policy goals. It is, for example, interesting to speculate about whether President Lyndon B. Johnson would have been viewed as epitomizing the imperial presidency if the United States had *won* the Vietnam War, since many of Johnson's acts during that conflict were comparable to those of President Roosevelt during World War II and President Abraham Lincoln during the Civil War.

The Executive Branch
and Foreign Affairs:
Locus of Decision Making

As explained in greater detail in Chapters 4 and 5, in the weeks following Iraq's invasion and occupation of Kuwait early in August 1990, President George Bush took the following actions. He denounced Baghdad's overt aggression and declared that its so-called annexation of oil-rich Kuwait would not be accepted by the United States and the international community. As commander in chief of the military establishment, President Bush ordered a massive and continuing buildup of U.S. armed forces in the Persian Gulf area; imposed a blockade against shipping to and from Iraq; called up reserve units to active duty; and promised to supply American military equipment to other threatened nations. Bush also pledged that the United States would defend Saudi Arabia and (by strong implication, at least) other states within the region that might be victims of new Iraqi aggression. Then, early in January 1991, the president asked Congress to approve offensive military operations against Iraq, which were subsequently undertaken. After the American-led coalition scored an overwhelming military victory, the Bush White House proclaimed a cease-fire and defined the terms that Baghdad would have to meet for the armistice to become permanent. Throughout the crisis, the president and his advisers met in formal and informal sessions with members of the news media and made radio and television appearances to explain his administration's approach to the Persian Gulf conflict. On the basis of public opinion polls and other evidence, the president's policy commanded the overwhelming support of the American people. On the diplomatic front, the Bush administration led a successful campaign to involve the long-moribund United Nations in the Persian Gulf crisis; and it was highly successful in forging and maintaining an international coalition to defend the Persian Gulf area.

This single example focuses attention upon the basic theme of this chapter: the crucial role of the president in the foreign policy process of the United States. As the nation entered its third century under the Constitution, the president of the United States was in some respects the most powerful official in the world. This was an ironic situation, because the nation's founders had been extremely wary of executive power. Little doubt exists that, in their minds, the dominant organ of the new system of government was to be Congress. Yet after two hundred years of experience in foreign affairs, the president has become what one commentator has called the "ultimate decider" and the "decision maker of last resort." [1]

In practice, all presidents depend upon a corps of official and unofficial advisers to assist them in managing foreign relations. Historically, the State Department has been the agency which, under the president's ultimate direction, is in charge of the foreign policy of the United States. Since World War II, however, the State Department has faced increasing competition from many other executive agencies—such as the Defense Department, the Central Intelligence Agency (CIA), and the president's own staff—that have become active in the foreign policy field.

As the subsequent discussion will show—and as was dramatically illustrated by the Iran-contra affair during President Ronald Reagan's second term—the achievement and maintenance of unity within the executive branch in dealing with foreign policy issues have sometimes been a challenge for national leaders. Various mechanisms and devices created since World War II—which will also be discussed—have thus far failed to solve the problem and have, in some respects, perhaps compounded it.

An even older problem confronting officials involved in foreign policy decision making is coordinating the actions of the executive and legislative branches. The two problems are related, for executive-legislative cooperation in foreign affairs is, to a significant degree, dependent upon the maintenance of unity among the leading members of the executive bureaucracy in dealing with foreign policy issues.

Concepts in Foreign Policy

Foreign policy refers to the external goals for which a nation is prepared to commit its resources. This definition distinguishes between a nation's foreign policy and a variety of hopes, visions, and dreams (such as universal democracy and perpetual peace) that may be espoused by individuals and groups within the society. Unless the objective—in the case of the United States, for example, protecting the security of members of the North Atlantic Treaty Organization (NATO) or preserving access to Persian Gulf oil supplies—involves some application of the economic, military, intellectual, or other resources of the nation, it cannot be seriously viewed as forming part of its foreign policy.

A closely related term is *foreign policy process.* This denotes a complex and often time-consuming series of steps by which officials in the executive and legislative branches formulate external goals or objectives and decide upon the most appropriate means for reaching them. More specifically, the foreign policy process may be thought of as entailing, in the usual case, six distinct steps or stages.

1. Officials, and often the public as well, perceive an external challenge or problem that is viewed as affecting the interests of the United States. This challenge might be evidence of Iraqi expansionism, human rights abuses by a foreign government, or a rising level of national armaments.

2. The president and his advisers attempt to identify the challenge clearly and to determine precisely how and to what degree the interests of the United States are affected by it. For example, what would be the effects of the new era in Soviet-American relations on European security, or of continuing political violence in South Africa, or of mounting economic problems in Mexico?

3. Executive officials formulate and consider alternative courses of action or *policy options* available to the United States for responding to the external challenge. They evaluate these options in the light of the likely consequences and implications of each. In the end, the president has the responsibility of choosing the course of action the government will pursue.

4. Steps are taken to implement or carry out the policy chosen by the president. Doing so may involve diplomatic moves by the State Department and U.S. ambassadors abroad; military programs and activities by the Department of Defense; intelligence studies and a variety of other operations by the CIA and other members of what is called the "intelligence community"; propaganda and informational programs by the United States Information Agency (USIA); economic measures by the Treasury Department; a new food aid program, in which the Department of Agriculture plays a key role; a new national energy policy; legislation or appropriations by Congress; and other possible steps to achieve the declared objective abroad. It is virtually certain that the achievement of any foreign policy goal today will require the collaboration of several executive agencies and some form of congressional participation, if only in the provision of funds.

5. The success of the policy in achieving its goals is reviewed. What major problems have been encountered in the attempt to realize the

policy's objectives? What steps could be taken to improve the policy or its implementation? Is there another option that, on balance, would be preferable? Efforts to answer such questions are made by the State Department (including U.S. officials overseas), the White House staff, and other executive agencies; by committees of Congress, which often investigate problems in the foreign policy field; by citizens' organizations and "think tanks" (such as the Council on Foreign Relations and the Rand Corporation); by foreign governments and political movements; and by individual citizens, political commentators, and informed students of the nation's diplomacy.

6. Policy makers determine the future of the policy. The decision may be to continue the existing policy largely unchanged; to modify it, in the belief that major changes are required; or to abandon it, on the grounds that it cannot achieve U.S. goals abroad. Thus, to take a hypothetical case, in the American approach to arms-control issues with the Soviet Union, the president and his advisers may decide that the nation's position on disarmament is in the main satisfactory and ought to be continued; or that substantial changes need to be made in current U.S. policy toward arms-control questions; or that the prevailing policy does not achieve American objectives abroad and ought, therefore, to be replaced by a totally new set of proposals designed to achieve the reduction of Soviet and American military arsenals.

It must be recognized that, like certain concepts in physics, such as "frictionless bearings" or a "perfect vacuum," the above model of foreign policy decision making is an ideal type, almost never found in its pure form in the real world of decision making. In reality, the foreign policies of the United States (and of other countries) sometimes are continued for no better reason than habit, bureaucratic momentum, or public resistance to change. President Dwight D. Eisenhower once said that it came as a great shock to him to discover that he could issue a presidential order to the bureaucracy—and nothing would happen. Nearly always, subjective and emotional factors influence policy decisions, as when President Lyndon B. Johnson said about a particular challenge abroad that it was "just like the Alamo!" Unquestionably also, the White House, the State Department, Congress, and other participants in the foreign policy process may and do develop strong vested interests in an existing policy. At every stage, misperception, erroneous information, and faulty interpretation of events abroad may influence the outcome of the decision-making process.

Former secretary of state Dean Acheson said, after he left office, that the exact process by which foreign policy decisions are actually made within the United States government is "unknown and unknowable." Former presidential adviser Clark Clifford called the process by which foreign policy decisions were arrived at by President Johnson "unfathomable." After North Korea invaded South Korea in late June 1950, President Harry S. Truman did not engage in a prolonged process of formal decision making before concluding that the United States must resist the attack; rather, the formal decision-making process was used to ratify the presidential decision after it had already been made. Critics charged that this was also frequently the case with decision making in the Vietnam War during the Johnson administration. At some point all presidents have demanded that their advisory machinery produce viewpoints and policy recommendations consonant with their own prior inclinations. Allowing for these qualifications, it is nevertheless the case that decision making in the foreign policy field generally approximates the sequence of steps that has been described.

Another concept in the field of foreign policy, one which has come to the fore especially since World War II, is *national security policy*. This embraces activities, both abroad and in domestic affairs, that are designed to protect the independence and integrity of the United States. At its most basic level, national security policy is concerned with the defense of the nation against actual and potential enemies. Construed more broadly, it involves preventing threats to national sovereignty, collecting and evaluating information about the behavior of potential enemies, creating and maintaining military alliances, and supplying friendly countries with arms and other forms of aid.

A famous Prussian general of the Napoleonic period, Karl von Clausewitz, has said, "War is the continuation of politics by other means." [2] One of the implications of this dictum is the idea that political and military relations among nations are two sides of the same coin. Political or diplomatic disputes sometimes lead to armed conflicts among nations; in turn, the results of war—and one nation's perception of another's military strength—crucially affect what diplomats are able to achieve at the conference table.

Awareness of these relationships led to the creation in 1947 of the National Security Council (NSC), the highest presidential advisory agency for national security policy. While NSC's membership has varied, its members currently are the president (who serves as chairman), the vice president, the secretary of state, and the secretary of defense. Other civilian and military officials may be, and frequently are, invited to participate in its deliberations. The NSC staff is directed by a presidential assistant. Beginning with the Eisenhower administration in 1953, the position was elevated into the presidential assistant for national security affairs. The best known and most influential occupant of this position was Henry Kissinger under the Nixon and Ford administrations. Kissinger converted the NSC staff into a kind of rival State Department; although he was not a member of the National Security Council, Kissinger operated as a de facto cabinet officer.

Conversely, in the Nixon-Kissinger era, the influence of the State Department declined significantly. While other national security advisers have been less influential than Kissinger, the position has become an extremely influential one in the foreign policy field. (It should be noted also that, in contrast to cabinet officers, the president's national security adviser is *not* confirmed in the position by the Senate.)

The NSC was created to integrate diplomatic, military, financial, and other factors into a unified national security policy for the United States. It is important to note that the NSC is solely an *advisory organ to the president.* Chief executives utilize the NSC in very different ways. Some, like President Dwight D. Eisenhower, have been strongly "staff oriented" in arriving at decisions and so have relied heavily upon the NSC. Others, like President Johnson, relied more frequently on informal advisers and friends. Under President Ronald Reagan, certain members of the NSC staff exercised a high degree of independence in efforts to achieve what they viewed as national goals abroad.

The membership of the NSC was deliberately composed by Congress to preserve and underscore a fundamental principle of the nation's constitutional system: civilian control over the military establishment. All members of the NSC are civilians, although military officers (such as members of the Joint Chiefs of Staff) may be invited by the president to attend NSC sessions. However, the president may also, and not infrequently does, consult the nation's top military commanders directly in the determination of national security policy and strategy.

Another important term in the field of foreign policy is *diplomacy.* This concept is somewhat ambiguous and often causes widespread public confusion. At the risk of oversimplification, we may say that it is frequently used in two different ways. Diplomacy can refer to the entire range of a nation's external relationships—routine diplomatic communications between governments, summit conferences among heads of state, the recognition of one government by another, cultural and scientific exchange programs, and so on. Alternatively, diplomacy often has a more limited connotation: the resolution of disputes and conflicts among nations by peaceful methods. In this latter sense, diplomacy is conceived of as a substitute for war and violence; it is a method of preventing the settlement of international quarrels with armed force.[3]

Americans have traditionally been suspicious of diplomacy and of the officials engaged in it. In the public mind, diplomacy is associated with Old World political values and machinations held to be at variance with the democratic ethos of the New World. One argument invoked to justify an isolationist stance in foreign affairs has been that Americans lacked skill and training in diplomacy; hence, in any encounter with the wily diplomats of the Old World, the United States would almost certainly lose. This point of view was reinforced by the results of several diplomatic conferences during World War II, such as the meetings at Yalta and Potsdam in 1945, which many Americans interpreted as diplomatic victories for the Soviet Union. This historical frame of mind no doubt contributes to the poor image that the State Department tends to have with the American public and with Congress.[4]

The President's Constitutional Authority

The preeminent position of the chief executive in the U.S. foreign policy process stems from two broad sources of power: those conferred by or implied in the Constitution; and those that are outgrowths of tradition, precedent, or historical necessity. Let us examine each of these categories in detail.

From the beginning of the republic, constitutional authorities have debated whether the Founders intended to make the conduct of foreign policy largely an executive responsibility, whether they meant for Congress to be the dominant organ, or whether they desired some kind of balance of power between the two branches.[5] Yet it is beyond contention that the intention of the Founders has been less important in determining what happened than numerous other influences, such as the impact of forceful personalities upon the presidential office, the crises confronting the nation at home and abroad, and the decisions of the Supreme Court. Irrespective of what the Founders desired, the tendency has been toward executive preeminence in nearly every aspect of the foreign policy process, a reality that has not been fundamentally changed since the end of the Vietnam War.

The constitutional position of the president in foreign affairs rests upon several important provisions. Article II, Section 1 vests the executive power of the government in the president. It also requires that the president take an oath to "preserve, protect and defend the Constitution of the United States," implying a responsibility for the preservation of national security. Sections 2 and 3 of this article specify the president's powers, of which the most relevant to foreign policy are that the chief executive serves as commander in chief of the army and navy, can make treaties with foreign governments with the advice and consent of the Senate, can appoint ambassadors and other representatives of the United States abroad, and can "receive ambassadors and other public ministers" of other governments.

Commander in Chief

The Constitution (Article II, Section 2) also designates the president as "Commander in Chief of the Army and Navy"—which today also includes the air force. Like other constitutional provisions, this grant of authority engendered much controversy. Does it mean that the president should function symbolically or ceremonially as head of the armed forces (like the British monarch in modern history), while leaving the determination of military strategy and the deployment of the armed forces to others, possibly to Congress? (The case studies in Chapter 5 focus upon the demands and behavior of Congress regarding the use of the armed forces for foreign policy ends.) Or does it mean that the chief executive actually determines military strategy and tactics?[6]

American diplomatic experience has left no doubt about the answer. Successive presidents since Lincoln have interpreted their authority in this realm broadly and dynamically. Their position as commander in chief of the armed forces has become one of their most influential powers in the foreign policy field. Over the course of its history, the United States has been involved in more than 125 "undeclared wars" and other instances of violent conflict abroad conducted under presidential authority. For example, in 1846 President James K. Polk ordered the army to occupy disputed territory along the Rio Grande, unquestionably (and almost certainly by intent) provoking Mexico into war. Early in the twentieth century, despite strong congressional opposition, President Theodore Roosevelt sent the American navy on a cruise around the world. (His implicit objective was to impress Japan with U.S. naval might.) On his own authority, President Franklin D. Roosevelt ordered the navy to shoot on sight any German submarines that entered the hemispheric "security zone." President Truman personally made the decision to use two atomic bombs against Japan in 1945; in 1950 he again ordered U.S. armed forces in the Pacific to repel North Korea's thrust into South Korea, thereby involving the United States in one of the most prolonged and expensive undeclared wars in its history.

Early in his administration, President Eisenhower threatened Communist China and North Korea with the possible use of nuclear weapons if they resumed hostilities in the Korean conflict. Eisenhower was also the first of several chief executives to make major military commitments to the government of South Vietnam, ultimately leading to massive U.S. involvement in the conflict between North and South Vietnam.

In the most dangerous cold war encounter since World War II, President John F. Kennedy in 1962 presented the Soviet Union with an ultimatum demanding the removal of its nuclear missiles from Cuba. Kennedy placed the U.S. air force on worldwide alert and interposed the navy between Cuba and the Soviet ships that were apparently bringing new missiles to the island. Little doubt exists that Kennedy was prepared to use whatever degree of force was required to eliminate this Soviet threat.[7]

During the closing months of his administration, following the Soviet invasion of Afghanistan, President Jimmy Carter issued the so-called Carter Doctrine, pledging the United States to defend the security of the oil-rich Persian Gulf area—a commitment reaffirmed by Presidents Reagan and Bush. (President Bush's decision to resist Iraqi aggression against Kuwait and possibly against Saudi Arabia, for example, led to one of the largest American military buildups witnessed in many years.) A few weeks after his pronouncement, President Carter ordered the Pentagon to undertake a mission designed to rescue U.S. citizens being held as hostages in Iran. Congress and the American people were not informed of this mission until after it had been launched and had failed to achieve its objective.[8]

A president's decision *not* to use armed force, or to terminate military hostilities and enter into negotiations for a truce or for a peace treaty, can have significant effects upon the nation's relationships with other countries. This was illustrated by President Carter's refusal to embroil the United States in several conflicts in black-ruled African countries. After first deciding to intervene militarily in Lebanon's troubled political situation, President Reagan later withdrew the nation's forces from that country.

With the concurrence of the Senate, the president also appoints and promotes high-level military officers; and on his own authority, he can relieve military commanders of their posts, as President Truman did in his widely publicized dismissal of Gen. Douglas MacArthur during the Korean War and as President Bush did when he relieved the air force chief of staff of his position in 1990. While ultimate authority to determine the size and nature of the U.S. military establishment resides with Congress, the president plays a crucial role in that decision. The president's statements—the budget message to Congress, along with many other communications to the legislative branch and the testimony provided to congressional committees by executive branch officials—usually have a decisive impact upon legislative attitudes and behavior. During 1990, for example, a prolonged "budget summit" involving executive and legislative officials had major and long-term implications for military spending, foreign aid programs, and other aspects of foreign affairs.

Treaty-making Power

Article II, Section 2 of the Constitution gives the president the power, "by and with the Advice and Consent of the Senate, to make treaties, provided two-thirds of the Senators present concur." The ability of the chief executive to enter into formal agreements with other countries in the form of treaties—and less formal accords and understandings by means of executive agreements—is another influential tool of presidential leadership.

Controversy has always surrounded the meaning and requirements of this constitutional provision. For example, is the process of negotiating treaties an exclusively executive function, or does the "advice and consent of the Senate" mean that the Senate plays a role in the negotiation process, as well as the ratification of treaties? Again, diplomatic experience provides the answer. Presidents have nearly always taken the view that the executive branch "makes" or negotiates treaties and then submits them to the Senate for its consideration. In the post-World War II period, senators (and occasionally even representatives) have been invited by the White House to participate in international negotiations. This practice reached its zenith in the negotiations on the UN Charter and on treaties with the Axis powers after World War II. Moreover, the case study on arms control (Chapter 3) provides other examples of the phenomenon.

After a treaty has been negotiated and signed by the parties to it, the agreement is submitted to the Senate for its consideration. At this stage, the Senate has several choices. After deliberation and debate, the Senate can *approve* the treaty by the required two-thirds majority. (Throughout American history, the vast majority of treaties has received senatorial approval.) Conversely, the Senate can *reject* the treaty, by failing to give it a favorable two-thirds vote. In reality, the Senate very rarely takes this course of action. Then the Senate may *change* the treaty, by attaching amendments, reservations, and understandings to it.*

After the Senate has approved a treaty, it must be signed and *proclaimed* by the president before it becomes law. It is a popular misconception to say that the Senate "ratifies" treaties. The Senate plays a key role in the ratification process, but in the end the treaty becomes law only after it has been proclaimed by the president and accepted by the other parties to it.

Throughout the entire process of treaty making, the chief executive retains the initiative. The president decides to undertake the negotiations, appoints the negotiators and monitors their work, approves the treaty's provisions and submits it to the Senate, and proclaims the

---

* An *amendment* to a treaty changes its language and provisions, thereby probably requiring its renegotiation with the other parties to it. *Reservations* and *understandings* specify the American interpretation of its provisions. For example, in several international agreements, the United States has specified that the accord does not supersede the Monroe Doctrine, under which Washington has historically protected the defense of the Western Hemisphere. In Senate deliberations on the SALT II arms limitation agreement with the Soviet Union in 1979, several senators insisted upon an understanding that the Soviet Union would adhere to pledges (given orally) not to expand certain components of its military strength.

treaty as law. At any stage the president may withdraw the treaty from active Senate deliberation, or the president may refuse to proclaim a treaty that has already been approved by the Senate, if the White House believes its provisions are detrimental to the national interest. This was the action taken by President Woodrow Wilson toward the Treaty of Versailles, because of the objectionable amendments and resolutions added to it by the Senate.

Can a president also terminate an existing treaty? This question was posed by the action of the Carter administration in December 1978 when it established full diplomatic relations with the People's Republic of China and concurrently notified the Republic of China (Taiwan) that the security treaty with that government would be allowed to lapse. Predictably, Carter's action precipitated considerable public and congressional opposition. Since the security pact with Taiwan had been approved by the Senate, some legislators argued that it could be terminated only with the concurrence of the Senate or of Congress as a whole. Initially, this viewpoint was supported by a U.S. district court, but on December 13, 1979, by a vote of 7-2, the Supreme Court reversed the decision, holding that the president had the constitutional authority to terminate the defense pact with Taiwan. In writing about the decision, four members of the Court held that the controversy was a political question that was not subject to judicial determination and that had to be resolved between the president and Congress.[9]

Another issue that has arisen is: Who has the power to interpret (or reinterpret) the meaning of treaties between the United States and foreign nations? Predictably perhaps, executive officials have contended that this power also belongs to the president, while many legislators have taken the position that it belongs to the Senate (or, as some view it, to the Senate and the president, jointly). This issue will be examined further in the case study of arms control.

Executive Agreements

Several meetings between President Bush and Soviet president Mikhail Gorbachev led to a wide range of agreements or understandings. These covered such diverse subjects as the future of Communist governments in Eastern Europe, the reunification of Germany, disarmament accords between the two superpowers, Soviet military and other forms of assistance to Nicaragua, and Moscow's role in American-led efforts to respond to Iraqi expansionism in the Persian Gulf area. At a lower level, Secretary of State James Baker and other executive officials arrived at additional understandings with their Soviet counterparts, in the new "post-cold war era."

These understandings provide merely recent examples of what are sometimes called *executive agreements* between governments.* Although executive agreements are not mentioned in the Constitution, they have a venerable tradition going back to the earliest days of the republic. Some of them have had a momentous effect on the course of American foreign relations. Some notable examples are President Franklin D. Roosevelt's destroyers-for-bases deal with Great Britain in 1940; the agreements with the Soviet Union and other allies during World War II (notably those reached at the Yalta and Potsdam conferences); a series of understandings, beginning in the Truman administration, by which the United States assumed a de facto commitment for the security of Israel; and the understandings between the United States, several Arab states, the European allies, and Japan to maintain the military security of the Persian Gulf region.

According to one estimate (and estimates vary widely), between 1946 and 1976 the United States entered into 7,201 executive agreements with foreign countries (excluding over 60 secret agreements that the State Department reported to Congress between 1972 and 1977)— far more than the number of treaties signed during the same period.[10] Few presidential prerogatives in foreign affairs have generated such concern on Capitol Hill in recent years as the practice of entering into such agreements without legislative knowledge, scrutiny, or concurrence. As Sen. J. William Fulbright, D-Ark., a former chairman of the Senate Foreign Relations Committee, lamented:

> The Senate is asked to convene solemnly to approve by a two-thirds vote a treaty to preserve cultural artifacts in a friendly neighboring country. At the same time, the chief executive is moving military men and materiel around the globe like so many pawns in a chess game.[11]

In 1972, Congress passed the Case Act, which requires that all executive agreements be reported to Congress. If Congress objects to an agreement, it may then take such action as seems warranted. Despite such legislation, experience since the 1970s does not indicate that Congress has yet been able to impose effective limits upon the president's power to enter into agreements with other governments.[12]

---

* Under the Constitution a distinction can be made between a treaty and an agreement (or compact) with other countries, although the differences are not always legally and practically clear. An *executive agreement* is an understanding between heads of state or made under their authority; it may be either written or oral; and many agreements ultimately require congressional approval (as in providing funds for their implementation) before they can become effective. Many executive agreements (for example, those related to the sale of surplus agricultural commodities abroad) are negotiated pursuant to authority delegated by Congress. These are sometimes described as *statutory agreements.*

Appointment Power

Article II, Section 2 of the Constitution also provides that the president "shall nominate, and by and with the Advice and Consent of the Senate, shall appoint Ambassadors [and] other public Ministers and Consuls." An ambassador serves as the alter ego of the head of state abroad; hence, it is expected that the president will select those individuals for this post who share his conception of the nation's role in foreign affairs. The same constitutional requirement also applies, of course, to the secretaries of state and defense, as to other cabinet heads, and to lower-level department officials, normally down to and including assistant secretaries. To date, however, the appointment of the president's national security adviser has not required confirmation by the Senate.

As they have with the treaty power, resourceful chief executives throughout U.S. history have discovered methods for circumventing limitations upon their appointment power. One such device is for the president to make an interim appointment; the individual so appointed may hold office and perform important duties while the Senate is not in session. After the Senate reconvenes, the president has three choices: he may submit the name of the interim appointee for confirmation; he may allow the interim appointee's period of service to end and may nominate another individual (perhaps one more acceptable to the Senate) for the position; or he may decide not to fill the position at all.

The chief executive may also, and frequently does, use cabinet officers to undertake diplomatic assignments. In 1979, President Carter relied upon Secretary of the Treasury Michael Blumenthal to arrive at certain understandings with the People's Republic of China before the United States opened an embassy in that country.[13] During the Bush administration, the secretary of state, the secretary of defense, and the secretary of the treasury were active in enlisting the assistance of other nations in supporting the effort to oppose Iraqi expansionism in the Persian Gulf area.[14]

The appointment of personal representatives is another device presidents have used to bypass senatorial confirmation of diplomatic officials. During World War II, President Franklin D. Roosevelt relied heavily upon his personal aide, Harry Hopkins, to conduct negotiations both with Great Britain and with the Soviet Union. The distinguished public servant W. Averell Harriman served as the personal representative of several presidents during and after World War II. In the Reagan administration, presidential envoy Philip C. Habib spent several months in efforts to gain a peace agreement in strife-torn Lebanon.[15] From time to time presidents have also used the vice president—and sometimes the first lady—as diplomatic envoys.

Recognition of Foreign Governments

Article II, Section 3 of the Constitution gives the president the power to "receive Ambassadors and other public Ministers" from foreign countries. The power of the president to recognize other governments is derived from this provision.

In normal diplomatic relations between two nations, each gives formal recognition to the legitimacy of the other's government by the exchange of ambassadors (or ministers) between them and the establishment of embassies (or legations). Therefore, the decision as to whether to receive diplomatic representatives from other countries—and, hence, to accord formal recognition to their governments—belongs solely to the president. In practice, the Senate can frustrate the exercise of this power, as when it refused to confirm President Truman's designated ambassador to the Vatican, but such cases are exceptional. On the other hand, President Franklin D. Roosevelt decided to accord formal diplomatic recognition to the Soviet Union in 1933, after its Communist regime had been in existence for more than fifteen years. At the end of 1978, President Carter recognized the People's Republic of China, thereby ending the long period of estrangement that had existed between the two countries.

For many years two theories have existed about the criteria that should be employed in deciding whether the president should recognize another government. What might be called the classic international law conception holds that such recognition should depend primarily upon whether the government in question is stable, has established its authority throughout the country, and is fulfilling its international obligations. If so, it should be recognized, irrespective of the nature of its government or its ideological system. Applying this traditional standard, most governments, unlike the United States, recognized the People's Republic of China soon after the end of the Chinese civil war in 1949.

The other view—the Wilsonian or distinctively American approach—holds that recognition should depend upon the nature and character of the government in question. Specifically, it relies upon such criteria as whether the government enjoys popular support, whether it respects the rights of its citizens, and whether its conduct accords with international law. In 1913, President Woodrow Wilson invoked such principles when he refused to recognize the new government of Mexico, headed by Victoriano Huerta (a regime Wilson called "a government of butchers"). Basically the same reasons dictated America's refusal for many years to recognize the Communist regimes in the Soviet Union and China. The same consideration dictated Washington's refusal to recognize the government of Panama under the regime of Manuel

Noriega, who was in time arrested and extradited to the United States as a major drug dealer.

If the president can recognize foreign governments, he can by the same token withdraw or withhold recognition. In 1990, President Bush refused to recognize—to accord legitimacy to—Iraq's absorption of Kuwait. The White House continued to recognize the Kuwaiti government-in-exile as the nation's rightful governing authority. In extreme cases, presidents have sometimes dramatically severed diplomatic relations with another country, as President Woodrow Wilson did with Imperial Germany before the United States entered World War I. Another presidential option is to withhold recognition for an indefinite period, perhaps until a country achieves internal political stability or modifies its behavior. Alternatively, the president can send a warning to another country by calling the American ambassador home "for consultation." President Carter, for example, recalled the U.S. ambassador to Moscow, Thomas J. Watson, to express anger at the Soviet Union's invasion of Afghanistan. Conversely, the president can require foreign diplomats in the United States to leave the country if their state's behavior becomes unacceptable to the White House.

Informal Techniques of Leadership

In addition to these constitutional powers, the chief executive possesses certain informal and extraconstitutional techniques for the management of foreign affairs. Five of these are especially important.

First, the president has unequaled access to the information sources required for effective decision making. Information is available to the White House from many sources, including departments and agencies within the executive branch, embassies and other overseas posts, the intelligence community, and foreign governments. The scope and nature of the information at the president's disposal about events and tendencies abroad are among his most influential resources for affecting the course of American diplomacy. Moreover, presidents are often able to withhold this information even from Congress under the doctrine of executive privilege.* However, as we shall see more fully in Chapter 2, the legislative branch has made increasing efforts to acquire

---

* Under this doctrine, the president and his principal aides cannot be compelled to testify before Congress, or to make papers and other records public, if to do so would impair the confidentiality of advice given to the president or would be damaging to national security. Members of Congress sometimes oppose particular applications of this doctrine or accuse presidents and their subordinates of abusing it. Nevertheless, Congress has generally acknowledged the necessity of the doctrine for the successful, orderly, and secure operation of the federal government.

its own sources of information in order not to remain dependent upon information supplied by executive officials.

Second, a noteworthy trend in the evolution of the presidency has been the growing importance of the chief executive's role as a *legislative leader.* Article II, Section 3 of the Constitution requires the president periodically to provide Congress with "information of the State of the Union." His annual State of the Union address, however, is merely one among literally hundreds of messages and recommendations sent from the White House to Capitol Hill. Even more important may be the president's Budget Message, normally a document of several hundred pages, containing detailed recommendations for expenditures in all spheres of domestic and foreign governmental activity. As a rule, Congress uses these recommendations as a guide to its own deliberations. Although in the end it may depart from them in some respects, congressional action is massively influenced at all stages by the wishes of the president.

After Congress has approved a budget, the president still possesses discretion in the administration of the funds available to the executive branch. For example, after encountering considerable opposition to his request for expanded economic and military aid to El Salvador in 1983, President Reagan and his advisers stated that by "reprogramming" budgetary allocations and shifting funds from one program to another they would manage to acquire the funds the White House needed to achieve the administration's goals in Central America.[16] Such tactics, it must be emphasized, may be successful in the short run, but where funds are involved in the long run the president is dependent upon congressional willingness to provide them. Some recent presidents have also impounded (or refused to spend) funds appropriated by Congress for diplomatic purposes not approved by the White House. The frequent use of this power by President Richard Nixon led Congress to pass the Congressional Budget and Impoundment Control Act of 1974, which limited the chief executive's discretion in this realm.

The ability of a chief executive to "manage" Congress—or to maintain at least minimally collaborative relations with it—has become a major criterion by which the success of a president is measured. Even by his own admission, President Carter neglected his legislative responsibilities. Both his domestic and his foreign policy programs suffered from that neglect. On the other hand, President Reagan's reputation as the "Great Communicator" during his first term owed much to his ability to persuade an often reluctant Congress to support his policies.[17] President Bush's diplomatic moves also enjoyed a high level of congressional support—a result, in part, of the fact that they were approved by a substantial majority of the American people.

Third, perhaps the most effective technique available to the president for managing foreign relations is the ability to influence public opinion. Even before the era of modern communications media, chief executives understood the potency of this tactic. President Theodore Roosevelt once observed:

> People used to say to me that I was an astonishingly good politician and divined what the people are going to think. . . . I did not "divine" how the people were going to think; I simply made up my mind what they ought to think, and then did my best to get them to think it.[18]

As a molder of public opinion at home and abroad, the president is in a uniquely favorable position vis-à-vis Congress and other potential rivals. Routinely, the activities and statements of the chief executive are given extensive coverage by the news media. The president's actions and statements dominate the news outlets; responses by rival political figures to major presidential addresses, for example, usually attract only a fraction of the audience that heard the president. When the White House believes it desirable, the president can almost always obtain time on national radio and television to inform the public about a crisis or some significant development in foreign affairs and describe the steps he proposes to take to deal with it. According to one informed student of public opinion, once a president has made a foreign affairs decision that becomes known to the public, he automatically receives the support of at least 50 percent of the people, irrespective of the nature of the decision.[19] Despite recent fears of the imperial presidency, the American people continue to believe that the president is and should be in charge of foreign policy. Conversely, as the demise of the Carter administration suggested, they have little forbearance for a chief executive who appears to be indecisive and to have lost control of events abroad.

At one time or another, every president in the past sixty years has been accused of managing the news to achieve his foreign policy objectives.[20] President Franklin D. Roosevelt used his radio "fireside chats" with extraordinary effectiveness to rally public opinion behind his policies. During the Cuban missile crisis in 1962, President Kennedy made a dramatic national TV speech, informing the nation about the construction of Soviet missile sites in Cuba and presenting his strategy for responding to the threat. During the early 1980s, President Reagan repeatedly relied upon his communication talents to rally public support behind his program for substantial military expansion. And on frequent occasions during the Persian Gulf crisis, President Bush made appeals at home and abroad for support of his diplomatic and military strategies.

Fourth, one of the oldest bases of the president's power is his role as a political leader. Normally, a president is automatically acknowledged to be the leader of his political party. Congressional, state, and local candidates usually value his endorsement in their political campaigns, and there may be considerable pressure on them to support the president's policies in order to win that endorsement. The president can also make many "patronage" appointments to federal office (though the number of these appointments has declined over the past half-century), and he is naturally inclined to favor political friends and allies. Moreover, White House influence can be useful to legislators and others in dealing with the federal bureaucracy. Perhaps most crucially, leaders and members of the president's party are constantly aware that the results of the next presidential election will depend substantially upon the president's record in dealing with major internal and external issues.

Finally, the president is sometimes able to commit the nation to a position or course of action in foreign affairs regardless of what others may wish. This power was vividly illustrated by President Theodore Roosevelt's actions in building the Panama Canal. Roosevelt was determined to "make the dirt fly" in Panama—that is, to get the canal built despite the opposition of legislators and others. He authorized construction to begin even before the Senate had approved the Hay-Bunau-Varilla Treaty (1904), which gave the United States the right to construct a canal across the Panamanian isthmus. He later noted:

> If I had followed traditional, conservative methods I would have submitted a dignified State paper . . . to Congress and the debates on it would have been going on yet; but I took the Canal Zone and let Congress debate; and while the debate goes on the Canal does also.[21]

During the crisis over the Soviet threat to Greece in 1947, President Truman committed the United States to a policy of "containment" of communism, and in a speech on the Senate floor, Sen. Arthur H. Vandenberg, R-Mich., declared:

> The overriding fact is that the President has made a long-delayed statement regarding Communism on-the-march which must be supported [by Congress] if there is any hope of ever impressing Moscow with the necessity of paying any sort of peaceful attention to us.[22]

In short, once the chief executive has put a policy in motion, it is extremely difficult for Congress or public opinion to repudiate it. After President Bush, for example, committed the United States to a policy of opposition to Iraqi aggression in the Persian Gulf region, Bush's critics faced massive obstacles to opposing the policy successfully without repudiating the American chief executive in the eyes of the world and undermining the credibility of the nation's diplomacy.

Even beyond both constitutional grants of authority and informal modes of executive leadership is this reality: the president of the United

States is the head of state and the leader of perhaps the most powerful nation known to history—the dramatically visible symbol of that nation. In contrast to the way in which it structures the other two branches of the government, the Constitution vests the executive power of the United States *in a single person:* the president. Sometimes, for example, as in President Kennedy's dramatic presence at the Berlin Wall, the chief executive makes or asserts the nation's foreign policy in a way in which rivals find it nearly impossible to challenge successfully. For millions of people at home and abroad, the White House serves as the focal point of decision making in the U.S. government. When citizens ask, "Who is in charge here?" they almost immediately, perhaps instinctively, answer, "The president." It is to the Oval Office that they look for dynamic leadership in formulating responses to external problems. Implicitly—and, no doubt in many cases reluctantly—even Congress concedes that it is incapable of providing the kind of unified and decisive leadership required to navigate the troubled waters of international relations safely in the late twentieth century.

The Foreign Policy Bureaucracy

Within the executive branch, many entities other than the White House are involved in the making of foreign policy. Chief among these is, of course, the State Department, but account must also be taken of the intelligence community, the military establishment, and a host of other agencies.

The State Department

The executive agency most broadly and directly concerned with foreign affairs is the Department of State, headed by the secretary of state, who is generally regarded as the highest ranking cabinet officer. Under the authority of the president, the department conducts relations with more than 150 other independent nations around the world, with international organizations such as the United Nations, and with regional bodies such as the Organization of American States (OAS). It operates more than 150 embassies and diplomatic missions overseas, as well as some 140 consular posts. Yet the State Department's operating budget has always been one of the smallest of any executive agency. In the 1989 fiscal year, for example, it was $1.95 billion—considerably less than 1 percent of the funds allocated to the military.

Traditionally, the State Department's primary concern has been political relations with other countries. Its five regional bureaus, plus another bureau for international organization affairs, serve as the channels for communicating policy decisions to U.S. embassies abroad and for receiving communications from them. Since World War II, there has also been a significant expansion in the department's functional bureaus, those that deal with problems and issues cutting across national boundaries. For example, the department now has a bureau that is concerned with the impact of public opinion on foreign policy, and another for oceans and international environmental and scientific affairs. Two recent additions have been bureaus for human rights and humanitarian affairs and for international refugee affairs.[23]

Another postwar development has been the department's recognition of a growing congressional role in foreign policy. An assistant secretary for congressional relations is now assigned specific responsibility for maintaining constructive relations with Congress, and this function has become an increasingly important and time-consuming dimension of State Department activities. The Office of Congressional Relations collects and analyzes information on legislative attitudes toward foreign policy issues; it provides services requested by members of Congress, such as foreign travel arrangements; and, when required, it plays a prominent role in White House lobbying on Capitol Hill for the president's foreign policy program. State Department services to Congress sometimes take curious forms. Former secretary of state Acheson pointed out that legislators often feel compelled for domestic political reasons to oppose certain external programs, such as foreign aid. In one case the department helped a legislator resolve that dilemma "by the promise of a powerful speech against the foreign aid bill when it came up for final vote in the House. We [the State Department] duly wrote it and all parties profited!"[24]

In 1961, Congress established the Agency for International Development (AID) to administer bilateral economic aid programs. Initially it was housed within the State Department; later, it was made part of the International Development Cooperation Agency. While it is thus administratively separate from the State Department, in carrying out its mission AID still takes its policy guidance from the department.

Routinely, newly elected presidents announce that they regard the secretary of state as their chief foreign policy adviser and expect this official to provide overall direction to the government's activities in foreign affairs. Yet in practice, a decline in the State Department's preeminence in the foreign policy field since World War II has been evident to all observers. The department's reputation with the White House, with other executive agencies, with Congress, and often with other governments has been chronically poor. In the minds of some presidents, the State Department has epitomized bureaucratic inertia, devotion to tradition, and lack of imagination.[25] Ever since the administration of President Franklin D. Roosevelt, presidents have been prone to bypass the State Department, using one device or another to make crucial decisions without consulting it.[26] As we shall see, coordinating mechanisms, like the National Security Council, have emerged as powerful rivals to the State Department for dominance in the foreign policy field. Indeed, at times (and the Reagan administration provided a dramatic example) a condition of anarchy has appeared to exist among the executive agencies involved in foreign relations.

The erosion of the State Department's position can be explained by many factors and developments. Critics of the department have complained that it has failed to adapt its procedures and ideas to a rapidly changing world, leaving the White House no choice but to look elsewhere for creative policy recommendations. The involvement of an increasing number of other executive agencies in foreign relations has diluted the State Department's authority and responsibility. Finally, unlike other departments and agencies of the national government, the State Department suffers from the disability of having no domestic constituency to argue or lobby for its programs and activities abroad. In fact, its policies toward the Soviet Union or South Africa or Israel often engender strong *negative* reactions by pressure groups within the United States. What such groups are against is often considerably clearer than what they are for.[27] On Capitol Hill, the State Department is likely to be regarded by legislators as a troublemaker, for it advocates costly foreign economic and military aid programs, which are frequently unpopular with the voters.

The Intelligence Community

The agencies and bureaus that collect and analyze information on foreign affairs for the executive branch are collectively known as the *intelligence community*. As specified in Executive Order 12333, issued by President Reagan on December 4, 1981, the intelligence community consists of the Central Intelligence Agency; the National Security Agency; the Bureau of Intelligence and Research in the Department of State; the Defense Intelligence Agency and the intelligence offices of the army, navy, air force, and marine corps in the Department of Defense; the Federal Bureau of Investigation; intelligence offices in the Department of Energy and the Department of the Treasury; and "staff elements of the Director of Central Intelligence."[28]

Intelligence is a minor part of the activities of some of these agencies in terms of their budget and personnel, even though it may be important in the total flow of information. The function that makes the FBI part of the intelligence community is counterintelligence—that is, the identification of covert foreign agents in the United States and the defeat of foreign efforts at espionage and subversion. The main contribution of the Treasury Department is economic, financial, and monetary information.

As every reader of the daily headlines is aware, in recent years public controversy has surrounded the activities of the CIA and other members of the intelligence community. Charges have been made that intelligence agencies have sought to assassinate political leaders abroad; that they have supported attempts to overthrow foreign governments; and that they have infringed upon the rights of U.S. citizens. On the other hand, the intelligence agencies have also encountered criticisms (particularly after the Iranian revolution in 1979) that they have failed to provide policy makers with objective and up-to-date estimates that would have enabled them to anticipate major developments abroad and to respond effectively to them.

Two general observations about intelligence activities in the United States are worth making here. First, today, as in the past, the intelligence function is recognized by officials in both the executive and the legislative branches, and by a majority of citizens, as essential to the national security and to the achievement of diplomatic objectives. The CIA was established in 1947 in large part because of vivid recollections by the American people and their leaders of the military disaster at Pearl Harbor, which was (rightly or wrongly) viewed as the result of an intelligence failure. Most informed Americans are aware of the adverse consequences of a crippled or inadequate intelligence service. In 1983, a terrorist attack against U.S. marines in Lebanon, resulting in the death of 241 men, dramatically called attention to the dangers implicit in a lack of advance information. Again in 1990, neither the CIA nor any other intelligence agency (such as the Mossad, the Israeli intelligence agency) alerted the White House to the strong likelihood of an Iraqi attack against Kuwait.

Second, the need for effective intelligence operations conflicts with such traditional democratic concepts as open diplomacy, freedom of the press, and public disclosure of information, which are no less important in the foreign policy process. The tension in a democracy between these two kinds of requirements is real, continuing, and perhaps inescapable. If, as is suggested in Chapter 6, congressional efforts to monitor and regulate intelligence operations have been less than satisfactory, the reason may be that the dilemma has no simple or easy solution.

Propaganda and Informational Programs

Another executive agency that plays a key role in foreign affairs is the United States Information Agency (USIA). Like AID, USIA is administratively separate but takes its policy guidance from the State Department. Its mission is to conduct propaganda and informational programs abroad on behalf of the United States. Perhaps its best known activity is the Voice of America, the nation's worldwide radio network. In addition, the USIA engages in a variety of other activities and programs, such as the production and distribution of films; the preparation of press releases; the sponsorship of cultural, scientific, and other kinds of exhibits and lectures; and the operation of cultural centers and libraries overseas.

Ever since its creation in the early postwar period, controversy has surrounded the mission of the USIA, growing out of the conflict between two conceptions of the agency's mission. One view holds that it was intended to be primarily a propaganda instrument of the government, and as such, its dominant function ought to be to portray the internal and external policies of the United States in the most favorable light possible. The other conception is that USIA's principal mission is to engage in a "campaign of truth," as the program was designated by the Truman administration, and it should therefore be factual and objective in its depiction of the United States, with no attempt to gloss over shortcomings and failures. The underlying assumption of this latter approach is that objectivity is "the best propaganda" for a democratic nation. The conflict between these two schools of thought has impeded the effectiveness of U.S. propaganda and informational campaigns in the past and will likely continue to do so in the future.[29]

The Military Establishment

Among national policy makers and informed citizens, World War II produced a realization that was not always present in earlier eras of U.S. diplomacy: the military establishment plays a vital role in the foreign policy process. Previously, both civilian and military officials tended to separate political and military questions sharply, as illustrated by President Franklin D. Roosevelt's view that the resolution of political questions arising during the war ought to await the outcome of military hostilities.[30] After the end of the war, when a new political-military conflict known as the cold war had erupted among the erstwhile allies, American officials recognized the indissoluble link between these two aspects of national policy. Again in the early 1990s, a victory by the American-led coalition in the Persian Gulf region did not ensure achievement of Washington's long-term political objective of peace and security in the Middle East.

Following a prolonged study, the Department of Defense was created in 1947, and other reforms of the military establishment were undertaken. While the traditional pattern of separate military services was preserved, they were placed under the jurisdiction of a single department, headed by a civilian secretary of defense. The Joint Chiefs of Staff, consisting of the commanders of each of the military branches and a chairman, was created to formulate unified military strategy.

By the late 1980s, some 2.2 million men and women were serving in the armed forces of the United States. For fiscal year 1989, the Reagan administration asked Congress to appropriate $332 billion to operate the Department of Defense.[31] For fiscal year 1991, the Bush White House proposed a national defense budget of some $296 billion—a reduction of around $11 billion from the previous year. Within a few months, however, military spending projections were upset by the enormous costs involved in the Persian Gulf War (see Chapter 5). Washington hoped, however, to recover a major portion of this expense from the other members of the allied coalition opposing Iraqi expansionism. The war aside, sentiment was strong on Capitol Hill for more drastic reductions in military spending. Even executive officials conceded that, in the light of the fundamental improvement in Soviet-American relations, substantial savings in the military budget ought to be possible in the years ahead. At the same time, the conflict in the Persian Gulf had also called attention to the crucial role of what might be called high technology weapons systems, which are often extremely expensive. The war also demonstrated the desirability of more and better means of transporting the nation's armed forces to possible trouble spots.

During all the nation's post-World War II military conflicts, however, U.S. public opinion and governmental policy remained supportive of one basic constitutional principle. A civilian, the president, is the commander in chief of the armed forces; the members of the National Security Council are civilian officials; the secretary of defense is a civilian; and the overall foreign policy process remains under civilian control. No convincing evidence exists that the fundamental constitutional principle of civilian control over the armed forces is in jeopardy. During the Persian Gulf War, for example, it was clear on several occasions that, irrespective of their personal views or initial policy recommendations, the nation's highest military officials unhesitatingly carried out policy as decided upon by the president.

Other Executive Agencies

A striking and highly significant development since World War II has been the increased interest and involvement in foreign relations by many departments and agencies within the executive branch other than those that have been discussed so far. The departments of Agriculture, Commerce, Defense, Treasury, Transportation, Interior, Energy, and Labor all have responsibility for problems with a foreign policy dimension. For example, the Agriculture Department has played a pivotal role for many years in the Food for Peace program, which ships food products to needy countries; it promotes agricultural exports to countries such as Japan; and it has sent hundreds of experts abroad to assist less-developed societies in raising their agricultural output. As has always been the case, the Commerce Department seeks to expand American business, investment, and trade opportunities abroad. The Treasury Department is concerned with fiscal and monetary issues, such as the soundness of the dollar overseas. The Transportation Department has some responsibilities in the determination of international airline routes. The Energy Department is keenly interested in preserving the nation's access to foreign supplies of fuel, such as petroleum products and natural gas. Even the Interior Department conducts programs that impinge upon foreign affairs, such as water reclamation projects involving the United States and Mexico.

A growing number of smaller and less publicized federal agencies have functions giving them a role in foreign relations. The National Aeronautics and Space Administration (NASA) sponsors programs that affect the global balance of military power and America's ability to monitor the military activities of other countries. The Arms Control and Disarmament Agency is responsible for preparing reports and recommendations to the president on arms-limitation proposals.

This proliferation of executive agencies involved in foreign affairs has had a parallel in Congress, as we shall see more fully in Chapter 2. Today there is hardly a legislative committee or subcommittee whose work does not relate in some way to foreign affairs, and the result is a serious potential for conflict between the White House and Congress on foreign policy questions. This poses an increasingly difficult problem for the creation and maintenance of unified governmental efforts abroad.

Coordination of Foreign Policy

Senator Vandenberg once told officials of the Truman administration that members of the Republican party wanted to cooperate with the White House on behalf of a "bipartisan foreign policy," but they could do so only with "one secretary of state at a time." The problem to which the senator alluded has become more acute since that time. The Carter administration's response to the collapse of the Iranian monarchy in 1979, for example, became, in the words of one report,

> the subject of fierce internal debate [within the executive branch], with many officials asserting that interagency disputes and bureaucratic compromises have hampered the efforts of Mr. Carter and his top advisers to fashion and carry out an overall strategy.[32]

According to former secretary of state Alexander Haig, conflicts among President Reagan's chief foreign policy advisers were such that the United States had become a "ghost ship" drifting aimlessly upon the sea of international relations. Other studies of the Reagan administration have concluded that at times, the term *anarchy* could accurately be used to describe relations among executive officials and agencies.[33]

There have, of course, been examples of an impressive degree of unity in the White House's approach to major foreign policy issues. An outstanding one was the Kennedy administration's handling of the Cuban missile crisis in 1962. Its response to the discovery of nuclear-armed Soviet missiles in Cuba was a model of diplomatic decision making; and yet in the early stages of the crisis, there was considerable disagreement among President Kennedy's advisers over what actions to take. Ultimately, the members of Kennedy's foreign policy team did reach substantial unanimity on the course of action to be followed, and this was unquestionably one of the factors contributing to the achievement of U.S. goals in the crisis. In the Bush administration, a substantial consensus appeared to exist among the president and his advisers concerning the main lines of the nation's external policy.

Presidents and Their Advisers: Four Models

On the basis of historical experience, it is possible to identify four reasonably distinct patterns or models of relationships between chief executives and their foreign policy advisers. Each pattern has both assets and liabilities for the effort by the United States to achieve its foreign policy objectives.

1. *The president as his own secretary of state.* This model is associated particularly with the presidency of Franklin D. Roosevelt. FDR was, in some respects, the most charismatic and politically adroit chief executive in U.S. history. Although he possessed only limited background and experience in the foreign policy field, as time passed he increasingly took the conduct of external affairs into his own hands. For example, Roosevelt had almost unlimited confidence in his ability to arrive at lasting agreements with "Uncle Joe" Stalin, and, more generally, to create the kind of new world order he hoped would follow World War II. FDR's secretary of state, Cordell Hull, therefore largely confined his efforts to a few assigned areas of foreign policy, such as generating support on Capitol Hill for Roosevelt's diplomatic moves and cultivating cordial relations with Latin America. The president himself made crucial foreign policy decisions, often without even consulting the State Department; negotiated with foreign leaders; attended summit conferences; and otherwise conducted foreign relations. Hull and other members of FDR's inner circle were often left in ignorance of the president's foreign policy moves and intentions. Any coordination of the

administration's foreign policy activities (and frequently there was very little) was provided by Roosevelt himself.

FDR's determination to be his own secretary of state undoubtedly added to the burdens of his office, contributing to his declining health and vitality. Moreover, many diplomatic historians believe that a number of Roosevelt's diplomatic decisions reflected a lack of understanding of key international issues and were detrimental to U.S. interests. His penchant for secrecy meant that there was no immediate accountability to Congress and the electorate for foreign policy moves. At the same time, it must be remembered that FDR led the nation during wartime, when a high degree of secrecy customarily surrounds military and diplomatic moves. It must also be noted that, in the U.S. constitutional system, a president is free to function as the secretary of state at any time, and nearly all presidents in fact do so at some stage.

2. *The hierarchical model.* This pattern is illustrated by the approach to diplomatic decision making taken by President Truman. Truman had even less experience in foreign affairs than Roosevelt, but unlike his predecessor, he did not hesitate to acknowledge his limitations in this respect. Truman followed the ritual of declaring that his secretary of state would be responsible for the conduct of foreign relations, under his own direction. However, in contrast to most presidents, Truman actually adhered to this principle. Time and again he defended his secretary of state from critics inside and outside the government and supported him against rival claimants within the executive branch. This State Department-centered model of decision making clearly has advantages, as shown by the fact that the Truman administration accomplished some of the most noteworthy diplomatic feats of the post-World War II era.

In this model, the president assumes ultimate responsibility for directing foreign affairs, but he delegates the day-to-day conduct of foreign relations to the secretary of state, who in turn relies upon the State Department bureaucracy for expertise and guidance. The secretary of state is also given the authority to coordinate foreign policy activities throughout the executive branch. (The National Security Council was created during Truman's administration, but its role in foreign policy decision making was minimal during his term of office; he was known to be unenthusiastic about the NSC mechanism.) It may be seriously questioned whether, with the widening circle of executive agencies involved in foreign policy decision making, it is any longer possible to return to this model.

3. *The consensual model.* The Johnson administration of the 1960s is a good illustration of this pattern. Its outstanding trait was the overt unanimity among the president's foreign policy advisers in formulating policy toward the Vietnam War and most other developments abroad.

Under the tragic circumstances of his accession to the presidency, LBJ believed that he was obliged to continue the diplomatic policies of his predecessor, and President Kennedy had left no doubt that he viewed Communist control of Southeast Asia as highly detrimental to U.S. diplomatic and security interests. President Johnson was determined to prevent that development.

Despite his background of service in Congress, LBJ possessed little firsthand knowledge or experience in the sphere of foreign relations. Moreover, as a product of the populist political tradition, he was suspicious of the State Department and of foreign affairs generally—a realm populists believed to be a distraction from the principal business of domestic affairs. President Johnson defined his chief goal as the creation of the Great Society in the United States.

LBJ also valued loyalty among his aides; he expected unwavering support from them, and he did not take kindly to evidence of dissent from his administration's policies. The result was what some commentators have called "groupthink," a more or less forced and virtually monolithic agreement among his advisers. For several years, Johnson used techniques of direct and indirect coercion to maintain this show of unity, but the result was to prevent full and frank discussion by executive officials of controversial foreign policy issues—above all, the Vietnam War. Dissenters, such as Under Secretary of State George Ball, found themselves ostracized and increasingly relegated to the sidelines. Failing to get a hearing for their views within LBJ's official family, some dissenters resorted to leaks to the press in order to present their ideas and policy recommendations. Adherence to this model of decision making contributed to the perpetuation of a policy abroad that, in the end, resulted in a dramatic and serious diplomatic defeat for the United States.

4. *The rival State Department model.* The diplomatic record of the Nixon administration illustrates the fourth approach to foreign policy decision making. As a chief executive who was keenly interested in foreign policy, and who had acquired impressive experience in this sphere, President Nixon had decided by the 1970s that fundamental changes were called for in the nation's approach to external problems. (Many of Nixon's substantive proposals were contained in what came to be called the Nixon Doctrine.) He was extremely suspicious of the State Department and doubted its ability to provide the diplomatic leadership required in the era following the Vietnam War. Accordingly, Nixon selected as his national security adviser Henry Kissinger, who possessed outstanding academic credentials, had a clear conception of the direction in which he believed U.S. foreign policy ought to move, and had the ambition and skill needed to make his viewpoints prevail in the inevitable bureaucratic infighting. Like Nixon, Kissinger doubted both the ability

and the willingness of the State Department to provide creative diplomatic leadership. Meanwhile, President Nixon appointed a largely unknown individual, William P. Rogers, to head the State Department, in the deliberate expectation that Rogers would be a weak and ineffectual secretary of state. In the Nixon White House, therefore, Kissinger quickly emerged as the principal spokesman, articulator, negotiator, and highly visible public symbol of the administration's foreign policy.

This White House-centered model of decision making signified the fact that the president was extremely interested in foreign affairs, was actively involved in the decision-making process, and was determined to impose central direction and coordination upon the nation's diplomatic activities. Kissinger created and operated the "rival State Department" with President Nixon's full encouragement and support. Yet, as many legislators and commentators complained at the time and afterward, Kissinger had never been confirmed in his position by the Senate, and he often conducted himself as though he had no real accountability to Congress or the American people for his performance. To this day, the State Department has not regained the status it enjoyed in an earlier era, and perhaps it never will.

Three observations may be made about the decision-making models considered here. First, presidents are free to use their advisers in any way they choose. Congress may create new administrative structures, like the NSC, but it cannot determine how—or even whether—a particular president will utilize such mechanisms in the decision-making process.

Second, a president may use different models at different times. For example, President Truman did rely somewhat more upon the NSC toward the end of his tenure in office than he had earlier.

Third, coordinating mechanisms and devices are perhaps in the end less important than individuals in determining whether the executive branch achieves and maintains a high degree of unity in dealing with foreign policy problems. No one of these models per se guarantees unity among the major participants in the foreign policy process, nor is one inherently superior to the others. The model that is employed, and the contribution that it makes to the foreign policy process, will to a considerable degree be determined by a particular president's administrative style and preferences. In the final analysis, durable unity within the government on foreign policy questions will likely be a function of a widely shared conviction that the policy adopted best promotes the interests of the United States in foreign affairs.

Notes

1. Roger Hilsman, *The Politics of Policy Making in Defense and Foreign Affairs* (New York: Harper and Row, 1971), 18. Recent studies focusing

upon the presidency include the following: Cecil V. Crabb, Jr., and Kevin V. Mulcahy, *Presidents and Foreign Policy Making: FDR to Reagan* (Baton Rouge: Louisiana State University Press, 1990); Barbara Kellerman and Ryan J. Barilleaux, *The President as World Leader* (New York: St. Martin's, 1990); Carnes Lord, *The Presidency and the Management of National Security* (New York: Free Press, 1988); James P. Pfiffner and R. Gordon Hoxie, *The Presidency in Transition* (New York: Center for the Presidency, 1991); Richard E. Neustadt, *Presidential Power and the Modern Presidents: The Politics of Leadership from Roosevelt to Reagan* (New York: Free Press, 1990); Sidney M. Milkis and Michael Nelson, *The American Presidency: Origins and Development, 1776-1990* (Washington, D.C.: CQ Press, 1990); Nigel Bowles, *The White House and Capitol Hill: The Politics of Presidential Persuasion* (New York: Oxford University Press, 1987).

2. Clausewitz was the author of the celebrated treatise *On War,* in which he examined the relationships between armed conflict and the political process. For an illuminating condensation of his thought, see Roger A. Leonard, ed., *Clausewitz on War* (New York: Capricorn, 1968). For more detailed studies of national security policy, see R. Gordon Hoxie, *Command Decision and the Presidency: A Study in National Security Policy and Organization* (New York: Center for the Presidency, 1989); Frederick H. Hartmann and Robert L. Wendzel, *Defending America's Security* (Washington, D.C.: Pergamon, 1988); Peter Mangold, *National Security and International Relations: The Search for Security* (New York: Routledge, Chapman and Hall, 1990); Cecil V. Crabb, Jr., and Kevin V. Mulcahy, *American National Security: A Presidential Perspective* (Pacific Grove, Calif.: Brooks/Cole, 1990); and Cynthia Watson, *U.S. National Security Policy Groups* (Westport, Conn.: Greenwood Press, 1990).

3. For a more detailed discussion of the meaning and connotations of diplomacy, see Elmer Plischke, "The New Diplomacy: A Changing Process," *Virginia Quarterly Review* 49 (Summer 1973): 321-345.

4. For fuller elaboration of this point, see the discussion on the "different worlds" that the State Department and Congress occupy, in Smith Simpson, *Anatomy of the State Department* (Boston: Houghton Mifflin, 1967), 152-183.

5. For a succinct discussion of this longstanding controversy, see the report prepared by the Library of Congress for the House Foreign Affairs Committee, *Background Information on the Use of the United States Armed Forces in Foreign Countries,* 91st Cong., 2d sess., 1970. A more detailed treatment of the significance of individual constitutional provisions is provided in *The Constitution of the United States of America: Analysis and Interpretation* (Washington, D.C.: Library of Congress, 1973).

6. A useful compendium of conflicting interpretations of the president's authority over the armed forces is provided in Senate Foreign Relations Committee, *Hearings on the War Powers Legislation,* 92d Cong., 1st sess., 1971. See also Pat M. Holt, *The War Powers Resolution: The Role of Congress in U.S. Armed Intervention* (Washington, D.C.: American Enterprise Institute, 1978).

7. For further discussion of the use of armed force to achieve national goals abroad, see Gregory A. Fossedal, *The Democratic Imperative: Exporting the American Revolution* (New York: Basic Books, 1989); Edward K. Hamilton, ed., *America's Global Interests: A New Agenda* (New York:

W. W. Norton, 1989); Benjamin Frankel, *In the National Interest: A National Interest Reader* (Lanham, Md.: University Press of America, 1989); George Weigel, *American Interests, American Purposes* (Westport, Conn.: Greenwood Press, 1989); and Wesley T. Wooley, *Alternatives to Anarchy: American Supranationalism since World War II* (Bloomington: Indiana University Press, 1988).

8. The context, meaning, and implications of the Carter Doctrine are discussed in Cecil V. Crabb, Jr., *The Doctrines of American Foreign Policy: Their Meaning, Role, and Future* (Baton Rouge: Louisiana State University Press, 1982), 325-371. The ill-fated mission to rescue the hostages in Iran is discussed in detail in Jimmy Carter, *Keeping Faith: Memoirs of a President* (New York: Bantam, 1982), 459-513.

9. See the column by James Reston in the *New York Times*, December 20, 1979, and the editorial, "Unmaking a Treaty," January 20, 1980. See also *Congressional Quarterly Weekly Report*, December 15, 1979, 2850.

10. Loch Johnson and James M. McCormick, "Foreign Policy by Executive Fiat," *Foreign Policy* 28 (Fall 1977): 118-124. This article provides a comprehensive and illuminating discussion of presidential reliance upon executive agreements since World War II and of Congress's response to that practice.

11. Ibid., 118.

12. Ibid., 118.

13. *New York Times*, March 2, 1979.

14. See the discussion of the allied contribution to the Persian Gulf defense effort in *Newsweek*, "Special Issue," Spring/Summer, 1991, 39-40; dispatch by Thomas L. Friedman and Patrick E. Tyler in *New York Times*, March 3, 1991; and *Time*, November 12, 1990, 34.

15. See W. Averell Harriman and Elie Abel, *Special Envoy to Churchill and Stalin: 1941-1946* (New York: Random House, 1975); Hamilton Jordan, *Crisis: The Last Year of the Carter Presidency* (New York: G.P. Putnam's Sons, 1982); and, for reports on Habib's diplomatic activities in the Middle East, *New York Times*, July 23 and November 2, 1982.

16. President Reagan's budgetary maneuvers in responding to upheaval and violence in Central America are discussed by Tom Wicker in the *New York Times*, March 1, 1983.

17. For more detailed discussion of lobbying by governmental agencies, see *The Washington Lobby*, 4th ed. (Washington, D.C.: CQ Press, 1982).

18. More extensive discussions of the role of public opinion in shaping foreign policy decisions are Roderick P. Hart, *The Sound of Leadership: Presidential Communication in the Modern Age* (Chicago: University of Chicago Press, 1987); Symposium "The Media and the Presidency," *Presidential Studies Quarterly* 16 (Winter 1986); Irving Crespi, *Public Opinion, Polls, and Democracy* (Boulder, Colo.: Westview Press, 1989); George Edwards III and Stephen J. Wayne, *Presidential Leadership: Politics and Policymaking* (New York: St. Martin's, 1990); Eugene Wittkopf, *Faces of Internationalism: American Public Opinion and Foreign Policy* (Durham, N.C.: Duke University Press, 1990); Thomas Bodenheimer and Robert Gould, *Rollback: Right-Wing Power and U.S. Foreign Policy* (Boston: South End Press, 1989); and Mohammed E. Ahrari, ed., *Ethnic Groups and U.S. Foreign Policy* (Westport, Conn.: Greenwood Press, 1987).

19. Daniel Yankelovich, "Farewell to 'President Knows Best,'" *Foreign Affairs* 57 (1978): 670. Yankelovich contended that "automatic" public approval of presidential leadership in foreign affairs was declining, but President

Reagan subsequently utilized his skills as a communicator in convincing the American public that he would reverse the decline of the nation's power abroad. For an analysis of these skills, see John Herbers, "The President and the Press Corps," *New York Times Magazine,* May 9, 1982.

20. The subject is examined in Doris A. Graber, *Media Power in Politics* (Washington, D.C.: CQ Press, 1984); Robert B. Sims, *The Pentagon Reporters* (Washington, D.C.: National Defense University, 1985); William A. Dorman and Mansour Farhang, *The U.S. Press and Iran: Foreign Policy and the Journalism of Deference* (Berkeley: University of California Press, 1987); Brigitte L. Nacos, *The Press, Presidents, and Crises* (New York: Columbia University Press, 1990); Daniel C. Hallin, *The "Uncensored War": The Media and Vietnam* (Berkeley: University of California Press, 1989); and Brent Scowcroft, *Reflections on the Role of the Media* (Washington, D.C.: Georgetown University Institute for the Study of Diplomacy, 1988).

21. Quoted in Thomas A. Bailey, *A Diplomatic History of the American People,* 8th ed. (New York: Appleton-Century-Crofts, 1969), 497.

22. Arthur H. Vandenberg, Jr., ed., *The Private Papers of Senator Vandenberg* (Boston: Houghton Mifflin, 1952), 344.

23. For a provocative analysis of the State Department since World War II, see Barry Rubin, *Secrets of State: The State Department and the Struggle over U.S. Foreign Policy* (New York: Oxford University Press, 1985).

24. Dean Acheson, *Present at the Creation: My Years in the State Department* (New York: W. W. Norton, 1969), 93.

25. Perhaps no modern president was more inclined in this direction than Kennedy; see Theodore C. Sorensen, *Kennedy* (New York: Harper and Row, 1965), 287-290.

26. A recent example was the Carter administration's diplomacy during the Iranian crisis of 1979. According to one report, the president sent a high-ranking U.S. military officer attached to NATO to confer directly with Iranian military leaders; this official "was told by the White House to bypass the United States Embassy" in Tehran. Nor was the embassy informed about discussions between members of the White House staff and Iranian diplomatic officials in the United States. See the dispatch by Richard Burt in the *New York Times,* January 12, 1979.

27. For a more detailed analysis of the State Department's postwar decline, see Robert Pringle, "Creeping Irrelevance at Foggy Bottom," *Foreign Policy* 29 (Winter 1977-1978): 128-140.

28. *Weekly Compilation of Presidential Documents,* vol. 17, no. 49, 1336-1348. One commentator has pointed out that the concept of the intelligence community is actually rather amorphous, since nearly every executive agency engages in some form of information gathering. Some informative studies of American intelligence organization and operations are the following: Jeffrey T. Richelson, *The U.S. Intelligence Community* (Cambridge, Mass.: Ballinger, 1985); Roy Godson, ed., *Intelligence Requirements for the 1990s* (Lexington, Mass.: Lexington Books, 1989); Bruce D. Berzowitz and Allan E. Goodman, *Strategic Intelligence for American National Security* (Princeton: Princeton University Press, 1989); Rhodi Jeffreys-Jones, *The CIA and American Democracy* (New Haven: Yale University Press, 1989); and Loch K. Johnson, *America's Secret Power: The CIA in a Democratic Society* (New York: Oxford University Press, 1989).

29. Background on U.S. propaganda and informational programs since World War II is provided in John W. Henderson, *The United States Information*

Agency (New York: Praeger, 1969); and Terry L. Deibel and Walter R. Roberts, *Culture and Information: Two Foreign Policy Functions* (Beverly Hills, Calif.: Sage, 1976). Recent information on the USIA's activities and programs may be found in Senate Committee on Foreign Relations, *Certain USIA Overseas Activities,* 98th Cong., 1st sess., 1983, S. Rept. 1983; and in House Committee on Foreign Affairs, *Oversight of the U.S. Information Agency,* 98th Cong., 2d sess., 1984. Useful commentaries are Frank A. Ninkovich, *The Diplomacy of Ideas: U.S. Foreign Policy and Cultural Relations* (New York: Cambridge University Press, 1981); Morrell Heald and Lawrence Kaplan, *Culture and Diplomacy* (Westport, Conn.: Greenwood Press, 1979); Garth Jowett and Victoria O'Donnell, *Propaganda and Persuasion* (Newbury Park, Calif.: Sage, 1986); and Leo Bogart, *Premises for Propaganda* (New York: Free Press, 1976).

30. See Gaddis Smith, *American Diplomacy during the Second World War* (New York: John Wiley, 1966), 12-16. For an expression of this viewpoint by a high-ranking military leader, see Omar N. Bradley, *A Soldier's Story* (New York: Holt, Rinehart and Winston, 1951), 536.

31. Helpful studies of major challenges facing the American military establishment are David C. Hendrickson, *Reforming Defense: The State of American Civil-Military Relations* (Baltimore: Johns Hopkins University Press, 1988); Helga Haftendorn and Jakob Schissler, *The Reagan Administration: Toward a Reconstruction of American Strength* (Hawthorne, N.Y.: Aldine de Gruyter, 1988); Kenneth L. Adelman and Norman R. Augustine, *The Defense Revolution* (San Francisco: ICS Press, 1990); Philip Webber, *New Defense Strategies for the 1990s: From Confrontation to Coexistence* (New York: St. Martin's, 1990); and Joseph Kruzel, ed., *American Defense Annual, 1989-1990* (Lexington, Mass.: Lexington Books, 1989), as well as the other annual volumes in this valuable series.

32. Dispatch by Richard Burt, *New York Times,* January 12, 1979.

33. Alexander Haig, *Caveat: Realism, Reagan, and Foreign Policy* (New York: Macmillan, 1984). Haig's tenure as President Reagan's first secretary of state was marked by continuous squabbling among cabinet heads and White House aides; after eighteen months in office, he resigned and was replaced by George Shultz.

CHAPTER 2

Congress and Foreign Affairs:
Traditional and Contemporary Roles

In mid-October 1987, the Senate passed a $3.6 billion authorization bill to finance the operations of the State Department for the next fiscal year. During the course of debate on this measure, ninety-eight amendments were offered, of which eighty-six were adopted. As one report expressed it, these amendments enabled legislators to express "outrage, support, concern and frustration" about almost every conceivable aspect of American foreign relations. One amendment called upon the president to seek reimbursement from those nations (chiefly the NATO allies and Japan) whose ships were being protected by the U.S. navy in the Persian Gulf. Another exempted anticommunist newspapers and other publications from the U.S. trade boycott against Nicaragua. Another amendment demanded that the president close the offices operated by the Palestine Liberation Organization (PLO) in Washington and New York City. Meanwhile, congressional dissatisfaction with the condition of the nation's foreign policy was expressed in another way: Congress made a deeper cut in the State Department's operating budget than had been made in some thirty years—a reduction that the department said would require large-scale layoffs of personnel. (It was observed, however, that the $84 million reduction in funds represented less than half the cost of a single B-1 bomber.)[1]

These actions illustrated the determination of the legislative branch to play a greater role in the foreign policy process. Since the Vietnam conflict especially—because of the belief that actions by the "imperial presidency" were in large measure responsible for American involvement in that traumatic episode—legislators have been determined to take back what many of them view as the historic prerogatives of Congress in foreign, no less than in domestic, policy. They want Congress to be accepted as a "partner" with the president in the conduct of foreign relations.[2]

Congressional Assertiveness:
The Challenge and the Problems

All informed students of recent U.S. foreign relations are aware that the milestones in the nation's diplomacy in the years after World War II—establishment of the UN (1945), the Greek-Turkish Aid Program (1947), the Marshall Plan for European recovery (1948), the NATO treaty (1949), and the Point IV program of aid to the developing countries (1949)—emerged as the result of collaboration between executive and legislative policy makers. Over the next twenty years, however, congressional influence in foreign relations declined, reaching its nadir at the time of the Vietnam War. Yet by the mid-1970s, presidents Nixon and Ford—joined sometimes even by some legislators—were complaining about the "restraints" that Congress was trying to impose upon the executive branch's ability to respond to foreign crises. During the 1980s, President Reagan similarly deplored legislative efforts to limit his freedom of action in Central America and the Middle East.

According to an informed commentator, Congress has "always been uncertain about its role in the field of foreign affairs." [3] Can Congress become a dynamic and effective force in foreign relations? Can it, as some proponents of a more influential legislative role advocate, operate as a full partner with the president in foreign affairs? A revitalization of legislative influence in external affairs faces numerous major and minor obstacles.

There is, first of all, a problem that has impeded effective legislative participation in the foreign policy process for more than two centuries—since even before the founding of the republic—and may be a more formidable obstacle today than at any other stage in American history. In 1777, the Continental Congress established a five-member Committee for Foreign Affairs to conduct external relations. Yet, as one study found, "partisanship and personalities, frequent changes in personnel and the use of special committees, impaired the efficient functioning of the committee and made a coherent policy impossible." Legislative management of foreign relations was characterized by "fluctuation, . . . delay and indecision." As much as any other single factor, it was the mismanagement of foreign affairs *by Congress* that led to the calling of the Constitutional Convention in 1787.[4]

Contemporary evidence indicates that the same conditions—a diffusion of power and responsibility in Congress and an inability to coordinate its activities in foreign affairs—are no less present today than they were then.[5] Indeed, they may have become worse since the end of World War II, as political party ties have weakened, the power of committee chairmen has declined, the number of legislative subcommittees has proliferated, and individual legislators increasingly attempt to leave their mark on selected areas of foreign policy. Sen. Barry Goldwater, R-Ariz., upon retiring from the Senate after many years of service, said, "If this is the world's greatest deliberative body, I'd hate to see the worst!" [6]

A few figures and examples will reinforce and illustrate the point. During an investigation by the Senate Foreign Relations Committee of the Johnson administration's conduct of the Vietnam War, one member remarked, "There are nineteen men on [the committee], and they represent 21½ viewpoints." [7] During the 1970s, the Carter administration's foreign policy efforts were beset by the divisions on Capitol Hill. Distrustful of the Soviet Union, conservative groups in Congress opposed attempts to arrive at agreements with Moscow, such as the SALT II treaty. By contrast, liberal legislators were calling for large reductions in the national defense budget. A third group demanded across-the-board reductions in all federal spending.[8]

During the first session of the 99th Congress (1985), the Senate had sixteen standing (or permanent) committees, and nearly all of them claimed jurisdiction over some aspect of foreign policy. The Senate, lamented one experienced legislator, "has 100 separate power centers." [9]

The situation is similar in the House of Representatives. In the drafting of a trade bill in 1986, six different standing committees played a significant part. In addition to the Foreign Affairs Committee, they were Ways and Means; Banking, Finance, and Urban Affairs; Energy and Commerce; Education and Labor; and Agriculture.[10] When Congress was called upon in the 1970s to respond to the energy crisis precipitated by the suspension of oil shipments from the Persian Gulf area, the House leadership discovered that more than *eighty subcommittees* had jurisdiction over some aspect of the energy problem, leading to the observation that the term "subcommittee government" could be used to describe the operations of the legislative branch.[11]

Congress's Constitutional Powers

Like the executive branch, Congress has both formal constitutional and extraconstitutional prerogatives. For the Founding Fathers, Congress was unquestionably viewed as the dynamic organ of government, as the voice of the people, and as the depository of democratic ideals. For a number of reasons—not least, their colonial experience—they were profoundly suspicious of executive power. The American people and their delegates to the Constitutional Convention mostly believed that the abuse of power by executive officials (by King George III, the British prime minister, and the royal colonial governors) was largely responsible for the American Revolution. It is noteworthy that the powers and responsibilities of Congress are described in the first article of the Constitution; they are also specified in much greater detail than those of the president or the judiciary.

Did the Founding Fathers expect Congress to play the leading role in foreign as well as domestic affairs? Or, as the Supreme Court held in 1936, did they understand that these were two realms?[12] Constitutional authorities have debated this question for some two hundred years, and even today the answer remains unclear.* As Thomas Jefferson, the nation's first secretary of state, said, "The transaction of business with foreign nations is executive altogether."[13] The experience of President George Washington in trying to arrive at a unified position within the national government on the Jay Treaty with England in 1794 underscored his point. The treaty was approved only after "stormy sessions" in both houses of Congress.[14]

In any case, the Founders gave the legislative branch important constitutional duties in the foreign policy field. Of the eighteen powers given to Congress in Article I, Section 8, seven affect foreign policy directly; others are enumerated in Article II. Four of Congress's foreign policy powers are especially important. Two of them belong to the Senate alone, creating for it a unique role in the foreign policy process: giving advice and consent to treaties and confirming the executive's appointments. The other two are exercised jointly by the House and Senate: the power to raise and appropriate funds and the power to declare war.

Advice and Consent Prerogative

As we have already seen, the Constitution provides that the president may make treaties "by and with the Advice and Consent of the Senate . . . provided two-thirds of the senators present concur." Why did the Framers require that agreements with other countries must receive a two-thirds majority vote in the Senate, when a simple majority was deemed sufficient for all other legislative acts (except impeachments and the overriding of vetoes)? The answer appears to be that this

---

* Many commentators on American diplomacy draw a distinction in roles between the executive and the legislative branches in making and conducting foreign policy. Yet this traditional distinction is becoming increasingly difficult to draw and maintain in practice. The *conduct* of foreign policy—involving such questions as how foreign aid is actually administered or whether the president should use armed force to achieve a particular foreign policy objective—is not a matter that Congress today is willing to leave solely to the executive branch. In other words, how the White House *conducts* foreign policy will affect legislative attitudes and behavior in the *making* of foreign policy.

provision reflected the isolationist sentiments of the Founders—a "congenital distrust of Europe"—and illustrated the people's determination that the nation's involvement in international politics would remain extremely limited.[15]

Another question is why congressional participation in treaty making was limited to the Senate alone. From their experience under the Articles of Confederation, the Founders had become painfully aware of the consequences of foreign policy mismanagement by the entire Congress. The smaller, indirectly elected (until 1913), and more mature Senate—capable of resisting the whims of public opinion—was expected to serve as a kind of council of state to advise the president on foreign relations.

As noted in Chapter 1, the ratification of international agreements by the United States government is a multistage process, in which the Senate plays a critical role. It acts upon treaties submitted to it by the president, but it does not, as is often believed, "ratify" them.[16] It gives (or withholds) its "advice and consent," but treaties become part of "the supreme law of the land" (as they are designated in Article VI of the Constitution) only when they have been approved by a two-thirds vote in the Senate *and* proclaimed by the president.

Throughout the course of U.S. history, the vast majority of treaties has been approved by the Senate. Between 1789 and 1982, only nineteen treaties were rejected by the Senate, out of some 1,400 submitted to it.[17] (In some cases, the Senate neither approves nor disapproves a treaty; it simply refuses to act upon it. This is equivalent to rejection.) Occasionally, the threat of an adverse vote can induce a president to withdraw White House support for a treaty under Senate consideration, as occurred when President Carter in effect withdrew the SALT II arms-control agreement with the Soviet Union in 1980. Although SALT II is, technically speaking, still "before" the Senate, senators know that a treaty cannot go into effect without the support of the president.

For several years after World War II, it was common practice for the president to appoint senators to serve as members of the team that negotiated important treaties. This device went far toward assuring bipartisan support for the agreement. This practice, however, appears to have fallen into disuse in more recent years. Legislators have even undertaken diplomatic negotiations on their own, sometimes in the face of expressed presidential opposition to their actions, as we shall see in Chapter 9.

Another dimension of the treaty-making process became a matter of controversy between executive and legislative officials in the late 1980s. This was the issue of the *interpretation* of existing treaties. As will be explained in Chapter 3, certain provisions of the Anti-Ballistic Missile Treaty of 1972—especially those related to the development of a space-based defense system ("Star Wars") by the United States—had become matters of great contention between the Reagan White House and its critics. President Reagan's position was twofold: he contended that the construction of a Star Wars system was permissible under the 1972 treaty and that the interpretation of the terms of this or any other treaty is an exclusively executive prerogative. Opponents of Star Wars on Capitol Hill argued that the system would violate the ABM agreement. Even so staunch a supporter of a strong defense establishment as Sen. Sam Nunn, D-Ga., said that the Senate was entitled to interpret the meaning of any treaty to which it has given its consent. At a minimum, the Senate and White House jointly should agree upon a treaty's meaning. President Reagan, however, showed no sign of being deterred by such legislative sentiments from moving ahead with the development of the Star Wars system.

The Senate's role in the treaty-making process has given the upper chamber a distinctive and prestigious position in foreign affairs. It was Senate opposition that led to U.S. rejection of membership in the League of Nations after World War I; and during the interwar period, powerful voices in the Senate expressed the isolationist sentiment that actuated the nation's foreign policy. During and after World War II, influential senators such as Vandenberg and Tom Connally, D-Texas, cooperated with the Roosevelt and Truman administrations to lay the foundation for the active internationalist role that the United States assumed after 1945.[18] In the 1960s, the Senate (more specifically, the Senate Foreign Relations Committee) again took the lead in congressional opposition to the nation's role in the Vietnam War.

Throughout most of the nation's history, the House of Representatives was content to play a subordinate role in the foreign policy process. Membership on the House Foreign Affairs Committee was largely viewed as a symbolic assignment that few legislators coveted. As late as 1970, the chairman of the Foreign Affairs Committee expressed the opinion that the committee should normally support the executive branch's foreign policy positions.[19]

A noteworthy trend in recent years, however, has been an effort by the House to reverse this traditional role. Even though the House has no formal constitutional responsibility in treaty making, it has sought to use other powers, such as its predominant position in the appropriations process, to exert its influence in foreign relations. This viewpoint was illustrated in the remarks of Rep. John D. Dingell, D-Mich., early in 1979 in connection with the Panama Canal treaties:

> We in the House are tired of you people in the State Department going to your tea-sipping friends in the Senate. Now you good folks come up

here and say you need legislation [to implement the treaties] after you ignored the House. If you expect me to vote for this travesty, you're sorely in error.[20]

Later, President Reagan's critics in the House demanded that he adhere to the provisions of the (unratified) SALT II treaty. They threatened to enact this demand into law, perhaps as an amendment to the Defense Department's budget, if the president refused to comply.[21]

Senators resent these efforts by the House to intrude upon their historic domain, and they continue to guard their constitutional prerogatives in the treaty-making process jealously. Sen. Frank Church, D-Idaho, a former chairman of the Senate Foreign Relations Committee, said of the representatives' actions, "Their nibbles end up being big bites, and we [are] being bitten to death."[22]

Confirmation Prerogative

The other (and much less influential) senatorial prerogative is the power to confirm executive appointments. In the minds of the Founders, this power and the power to approve treaties were interrelated. The Senate was expected to play a key role in the appointment of the officials who would engage in treaty negotiations. The Senate would thereby acquire a voice in framing the instructions given to these officials.[23] Within a relatively short time, however, this linkage broke down. Throughout U.S. history, the Senate has generally given routine approval to the president's diplomatic appointees. In 1981, for example, a not untypical year, out of 106,616 nominations for appointments by the president that were received by the Senate, 105,284 were confirmed, 33 were withdrawn, and 1,299 were left unconfirmed by the end of the legislative session. No nominee was rejected outright.[24] As a rule, the Senate operates upon the principle that an incumbent president is entitled to have a team in which he has confidence and whose members will support his program.

Occasionally, of course, the rule is broken. Early in his first term, President Reagan nominated Ernest W. Lefever to be assistant secretary of state for human rights and humanitarian affairs. A number of legislators and public groups questioned Lefever's dedication to the cause of international human rights. In the face of virtually certain senatorial rejection of his candidate, President Reagan withdrew Lefever's nomination.[25] Several years later, President Reagan nominated Robert M. Gates to serve as director of the Central Intelligence Agency. Because of his involvement in the Iran-contra affair, Gates was widely opposed within Congress, and President Reagan also withdrew his name from further consideration.[26]

Power of the Purse

What has historically been called the "power of the purse"—the weapon used by the British Parliament to establish its primacy over the monarchy—consists of two interrelated prerogatives: the power to *raise revenue* (by means of taxes, tariffs, and loans), granted to Congress in Article I, Section 8; and the power to determine how the funds shall be *spent,* in accordance with the stipulation in Article I, Section 9 that "no money shall be drawn from the Treasury, but in Consequence of Appropriations made by law."

Since all federal expenditures must be approved by Congress, it may increase funds for particular programs above White House recommendations; it may refuse to grant the funds needed for carrying out certain programs and policies; it may provide the required funds with the proviso that certain conditions be met; it may terminate programs already in existence; and it may exercise legislative oversight of programs, investigating such questions as whether they are achieving their objectives or whether their continuation is in the national interest.

A few brief examples will illustrate the scope and importance of the power of the purse in shaping external policy. In 1986, Congress reduced the Reagan administration's proposed defense budget by $17.6 billion—the largest cut in the White House's recommended defense budget in many years. Congress at first refused to accept President Reagan's request for funds to produce the Pershing II and MX missile systems; although funds for these systems were later restored, the amounts were smaller than had been requested. In the same year, the House nearly passed a resolution calling upon the executive branch to negotiate a freeze on nuclear testing with the Soviet Union (it was defeated by one vote). Congress also placed a ceiling of 315,000 on the number of U.S. troops that could be stationed in Western Europe; and in a related move, it made a moderate reduction in the financial contribution by the United States to the NATO defense program—thereby indicating the existence of widespread dissatisfaction on Capitol Hill with the level of contributions to NATO by other members of the alliance.

In succeeding years, Congress refused to approve—or placed very severe restrictions upon—military aid to the Nicaraguan contras, despite President Reagan's repeated insistence that support for them was essential to achieve the nation's diplomatic and security goals in the Western Hemisphere. In mid-1986, the House finally approved the president's request. The vote margin was only twelve votes, and the administration won this narrow victory only after an intensive "lobbying blitz" directed at wavering members of the House.[27] The following year, because of the revelations accompanying the Iran-contra affair, the Reagan administration's program of aid to the contras once again came under fire on Capitol Hill. When the evidence left little doubt that executive officials had evaded or violated the law in their efforts to support the contras, many legislators appeared determined either to cut off U.S. funds to the contras entirely or to impose extremely stringent limitations on their use.

In 1986, Secretary of State Shultz complained vociferously about the budgetary cuts made by Congress in the administration's foreign policy programs. Shultz declared his intention to "drop everything else" in order to lobby for restoration of the funds. He asserted that the budget reductions by Congress impaired the nation's ability to promote democracy and economic progress in such countries as the Philippines, South Korea, and Thailand and jeopardized the ability of the United States to protect its embassies and citizens abroad from attacks by terrorists. In Shultz's assessment, Congress's action amounted to a "tragedy for U.S. foreign policy and national security." [28]

During President Reagan's second term, legislators used the annual debate over the Defense Department budget as another occasion for assertiveness in the foreign policy field. In 1987, for example, some of them expressed their opposition to the Star Wars proposal; others demanded that the White House move ahead energetically in the effort to arrive at an arms control agreement with the Soviet Union that would reduce the number of intermediate-range missiles in Europe. A number of Democrats in the Senate threatened to filibuster the defense spending bill unless their demands were accepted by the president. In turn, Republicans filibustered to keep Democratic demands out of the bill. Other critics of President Reagan's diplomacy threatened to reduce drastically the proposed $303 billion defense budget unless executive officials were more responsive to congressional complaints.[29]

During the same period, Congress voted to suspend U.S. aid to Pakistan, in an expression of legislative displeasure with that nation's apparent determination to acquire a nuclear arsenal. Some legislators were searching for a way to express their dissatisfaction with the Reagan administration's policies in the Persian Gulf area—especially its failure to involve Congress in the making of key decisions, some of which risked the possibility that the United States would become actively engaged in military hostilities.[30]

Authorization and Appropriations Process. Federal programs that require expenditures for their implementation must be approved by Congress in two stages. As an example, take the annual foreign aid budget. The first major step in the process is for the program to be considered by the Senate Foreign Relations Committee and the House Foreign Affairs Committee. Theoretically, in the *authorization phase* these committees are concerned with such questions as: Does foreign assistance promote the diplomatic interests of the United States? Are particular foreign aid projects (in Bolivia, say, or Morocco, or India) justified? Is there a strong likelihood that the objectives of the program can be achieved? Following committee consideration and recommendation, authorization bills must be approved by the full House and the full Senate. If the bills differ, the two houses must agree upon a common measure before the authorization becomes law and this stage is completed.

Next, the foreign aid program must go through the *appropriations stage,* in which the funds are actually provided for its implementation. This is the province of the House and Senate appropriations committees. Custom has established that the House committee plays the dominant role in the appropriations process, and in the postwar period it has had a decisive voice in certain aspects of American foreign policy.

Theoretically, neither the House nor the Senate Appropriations Committee is concerned with the merits of a program that has already been authorized by Congress. The appropriations committees are supposed to concentrate upon such matters as whether sufficient revenues are available to finance the authorized programs. In practice, however, the jurisdictional and political lines between the appropriations committees and the authorizing committees have become indistinct, to the point of disappearing entirely. Between 1955 and 1965, for example, the foreign aid program encountered its most formidable opposition on Capitol Hill from the Foreign Operations Subcommittee of the House Appropriations Committee, headed by Rep. Otto Passman, D-La., an outspoken and determined opponent of foreign aid. Each year the subcommittee subjected the foreign aid authorization to "Passmanization," a process of making massive cuts in the program. Passman accused executive policy makers of attempting to "grab the check," that is, forcing U.S. taxpayers to pay for all the social and economic needs of the world.[31]

By custom, the Senate Appropriations Committee functions as a "court of review" for the actions taken by its counterpart in the House. As a rule, some—occasionally most—of the cuts made by the House in foreign aid (and other programs) are restored by the Senate committee. The final amount in the appropriation bill must then be set by another agreement between the two chambers.[32]

Problems of Budgetary Procedures.   Students of the national legislative process, as well as many members of the House and Senate, have long recognized and deplored the fact that Congress's handling of the budget is fragmented and lacking in any sense of priority among the literally hundreds of budgetary categories. In an effort to remedy these longstanding defects, in 1974 Congress enacted the Budget and Impoundment Control Act.³³ This act created budget committees in the House and the Senate, whose responsibility it would be to prepare a tentative, and later a final, budget for each chamber. The latter would reflect decisions about spending priorities and would balance total expenditures against anticipated governmental revenues.

Without entering into a detailed analysis of the effects of this act, it may be noted that this attempt at budgetary control has thus far failed to achieve its objectives. Some observers, in fact, believe that the changes have made foreign policy measures, such as the foreign aid program, even more vulnerable on Capitol Hill than they were before. The process of budgetary accommodation now required, in the view of one commentator, "has the greatest impact on the weakest programs," making foreign aid "a prime target" (especially in a national election year). Lacking a strong domestic constituency, foreign aid is always a tempting target for budget cutters.

By many criteria, the power of the purse has been and remains the most potent weapon available to Congress for determining public policy. Yet even in the post-Vietnam era of congressional activism, it remains an underutilized instrument of legislative influence in foreign affairs. As we observed in Chapter 1, resourceful presidents can usually get access to funds for foreign policy undertakings, at least in the short run, by using emergency funds at their disposal, by reprogramming budgeted funds, and by other devices. Under the terms of an agreement reached between the White House and Congress in 1990, legislative discretion with regard to the budget was significantly curtailed. Ultimately, the threat or actuality of reduced appropriations can of course restrain the president or compel changes in his conduct of foreign relations. In the long run, all chief executives are aware that nearly every worthwhile program in foreign affairs requires funds for its implementation; if Congress does not provide those funds, the program has no future.

War Powers Prerogative

Constitutional Powers.   Four consecutive provisions of Article I, Section 8, of the Constitution comprise the war powers of Congress. These confer the powers to "declare war," to "raise and support armies," to "provide and maintain a navy," and to "make rules for the government and regulation" of the armed forces. These provisions have served as the basis for forceful assertions of the congressional will in external policy.

Declarations of War.   Although the Constitution grants to Congress the power to declare war, several developments in modern international relations have combined to render this legislative prerogative largely a formality. In contrast to international practice for several centuries before the Constitution was drafted, in modern history nations have seldom declared war before engaging in hostilities. When Congress does issue a declaration of war (which it does rarely), the declaration simply recognizes that a condition of warfare *already exists;* it is not an occasion for Congress to debate whether hostilities *ought* to exist.

Indeed, more than a century ago the Supreme Court held in a landmark case that the existence of a state of war depended upon prevailing conditions; the president was not required to await a declaration of war from Congress before responding to external threats.[34] Chief executives, especially in modern times, have frequently referred to "functional equivalents" of a declaration of war. Examples are the passage of the 1964 Gulf of Tonkin Resolution, which approved the president's use of armed force in responding to threats to U.S. security interests in Vietnam, and (during the Vietnam War) congressional enactment of the draft and the defense budget.[35] Following such precedents, President Bush did not ask Congress to declare war when he committed the nation to oppose Iraqi expansionism in the Persian Gulf area in 1990. Several months after the crisis erupted, he did request legislative authority to undertake offensive operations after Baghdad refused to withdraw its forces from Kuwait. After Congress granted this request, some legislators themselves commented that the House and Senate had passed the functional equivalent of a declaration of war, despite legislative opposition to the idea on the basis of experience in the Vietnam conflict.

Of the more than 125 violent encounters in which the United States has been engaged, only 5 have involved declarations of war by Congress. Most of these incidents of armed conflict have involved major or minor episodes in which the president or a local U.S. official employed the armed forces for foreign policy ends. Neither of the two prolonged and costly military engagements since the end of World War II—the Korean War (called a police action by the Truman administration) and the Vietnam War—was formally declared to be a war by Congress, primarily because the incumbent president did not request Congress to do so.

The creation of a worldwide network of military alliances since World War II has also eroded the power of Congress to declare war. Article 5 of the NATO agreement, for example, provides that the parties shall regard an attack upon one signatory as an attack upon all of them—a provision which, according to many commentators, is tantamount to the threat of "automatic war" by the United States. Despite laments on Capitol Hill about the tendency of modern presidents to bypass Congress in decisions to employ the armed forces abroad, some legislators have said that a declaration of war in each case involving military hostilities abroad would be inadvisable, since it might turn a limited war into a global nuclear conflict.[36]

Separation of Powers. During the drafting of the Constitution, Congress was at first given the power to "make" war. This language was later changed to grant Congress the power to "declare" war. Suspicious as they were of executive power, the Founders recognized that the successful prosecution of a war would require *both* executive and legislative participation; one branch alone could not "make" war. (No one was more mindful of this than George Washington, who had endured many frustrating experiences trying to get coordinated policy and effective support from the Continental Congress during the Revolutionary War.) Accordingly, in the Constitution the chief executive is also given important military powers. In particular, the president is designated commander in chief of the armed forces. As with other constitutional issues, the precise balance or allocation of war powers between the two ends of Pennsylvania Avenue has been determined more by experience, precedent, and circumstances than by the intentions of the Founders or by contending legal theories. In this case, the overall tendency has been for legislative prerogatives to be eclipsed by executive initiative and leadership.

Included in the legislative war powers is the authority for Congress to "raise and support armies" and "provide and maintain a navy." Reflecting the American people's aversion to a standing army, the Constitution prohibits Congress from making appropriations for the army for longer than two years. (No such limitation exists with regard to naval appropriations.) This stipulation assured that the questions of the size and character of the armed forces would be subject to frequent legislative review.

Throughout modern history, Congress has seldom used its power over the military establishment to its fullest potential for the purpose of influencing the course of American diplomacy. From the end of World War II until the termination of the Vietnam War, the tendency was for Congress to provide the kind of armed forces requested by the White House. From the end of the Vietnam conflict until the late 1970s, defense spending was deemphasized in favor of expanded domestic programs. Toward the end of President Carter's term, however, a significant expansion in the national defense budget began, as a result of the revolution in Iran and the Soviet invasion of Afghanistan.[37] Despite widespread expectations to the contrary, the end of the cold war did *not* witness a substantial decrease in national defense spending. New global and regional challenges—most dramatically, the Persian Gulf War— entailed heavy military expenditures; and, as always, the cost of advanced new weapons systems appeared to continually increase. As in the always controversial matter of closing military bases, Congress in fact was often under intense public pressure *not* to reduce military expenditures.

The War Powers Resolution.   Mounting legislative dissatisfaction with the president's use of the armed forces for foreign policy ends was forcefully demonstrated in 1973, when Congress passed the War Powers Resolution over President Nixon's veto.[38] This resolution will be more fully discussed in Chapter 5, but a few general observations should be made here.

The resolution declared that its purpose was to ensure that the "collective judgment of both the Congress and the President will apply to the introduction of United States Armed Forces into hostilities," or into situations in which hostilities are believed to be imminent. Accordingly, it required that congressional consent be obtained for the prolonged use of U.S. troops in foreign conflicts; otherwise the president would be required to withdraw American forces.*

Experience with the War Powers Resolution since 1973 provides little evidence to support the idea that such congressionally imposed legal constraints are effective in limiting the president's reliance upon armed force abroad. As we shall see, during the Persian Gulf crisis, for example, little or no reference was made to the resolution. This fact lends credence to the idea that other legislative efforts to influence the presidential conduct of foreign affairs have a considerably greater impact upon executive behavior than does the War Powers Resolution, whose actual importance in the American foreign policy process now seems minimal.

In recent years, chief executives have taken somewhat different positions regarding their authority over the armed forces. Presidents Ford and Carter acknowledged the legality of congressional restrictions on this authority, such as those contained in the War Powers Resolution, but nevertheless objected to them.[39] Other presidents, such as Johnson, Nixon, Reagan, and Bush, have insisted that this authority was derived *from the Constitution* and therefore could not be limited by

---

* One provision of the resolution was nullified by the Supreme Court's 1983 decision, in an unrelated case, regarding the legislative veto. *Legislative veto* is the name given to the procedure whereby Congress *permits* executive officials to engage in certain specified activities (such as the president's commitment of the armed forces abroad), unless and until Congress revokes his authority to do so. Normally, Congress's "veto" of executive actions is cast on a case-by-case basis, as was contemplated by the provisions of the War Powers Resolution. The Court held that the legislative veto was an unconstitutional exercise of legislative power, since the Constitution specifically provided for the procedures that must be followed (that is, passage by both houses of Congress and the signature of the president) for the enactment of legislation. The decision affected numerous pieces of legislation. (See *Immigration and Naturalization Service v. Chadha*, 462 U.S. 919 [1983]).

statutes or congressional resolutions. President Reagan, for example, complied with the resolution only nominally or not at all. In September 1982, for example, he ordered that a detachment of 1,200 marines be sent to Lebanon to engage in "peacekeeping." He did not request congressional consent for this action. As the weeks passed, President Reagan and his advisers contended that withdrawal of the forces would raise serious questions about the nation's credibility and staying power under adverse conditions and would thus endanger national security and global peace. He also pointedly informed his critics that, if he were compelled to withdraw the troops, the responsibility for Communist gains in this and other areas would rest with them. Influenced by such arguments, Congress did sanction the marines' presence in Lebanon for eighteen months, pursuant to the War Powers Resolution—although the president withdrew them before that time, following a terrorist attack in which 241 marines were killed.[40]

In the Persian Gulf crisis of 1987, the Reagan White House sent a naval contingent to protect Kuwaiti oil tankers from attack. Initially the president insisted that there was no danger that U.S. forces would become involved in hostilities and that the War Powers Resolution therefore did not apply. Similarly, President Bush ordered the armed forces of the United States to defend the Persian Gulf area. In these and other cases, the president's critics found themselves in a dilemma: either to support or acquiesce in the president's action, even though they doubted its wisdom, or to oppose it and risk being blamed for a possible military or diplomatic failure.

The problem that the War Powers Resolution addressed was in many respects analogous to that confronting the United States during the 1930s, when Congress sought to keep the nation out of World War II by passing the Neutrality Act. In the end, that effort failed. Legal attempts to keep America out of the hostilities were inadequate to protect the nation's diplomatic and security interests.

Other Economic Powers

The Constitution confers upon Congress certain general economic powers, several of which are important in the conduct of foreign relations. These include the power to levy and collect taxes, to impose tariffs upon imports, to borrow money, to regulate interstate and foreign commerce, and to coin money and regulate its value. The significance of these powers has greatly increased as a result of the steady growth in the federal budget and the part played by the budget in the national economy. For example, legislative measures to control domestic inflation are a major influence in determining the value of the dollar overseas; they also influence such intangible but crucial developments as the degree of confidence that foreign governments have in U.S. leadership.

Few of the economic prerogatives of Congress have more significant implications for foreign policy than its power to regulate commerce, examined more fully in Chapter 7. The trade wars among the states under the Articles of Confederation had led to economic turmoil and instability—a primary reason why the Constitutional Convention was assembled. Congress, therefore, was given the exclusive power to regulate trade both among the states and between the United States and foreign countries.

Beginning with the Reciprocal Trade Program inaugurated by the Roosevelt administration, the United States has sought to maximize its foreign trade on the basis of reciprocal tariff concession agreements with other countries. Congress grants the president considerable discretion to negotiate these and other trade agreements. It also periodically engages in major revisions of the trade laws, often at the instigation of domestic industries that claim they are threatened by rising imports (automobiles from Japan, textiles from Hong Kong, fruits and vegetables from Mexico). Labor unions, farmers, business groups, and others seeking to improve their competitive positions add to the pressures on Congress to act in matters of trade. On several occasions in recent years, for example, the House and Senate have used various means to convey to Japan their concerns about the rising volume of Japanese exports to the United States and Tokyo's resistance to expanded U.S. sales in the Japanese market.[41] Such congressional warnings are sometimes welcomed by the president and his advisers when they are trying to win new trade concessions from other countries.

Incident to its power to regulate commerce, from time to time Congress investigates the behavior of U.S. business firms overseas. In recent years, it has inquired into allegations that American corporations bribed officials in other countries to obtain preferential consideration. Political intervention in the affairs of Chile by the International Telephone and Telegraph Company has also elicited detailed legislative investigation.[42]

Today, virtually all foreign policy activities have an economic dimension. Even with regard to ideological and ethical issues, such as human rights in the Soviet Union and racial equality in South Africa, Congress has used trade concessions, boycotts, and other economic instruments in its efforts to influence the course of events.[43]

The Oversight Function

Since the mid-nineteenth century, many students of the legislative process have pointed out that, in the words of one of them, "control of the government—the oversight function—is probably the most important task the legislature performs." As a result, "the bureaucracy lives under the heavy frown of congressional supervision all the time." [44] Although it is not specifically mentioned in the Constitution, the congressional power of investigation is a basic legislative function, one that Congress has relied upon repeatedly to influence foreign affairs. During the 1930s, for example, the investigation carried out by the Nye Committee into the nation's participation in World War I had a major impact on public opinion, strongly reinforcing the existing isolationist mentality.[45] During World War II, the Truman Committee (the Special Senate Committee Investigating the National Defense Program, headed by then-senator Harry S. Truman, D-Mo.) investigated problems related to the war effort; this committee's work was widely cited as a model of constructive investigation by Congress.[46]

In the early postwar period, committees of the House and Senate examined political, social, and economic conditions in Europe, and their reports played key roles in formulating the Greek-Turkish Aid Program (1947), the Marshall Plan (1948), and NATO (1949). Later, Congress looked into the question of why the United States "lost" China to communism. These inquiries yielded few positive results and impaired morale in the State Department and other executive agencies for many years.[47] One of the most influential legislative inquiries in recent times was conducted during the late 1960s by the Senate Foreign Relations Committee on America's participation in the Vietnam War. This exhaustive and well-publicized review served as a focus for the emerging internal opposition to the war and was a major factor in the Nixon administration's decision to bring the conflict to an end.

During the late 1980s, revelations associated with the Iran-contra affair led to exhaustive investigations of the Reagan administration's activities in the Middle East and Central America. These inquiries directed the attention of the news media and the public to the administration's policy in Central America; brought censure of the intelligence agencies for certain of their activities (such as mining Nicaraguan harbors); strongly communicated legislative uneasiness about certain forms of interventionism by the United States in the affairs of Latin American nations; and focused attention upon certain ill-advised, and in some cases illegal, activities engaged in by President Reagan's aides.[48]

Informal Methods of Legislative Influence

In addition to its constitutional prerogatives, Congress has evolved several informal, but sometimes extremely effective, methods of influencing the course of foreign relations. One of these is the ability of the House or Senate (or both) to pass resolutions expressing the opinions of legislators on diplomatic issues.*

One way in which members of Congress inform themselves about foreign affairs is by making trips abroad for the purpose of firsthand observations. These trips are often referred to as junkets, with the implication that there is a large element of recreation in them. Shortly before the Memorial Day weekend in 1983, for example, it was reported that a number of legislators "were enjoying springtime in Paris—and Rome and Berlin and Athens and Budapest and Brussels and Prague and Geneva." Altogether during this period, fifty-nine representatives and seven senators were traveling to sixteen different countries (plus Puerto Rico), studying such diverse topics as the prospects for peace in the Middle East, Soviet advances in aircraft and technology (as seen at the Paris Air Show), and the possibility for negotiations among rival political factions in Central America.[49] One former State Department official has said that trips of this kind, despite their reputation, are extremely valuable; not only do they broaden legislators' horizons, but they also help Congress to be less dependent upon executive officials for their information about major developments abroad.

Sometimes, foreign governments encourage legislators to visit their countries in order to be better able to exert influence upon them.[50] One particularly newsworthy case occurred in 1987, when, at the invitation of the Soviet government, three members of the House and their staff visited a highly controversial, and hitherto secret, radar installation at Krasnoyarsk. The Soviet purpose was evidently to convince legislators that, contrary to the contention of President Reagan and his advisers, the installation did not violate the ABM Treaty; in so doing, the Soviets hoped to reduce support on Capitol Hill for the Star Wars scheme.[51] In 1990, the Kremlin admitted that this installation *did* violate the ABM treaty.

Although the era of great oratory may have ended on Capitol Hill (and elsewhere), speeches by individual legislators are newsworthy and can sometimes have a potent effect on U.S. foreign policy. One conspicuous example was a widely publicized speech by Sen. J. William Fulbright, D-Ark., criticizing the diplomacy of the Johnson administration in the Dominican Republic.[52] A different sort of example was provided by Sen. Jesse Helms, R-N.C., an outspoken and ultraconserva-

---

* Resolutions expressing the opinions of one or both houses of Congress may take various forms. A *concurrent resolution* conveys the opinion of both houses on a particular question. However, it is not law and thus does not require the president's signature. Similarly, a *sense of the House* or a *sense of the Senate* resolution may express the viewpoint of one chamber on a question. Although executive policy makers are interested in congressional sentiment, they are not bound by such resolutions.

tive senator, who evidently believed that President Reagan had to be "saved" from his own advisers. Helms not only made numerous speeches—sometimes amounting to filibusters—in the Senate, but he also raised questionable allegations about the activities of executive officials and used the rules of the Senate to block presidential nominations to diplomatic posts.[53] The Persian Gulf crisis in 1990-91 also served as the occasion for legislative oratory on the origins, nature, and future of the conflict.

Congress and Postwar Diplomacy

Since the late 1960s Congress has exhibited a new dynamism and militancy in exerting its prerogatives in external affairs. For the first two decades after World War II Congress was largely content to leave the management of foreign relations to the executive branch—thereby providing impetus for the emergence of the imperial presidency; when it did play a significant role in foreign relations, Congress normally supported the diplomatic policies and programs advocated by the White House. Recalling the decisive impact upon American diplomacy Congress had in earlier periods of the nation's history and concerned about the steady accretion of executive power, many members of the House and Senate have advocated a return to a more influential role in the realm of external policy.

Congress's dynamic involvement in the foreign policy process must be viewed from the perspective of the diplomatic experience of the twentieth century. The post-Vietnam War era of legislative assertiveness in foreign relations, for example, may be regarded as another stage in the "democratization" of American diplomacy that began under President Wilson. Although his own behavior was not always consistent with his expressed principle, Wilson believed in "open covenants, openly arrived at," in involving public opinion decisively in the foreign policy process, and in other measures designed to make the conduct of diplomacy compatible with America's democratic values. As the branch of government most representative of the people (as many legislators believe), Congress can justify its diplomatic assertiveness by reference to such Wilsonian principles. The perspective of history also reminds us that there have been many earlier periods of congressional activism in foreign relations—such as the era of the Spanish-American War and the decade of the 1930s. In the latter period, not even President Franklin D. Roosevelt—one of the nation's most skilled political leaders—was able to impose his will upon a Congress strongly attached to isolationism.

Since the end of the Vietnam War, Congress's *desire* to play a more independent and decisive role in the foreign policy process has been demonstrated on many occasions. The case studies that follow will provide numerous and varied examples of this legislative impulse. Much less evident, however, has been the *capacity* of Congress to manage foreign relations or even, for that matter, to serve as a full partner with the executive in foreign policy decision making. Judged by the recent evidence of the Persian Gulf crisis, the gap between the desires of Congress and its capabilities remains vast—so wide as to leave the president in effective control of the foreign policy process. The reasons for this phenomenon will be identified and explained in detail in Chapter 9.

Notes

1. Dispatches by Nathaniel C. Nash and Elaine Sciolino, *New York Times,* October 12, 1987.
2. Detailed studies highlighting congressional activism in foreign policy in recent years are Alan Platt and Lawrence D. Weiler, *Congress and Arms Control* (Boulder, Colo.: Westview Press, 1978); Robert A. Pastor, *Congress and the Politics of U.S. Foreign Economic Policy: 1929-1976* (Berkeley and Los Angeles: University of California Press, 1980); Thomas M. Franck and Edward Weisband, *Foreign Policy by Congress* (New York: Oxford University Press, 1979); Loch Johnson, *The Making of International Agreements: Congress Confronts the Executive* (New York: New York University Press, 1984); Douglas C. Waller, *Congress and the Nuclear Freeze* (Amherst: University of Massachusetts Press, 1987); Richard G. Lugar, *Letters to the Next President* (New York: Simon and Schuster, 1988); Thomas E. Mann, ed., *A Question of Balance: The President, the Congress and Foreign Policy* (Washington, D.C.: Brookings Institution, 1990); Natalie H. Kaufman, *Human Rights Treaties and the Senate: A History of Opposition* (Chapel Hill: University of North Carolina Press, 1990); and Cynthia J. Arnson, *Crossroads: Congress, the Reagan Administration and Central America* (New York: Pantheon, 1989).
3. Holbert N. Carroll, *The House of Representatives and Foreign Affairs* (Pittsburgh: University of Pittsburgh Press, 1958), 3.
4. Paul A. Varg, *Foreign Policies of the Founding Fathers* (East Lansing: Michigan State University Press, 1963), 46-66; and Albert C. V. Westphal, *The House Committee on Foreign Affairs* (New York: Columbia University Press, 1942), 14-15.
5. For detailed examinations of the problems impeding Congress's role as an effective legislative body, see Richard Bolling, *House Out of Order* (New York: E. P. Dutton, 1965); Joseph Clark, ed., *Congress: The Sapless Branch* (New York: Harper and Row, 1964); Joseph Clark, ed., *Congressional Reform: Problems and Prospects* (New York: Thomas Y. Crowell, 1965); and Roger H. Davidson et al., *Congress in Crisis: Politics and Congressional Reform* (Belmont, Calif.: Wadsworth, 1966).
6. *Congressional Quarterly Weekly Report,* January 3, 1987, 3-4.
7. See the dispatches by John W. Finney, *New York Times,* November 16, 1965, and February 26, 1967; and Marvin Kalb, "Doves, Hawks, and Flutters in the Foreign Relations Committee," *New York Times Magazine,* November 19, 1967.
8. *Congressional Quarterly Almanac,* 1977, 319.

9. *Congressional Quarterly Almanac, 1985,* 18G-34G; Sen. Daniel J. Evans, D-Wash., as quoted in a dispatch by Steven V. Roberts, *New York Times,* February 26, 1986.
10. *Congressional Quarterly Weekly Report,* May 24, 1986, 1154.
11. *Congressional Quarterly's Guide to Congress,* 3d ed. (Washington, D.C.: CQ Press, 1982), 451, 471.
12. In *United States v. Curtiss-Wright Export Corp.,* 299 U.S. 304 (1936), the Supreme Court made a fundamental distinction between the powers of the executive in domestic and foreign affairs, emphasizing that they were vastly greater in the latter than in the former.
13. Francis O. Wilcox, *Congress, the Executive, and Foreign Policy* (New York: Harper and Row, 1971), 146.
14. Julius W. Pratt, *A History of United States Foreign Policy* (Englewood Cliffs, N.J.: Prentice-Hall, 1955), 79-80.
15. Dexter Perkins, *The American Approach to Foreign Policy* (New York: Atheneum, 1968), 191.
16. Sometimes even legislators themselves become confused on this point. Thus, in 1987, Sen. Robert C. Byrd, D-W.Va., asserted that "the last word in this [process of approving treaties] is ratification of the treaty by the Senate."
17. *Guide to Congress,* 291-292. For historical background on senatorial action on treaties, see W. Stull Holt, *Treaties Defeated by the Senate* (Baltimore: Johns Hopkins University Press, 1933).
18. The senatorial contribution to U.S. foreign policy during this period is described in Arthur H. Vandenberg, Jr., ed., *The Private Papers of Senator Vandenberg* (Boston: Houghton Mifflin, 1952).
19. This was the view of Rep. Thomas E. Morgan, D-Pa., as cited in Wilcox, *Congress, the Executive, and Foreign Policy,* 6.
20. *U.S. News & World Report,* March 19, 1979, 46. For a detailed discussion of efforts by the House to compel the Reagan White House to undertake negotiations with rebel groups in Central America, see the dispatches by Martin Tolchin, *New York Times,* May 12 and May 13, 1983.
21. See the dispatches by Steven V. Roberts, *New York Times,* June 11, 1986 and October 1, 1987, and by Michael R. Gordon, *New York Times,* February 7, 1987.
22. Quoted in Loch Johnson and James M. McCormick, "Foreign Policy by Executive Fiat," *Foreign Policy* 28 (Fall 1977): 133.
23. See the study prepared by the Library of Congress for the Senate Foreign Relations Committee, *The Senate Role in Foreign Affairs Appointments,* 92d Cong., 1st sess., 1971, 3-10.
24. *Guide to Congress,* 207.
25. Ibid., 210.
26. *Congressional Quarterly Weekly Report,* March 7, 1987, 418-419.
27. *Newsweek,* July 7, 1986, 20-22.
28. See the dispatch by Bernard Gwertzman, *New York Times,* May 12, 1986.
29. Dispatch by Jonathan Fuerbringer, *New York Times,* September 12, 1987.
30. See the Associated Press dispatch by Tim Ahern, *Baton Rouge Morning Advocate,* October 2, 1987.
31. Dispatch by Peter Finney, Jr., *Baton Rouge Morning Advocate,* March 3, 1979, and Elizabeth B. Drew, "Mr. Passman Meets His Match," *Reporter,* November 19, 1964, 40-43.
32. For further information on the appropriations process, see Richard F. Fenno, "The House Appropriations Committee as a Political System,"

American Political Science Review 56 (June 1962): 310-324; and Jeffrey L. Pressman, *House vs. Senate: Conflict in the Appropriations Process* (New Haven: Yale University Press, 1966).

33. See Lawrence C. Dodd and Bruce Oppenheimer, eds., *Congress Reconsidered* (New York: Praeger, 1977), 163-192. The right of the chief executive to impound funds appropriated by Congress is examined in detail in "Controversy over the Presidential Impoundment of Appropriated Funds," *Congressional Digest* 52 (April 1973): 65-96. More recent commentaries are John W. Sewell and Christine E. Contee, "Foreign Aid and Gramm-Rudman," *Foreign Affairs* 65 (Summer 1987): 1015-1037; Allen Schick, *Making Economic Policy in Congress* (Washington, D.C.: American Enterprise Institute, 1983); and Howard Shuman, *Politics and the Budget* (Englewood Cliffs, N.J.: Prentice-Hall, 1984).

34. The *Prize Cases*, 67 U.S. (2 Black) 635 (1863).

35. For the views of some presidents concerning their authority over the armed forces, see Senate Foreign Relations Committee, *Hearings on War Powers Legislation*, 93d Cong., 1st sess., 1973, 167-172.

36. Sen. Jacob K. Javits, R-N.Y., said that it would have been "most unfortunate" if Congress had declared war in the Vietnam conflict, for such an act would have had "unforeseeable consequences." See Jacob K. Javits, "The Congressional Presence in Foreign Relations," *Foreign Affairs* 48 (January 1970): 226.

37. Recent studies of efforts by Congress to influence the nation's military policy are Douglas C. Waller, *Congress and the Nuclear Force* (Amherst: University of Massachusetts Press, 1987); and Michel Barnhart, ed., *Congress and United States Foreign Policy: Controlling the Use of Force in the Nuclear Age* (Albany: State University of New York Press, 1987); Jeffrey Record, *Beyond Military Reform: American Defense Dilemmas* (Washington, D.C.: Pergamon/Brassey's, 1988); and J. Ronald Fox, *The Defense Management Challenge: Weapons Acquisition* (Boston: Harvard Business School Press, 1988).

38. The background of the resolution is discussed in Gerald R. Ford, *A Time to Heal* (New York: Harper and Row and the Reader's Digest Association, 1979), 249-252, 280-283. See also Pat M. Holt, *The War Powers Resolution: The Role of Congress in U.S. Armed Intervention* (Washington, D.C.: American Enterprise Institute, 1978); and Marc E. Smyrl, *Conflict or Codetermination? Congress, the President, and the Power to Make War* (Hagerstown, Md.: Ballinger, 1988).

39. President Ford's views on the War Powers Resolution are contained in Ford, *A Time to Heal*, 251-253, 279-283. President Carter's account of the Iranian hostage crisis indicates little or no concern about the provisions of the War Powers Resolution; for example, late in 1979 Carter decided to "make a direct military attack" against Iran if the hostages were harmed. See Jimmy Carter, *Keeping Faith: Memoirs of a President* (New York: Bantam, 1982), 466.

40. Sen. Thomas F. Eagleton, D-Mo., declared that President Reagan effectively nullified the provisions of the War Powers Resolution when he ordered the marines into Lebanon, yet even he conceded that if the president had asked for congressional approval of this step, it would have been granted. See *New York Times*, November 17, 1982. For a discussion of congressional viewpoints on the Lebanese crisis, see *Congressional Quarterly Weekly Report*, April 23, 1983, 777.

41. See the discussion in "How Not to Write a Trade Law," *U.S. News & World Report,* October 5, 1987, 48-50; and the analysis of congressional viewpoints on a new trade bill in *Congressional Quarterly Weekly Report,* April 25, 1987, 765-771. More detailed treatment of legislative behavior on trade questions may be found in I.M. Destler, *American Trade Politics: System under Stress* (Washington, D.C.: Institute for International Economics, 1986); Darrell M. West, *Congress and Economic Policymaking* (Pittsburgh: University of Pittsburgh Press, 1987); Theodore H. Moran, "International Economics and National Security," *Foreign Affairs* 69 (Winter 1990/91): 74-91; and C. Fred Bergsten, *America in the World Economy: A Strategy for the 1990s* (Washington, D.C.: Institute for International Economics, 1988). See also Benjamin I. Cohen, *In Whose Interest? International Banking and American Foreign Policy* (New Haven: Yale University Press, 1986).

42. On the activities of IT&T in Chile, see Senate Foreign Relations Committee, *Multinational Corporations and United States Foreign Policy,* 93d Cong., 1st sess., March 20-April 2, 1973, pts. 1 and 2.

43. For an informative discussion of Congress's use of its economic powers in the foreign policy field, see Richard H. Ullman, "Human Rights and Economic Power: the United States versus Idi Amin," *Foreign Affairs* 56 (April 1978): 528-543. Congress's economic actions in connection with South Africa are discussed in *Congressional Quarterly Almanac, 1985,* 83-90.

44. Ralph K. Huitt, "Congress, the Durable Partner," in Sidney Wise and Richard F. Schiers, eds., *Studies on Congress* (New York: Thomas Y. Crowell, 1969), 45.

45. Wayne S. Cole, *Senator Gerald P. Nye and American Foreign Relations* (Minneapolis: University of Minnesota Press, 1962).

46. Donald H. Riddle, *The Truman Committee: A Study in Congressional Responsibility* (New Brunswick, N.J.: Rutgers University Press, 1964), and Wilfred E. Binkley, *President and Congress* (New York: Alfred A. Knopf, 1947), 268-269.

47. A useful source on congressional investigations is Arthur M. Schlesinger, Jr., and Roger Burns, eds., *Congress Investigates: A Documented History, 1792-1974,* 5 vols. (New York: Chelsea House, 1975).

48. For detailed examination of one specific investigation by Congress, see Loch Johnson, *A Season of Inquiry: Congress and Intelligence* (Chicago: Dorsey, 1988).

49. UPI dispatch by Ira R. Allen, *Baton Rouge Morning Advocate,* May 30, 1983. See also Senate Foreign Relations Committee, *Congress and United States-Soviet Relations,* 94th Cong., 1st sess., 1975, for a summary of a conference between members of the Senate and of the Supreme Soviet, at which a variety of diplomatic issues were discussed.

50. A discussion of efforts of this kind by President Anwar al-Sadat of Egypt is available in Stanley F. Reed, "Dateline Cairo: Shaken Pillar," *Foreign Policy* 45 (Winter 1981-1982): 176. For more recent examples, see *New York Times,* August 14, 1984.

51. *Congressional Quarterly Weekly Report,* September 19, 1987, 2230-2231.

52. *Congressional Record,* 89th Cong., 1st sess., 1965, S23855-S23865.

53. See the dispatches by Phil Gailey, *New York Times,* May 14, 1986, and Steven V. Roberts, August 4, 1986; and *Newsweek,* August 4, 1986, 15.

PART II

Congress Confronts
the Issues

We now turn our attention from the general pattern of interaction between Congress and the president in the foreign policy process to six case studies of policy making. The concrete issues selected for examination illustrate Congress's changing perceptions of its role in foreign policy making and how the executive branch and public opinion shape these perceptions.

Chapter 3 examines legislative action on the Soviet-American Anti-Ballistic Missile Treaty of 1972. This case study shows how the Senate deals with an important international agreement, how it exercises its constitutional responsibilities in the treaty-making process, and where some of the possibilities of conflict with the executive lie. Long after the treaty was ratified, a controversy over its interpretation raised new issues of executive-legislative relations.

Chapter 4 deals with the Arab-Israeli conflict in the larger context of turbulent Middle East politics and U.S. military relations with the government of Saudi Arabia. The case provides an illuminating example of congressional reliance upon the power of the purse to influence foreign policy. It also highlights the role and activities of pressure groups in U.S. foreign relations.

Chapter 5, "The Armed Forces," recounts ways in which Congress has attempted to draw the line between the constitutional power of the president as commander in chief and the constitutional power of Congress to declare war. The chapter emphasizes the essential pragmatism of the congressional approach.

In Chapter 6, the legislative oversight role of Congress is considered in reference to the intelligence community. Perhaps nothing better illustrates the evolving attitudes in Congress toward its role in foreign policy than the change in its relationship to the intelligence community. The congressional approach went from almost total neglect to item-by-item scrutiny of the intelligence budget. But as the Iran-contra affair was to indicate, legislative controls achieved only partial effectiveness.

Chapter 7 examines one of Congress's increasingly important prerogatives in the foreign policy field: its economic powers—specifically, the legislative role in dealing with trade issues. In many respects, the economic powers of Congress are among its most potent for influencing the course of external policy.

Finally, Chapter 8 traces the development of human rights and the promotion of democracy as an element in U.S. foreign policy. Congress took the initiative in forcing concern for human rights on the Nixon administration, but it was President Reagan who adopted the broader goal of promoting democracy.

CHAPTER 3

The Anti-Ballistic
Missile Treaty

The Anti-Ballistic Missile (ABM) Treaty combines in one issue several aspects of Congress's involvement in foreign policy. First, it is an example of the Senate's constitutional role in the treaty-making process—that is, the giving of its advice and consent to ratification. Second, it shows how both the Senate and the House fulfill their constitutional role of helping to determine the national defense posture and strategy. In this case, the basic question was—and is—whether to defend the country against nuclear attack by destroying the enemy's weapons before they can land or whether to rely instead on the capability to deliver an overwhelming retaliatory blow after an attack has taken place. Third, the treaty is unusual in that, long after it was ratified, it provoked a new struggle between the executive and legislative branches. The dispute was over whether the president can reinterpret an existing treaty without reference to the Senate, a question that involves the basic institutional relationships between the president and the Senate in the process of reaching and maintaining agreements with other countries. The dispute carried over in an acrimonious debate about the Treaty on Intermediate Nuclear Forces (INF), which was also a landmark in that it provided for elimination (not simply limitation) of an entire class of weapons. Finally, the performance of high-tech American weapons during the whirlwind Persian Gulf War added yet another dimension to the debate.

Background

The nuclear age, which began so dramatically with the bombing of Hiroshima in 1945, confronted military strategists with wholly new problems. This new weapon seemed to be as close as the human race could come to ultimate destruction—a weapon, moreover, against which there was perhaps no defense. There is a long military history of improvements in offense leading to improvements in defense, but the atom bomb made reasonable people wonder if that was any longer possible. Other people, equally reasonable, have thought that it might be, or that the effort to find a defense against nuclear weapons should at least be made.

Another facet of the nuclear age was that it called into question the traditional way of planning force structure. For millennia, it had been taken as a given that more was better: if the enemy had a thousand spears, you needed more than that. This principle was now called into question. If you could destroy the enemy with x number of bombs, it did not matter if the enemy had $2x$ and you certainly did not need $3x$. This new principle came to be called the *doctrine of sufficiency*.

Finally, there was the problem of the relationship between nuclear and conventional weapons. In the late 1940s and early 1950s, as the cold war changed the United States and the Soviet Union from allies to adversaries, U.S. military planners had to contend with an overwhelming Soviet conventional superiority. It had initially been expected that the newly organized United Nations would deal with global conflicts, but this expectation was short-lived. In the United States, it was politically unacceptable to maintain the World War II level of mobilization, and the Soviet Union had a bigger population, anyway. The solution that was adopted was to offset Soviet conventional superiority with nuclear weapons.

Soon, however, the Soviet Union acquired nuclear weapons, too. The premise of Western strategy was that the Soviets knew that if they attacked the West, the United States would launch a devastating nuclear counterblow. It did not take long before the Soviet Union became capable of carrying out a similar retaliation against a U.S. attack. Thus, there developed what was at first called the *balance of terror* and later became formalized in the arcane language of nuclear strategy as mutual assured destruction, with the ominous acronym MAD. This doctrine held that each side was able to wreak an unacceptable level of destruction on the other even after absorbing a first strike. As greater numbers of new and more powerful weapons, with new and longer-range delivery systems, were added to inventories on both sides, the assurance seemed to increase.

The strategy of mutual assured destruction was also based on the premise that there was no effective defense against nuclear weapons. Even bombs dropped from airplanes, such as those that destroyed Hiroshima and Nagasaki in 1945, were so powerful that if only one penetrated an antiaircraft defense, a city was lost. If the bombs were delivered by missiles traveling at speeds of thousands of miles an hour, defense did indeed appear hopeless. The only deterrence then became certain knowledge of instant "massive retaliation," in Secretary of State John Foster Dulles's phrase.

Nuclear Arms Control Efforts

In the immediate aftermath of World War II, the United States, which then held a monopoly on nuclear weapons, proposed in the United Nations that an international authority be created to control production of fissionable material, that there be international licensing and inspection of peaceful nuclear facilities, and that no nation be allowed to possess nuclear weapons or production facilities. This was the Baruch Plan, named for its principal author, Bernard Baruch, a financier and adviser to presidents. The Soviet Union at the time was well on the way to developing its own nuclear weapons (it produced its first in 1949) and was also at the peak of the paranoia that gripped it during the Stalin era. It rejected the U.S. proposal.

Throughout the 1950s, one arms-control conference followed another without significant result. The 1960s, however, saw a series of modest accomplishments. In 1963, the Limited Test Ban Treaty entered into force, prohibiting nuclear tests in the atmosphere, in outer space, and underwater. Underground tests were also banned if they would vent radioactive debris beyond the national borders. The treaty was aimed not so much at controlling nuclear weapons as at protecting the environment from the radioactive fallout of tests, but it was widely hailed as a useful first step.

This treaty was followed in 1967 by a treaty banning nuclear weapons from outer space; in 1968 by the nonproliferation treaty, in which nuclear states agreed not to transfer weapons to non-nuclear states and non-nuclear states agreed not to acquire such weapons; and in 1971 by the seabed arms control treaty, banning nuclear weapons from the ocean floor. (The Antarctic Treaty of 1959, the principal purpose of which was to internationalize the Antarctic, also banned nuclear weapons from that continent, along with military bases in general.)

Thus, a quarter-century after the Baruch Plan had been put forward, the nations of the world had done no more than nibble around the edges of the problem of controlling nuclear weapons. Sen. Eugene J. McCarthy, D-Minn., observed that the weapons had been banned from outer space, from the ocean floor, and from the Antarctic, where nobody intended to put them anyway; why not, he asked, ban them from places where they might hurt somebody? The stage was set for the Strategic Arms Limitation Talks, generally known by the acronym SALT. This is where nuclear weapons and the effort to build defenses against them would come together.

Beginnings of the Anti-Ballistic Missile

Despite the general assumption that there was no reasonable prospect of an effective defense against nuclear weapons, the army began a research program on anti-ballistic missile defenses in 1954, initially as an extension of its work on antiaircraft defense. That was at a time when missiles had relatively short ranges; intercontinental missiles did not yet exist.

Presidents Dwight D. Eisenhower, John F. Kennedy, and Lyndon B. Johnson all resisted the army's antimissile research program, mainly on the ground that it took budgetary and other resources away from more pressing needs. But, curiously in the light of subsequent events, the program found friends in Congress. In 1957, the year in which the Soviet Union acquired intercontinental ballistic missiles, Congress approved $137 million more than had been requested for ABM research.

The framework within which the ABM program was being considered changed in the middle 1960s, when it was learned that the Soviet Union was installing an ABM system of its own around Moscow. The question at once arose what the U.S. response should be. President Johnson stated the problem for both superpowers in a letter to Soviet Premier Aleksei Kosygin on January 21, 1967:

> I think you must realize that following the deployment by you of an anti-ballistic missile system I face great pressures from the Members of Congress and from public opinion not only to deploy defensive systems in this country, but also to increase greatly our capabilities to penetrate any defensive systems which you might establish.
>
> If we should feel compelled to make such major increases in our strategic weapons capabilities, I have no doubt that you would in turn feel under compulsion to do likewise. We would thus have incurred on both sides colossal costs without substantially enhancing the security of our own peoples or contributing to the prospects for a stable peace in the world.[1]

It may be noted that, in this letter, President Johnson made the point about a Soviet ABM that Moscow was later to make about a U.S. ABM—namely, that it would provoke an increase in offensive capabilities and thereby ratchet the arms race up another notch.

The U.S. Debate over Deployment

As Johnson had warned Kosygin, the Soviet ABM system increased pressures to deploy a similar system in the United States. The Johnson administration met these pressures with a curious in-between kind of policy. In September 1967, Defense Secretary Robert S. McNamara announced that the United States would begin to deploy a limited ABM system (which he said would cost $5 billion), not against the Soviet Union, but against China.[2] The Chinese had had nuclear weapons since 1964, but it was not expected that they would achieve an intercontinental missile capability before the mid-1970s.

In the view of its sponsors, the McNamara proposal, which was called Sentinel, had several advantages. It avoided the prohibitive expense of a nationwide system; it avoided the appearance of building toward a first-strike capability, which would certainly have been provocative to the Soviet Union; and yet it gave the impression that the United States was "doing something." On the other hand, as critics pointed out, what the United States was doing was defending against a threat (from China) that did not yet exist, while ignoring a threat (from the Soviet Union) that did exist.

Sentinel was initially welcomed by those members of Congress who had been pressing the Johnson administration to respond to the Soviet anti-missile defense of Moscow. In its report on the military construction authorization bill in 1968, the House Armed Services Committee said it "fully supports the Sentinel program," but also declared its "intense interest in the antiballistic missile defense of the United States"[3]—something that seemed to go far beyond Sentinel. Indeed, the Johnson administration had apparently created Sentinel as a buffer precisely against such a broader system. Years later, McNamara said it "was Congress-oriented, not China-oriented."[4] In announcing the decision to proceed with Sentinel, McNamara had warned against "the kind of mad momentum intrinsic to the development of all nuclear weaponry." The U.S. ABM, he said, should remain a "Chinese-oriented" light deployment and should not be expanded into a "heavy Soviet-oriented" system. The latter would provide "no adequate shield at all against a Soviet attack" and would merely induce the Soviet Union to increase its offensive capability. Clark Clifford, McNamara's successor as secretary of defense in the last year of the Johnson administration, continued to stress mutual assured destruction over defense.

A major fight began in Congress. On one side were those who wanted to use Sentinel as a building block for a full-blown ABM system. On the other were those who wanted no ABM at all. Virtually nobody supported, on its own merits, the concept of an ABM limited to defense against Chinese missiles or accidental launches of other missiles.

When the Nixon administration came to office in 1969, it renamed Sentinel Safeguard and gave it an expanded mission: to protect U.S. missile sites against Soviet or Chinese attacks. Defense Secretary Melvin R. Laird said that protection of cities was not feasible and that it was more important to protect the nation's retaliatory capacity. The first deployments of Safeguard were to be at Grand Forks Air Force Base in North Dakota and Malmstrom Air Force Base in Montana.

The Subcommittee on International Organization and Disarmament Affairs of the Senate Foreign Relations Committee, headed by Sen. Albert Gore, Sr., D-Tenn., held hearings on the ABM from March 6 to July 16, 1969. The witnesses were mainly scientists and academic experts who argued that the ABM would not work, that it was too expensive, and that it would give the Soviet Union the impression that the United States was seeking a first-strike capability. The administration found these arguments inconsistent: if the system would not work, it could not be provocative. Laird argued that it was the Soviet Union that was building a first-strike capability. Gore, in turn, declared Safeguard to be "a weapons system searching for a mission." [5]

The Senate debated the question of funds for the ABM from July 8 to August 6, 1969, in an atmosphere of tense emotion. On August 6, it divided 50-50 on an amendment by Margaret Chase Smith, R-Maine, to kill Safeguard. Under Senate rules, a proposition loses if the vote on it is tied, so Safeguard survived. In addition, Vice President Spiro T. Agnew voted against the amendment in exercise of his constitutional right to break a tie; the final vote was therefore 50 to kill Safeguard and 51 to keep it alive. This was the high-water mark of congressional opposition to the ABM, though opponents continued to attack the program in both the House and Senate, usually through efforts to limit or deny appropriations.

SALT I and II

In 1970, the SALT negotiations with the Soviet Union were proceeding, and a new argument crept into the debate over the ABM: whether it should be kept alive to be used as a bargaining chip in the negotiations. If it could be given up in return for a concession the United States wanted from the Soviet Union, some people said, it should not be unilaterally abandoned. This reasoning had been used before to keep weapons programs alive in the face of congressional opposition. It might indeed give the United States greater leverage in negotiations, but acquiring something for the principal purpose of giving it away is expensive; and if the other side recognizes that something is being used as a bargaining chip, the chip's value may substantially decrease, or the other side may come up with a bargaining chip of its own for which it will demand more concessions.

In fact, ABM did become the crucial element—or bargaining chip, some would say—in the SALT agreements that were signed in Moscow by President Nixon and General Secretary Brezhnev on May 26, 1972.

Henry Kissinger, then Nixon's national security adviser, said it explicitly: "The trade-off of Soviet willingness to limit offensive forces in exchange for our willingness to limit ABMs was the essential balance of incentives that produced the first SALT agreements."[6] Similarly, Nixon, in an address to Congress on his return from Moscow, said the negotiations had been successful because "over the past three years we have consistently refused proposals for unilaterally abandoning the ABM, unilaterally pulling back our forces from Europe, and drastically cutting the defense budget."[7] Fifteen years later, in 1987, President Reagan used the same reasoning to explain the success of his meeting with Soviet General Secretary Mikhail Gorbachev that led to the treaty eliminating intermediate-range nuclear forces.

The Nixon administration's willingness to limit ABMs in negotiations with the Soviet Union was largely induced by congressional and public opposition to the system. Ironically, it seemed at times that the SALT negotiators were rushing to give the ABM away before Congress killed it. If Congress had ended the program, it might not have been possible to extract the Soviet concessions that went into the SALT I treaty (as it came to be called when a second round of negotiations— SALT II—began). On the other hand, if Congress had not threatened to kill it, the Nixon administration might not have been willing to give it up—or might have gotten more in return for it. The administration itself was divided over the issue. The State Department and the Arms Control and Disarmament Agency vacillated between being lukewarm toward the ABM and being actively opposed to it. The Joint Chiefs of Staff were more enthusiastic for it than the civilians in the Pentagon. The intelligence community could not quite agree on the extent of the Soviet program.

Treaty Provisions

The SALT I or ABM treaty limited each party to two ABM systems, one for the national capital and one for a missile base (Article III).[8] These limitations did not apply to ABM systems or their components used for development or testing and located within recognized test ranges (Article IV), but in other respects, the treaty imposed severe limitations on testing or development. These activities were prohibited for systems or components that were sea-based, air-based, space-based, or mobile land-based. This language, by implication, permitted testing or development for systems that were fixed land-based, and for their components. In addition, the treaty prohibited testing and development of launchers capable of handling more than one interceptor missile at a time or those with automatic or other rapid-reload capabilities (Article V). The parties agreed not to convert non-ABM components to ABM uses or to test such components "in an ABM mode." Finally, they agreed not to deploy early warning radars "except at locations along the periphery of [the] national territory and oriented outward" (Article VI). A Standing Consultative Commission was established to consider questions arising out of the treaty's provisions (Article XIII).

Accompanying the treaty were seven "initialed statements"—that is, explanatory statements initialed by Nixon and Brezhnev (although technically not part of the treaty, these statements carry great weight); six "common understandings," statements agreed to during the negotiations that are less weighty than those initialed by the heads of state but recognized as controlling by both sides; and four unilateral statements by the U.S. negotiating delegation, elaborating its position but without any agreement or comment from the Soviet side. Most of these ancillary statements are highly technical (for example, dealing with the emitted power of phased-array radars), but some of them have been important in subsequent developments.

Initialed Statement [E] provided that if "ABM systems based on other physical principles and including components capable of substituting for ABM interceptor missiles, ABM launchers, or ABM radars are created in the future, specific limitations on such systems and their components would be subject to discussion" in the Standing Consultative Commission and to agreement pursuant to provisions for amending the treaty. For reasons that are not clear, the order of the statements was subsequently revised, and this one became [D]. Also, what had at first been called initialed statements became "agreed statements." What thus ended as Agreed Statement [D] later became one of the points of contention in the argument over whether the Reagan Strategic Defense Initiative threatened violation of the ABM treaty.

Common Understanding D (which later became C) was an agreement that the prohibition on mobile land-based ABM systems and components "would rule out the deployment of ABM launchers and radars which were not permanent fixed types." This also became the subject of a dispute over interpretation of the treaty.

An Interim Agreement on Strategic Offensive Arms was signed in Moscow at the same time as the ABM treaty proper. It was essentially a freeze on each country's strategic offensive missiles. No new fixed land-based intercontinental ballistic missile (ICBM) launchers were to be started, nor were old ones to be improved. Submarine-launched ballistic missile (SLBM) launchers were limited to those in being or under construction. A protocol dealt with specific numbers. It was stated to be the objective of the parties to conclude a further agreement with "more complete" measures within five years, the lifetime of the interim agreement.

Congressional Action

President Nixon sent the ABM treaty to the Senate on June 13, 1972, with a request for the Senate's advice and consent to ratification. There was little controversy. The Senate gave its approval on August 3 by a vote of 88 to 2. In the defense appropriation bill for fiscal year 1973, passed in 1972, Congress even denied funds for the ABM site allowed by the treaty to protect Washington. The other site that the treaty allowed, and that the United States had chosen to put at the Safeguard site in North Dakota, was about 90 percent complete when the treaty was signed.

On the day the president sent the ABM treaty to the Senate, he transmitted the interim agreement to both houses with a request for approval. In earlier times, the interim agreement might have been considered to be an executive agreement, signed under the president's constitutional powers to conduct foreign affairs and requiring no congressional action (see Chapter 1). Indeed, the president could unilaterally have done what the agreement required simply by not requesting, or by not spending, appropriations for further strategic missiles. However, when Congress created the Arms Control and Disarmament Agency in 1961, it provided in the authorizing legislation that "no action shall be taken under this or any other law that will obligate the United States to disarm or to reduce or to limit the Armed Forces or armaments of the United States, except pursuant to the treaty-making power of the President under the Constitution or unless authorized by further affirmative legislation by the Congress." [9]

The House was as enthusiastic about the interim agreement as the Senate had been about the treaty. A joint resolution approving it was passed August 28 by a vote of 329 to 7.

But controversy arose in the Senate. The debate revealed profound differences among senators in the way they viewed the U.S.-Soviet strategic balance and U.S.-Soviet relations in general. The argument was essentially over nuclear sufficiency versus nuclear parity or even superiority. In its report on the interim agreement, the Senate Foreign Relations Committee commented:

> The United States and the Soviet Union have at last reached a point at which sufficiency of weapons, rather than attempted superiority on both sides, can be the guiding principle in the quest for viable relationships. Each side now possesses such a plethora of strategic weaponry that each can now feel itself securely able to deter attack but not to initiate strategic nuclear attack....
>
> Sufficiency, or parity, which has replaced the policy of numerical superiority, has made computation of numbers far less germane. [10]

However, an important group of senators, led by Henry M. Jackson, D-Wash., saw the problem from a different perspective. Jackson said the thrust of the agreements was "to confer on the Soviet Union the authority to retain or deploy a number of weapons . . . that exceeds our own in every category, and by a fifty percent margin." [11] With a number of cosponsors, Jackson offered an amendment which "urges and requests the president to seek a future treaty that, inter alia, would not limit the United States to levels of intercontinental strategic forces inferior to the limits provided for the Soviet Union." The Nixon White House endorsed this, or at least acquiesced in it, but the Foreign Relations Committee rejected it by a vote of 11 to 0.

Sen. J. William Fulbright offered a substitute amendment providing that, in negotiations for a permanent treaty, the United States should seek agreement on the basis of "overall equality, parity and sufficiency" in the number of offensive weapons. Fulbright said Jackson was "not asking for equality between the United States and Russia." Rather,

> he means equality in specific weapons systems. . . . This . . . is a misconception of the whole effort . . . by both countries to bring about a degree of parity, or equality, in their overall strategic weapons systems, including not only the ICBMs, but aircraft, other forward-based nuclear weapons and . . . the nuclear submarines of our allies.

The kind of equality Jackson was talking about, Fulbright said, was "superiority—equality in one area [while] we are clearly superior in the others." [12]

On the floor of the Senate, the Fulbright substitute was rejected, 38 to 48, and the Jackson amendment was agreed to, 56 to 35. Both houses then approved the interim agreement, with this amendment included. [13]

Further Negotiations

At the end of the five-year period specified in the interim agreement, no new agreement had been signed. However, the limitations of the interim agreement continued to be observed by the tacit agreement of both sides while the SALT II negotiations proceeded. In large measure, the negotiating difficulties grew out of the asymmetries that had been at the heart of the Senate debate over the interim agreement. Finally, on June 18, 1979, a SALT II treaty was signed by President Carter and General Secretary Brezhnev in Vienna. It provided a complicated system of sublimits as well as counting rules, and it included a statement of principles for SALT III. President Carter sent the treaty to the Senate, and it was the subject of extensive hearings before the Foreign Relations Committee.

The central concern over the treaty had to do with verification: Could the United States be sure of Soviet compliance? But other difficulties arose as well. In August, intelligence agencies reported the presence of a hitherto unsuspected Soviet brigade in Cuba. Later intelligence assessments concluded that the brigade had been there for many years, but in the meantime U.S. apprehension of the Soviet Union was rekindled. Then, in December 1979, Soviet troops intervened in Afghanistan. This led President Carter to ask the Senate to suspend consideration of the SALT II treaty. The Senate complied.

The ABM Protocol

President Nixon journeyed to Moscow for another summit in the summer of 1974, at a time when his administration was encumbered by the unfolding revelations concerning the Watergate break-in. In these circumstances, both the United States and the Soviet Union were uncertain of the future and unwilling or unable to make significant long-term commitments. Nevertheless, one result of this meeting was a protocol further limiting what was permitted under the ABM treaty. (A *protocol* is an addendum to a treaty, usually dealing with a single point. It is roughly analogous to a codicil of a will.)

That treaty, as noted, had allowed each side two ABM sites—one to protect its national capital and one to protect a field of missiles. Neither party had fully availed itself of this allowance. The Soviet Union had an ABM defense around Moscow, but none around any of its missile fields. The United States had an ABM defense around its missile base at Grand Forks, but none around Washington (and, as we have seen, Congress had specifically prohibited the expenditure of funds for building one around Washington). The protocol signed in 1974 recognized this state of affairs and limited each side to one site which it could choose—either its capital or a missile base.

The Senate Foreign Relations Committee held sporadic hearings over the course of a year and then approved the protocol, with the remark that "it would have been preferable for the two sides to agree to the limitation of one complex each at the start." [14] The Senate gave its advice and consent to ratification without floor debate by a vote of 63 to 15 on November 10, 1975.

The Grand Forks site had been completed a month earlier. In the fiscal 1976 defense appropriation bill, Congress voted to put it in mothballs (except for the perimeter acquisition radar), thereby effectively abandoning the one ABM site to which the United States was still entitled. By that time, the Safeguard program had cost $6 billion, and all that remained was the radar unit.

The Strategic Defense Initiative

The idea of a defense against missiles died hard. The ABM treaty had scarcely been ratified before the army in 1973 presented what it called a "site defense system." This was an ABM to protect Minuteman ICBMs with short-range missiles, while Safeguard would provide areawide protection. In 1974, another system was offered, "advanced ballistic missile defense." In 1981, there was a program for research on laser-armed space satellites.

None of these programs generated congressional debates at all comparable to the earlier arguments over the ABM, but the concept remained controversial. Although one house of Congress or the other sometimes cut off funding for an ABM project, by the time the legislative process had run its course at the end of the year, something was almost always appropriated, though usually less than had been requested by the White House. This is a typical congressional response: when confronted with a program about which it is dubious, Congress gives something but not everything. Executive agencies know this and ask for more than they really need or expect.

A major new element was added to the debate when President Reagan proposed what he called the Strategic Defense Initiative (SDI) and what critics called Star Wars. The idea was to construct a kind of umbrella over the United States consisting of a network of space-based and space-launched laser and nuclear weapons with the capability of destroying hostile missiles in flight. According to one of the president's senior arms-control advisers, the idea grew from a private briefing on nuclear strategy that Reagan had received years before when he was governor of California. The point was made in the briefing that the nuclear standoff between the superpowers could be compared to two people each holding a pistol to the other's head; each was hostage to the other, and the size of the pistol did not much matter. Governor Reagan's response, as reported at a seminar in 1986, was, "Why don't we put on a helmet?" SDI was to be the nation's helmet. Indeed, it was to be everybody's helmet. If it worked (and nobody knew whether it would), Reagan offered to share the technology with the Soviet Union, though in the best of circumstances, the technology would not be available until long after he left office.

President Reagan presented the SDI concept to the country in a television speech on March 23, 1983, in which he said:

> I've become more and more deeply convinced that the human spirit must be capable of rising above dealing with other nations and human beings by threatening their existence. . . .
> Wouldn't it be better to save lives than to avenge them? Are we not capable of demonstrating our peaceful intentions by applying all

our abilities and our ingenuity to achieving a truly lasting stability? . . . Let me share with you a vision of the future which offers hope. It is that we embark on a program to counter the awesome Soviet missile threat with measures that are defensive. . . .

What if free people could live secure in the knowledge that their security did not rest upon the threat of instant U.S. retaliation to deter a Soviet attack, that we could intercept and destroy strategic ballistic missiles before they reached our own soil or that of our allies?[15]

The SDI proposal at once aroused a storm of controversy. The arguments were similar to those made years before with respect to the original ABM, but they were now raised to a higher intensity because of the escalation, both in cost and in technical sophistication, represented by the SDI. It was estimated that the first five years of research would cost $22 billion. Deployment would cost perhaps $500 billion or more. Harold Brown, a nuclear physicist who had been secretary of defense in the Carter administration, said that SDI might require a computer program of as much as 100 million lines.[16] The greater cost and complexity, it was now argued, would also be detrimental to the other components of the U.S. military establishment, in that both human and material resources would be diverted into the new project.

Otherwise, the same arguments that had been heard about the ABM were repeated. Just as it was once thought that nuclear weapons provided the ultimate offense, now SDI was said to offer promise of the ultimate defense. For precisely that reason, opponents replied, SDI could very well give the appearance of providing the United States with a first-strike capability. It would inspire the Soviet Union to seek ways to penetrate it and would therefore escalate the arms race to yet a higher level. SDI supporters argued, on the other hand, that the program was defensive and that, by definition, it threatened no one, particularly since it was accompanied by a presidential offer to share the technology.

Whatever the merits of these arguments, it soon became clear that the Soviet government was very disturbed. SDI became the sticking point on U.S.-Soviet arms-control negotiations. It was the rock on which the meeting between Gorbachev and Reagan in Reykjavik foundered in October 1986. Repeatedly, Gorbachev demanded that SDI be abandoned or limited; adamantly, Reagan refused. SDI, he said, was not a bargaining chip; he would not negotiate it away. (On at least one occasion, Reagan recognized the threat implicit in SDI. At the Geneva summit in 1985, he is reported to have told Gorbachev that it would be dangerous if just one side were to deploy a space defense.[17])

Treaty Interpretation

Before the debate in the United States could be fully developed over the question of the SDI on its own merits, two new and highly contentious issues were added—namely, at what point would SDI be constrained by the ABM treaty, and where in the government would that decision be made?

The first hint of these issues came from National Security Adviser Robert C. McFarlane on the "Meet the Press" television program October 6, 1985. McFarlane remarked that testing and development of ABM systems based on "new physical concepts" was "approved and authorized" by the SALT I treaty.[18] Before then, it had been taken for granted that SDI laboratory research was not covered by the treaty, but that when the SDI proceeded to testing (outside the laboratory), development, or deployment, the treaty did apply. It was not even certain in the early stages that SDI involved "new physical concepts"— nor, for that matter, what "new physical concepts" were.

The ABM treaty proper does not mention "new physical concepts." Agreed Statement [D] refers to "other physical principles" (without defining them) and says that if ABM systems involving such principles are created, then "specific limitations [on them] . . . would be subject to discussion . . . and agreement." The treaty itself is very clear in its prohibition of the development, testing, or deployment of other than fixed land-based systems (Article V).

One possible element of SDI was the use of space-based lasers to disarm enemy missiles, and this could be called a "new physical concept" or "other physical principle." Another possible element was the deployment of so-called kinetic kill vehicles—missiles which would disable enemy missiles by physically hitting them. These involved no new concepts or principles and were thus clearly prohibited by the ABM treaty, but they could also be in place earlier than the more exotic technologies using lasers or particle beams. This gave rise to a dilemma: if the United States did what could be done most quickly, it would have to deal sooner with the limitations imposed by the ABM treaty.

Administration Position

McFarlane's seemingly casual remark provoked a heated debate over a "broad" versus a "narrow" or "restrictive" or "traditional" interpretation of the ABM treaty. A few days after McFarlane's television appearance, President Reagan signed National Security Decision Directive 192, which in effect took both sides of the issue. As explained by Secretary of State Shultz in a speech two days later:

It is our view, based on a careful analysis of the [ABM] treaty text and the negotiating record, that a broader interpretation of our authority is fully justified. This is, however, a moot point; our SDI research program has been structured and . . . will continue to be conducted in accordance with a restrictive interpretation of the treaty's obligations.[19]

Actually, the administration had been considering this question internally for some time. On October 3, 1985, the legal adviser of the State Department, Abraham D. Sofaer, a former federal judge, produced a memorandum supporting the broad interpretation based on, among other things, the *negotiating record* of the treaty—that is, the collection of all the documents involved in the negotiations.[20] For the preparation of this memorandum, he relied mainly on some young lawyers new to his staff. He later disavowed this memo and wrote another one, which, however, reached the same conclusion.

Congressional Reaction

The issue prompted hearings on both sides of Capitol Hill, first by a House Foreign Affairs subcommittee and then by a Senate Armed Services subcommittee. The administration was represented by Sofaer and by Paul Nitze, who had been one of the treaty's negotiators—the only one still serving in the government. On the other side, the subcommittees heard from Gerard C. Smith, who had been head of the Arms Control and Disarmament Agency in the Nixon administration and who had been chief of the ABM treaty negotiating team. Smith was supported by John B. Rhinelander, who had been the team's legal adviser.

The issue gradually went beyond the question of the legally correct interpretation. SDI opponents wondered why, if the issue was indeed "moot," as Shultz had said, the administration was so insistent about it. Was it seeking to establish the validity of the broad interpretation against the day when it would want to conduct tests that were prohibited by the narrow interpretation? Some supporters of SDI wanted to move quickly to make the broad interpretation irreversible, so that it could not be abandoned by the new administration that would take office in 1989. The system probably could not be tested and certainly could not be deployed before then, but if the right to do so under the ABM treaty could be firmly established, SDI's political survivability would be improved.

The fundamental argument provoked by the Sofaer memorandum had to do with what Congress, and particularly the Senate, perceived to be their institutional prerogatives. Few issues arouse more fervor on Capitol Hill, and it was even greater in this case because Reagan, more than most presidents, was jealous of the prerogatives of his office. Sofaer had based his reinterpretation largely on the negotiating record, but senatorial requests to see that record were resisted. Finally, it was supplied, or at least enough of it to satisfy the Senate, but only after repeated delays had sorely tried senatorial patience. (The Shultz State Department thereby demonstrated that it had failed to learn the lesson that had also eluded the State Department under every other secretary at least since Dean Acheson: the department's relations with Congress would be greatly improved if it would supply promptly and graciously what it is eventually going to supply tardily and grudgingly.)

Administration officials insisted that the interpretation of a treaty was the prerogative of the president alone. Some senators, notably the minority leader, Robert J. Dole, R-Kan., supported this view, but others vigorously dissented. Sen. Sam Nunn, D-Ga., said it would amount to having "the Senate of the United States declare itself a potted plant . . . an ornament in the foreign policy arena, adorning but having no influence." [21] The Foreign Relations Committee called the reinterpretation "the most flagrant abuse of the Constitution's treaty power in 200 years." [22]

Confrontation

How some senators felt about reinterpreting the treaty depended on how they felt about SDI: those favoring SDI favored the reinterpretation; those opposing SDI opposed the reinterpretation. But there was another group, epitomized by Nunn, which thought that, regardless of SDI, reinterpretation amounted to a unilateral changing of the rules of treaty making. The Senate had thought the treaty meant one thing when it had approved it; now the Senate was being told that the treaty really meant something else. Further, the Senate was being told, in effect, that it did not even have a voice in the matter. This sounded to some not simply like reinterpretation by the president but like amendment by the president. Moreover, they said, the matter was without precedent. The Foreign Relations Committee declared that it was "aware of *no* instance in which a treaty was reasonably supposed by the Senate, when it consented to ratification, to mean one thing, and it was argued later by the Executive to mean something altogether different." [23] In this view, any reinterpretation of a treaty, like the treaty itself, should result from joint action by the president and the Senate. Nunn had warned the president about the potential consequences of acting unilaterally. In a letter of February 6, 1987, he wrote:

> I am concerned that absent due consultation, a unilateral Executive Branch decision to disregard the interpretation of the Treaty which the

Senate believed it had approved when the accord was ratified in 1972 would provoke a Constitutional confrontation of profound dimensions.[24]

The administration held to the reinterpretation (though without actually doing anything to violate the old interpretation), and the constitutional confrontation that Nunn had predicted began to take form. First, Nunn made a major speech in the Senate, which extended over three days (March 11, 12, and 13, 1987). He exhaustively analyzed the negotiating record he had been supplied, the record of Senate consideration, and the Sofaer memorandum. His conclusion was that, although there were some ambiguities in the negotiating record, they were not

> of sufficient magnitude to demonstrate that the Nixon administration reached one agreement with the Soviets and then presented a different one to the Senate. The preponderance of evidence in the negotiating record supports the Senate's original understanding of the treaty, that is, the traditional interpretation.[25]

Nunn's speech was followed by joint hearings by the Senate Foreign Relations and Judiciary committees. The purpose of the hearings was to consider a resolution on the subject by Sen. Joseph R. Biden, Jr., D-Del., chairman of Judiciary and the second-ranking Democrat on Foreign Relations. The Biden resolution set forth the legislative history of the ABM treaty in great detail and concluded that the broad interpretation "would be inconsistent with the provisions of the Treaty and would require an amendment to the Treaty." Further, the resolution declared, "no amendment to the ABM Treaty may occur without the agreement of the Parties and the advice and consent of the Senate." [26]

Biden assailed the administration view as being "a purposeful act of revisionist distortion." [27] On the other hand, Sen. Gordon J. Humphrey, R-N.H., said the president should withdraw from the ABM treaty altogether and carry the battle for anti-missile defenses to the public. Sen. Ernest F. Hollings, D-S.C., also consulted the negotiating record and announced his agreement with Sofaer.[28]

Despite the joint hearings, the Foreign Relations Committee had sole jurisdiction over the resolution and approved it on May 19, 1987, by a vote of 11 to 8. Nancy Landon Kassebaum of Kansas was the only Republican to vote for it, a fact that suggested there would be difficulty in bringing it to a vote in the Senate as a whole. The resolution was reported in September, but was not further considered in 1987. Other business was clogging the Senate calendar as the session moved to a close, and administration supporters made it plain they would mount a major fight against any effort to bring the resolution to a vote.

The Battle over Funding

The question of reinterpreting a treaty is an issue between the Senate and the president, and this particular reinterpretation involved a major issue of national defense as well. On this latter issue, the House joined the Senate in resorting to the congressional power of the purse. Members of the House generally approached the matter on the basis of the merits of SDI and thought that the issue of treaty reinterpretation was secondary. House opponents of SDI welcomed the reinterpretation issue as a further roadblock and House proponents deplored it for the same reason, but generally the House did not feel as institutionally involved as the Senate.

The first action came in the House Armed Services Committee in connection with the defense authorization bill. (For the distinction between authorization and appropriation, see Chapter 2.) The committee voted to require continued observance of the ABM treaty's traditional interpretation. The House passed the bill with the committee's restriction intact. The strength of feeling in the House was shown by a vote of 159 to 262 against a proposal to delete the restriction.

The Senate Armed Services Committee went further. It approved a provision, offered by Nunn and Sen. Carl Levin, D-Mich., prohibiting tests of anti-missile devices that were based in space or on aircraft, ships, or mobile ground vehicles unless the tests were approved by Congress. This prohibition was strongly opposed by the administration and set off a Republican filibuster, which went on throughout the summer of 1987.

The Senate spent a great deal of time in parliamentary skirmishing over the filibuster. Nunn served notice on the president that if the administration insisted on reinterpreting the ABM treaty, he would insist that the Senate be given the negotiating record of the treaty eliminating intermediate-range nuclear forces (INF), which was then close to being completed. (It was signed by Reagan and Gorbachev in Washington in December 1987.) "In effect," Nunn wrote to the president, "the Sofaer doctrine holds that if the Senate is misinformed by Executive Branch officials as to the meaning of a proposed treaty, that is simply too bad. ... If Congress relies upon the testimony of your administration as to the meaning of an INF treaty, it will be at its own risk." [29] Sen. Claiborne Pell, D-R.I., chairman of the Foreign Relations Committee, went further. He demanded the negotiating records for twenty treaties that were already pending before the committee.

Nunn finally broke the filibuster by threatening to keep the Senate from taking up the nomination of Robert Bork to the Supreme Court until after it had disposed of the defense bill. (The president had nominated Bork to fill a vacancy on the Court during the summer and had made Senate confirmation one of his highest priorities. The nomination became bitterly controversial and was eventually rejected by the Senate, but of course that was not foreseen at the time of Nunn's threat.) The Senate then voted 58 to 38 to table a motion to delete the Nunn-Levin amendment. To "table" a motion technically means only to set it aside, but in practice it is the functional equivalent of rejection; hence, when a motion to delete an amendment is tabled, the amendment remains intact.

Sen. Pete Wilson, R-Calif., called the Nunn-Levin amendment "the most glaring unilateral concession in the history of arms control." [30] Nunn, on the other hand, said that what he called the "Sofaer doctrine" was "the boldest assertion of executive power at the expense of the Senate as an institution that I've ever seen." Unless the administration repudiated Sofaer, Nunn continued, the Senate would have to review the entire negotiating record on all future treaties. Thus, he concluded, "in an effort to temporarily strengthen this president on the ABM treaty [the administration has] weakened the presidency as an institution." [31] Meanwhile, in the background was the threat of a veto if the president believed his powers were unduly limited.

In the end, the matter was compromised, and the basic issue was left unresolved. The bill that was sent to the president in late November replaced the Nunn-Levin amendment with a provision limiting anti-missile tests to those that the administration had previously announced would take place during the year ending September 30, 1988. All of these fell within the traditional or narrow interpretation of the ABM treaty. Both the president and Congress had made their points for another year. Congress achieved what it wanted—namely, limiting SDI tests to those permitted under the narrow interpretation. The president avoided a congressional restriction on his prerogatives; the limitation he accepted permitted him to do all that he had intended to do anyway. It was a classic example of how the legislative process works.

The Issue Recurs

The ABM dispute affected Senate consideration of the treaty on Intermediate Nuclear Forces (INF), which was signed in Washington by President Reagan and General Secretary Gorbachev December 8, 1987. This treaty was a landmark in arms control in three respects: (1) it provided for the elimination, as distinguished from the limitation, of a whole class of weapons—in this case, intermediate and shorter range missiles and launchers (those with ranges from 500 to 5,500 kilometers); (2) in providing for this elimination, it introduced the principle of asymmetrical reductions—that is, one party (in this case the Soviet Union) would give up more than the other party; and (3) it provided for on-site inspections to verify that the eliminations had in fact occurred.

As noted previously, differences over the ABM treaty had kept Reagan and Gorbachev from any agreement in Reykjavik in 1986. In Washington in 1987 they agreed in effect to postpone their ABM dispute in order to be able to sign the INF treaty. The result was a wordy paragraph in their joint statement which said that they would observe the ABM treaty "as signed . . . while conducting their research, development and testing as required." [32] But each leader shortly made it clear that he continued to hold to his earlier position. In January 1988, the United States submitted a new draft treaty in the continuing arms negotiations in Geneva, in which it insisted on the broad interpretation. Georgi M. Kornienko, a senior Soviet official visiting Washington, accused the United States of "disrespect" for the December Gorbachev-Reagan statement. [33]

The issue continued to resonate in the Senate. After considerable negotiation with a number of senators, Secretary of State Shultz provided a letter that satisfied Nunn. In it, the secretary gave assurances that executive-branch testimony could be regarded as authoritative without being incorporated in the Senate resolution of ratification. Shultz also promised that the Reagan administration would not adopt a different meaning for the treaty without the approval of the Senate.

On March 30, 1988, the Foreign Relations Committee voted 17 to 2 to report the treaty favorably to the Senate. By a vote of 12 to 7, the committee added the substance of Shultz's letter to Nunn as a condition in the resolution of ratification. The committee then went on to say in the resolution that any departure from this understanding would require "Senate advice and consent to a subsequent treaty or protocol, or the enactment of a statute." [34]

This became a major issue during Senate debate on the INF treaty in May 1988. The issue was still viewed as an institutional one involving the respective prerogatives of the president and the Senate, but a group of Republican senators argued that the Foreign Relations Committee's proposals would undermine the president and enhance the Senate at his expense.

Majority Leader Robert Byrd proposed a somewhat diluted compromise that attracted some Republican support, including that of Minority Leader Dole. The Byrd substitute contained a provision that the United States would not depart from the "common understanding" of the treaty's meaning except with the advice and consent of the Senate or through enactment of a law by both houses of Congress. [35]

The Senate agreed to the Byrd substitute, 72 to 27, on May 26, 1988. The following day, it tabled (that is, in effect rejected) two final efforts by Sen. Arlen Specter, R-Pa., to dilute the provision further. One of these would have defined "common understanding" as a "shared interpretation" that the Senate clearly relied on. It was tabled 67 to 30. The other disclaimed any intent by the Senate to change "the heretofore accepted constitutional law." [36] It was tabled, 64 to 33. The Senate then gave its advice and consent to the INF treaty, 93 to 5.

Reagan was determined to have the last word. Senate action came while the president was en route to yet another meeting with Gorbachev. From Helsinki, Reagan issued a statement: "I continue to have concerns about the constitutionality of some provisions of the resolution of ratification, particularly those dealing with interpretation." [37]

The Bush Administration

Nor did the change in administrations from Reagan to Bush or the collapse of communism in Eastern Europe end the debate about Reagan's Strategic Defense Initiative. The Bush administration developed a modification of SDI which it called Brilliant Pebbles. The "pebbles" would be clusters of small rockets in earth orbit. They would be designed to detect the launch of hostile missiles and to intercept and destroy them by impact. Some thought Brilliant Pebbles would violate the ABM treaty.[38]

Following the disintegration of the Warsaw Pact in 1989, the administration found new reasons to proceed with SDI. Defense Secretary Richard Cheney told the Senate Armed Services Committee in February 1990, "I think given the proliferation of ballistic missile technology in the third world and weapons of mass destruction that, by the end of the century, we will be in a position where we would like very much to have some kind of defensive system deployed against these capabilities." [39]

Sen. Strom Thurmond, R-S.C., strongly agreed "both because of the Soviet strategic missile threat and because of proliferation of ballistic missiles in third world countries." [40] But Sen. Albert Gore, Jr., D-Tenn., differed. In a statement reminiscent of his father's remark twenty years earlier about a weapon in search of a mission, Gore described the "effort to shift the SDI program from a defense against the Soviets to an *n*th country threat or a terrorist missile" as a problem of looking for a new perceived threat.[41]

The Persian Gulf War of 1991 added yet another new angle. The army's Patriot missile scored a series of successes, some of them seen on worldwide television, in intercepting and destroying Iraqi Scud missiles. Proponents of SDI seized on this success as an argument for pressing ahead with the more elaborate system. Former defense secretary Brown dismissed this as "partisan nonsense."[42] Senator Nunn simply pointed out that Patriot was entirely an army program and had nothing to do with SDI.

Two new elements entered the argument. Proponents of SDI stopped talking about reinterpreting the ABM treaty and started talking about renegotiating it. And more so than in the past, debate tended to center not on whether there should be an antimissile defense, but on what it should be like. Thus, Senator Nunn defined the issue:

> Whether it is better to devote our resources to near-term technology that can protect us against limited attacks that are much more likely to come from third countries or from some accidental or unauthorized launch, or whether on the other hand we are going to go for this very exotic system that will take a long, long time, a lot of money to develop and when we get through developing it, at least in the first stages, we are still not going to have anything like comprehensive defense.[43]

The issue was reopened in a bill to authorize supplemental appropriations to pay for the war and also to provide benefits for members of the armed forces who served in it. In the House, Rep. C. Christopher Cox, R-Calif., offered an amendment expressing the sense of Congress that the administration should negotiate an agreement with the Soviet Union to allow research, development, testing, and deployment of a defense against ballistic missiles. The amendment was rejected, 145 to 281, with little debate.

In the Senate, Sen. John W. Warner, R-Va., ranking minority member of the Armed Services Committee and a former secretary of the navy, offered an amendment that the administration should negotiate an agreement "which would clearly remove any limitations on the United States having effective defenses against ballistic missiles."[44] If this could not be done within two years, the president was to report to Congress his determination whether continued adherence to the ABM treaty was in the national interest.

Warner produced a letter from National Security Adviser Brent Scowcroft, giving the amendment the administration's blessing. Warner argued that fifteen or twenty developing countries might have a missile capability by the end of the century and that instability in the Soviet Union also increased the possibility of unauthorized or accidental use.

Nunn offered a substitute amendment which would increase the authorization for Patriot procurement by $224 million and reallocate $487 million more of SDI funds to accelerate research and development of ground-based sensors and interceptors designed for early deployment. The problem, Nunn said, was that although the president had announced in his State of the Union message that SDI was to be scaled back to provide defense against limited attacks, the SDI organization in the Pentagon was in fact "putting the money on long-term Brilliant Pebbles research, and they are cutting back drastically on near-term systems that are much more available for the next five to ten years." [45] After reflecting on the matter overnight, Warner withdrew his amendment (taking the Nunn substitute with it) the next day.

The issue continued to enliven consideration of the fiscal 1992 defense authorization and appropriation bills during the spring and summer of 1991. The administration recommended a first phase which it called Global Protection Against Limited Strikes (GPALS). This, it was said, could be in place by the end of the decade at a cost of $75 billion. Yet another new element was added in the form of budget constraints. The agreement between Congress and the Bush administration which ended (at least temporarily) the 1990 budget crisis provided that increases in spending had to be offset by decreases and that money could not be moved between defense and nondefense accounts. So the competition was heightened between the components of the defense budget.

The House Armed Services Committee set the lines which were substantially followed by the House in both the authorization and appropriation bills. The administration had requested $5.17 billion for ABM research in fiscal 1992; the committee approved $3.54 billion. Almost all of the reduction was accounted for by the total elimination of $1.61 billion for Brilliant Pebbles. At the same time, the committee approved $883 million (up from $603 requested) for work on an antitactical missile to be used against shorter-range attacks. It further transferred this program from the SDI office to the army. In the appropriation bill, the House reduced the antitactical missile funds to $787 million.

Some of the votes for the ABM reductions came from people who were opposed to the ABM. Other votes came from people who were perhaps not opposed to ABM at all but who simply favored other weapons more strongly. One such weapon was the V-22 Osprey, an aircraft ardently sought by the marine corps and the House delegations from Texas and Pennsylvania—where it would be made—but opposed by the Bush administration. ABM opponents picked up votes by posing the issue as a transfer of funds from ABM to Osprey. ABM's loss became Osprey's gain, and the administration lost on both counts.

The argument over interpretation of the ABM treaty appeared to be over. In an orchestrated barrage of speeches in the Senate June 6, supporters of SDI shifted their emphasis to renegotiation or abrogation of the treaty. Sen. Robert C. Smith, R-N.H., called the treaty "a growing national security liability." [46] Sen. Dan Coats, R-Ind., said the U.S. "should seek to modify the treaty to lift any restriction on research, development, and testing, and focus limitations solely on the deployment of weapons." This could be done, he said, "cooperatively with the Soviet Union in the defense and space talks." [47]

Conclusion

Taken by themselves, the ABM treaty of 1972 and its protocol of 1974 are routine examples of the way in which the president and the Senate share power in the treaty-making process. But there is far more to them than that. These agreements are at the heart of three issues that, in one form or another, have agitated U.S. defense policy since 1945.

First, there are the more or less technological questions. Is there any point in trying to construct a defense against nuclear weapons? Conversely, is there any justification for not trying? If a serious effort were made to provide effective defense, either through SDI or some other means, would it in fact lead to security? Or would it merely stimulate an adversary's search for more, and more powerful, offensive weapons? With or without a defense, how many nuclear missiles are enough? Finally, when the United States and the Soviet Union agreed in the ABM treaty not to construct nationwide ABM defenses, they agreed in effect to put their populations mutually at risk. Is this morally or strategically acceptable?

Second, there are the constitutional issues. The Constitution gives Congress the power to "provide for the common defense" and "to raise and support armies," and therefore Congress must have a role in searching for the answers to all these questions—but the Constitution also designates the president as commander in chief. Similarly, the Constitution gives the president the power to make treaties, but only with the approval of the Senate by a two-thirds vote. The issue of antimissile defense, as it evolved into the SDI, raised the question of how much flexibility the president has in interpreting a treaty after it has been made. The Reagan administration implied that the president's flexibility is virtually unlimited, while a majority of the Senate (and the House, too, for that matter) said it is constrained by the Senate's powers. Senator Nunn warned that Reagan's unyielding insistence on upholding what he saw as the powers of the presidency might be counterproductive, in that it would ultimately weaken the office. Something of the same thing occurred as a consequence of President Johnson's persistence in the face of congressional opposition to his Vietnam policy.

Third, the Persian Gulf War, which followed hard on the collapse of Communist power in Eastern Europe, raised new questions of grand strategy. What sort of weapons did we need to prepare defenses against?

The proliferation of weapons in the Third World and growing instability in both the Third World and the Communist world lent urgency to the search for answers.

All of these questions—technological, constitutional, and strategic—are worthy of serious national debate with the participation of the public at large as well as of Congress and officials of the executive branch. The institutional struggle that these issues provoked between Congress and the president was in part a demonstration of institutional jealousy on both sides—or ambition counteracting ambition, in the more elegant phrasing of the Federalist papers.[48] But this struggle was also a reflection of the fact that the larger issues were unresolved. There was no greater consensus in Congress about these larger issues than there was in the public. But in asserting its institutional prerogatives against those of the president, Congress kept the larger issues from being decided on presidential terms. It bought time for second thoughts and more debate. That is surely how the Framers intended the Constitution to work.

Notes

1. Lyndon Baines Johnson, *The Vantage Point: Perspectives of the Presidency, 1963-1969* (New York: Holt, Rinehart and Winston, 1971), 479-480.
2. The text of McNamara's speech is in *New York Times,* September 18, 1967.
3. House Armed Services Committee, *Military Construction Authorization.* 90th Cong., 2d sess., 1968, H. Rept. 90-1296 (H.R. 16703), 5.
4. In a conversation with John Newhouse November 12, 1987. Quoted in Newhouse, *War and Peace in the Nuclear Age* (New York: Alfred A. Knopf, 1989), 205.
5. *Congressional Quarterly Almanac, 1969,* 260.
6. Henry Kissinger, *White House Years* (Boston: Little, Brown, 1979), 208.
7. *Congressional Record,* 92d Cong., 2d sess., June 1, 1972, 19516.
8. 23 UST 3435; TIAS 7503. The texts of the treaty, the interim agreement, the agreed interpretations, and the unilateral statements, as well as useful related documents, are in House Committee on Foreign Affairs and Senate Committee on Foreign Relations, *Legislation on Foreign Relations through 1988,* vol. 5, *Treaties and Related Material* (Washington, D.C.: Government Printing Office, 1989), 196-217.
9. Arms Control and Disarmament Act of 1961, as amended, sec. 33 (22 USC 2573).
10. Senate Committee on Foreign Relations, *Agreement on Limitation of Strategic Offensive Weapons,* 92d Cong., 2d sess., 1972, S. Rept. 92-979, 5, 8.
11. *Congressional Record,* 92d Cong., 2d sess., August 11, 1972, 27935.
12. Ibid., September 7, 1972, 29725.
13. The Jackson Amendment is in sec. 3 of the joint resolution on the agreement, P.L. 92-448, approved September 30, 1972.
14. *Congressional Record,* 94th Cong., 1st sess., November 6, 1975, 35363.
15. *Weekly Compilation of Presidential Documents,* vol. 19, no. 12 (March 28, 1983): 447.

16. Harold Brown, "Is SDI Technically Feasible?" *Foreign Affairs* 64 (*America and the World, 1985*): 444.
17. Newhouse, *War and Peace in the Nuclear Age,* 387.
18. *Department of State Bulletin* 85 (December 1985): 33.
19. Ibid., 23.
20. The negotiating record includes summaries of the negotiating sessions, memoranda of conversations with representatives of the other government and of communications between the U.S. negotiators and the government in Washington, summaries of telephone conversations, and even travel vouchers and hotel bills. These records are, obviously, voluminous. Along with a great deal of dross, they also contain some very sensitive material and are very tightly held by the State Department. Nevertheless, they are usually viewed as being of no more than historical interest. The ABM treaty is the only instance since World War II when they have been an important subject of controversy or source of interpretation.
21. Dispatch by Helen Dewar, *Washington Post,* September 16, 1987.
22. Dispatch by R. Jeffrey Smith, *Washington Post,* September 21, 1987.
23. Senate Committee on Foreign Relations, *The ABM Treaty Interpretation Resolution,* 100th Cong., 1st sess., 1987, S. Rept. 100-164, 48 (italics in the original).
24. The full text of Nunn's letter is in *Congressional Quarterly Weekly Report,* February 14, 1987, 274.
25. *Congressional Record,* daily ed., 100th Cong., 1st sess., March 13, 1987, S3172. The full text of Nunn's speech is in Ibid., March 11, 1987, S2967-S2986; March 12, 1987, S3090-S3095; and March 13, 1987, S3171-S3173.
26. S. Res. 167, 100th Cong., 1st sess.
27. Senate Committee on Foreign Relations and Committee on the Judiciary, *The ABM Treaty and the Constitution, Joint Hearings,* 1987, 118.
28. Ibid., 109-112, 442-470.
29. *Congressional Quarterly Weekly Report,* September 5, 1987, 2127.
30. *Congressional Record,* daily ed., 100th Cong., 1st sess., September 16, 1987, S12142.
31. *Congressional Quarterly Weekly Report,* September 19, 1987, 2232.
32. Text in *Washington Post,* December 11, 1987.
33. Dispatch by Don Oberdorfer and R. Jeffrey Smith, *Washington Post,* January 30, 1988, A5.
34. Senate Committee on Foreign Relations, *The INF Treaty,* 100th Cong., 2d sess., Exec. Rept. 100-15 (April 14, 1988), 436 (resolution of ratification), 442 (Shultz's letter to Nunn). This report also contains much other useful material on treaty interpretation.
35. *Congressional Record,* daily ed., 100th Cong., 2d sess., May 26, 1988, S6724.
36. Ibid., May 27, 1988, S6884 and S6890.
37. *Weekly Compilation of Presidential Documents,* vol. 24, no. 22 (June 6, 1988): 683.
38. See, for example, remarks of Sen. Jeff Bingaman, D-N.M., in Senate Committee on Armed Services, unpublished transcript, February 1, 1990, 100.
39. Ibid., 103.
40. Ibid., 155.
41. Ibid., 136.
42. R. Jeffrey Smith and Dan Morgan, "SDI Ordered to Aim Lower, Scale Back," *Washington Post,* January 31, 1991.

43. *Congressional Record,* daily ed., 102d Cong., 1st sess., March 13, 1991, S3180.
44. Text in ibid., S3176.
45. Ibid.
46. *Congressional Record,* daily ed., 102d Cong., 1st sess., June 6, 1991, S7255.
47. Ibid., S7251.
48. *The Federalist,* no. 51.

CHAPTER 4

The United States in the Middle Eastern Vortex

Since the end of the Vietnam War, no region has presented the United States with as many diplomatic and military challenges as the Middle East. The region resembles the Balkans of the pre-World War I era: a zone of ongoing political turbulence and instability, producing a succession of major and minor conflicts.

Several factors have drawn the United States ever more deeply into the vortex of the Middle East. One of these is the region's strategic importance. It must be remembered that one of the decisive military campaigns of World War II—the Battle of North Africa—was waged in the region. Then there is the continuing dependence of the United States and other industrialized nations upon access to the oil supplies of the Persian Gulf area. Despite steps taken in recent years to change that reality, the United States, Western Europe, and Japan remain heavy consumers of Middle Eastern oil. For the industrialized nations, a prolonged lack of access to this vital energy source would unquestionably result in severe economic dislocations, dangerous threats to national security, and political crises.

America's longstanding ties to the State of Israel are another factor immersing the United States deeply in developments in the Middle East. For almost half a century, U.S. financial, military, and diplomatic support of Israel has been essential to that nation's continued independence and development. Meanwhile, Israel has continued to face ominous threats to its security and future independence.

Another crucial development involving the United States in the Middle East has been the decline of British power since World War II. In this and other regions, Britain's decline has presented difficult choices for policy makers in Washington. Since the nineteenth century, for example, Great Britain had assumed the burden of preserving peace and stability within the Persian Gulf region, an area that was often described as in the British sphere of influence. The erosion of British power has plainly left a power vacuum in the Middle East. If the United States does not "inherit" Britain's historic role as the preserver of peace and security within the region, then what other nation will do so? Candidates for the position have not been lacking. For a number of years after World War II, the Soviet Union sought to fill the vacuum. In the recent period, the clerically ruled revolutionary government of Iran also aspired to play the role. Then by 1990, it was clear that there was another powerful, perhaps even more dangerous, candidate: the government of Iraq, led by the politically ambitious and ruthless Saddam Hussein.

Among the many specific issues in America's post-World War II relations with the countries of the Middle East, three have been selected for detailed treatment in this chapter. These are the Arab-Israeli conflict; arms sales by the United States to Saudi Arabia and Jordan; and the major implications of the Persian Gulf crisis that began in August 1990.

U.S. Involvement in the Arab-Israeli Conflict

One of the most intractable problems of the post-World War II era has been the Arab-Israeli conflict. It has been particularly difficult for the United States because of contradictory interests—on the one hand, a deep commitment to the idea and the reality of a Jewish state; on the other, the importance of the Arab states because of their geography, their leadership of the Moslem world, American fears of Soviet influence, Arab oil reserves, and the strategic importance of the Persian Gulf area.

The foreign policy of the United States toward the Arab-Israeli conflict may be conveniently envisioned in four stages.[1] In the first, from the founding of the Zionist movement in the late nineteenth century until World War II, the United States had no official involvement in the Arab-Israeli controversy. Yet private citizens and groups—whose views were often supported by resolutions passed by the state legislatures and Congress—were active in behalf of Zionist goals.

In the second stage—during and after World War II, until the creation of the State of Israel on May 14, 1948—the Roosevelt and Truman administrations supported the establishment of a Jewish state in the ancient land of Palestine, and they endorsed other Zionist goals, such as expanded Jewish immigration to Palestine after the war.

The Middle East

For almost twenty years after Israel came into existence, American foreign policy in its third stage was overtly pro-Israeli. Economic and technical aid by the United States, along with military assistance and arms sales (often on highly advantageous terms for the Israelis), enabled Israel to survive, to absorb a steady stream of immigrants, and to create a high standard of living for its citizens. Governmental aid and loans to Israel were supplemented by a high level of private donations and other forms of aid by Jewish groups and other supporters of Israel in the United States.

Background

The State of Israel is the fulfillment of Zionism, or the idea of a Jewish state. Zionism as a political idea was developed and elaborated by Theodor Herzl at the end of the nineteenth century in his influential book *The Jewish State* (1896). For Herzl, Zionism was the answer to the pervasive anti-Semitism that, in his view, made the assimilation of Jews in Europe impossible.[2] The World Zionist Organization, with Herzl as its president, was established in Switzerland in 1897.

World War I gave momentum to Zionism, and World War II gave it fulfillment. In 1917, Lord Balfour, the British foreign minister, issued the now famous Balfour Declaration:

> His Majesty's Government view with favour the establishment in Palestine of a national home for the Jewish people, and will use their best endeavors to facilitate the achievement of this object, it being clearly understood that nothing shall be done which may prejudice the civil and religious rights of existing non-Jewish communities in Palestine, or the rights and political status enjoyed by Jews in any other country.[3]

A similar statement was adopted by the U.S. Congress as a joint resolution in 1922. Two points are to be noted. First, the reference in the Balfour Declaration was to a "national home for the Jewish people"— which was not necessarily the same thing as a Jewish state. Second, there was also a proviso against prejudicing the rights of the Arabs in Palestine, who comprised a substantial majority of the population. The Balfour Declaration was also incorporated into the British mandate for Palestine under the League of Nations.

As the mandatory authority administering Palestine on behalf of the League of Nations, Great Britain was increasingly caught in the crossfire between the Zionists, who wanted to create a Jewish state in the country, and the Arabs, who opposed the Zionist goal. As time passed, officials in London became increasingly preoccupied with the approach of World War II; they had neither the incentive nor the power to resolve the Palestinian problem. The Palestinian question became acute in the aftermath of World War II. The Zionists exerted pressure on London to enable survivors of the Holocaust—Nazi Germany's campaign to exterminate the Jews—not only to immigrate into Palestine, but also to establish a Jewish state there. On November 29, 1947, the United Nations General Assembly voted for a plan to partition an independent Palestine into separate Jewish and Arab states, tied together in an economic union, with the city of Jerusalem under direct UN trusteeship. While the Arabs rejected the partition proposal, the Zionists reluctantly accepted it, since the plan did grant them the long-awaited Jewish state.

On December 3, 1947, the British announced that they would consider their mandate from the League of Nations terminated on May 15, 1948. Both Jews and Arabs prepared for a war (called the first round in a series of military conflicts) that, in fact, did not wait until May. The state of Israel was proclaimed in Palestine at midnight, May 14. President Truman recognized it eleven minutes later.[4]

Throughout this period, in energetically supporting Zionist objectives, Truman acted largely on his own, although he received encouragement from many legislators. The State Department—viewed by Truman as dominated by "Arabists" who were under British influence—advised against his policy. Dean Acheson, undersecretary of state at the time, frankly stated in his memoirs, "I did not share the President's views on the Palestine solution." [5] Strong pro-Zionist pressures were coming from Capitol Hill. Postmaster General Robert Hannegan, charged with arranging Truman's reelection, supported the Zionists—who were themselves extraordinarily active. "I do not think I ever had as much pressure and propaganda aimed at the White House as I had in this instance," Truman wrote later.[6]

The Actors

Israel. In many respects, it is remarkable that Israel even exists today, and it is perhaps even more remarkable that it came into being only half a century after Herzl articulated modern Zionism. The Zionist dream has been made a reality only after a long and torturous history, which culminated in the horror of Hitler's Holocaust. Since its creation, Israel has engaged in four wars with the Arabs—the War of Independence (1948-1949), the Suez War (1956), the Six-Day War (1967), and the Yom Kippur War (1973). In the Persian Gulf War that erupted in August 1990, Israel sustained extensive damage from Iraqi Scud missile attacks. Since 1973, hardly a day has passed in which Israelis have not been subject to some kind of violent opposition or attack by the Arabs inside and outside of Israel's borders. By the 1990s, the *Intifada*—or armed resistance to Israeli rule by Palestinians in the West Bank and Gaza—was a daily reality of Israeli life. By the late 1980s, Israel had a population of just over 4 million people, vis-à-vis upwards of 200 million Arabs. Furthermore, Israel is almost totally lacking in natural resources.

Israel's defense strategy has been based on mobility, a high state of readiness, and superiority of weapons and training to offset Arab superiority in numbers. Nevertheless, Israel's military victories have not brought the country security, which remains as elusive today as in the late 1940s. Israel's extraordinarily high level of military expenditures (on a per capita basis, the highest in the world); its determination to acquire the latest and best military equipment; its insistence on retaining control of Jerusalem, the West Bank territories, and the Golan Heights in Syria—these provide tangible evidence of Israel's continuing sense of military vulnerability and isolation. Adding to the nation's predicament is a formidable array of internal problems, despite a high standard of living. In contrast to the biblical depiction of Palestine as a "land flowing with milk and honey," in reality it is largely desert or semidesert, with few mineral resources. Since 1948, Israel has consistently incurred a growing foreign trade deficit; high levels of inflation have been endemic; and Israel has become more dependent than ever upon a high volume of official and private aid from the United States, a condition that shows no sign of changing in the years ahead.[7] By 1991, some Israeli officials and observers indicated that the country would need new and massive allocations of American aid to preserve its security.

The Arabs.   While the Israelis, despite their nation's insecurity, are today brimming with pride over their accomplishments, the Arabs have long felt a sense of humiliation, outrage, and injustice. First of all, to their minds, in creating the State of Israel foreigners took over lands in Palestine that Arabs viewed as rightfully theirs, driving the inhabitants into a wretched existence as refugees. Second, despite their overwhelming numbers, the Arabs have suffered five crushing military defeats.

Yet it is unwise to generalize about the Arabs. Eight different countries are considered Arab (Egypt, Syria, Jordan, Lebanon, Iraq, Saudi Arabia, Yemen, and Kuwait), as are a series of tiny sheikdoms along the Persian Gulf and four North African states known collectively as the Maghreb (Algeria, Morocco, Tunisia, and Libya). There are other distinctions to be made among the Arab states: between rich (those with oil) and poor (those without oil); between those that are adjacent to Israel and those that are not; and among conservative, moderate, and radical regimes. Most Arabs do, of course, share a common religion (Islam) and a common language (Arabic), but this common ground has resulted in no more unity than Roman Catholicism and the Spanish language have produced in Latin America.

Throughout most of the period since 1948, opposition to Israel has been the principal unifying force throughout the Middle East, to the extent that there has been unity at all. Yet differences have also existed, ranging from intransigent radicalism to cautious moderation, even with respect to Israel. Indeed, one of the most serious splits in the Arab world since 1948 came about in 1979, when the other Arab states joined to ostracize Egypt because it had signed a peace treaty with Israel. As we shall see, the Persian Gulf crisis that erupted in 1990 clearly underscored these differences.[8]

The United States.   In their approach to the Arab-Israeli conflict, American policy makers have exemplified three different points of view toward the issue. The bureaucracy of the executive branch—represented principally by the State and Defense departments—has

Israel and the Occupied Territories

customarily tended to favor either a pro-Arab or an evenhanded approach to the question. State Department specialists on the Middle East (sometimes called the Arabists) tend to view the area primarily in terms of international, rather than domestic, politics. These officials have often seemed interested primarily in preserving cooperative relations with what they viewed as moderate Arab governments. In recent years, Egypt and Jordan—and for a time in the late 1980s, even Iraq— fell into this category.

Inevitably perhaps, the orientation of the White House has been more sensitive to domestic political considerations than have attitudes in the State or Defense departments. Yet since the early 1970s, incumbent presidents have also seen the necessity to maintain a more balanced approach to the Arab-Israeli problem and to preserve at least some kind of rapport with most Arab governments.

Congress has been, and remains, the most pro-Israeli actor of all in the American foreign policy process. This derives from several factors: the strength of the pro-Israeli lobby in the United States; the deep and sincere convictions of many legislators on the Palestine question; the impact of American public opinion, which has as a rule been overwhelmingly sympathetic to the Israeli position; and the general ineffectiveness of Arab attempts to influence American public opinion favorably.

In attempting to understand the Arab-Israeli conflict, it is essential to bear in mind that not all Jews are Zionists, and, of course, not all supporters of the Zionist cause are Jewish. Although the Zionist movement has its roots in the Jewish religious tradition, Zionism is essentially a political movement: its dominant goal has been the creation and (after 1948) the support and protection of the State of Israel. In the United States and other countries, Zionism has drawn support from people of many religious backgrounds and political beliefs. Nevertheless, the basic strength of the pro-Israeli lobby rests in the American Jewish community, whose continuing support of Israel has been vital to that country's survival as an independent nation.

Although the Jewish community in the United States numbers only some 6 million people (less than 3 percent of the American population), its political influence—especially on Capitol Hill—is greatly disproportionate to its numbers. By many criteria, the pro-Israeli lobby has been one of the most conspicuously successful pressure groups in the postwar American political system, serving as a model of effective lobbying. Many Arabs and their supporters in the United States believe that America's consistent support of, and identification with, Israel for over a generation has been "dictated" by the influence of the Zionist lobby on the news media, public opinion, and Washington generally, particularly Capitol Hill.[9]

In reality, the relationship between the activities of the Zionist lobby and American diplomacy in the Middle East is a highly complex one, involving a number of diverse elements. One of these is unquestionably the fact that Jewish individuals and groups in the United States tend to be especially active and involved politically. Furthermore, their interest is frequently translated into tangible and financial support for candidates who favor Israel's position. Morris Amitay, the former executive director of the American-Israel Public Affairs Committee (AIPAC) and principal spokesman for the lobby, has put it this way:

> A lot of these [uncommitted] Senators are from the Midwest, West, down South, and these [Jews] are some of the elite types of people that these Senators like to be with and talk to, besides the pull of actual contributions. I do not think anyone ever likes to be approached on the very gut political level. You look around at who the Jewish constituents are from sparsely inhabited states. They are teachers, they are doctors, they have invariably been involved some way in politics. They are usually respected people in the community, so you do not have to pitch it at the level of, "I contributed ten thousand dollars to your campaign—unless you do this you will make me unhappy and I will contribute to your opponent next time." At most it's implicit, and it is not even implicit a large percentage of the time.[10]

As a rule, politicians get elected and reelected less by pleasing people than by not offending them. It follows that a vocal, dedicated, and well-organized minority has more influence politically than an apathetic or indifferent majority. The success of the pro-Israeli lobby provides a striking illustration of the emergence and growing importance of single-issue politics in the United States.

The strength of the Zionist lobby also illustrates the role of ethnicity in the American political system. In demanding support for Israel, Jewish groups in the United States have followed the path taken by Polish-Americans, Greek-Americans, Irish-Americans, and other ethnic minorities in seeking to influence governmental policy toward the "old country."

In addition to these factors, the success achieved by the pro-Israeli lobby in the United States can be in part accounted for by an old axiom with which students of propaganda have long been familiar: the most effective propaganda motivates those toward whom it is directed (the target) to believe and act as they are already inclined to do. In propaganda strategy, this concept is known as *reinforcement*. In the case of American attitudes toward the Arab-Israeli conflict, this concept means that the pro-Israeli lobby has operated in an environment highly congenial to the achievement of its objectives. The values and norms of American society, for example, are derived from the Judeo-Christian tradition (there is no comparable "Islamic-Christian" tradition).

As the only Western-style democracy in the Middle East, Israel draws many of its political traditions and practices from the United States and Europe. The pioneers who founded the state of Israel (the Ashkenazim, or Jews of European origin) came from the West and believed in maintaining close ties with the United States and other Western nations. The accomplishments of Israeli society since 1948 in "making the desert bloom" also seem to many Americans a reenactment of their own frontier experience in the face of great odds and dangers. If Israel has received billions of dollars in official and private aid from the United States, the Israelis for their part have used this assistance effectively. Time and again since 1948 Israel has been widely referred to as the principal ally of the United States in the Middle East.

Through its embassy in Washington, as well as directly from Jerusalem, the Israeli government maintains close contacts with Congress and with pro-Israeli lobbying groups, principally AIPAC and an umbrella organization called the Conference of Presidents of Major American Jewish Organizations (Conference of Presidents, for short). Israeli prime ministers, foreign ministers, defense ministers, and other officials visit Washington frequently; Capitol Hill is a routine stop on their rounds, for informal meetings with key committees or with the House and Senate membership in general. These visiting officials almost always confer, as well, with the Conference of Presidents and with other prominent Jewish leaders. During a particularly tense period in the negotiations for the Israeli-Egyptian peace treaty, Prime Minister Menachem Begin met with two thousand Jewish leaders in New York on his way back to Jerusalem from Washington. Begin said to his audience, "You have great influence. Do not hesitate to use that influence." [11] It should also be noted that the American Jewish community has sometimes served as a voice of moderation in endeavoring to get the government of Israel to modify its policies.

The remarkable success of the pro-Israeli lobby in the United States can also be explained by reference to another factor: the relative weakness of a countervailing Arab lobby. Until the 1970s at least, pro-Arab groups faced a number of serious obstacles in their efforts to influence American attitudes in favor of their cause. These included: the relatively small size of the Arab-American community; the limited number of news outlets that were sympathetic to the Arab viewpoint; deep divisions among the Arab states and policy differences among Arab organizations; the authoritarian (sometimes, the totalitarian) nature of many Arab governments; and the lack of firsthand knowledge of the Arab world by most of the American people. Some of these factors have begun to change in recent years, as symbolized by the widespread admiration in the United States for Egypt's late president Anwar Sadat and the overall improvement in Egyptian-American relations. Yet even today, the Zionist lobby remains one of the most effective in the American political system.

The Arab-Israeli conflict has been a singular episode in American postwar foreign policy in another respect: in illustrating the phenomenon of lobbying *by foreign governments* to influence the diplomacy of the United States. Toward the Arab-Israeli issue, since 1948 American policy making has followed a familiar and often predictable pattern. The president overrules the executive bureaucracy; then Congress overrules the White House, compelling the president to call for more aid or otherwise be more generous toward Israel; in some cases, Congress has tried to prevent the chief executive from putting pressure on Israel to change its internal or external policies. Israeli officials have known that they could often successfully "appeal" the decisions of executive officials to Congress. Visits by the Israeli prime minister and other high-level officials to the United States have frequently had this objective as a primary goal. As the case study of the sale of arms to Saudi Arabia and Jordan will illustrate, in some instances these appeals to Congress have been directed at preventing or circumscribing diplomatic and military moves by the United States deemed favorable to the Arabs.

The Context of the AWACS Proposal

A few weeks after he entered the Oval Office in 1981, President Reagan proposed to Congress that the United States sell five Airborne Warning and Control System (AWACS) aircraft to Saudi Arabia. Reagan's request, which precipitated one of the most intense debates over American policy toward the Middle East witnessed since World War II, must be understood against a background of major tendencies and developments in the region, as these affected Washington's diplomatic interests.[12]

Since the late 1940s, Israel had been involved in five major military conflicts with Arab states, counting the Persian Gulf crisis. The first round of fighting grew out of the establishment of the State of Israel in 1948. Miraculously, the outnumbered Israelis defeated several Arab military forces, successfully founded the State of Israel, and greatly enlarged its borders.[13] The Suez crisis of 1956 was the second round in the Arab-Israeli contest. British, French, and Israeli troops invaded Egypt, quickly defeated its armed forces, and sought to depose President Gamal Abdel Nasser's government. Owing to the firm opposition of the Eisenhower administration, however, in time these foreign troops were withdrawn from Egyptian soil, and Israel was compelled to relinquish the territory occupied by its armed forces in the Sinai area.[14]

Animosity between Israel and the Arab states continued; it reached a new level of violence in the third round of hostilities, which erupted on June 5, 1967. The ensuing Six-Day War was an overwhelming military triumph for Israel. Relying upon a preemptive strike, Israel's air force largely wiped out the Egyptian air force on the ground, leaving Egyptian armor in the Sinai defenseless against Israeli air and ground attacks.

Israeli military superiority also defeated the smaller armed forces of Syria and Jordan.[15]

The Six-Day War had far-reaching consequences for nations inside and outside the Middle East. As a result of the conflict, Israel greatly expanded its borders, extending them to the Suez Canal and to the strategic Golan Heights in the north. Another outcome of this conflict was that the Arab enemies of Israel—after sustaining three defeats in orthodox military engagements—now relied increasingly upon guerrilla warfare, carried out particularly by the PLO, to achieve their goals.[16]

Two other developments growing out of the Six-Day War directly involved Saudi Arabia and its relations with the United States. As a result of its victory, Israel officially annexed the city of Jerusalem (from 1948 until 1967 the Old City had been under Jordanian authority). Israeli officials asserted that the annexation of the Old City was a *fait accompli* that was nonnegotiable. Later, Israel proclaimed Jerusalem its capital. While Arabs generally were incensed by Israel's action, it was especially offensive to Saudi Arabia. Controlled by the rigidly orthodox Wahhabi sect of Sunni Islam, its government has long served as the custodian of the religious shrines most sacred to Sunni Moslems. Next to Mecca and Medina, Jerusalem (according to Sunni tradition, the site from which Mohammed ascended into heaven) is the third holiest shrine in Islam. Following the 1967 war, therefore, Saudi Arabia became actively involved in the Arab-Israeli conflict for the first time. With a relatively small military establishment, Saudi Arabia's main contribution to the Arab campaign against Israel consisted of subsidies provided to the PLO and certain Arab governments (such as Jordan and Syria).[17]

Another far-reaching consequence of the Six-Day War was the discovery of what came to be called "oil power" and reliance upon it to achieve Arab diplomatic objectives. Arab oil producers ceased production during the 1967 war in an attempt to bring pressure to bear on the United States and other Western nations viewed as sympathetic to Israel. The discovery of oil power in 1967 was important for two reasons: it established a precedent that the oil-producing states of the Middle East were to use with telling effect in their next confrontation with Israel (1973); and it underscored the mounting vulnerability of the United States, Western Europe, Japan, and other advanced nations to an oil embargo—a lesson the industrialized nations were to learn again painfully in the early 1990s.

After the 1967 conflict, tensions between Israel and its Arab adversaries continued to engender instability, violence, and the prospect of a fourth round of direct military hostilities in the Middle East. With Soviet assistance, Egypt, Syria, and Iraq were rebuilding their military establishments.[18] Arab governments showed no inclination to accept Israel or to arrive at a resolution of outstanding differences with it. The PLO and other anti-Israeli political movements continued to rely on guerrilla attacks and terrorist incidents to express their militant opposition to Israel.

As time passed, most informed observers predicted that a new wave of hostilities would engulf the Middle East. It came on October 6, 1973, when the fourth round (called by Israelis and Americans the Yom Kippur War and by Arabs the Ramadan War) in the Arab-Israeli conflict erupted. In well-executed surprise attacks, Egyptian forces struck the Bar Lev Israeli defense line in the Sinai region, while Syrian troops attacked Israeli defense forces in the Golan Heights; in these initial thrusts, the Arabs inflicted heavy losses on the Israeli military establishment. After their tank losses were replaced by a massive American airlift, Israeli troops ultimately reversed the tide of battle. In the final stage, Israeli officials were restrained by Washington from threatening the Syrian capital, Damascus, and from mounting attacks aimed at Egyptian territory west of the Suez Canal.[19]

In the sense that Israeli forces were ultimately victorious on the battlefield, the Yom Kippur War again demonstrated Israel's military superiority over its Arab enemies. Yet the war shattered several myths: that Arab troops would not fight; that Arab governments were incapable of planning a surprise attack that would escape early detection by Israel's vaunted intelligence service; and that Israeli forces were invincible on the battlefield. For Arabs, the 1973 war immensely bolstered their self-confidence and morale. Throughout the Arab world, it was viewed as a moral victory for the Arab cause.

For the United States, perhaps the most far-reaching consequence of the Yom Kippur War was that the Arab states had acquired a new weapon—oil power—in their struggle against Israel. After the conflict erupted, the oil-producing states of the Middle East imposed an embargo on oil shipments. Saudi Arabia alone accounted for some 42 percent of the region's output. The five-month-long embargo cost the United States between $10 and $20 billion in income lost because of decreased production. Western Europe and Japan—which derived 75 percent or more of their oil imports from the region—were even more adversely affected. If it had continued for several months, the embargo could have resulted in devastating economic—and ultimately, even political—consequences for the industrialized nations. The 1973 war graphically underscored America's economic dependence upon the Middle East and called attention to the crucial importance of cordial Saudi Arabian-American relationships.[20]

The Elusive Search for Peace

Yet the 1973 war in the Middle East did little to remove the underlying sources of tension between Israel and the Arab states. Its victory was extremely costly for Israel in terms of casualties sustained and the financial burden of the war. Israeli officials might well have recalled Napoleon's observation after one of his triumphs on the battlefield: "Many more victories like that, and I am undone!"

Some Arab governments—Anwar Sadat's Egypt was the leading example—concluded on the basis of the 1973 war that another direct military encounter with superior Israeli military power was futile and irrational. President Sadat believed that Egypt and Israel must resolve their differences so that the Egyptian government could devote its attention primarily to internal needs.

The Yom Kippur War also unquestionably affected official and popular attitudes in the United States toward the Israeli and Arab positions. By the mid-1970s, as even the Israelis and some Arabs acknowledged, American opinion had become less overtly pro-Israeli, more critical of specific Israeli policies and behavior, and more inclined to demand flexibility from Israel's leaders in efforts to stabilize the Middle East.[21]

Prospects for peace in the Middle East were greatly enhanced by President Sadat's historic visit to Jerusalem on November 19, 1977. This meeting was followed by bilateral discussions between Israeli and Egyptian officials and by Prime Minister Begin's visit to Egypt at the end of 1977. President Carter invited Sadat and Begin to the presidential retreat at Camp David to resume the peace talks under American auspices.[22] Israeli and Egyptian officials alike were aware that—at a time when both governments urgently needed additional foreign assistance—progress in resolving the Arab-Israeli dispute would unquestionably make Washington more receptive to expanded aid for their respective nations.

For almost two weeks—in some of the most complex and difficult diplomatic negotiations in modern history—Sadat, Begin, and Carter, with their aides, endeavored to resolve Israeli-Egyptian disagreements. Time and again, Carter reminded Sadat and Begin of the possibly dire consequences of failing to reach a peaceful settlement. Finally, Sadat and Begin signed two draft accords on September 17, 1978, but not until March 26, 1979, was a treaty signed, inaugurating an era of peaceful relations between the two countries.

Despite the Camp David agreements, events soon made it clear that many obstacles lay in the path of an overall Arab-Israeli settlement. Except for Egypt, the enmity of Arab countries toward Israel was undiminished; the PLO and other anti-Israeli groups kept up their opposition to Zionism; and the buildup of military forces by Israel's enemies continued. A momentous event was the assassination of President Sadat on October 6, 1981. Perhaps more than any other single development, this signified the deep hostility and resentment toward Israel within the Arab world and the frustration that many Arabs felt about the inability of their leaders to pursue effective internal and external policies.[23]

The Saudi-American Diplomatic Connection

By the 1980s, three major segments of Arab opinion toward Israel and toward what Arabs viewed as Israel's sponsor, the United States, could be identified. As we have already observed, one point of view was exemplified by Egypt—the only Arab nation willing to sign a peace treaty with Israel. After Camp David, Egypt's influence within the Middle East dropped sharply, although by the late 1980s Cairo had begun to regain its former position among the Arab states. A second group comprised the Rejectionist Front, which consisted of the Arabs who remained implacably opposed to Israel. Led by Syria, Iraq, Libya, and several factions within the PLO, this group tended to be overtly anti-American; often they were recipients of massive Soviet economic, military, and other forms of assistance.

The third group consisted of moderate Arab opinion, illustrated by the position of Saudi Arabia and Jordan on the Arab-Israeli conflict and related regional issues. This attitude envisioned the ultimate possibility of peace with Israel, provided that the government of Israel made a number of fundamental concessions designed to satisfy Arab grievances and to guarantee Arab rights. Key questions related to Israel's readiness to grant true political autonomy to the Arab inhabitants of the occupied West Bank; to return the Old City of Jerusalem to Arab jurisdiction; and, above all, to accept a Palestinian homeland whose territory would include some parts of Israel.

The central role of Saudi Arabia in achieving American diplomatic objectives in the Middle East was emphasized by another climactic event: the collapse of the Iranian monarchy in January 1979. This event ranks as one of the most serious American diplomatic reverses in the postwar period; it was followed by the emergence of an outspokenly anti-American regime in Iran, headed by the Ayatollah Ruhollah Khomeini, whose power base was the Shi'ite clergy. Viewing the United States as the "Great Satan," Khomeini and his followers were determined to eliminate Western influence from the Persian Gulf area and to overthrow governments (such as Saudi Arabia's) that were friendly with the United States.[24]

In foreign relations, the Islamic-based government of Iran called for revolution in other states throughout the Persian Gulf area; supported the PLO and other enemies of Israel (while concurrently selling oil to the Israeli government); denounced Soviet intervention in Afghanistan and Communist machinations within Iran; and fought an exhausting eight-year war against Iraq, whose forces invaded Iran in September 1980. Prolonged political turbulence in Iran, coupled with the Soviet invasion of Afghanistan at the end of 1979, called into question the future stability of the entire Persian Gulf area and of Western access to its vital oil reserves.

Confronted with these dangers, President Carter issued a Carter Doctrine in his State of the Union message to Congress on January 23, 1980. This pronouncement declared the defense of the Persian Gulf area vital to the security and well-being of the United States, and it pledged America to defend the area from forces that might endanger its security. While the Carter Doctrine was directed specifically at the Soviet Union— it was an explicit warning to Moscow not to extend its hegemony in Afghanistan to adjacent countries—informed students of the Middle East were aware of two other forces that might jeopardize the security of the Persian Gulf area.[25] One of these was the revolutionary movements (such as those sponsored by Iran and the Ba'ath party in Iraq) aimed at radicalizing the governments adjoining the Persian Gulf. The other potential threat was the possibility of a new round in the Arab-Israeli conflict. In effect, President Bush invoked the Carter Doctrine against Iraq when it threatened the security of the Persian Gulf region in 1990.

Washington's ties with Saudi Arabia antedated the Iranian revolution and the issuance of the Carter Doctrine. Before 1932, when the Kingdom of Saudi Arabia was proclaimed under its first ruler, Ibn Saud I, the traditional homeland of the Arabs was little more than a collection of primitive Bedouin tribes, whose main pursuits appeared to be nomadism and warfare.[26] Ibn Saud succeeded in uniting the tribes under his leadership and in defeating his rivals. Throughout his long rule (Ibn Saud died in 1953), the kingdom was largely governed by tribal customs and traditions and in accordance with the fundamentalist Wahhabi religious principles professed by its leaders and the vast majority of its people.*

---

* The Wahhabi sect of the Sunni branch of Islam (with the Shi'ite branch, one of the two great divisions of Islam) derived from the life and thought of Mohammed ibn Abd al-Wahhab (1703-1791). His movement represented a reaction against the corruption and adulteration of the pure and revealed Islamic faith by foreign religious ideas and philosophical concepts, and even by Islamic movements (like Sufism) deemed at variance with the Koran. Thus, Wahhabism demanded a return to the original and literal tenets of Islam; Wahhabis have been called the Puritans of Islam and the custodians of religious fundamentalism. In practice, as it has evolved in Saudi Arabia, Wahhabism calls for literal adherence to Koranic requirements in such spheres as religious rites, treatment of criminals, and the status of women. See Bayly Winder, *Saudi Arabia in the Nineteenth Century* (New York: St. Martin's, 1965), 8-15; and John B. Christopher, *The Islamic Tradition* (New York: Harper and Row, 1972), 158-162.

The most crucial development during Ibn Saud's reign was the discovery of oil in Saudi Arabia in the early 1930s and the establishment of the oil industry by the Arabian American Oil Company (Aramco). Saudi Arabia was officially neutral in World War II, although it did assist the Allied cause during that conflict. When Ibn Saud I died, he was succeeded by his son, Ibn Saud II. The new king's extravagances and lack of interest in the welfare of the country finally led the Saudi royal family to depose him late in 1964, in favor of Crown Prince Faisal, who ruled until his assassination early in 1975.

King Faisal was a devout Moslem and was devoted to his country's modernization and welfare. Under his rule, the bulk of the oil income was allocated to national development. After Faisal's death, the infirm King Khalid ruled until his death in June 1982. His successor was the present ruler of Saudi Arabia, King Fahd.

Among the governments of the Middle East, Saudi Arabia is the epitome of oil power. Its oil reserves are estimated as high as 500 billion barrels (three times those of the United States). At full production, Saudi Arabia can ship upwards of 10 million barrels of oil daily into the world market, although in recent years its actual production has sometimes been no more than one-third of that amount. As a rule, Saudi Arabia has been the most influential member of the Organization of Petroleum Exporting Countries (OPEC).[27] In the deliberations of OPEC, Saudi Arabia acquired a reputation for moderation and restraint. In contrast to some other members, for example, Saudi officials appeared to understand that using oil power to precipitate economic chaos in the West would in the end also engender severe economic and political problems in the Middle East.[28]

The AWACS Proposal

In what was to become the first major test of his authority in the foreign policy field, President Ronald Reagan in April 1981 disclosed his administration's intention of selling five advanced AWACS aircraft,* valued at $5.8 billion, to the government of Saudi Arabia. Under the terms of the Arms Export Control Act (P.L. 90-629), Congress had thirty days within which to disapprove of (or veto) foreign arms sales through resolutions passed by majority votes in both the House and the

---

* Officially known as Airborne Warning and Control System aircraft, AWACS planes were advanced aircraft equipped with several forms of modern radar, designed to provide early warning of approaching enemy aircraft and missiles. As the Iraqi-Iranian war spread to the Persian Gulf area, these aircraft played a crucial role in defending Kuwait and Saudi Arabia, along with American and other neutral shipping, from attack, chiefly by Iranian aircraft and missiles. During the Persian Gulf crisis of 1990-1991, they provided warning of impending Iraqi air attacks.

Senate. Following established custom, the Reagan administration had provided Congress with informal notification of the proposed AWACS sale, but formal notification of this intention was not sent to Capitol Hill until October 1. Congress, therefore, had until October 30 to disapprove the transaction or the president would be free to complete it. In addition to the AWACS planes, the White House proposed to sell Saudi Arabia equipment for F-15 fighter aircraft; several KC-707 tanker aircraft, valued at some $2.4 billion; and 1,177 AIM-9L air-to-air missiles, costing approximately $200 million. Another item in the package (devices for improving the offensive striking power of the F-15s) was dropped after the government of Israel expressed outspoken opposition to it.[29]

On August 5, President Reagan in a letter to Congress called the AWACS transaction one of the "essential elements" in his Middle Eastern policy.[30] A few days later, Under Secretary of State James Buckley said that the AWACS transaction would contribute to achieving four major American goals in the Persian Gulf region. First, it would help preserve the nation's continued access to Middle East oil. Second, it would serve as a deterrent to Soviet influence in the area. Third, it would enhance the security of nations friendly to the United States, including Israel. Fourth, it would demonstrate America's "constancy" and "resolve" in protecting the security of nations bordering the Persian Gulf.[31] As the Persian Gulf crisis in 1990-1991 demonstrated, the close military ties between the United States and Saudi Arabia were essential in preserving the security of the region.

Lobbying Activities

The AWACS case precipitated some of the most intense lobbying activities witnessed on a foreign policy question since World War II. Major participants in this campaign included the government of Israel and its supporters within the United States, the government of Saudi Arabia and those groups favoring its position, and officials of the Reagan administration.

Predictably, the response of the pro-Israeli lobby to the AWACS proposal was vociferously adverse. Prime Minister Begin informed State Department officials that making AWACS aircraft available to Saudi Arabia would "present a very serious threat" to the security of his nation.[32] As the weeks passed, blocking the AWACS transaction became the primary goal of the Israeli lobby in the United States. Spearheaded by AIPAC, the pro-Israeli lobby undertook a grass-roots campaign to rally public opinion against the sale and to direct popular sentiment against it to executive and legislative officials in Washington. The Israeli lobby concentrated on convincing members of the House and

Senate that the AWACS sale was in neither America's nor Israel's interests.[33]

Arguments advanced against the AWACS sale included the following: (1) in view of the political instability of the Persian Gulf area, the aircraft might fall into the hands of governments or political groups that would use them against Israel or the United States; (2) Saudi Arabia, with its limited armed forces, did not need sophisticated weapons like AWACS and the other advanced military hardware it had requested from the United States; (3) the provision of these weapons to Saudi Arabia could well add to its political instability, leading to the kind of domestic opposition that had toppled the Iranian monarchy; and (4) to match Saudi Arabia's intensified defense efforts, Israel would be required to embark on a new round of military spending that would further damage its economy.

A noteworthy feature of the AWACS case was that—perhaps for the first time in the history of the Arab-Israeli conflict—the pro-Israeli lobby found itself pitted against a skillful and effective pressure campaign conducted by the Arab lobby in support of the AWACS transaction. By the 1970s, moreover, American attitudes toward the Arab-Israeli dispute had clearly begun to change. After four military victories since 1948, Israel no longer appeared to many Americans as the underdog in the Arab-Israeli contest. Arab imposition of the oil embargo during the 1973 war and the consequent rapid increases in the price of oil imports from the Middle East served as forceful reminders to Americans of their vulnerability and dependence upon the oil reserves of the region. By the end of the decade, Soviet gains in the vicinity of the Persian Gulf and on its western flank (as in eastern Africa) focused American attention once more on the region's strategic importance. Under these circumstances, foreign governments and organizations in the United States that advocated the AWACS sale found conditions favorable for their activities.

For many years, pro-Arab groups in the United States had found their lobbying activities hindered by several factors that diminished their political impact. Among these were the overall American ignorance of the Middle East; the continuing schisms that perpetuated suspicions and rivalries among Arab governments and political movements; the negative feelings of many Americans toward oil corporations and their links with Arab states; and the relative smallness of the Arab-American community (some 2 million people, most of Lebanese extraction).

Yet the Arab lobby also possessed strengths that had slowly enhanced its effectiveness as a pressure group. Led by the National Association of Arab Americans (NAAA), the Arab lobby had unquestionably become more skillful in its public relations and media campaigns designed to make Americans more receptive to Arab viewpoints.

The NAAA's mailing list was growing steadily and its budget was increasing. Several Arab governments retained former legislators, such as J. William Fulbright, to represent their interests in the United States. Saudi Arabia was represented by Frederick Dutton, who had been a State Department official during the Kennedy administration. For several years, a few legislators, such as Sen. James Abourezk, D-S.D. (who was of Lebanese background and who became active in the NAAA after he left the Senate in 1979), had been willing to champion the Arab cause on Capitol Hill. Even so, developments such as the internecine strife among various Arab groups in Lebanon remained a serious obstacle to unified Arab lobbying activities in the United States.[34]

For several months, the Arab lobby undertook a public relations and media campaign emphasizing the importance of the AWACS sale for cooperative Saudi-American relations. Certain actions by the government of Israel—such as its bombing attack against a nuclear installation in Iraq in the summer of 1981 and its intensive bombing of the city of Beirut several weeks later (in which some three hundred people were killed)—reinforced the Arab contention that the Saudi military establishment needed the AWACS planes and related military equipment.

Congress Considers the AWACS Proposal

From the beginning, it was evident that the AWACS proposal faced formidable opposition in the House and Senate. As expected, opposition to the AWACS sale was especially intense in the Democratic-controlled House of Representatives, where pervasive fears existed that the move would endanger Israel's security. On October 14, 1981, by a vote of 301 to 111, the House passed a resolution (H. Con. Res. 194) disapproving the AWACS transaction. (In order to block the sale, it must be remembered, majorities in both the House and Senate had to vote against it; otherwise, the president was free to conclude the transaction.) Although prospects did not initially appear encouraging, the White House now turned to the Senate for the support it needed to complete the AWACS transaction.[35]

On October 15, the Senate Foreign Relations Committee voted 9 to 8 against approving the proposed AWACS sale. It is illustrative of the divisions within Congress on foreign policy issues that on the same day the Senate Armed Services Committee voted 10 to 5 in favor of providing the AWACS aircraft and other military equipment to Saudi Arabia. As events proved, sentiment in the full Senate on the AWACS question was closely divided. Before the issue reached the Senate floor, President Reagan and his aides renewed their efforts to gain the support of wavering senators. A presidential promise to provide Israel with radar-jamming equipment reassured several senators that the AWACS planes would not jeopardize Israel's security. The White House also pledged that providing the AWACS planes to Saudi Arabia would not be followed by a large-scale military buildup in the Persian Gulf area. At the administration's initiative, three former chief executives— Presidents Nixon, Ford, and Carter—endorsed the AWACS proposal as a move that would promote American diplomatic interests in the Middle East and pose no threat to Israel's security.[36]

The climax came on October 28, when after prolonged and heated debate the Senate voted on the AWACS transaction. Ultimately, the outcome was an impressive, if narrow, victory for the Reagan administration. The Senate failed, by a vote of 48 to 52, to join the House in disapproving the AWACS transaction. Crucial to the outcome was the fact that President Reagan and his aides had persuaded seven new Republican senators to change their positions and to support the White House proposal. In the end, President Reagan was granted the authority he requested to provide an $8.5 billion arms sale package, including the AWACS aircraft and related military equipment, to the government of Saudi Arabia.[37]

Other Arms-Sale Proposals

As events indicated, the AWACS case proved to be not the last in a series of instances in which the president and Congress were required to face the issue of American arms sales to Arab countries. During the first half of 1984, the Reagan White House authorized the shipment of four hundred Stinger antiaircraft missiles to the Saudi government, primarily for defense against the growing Iranian threat. Predictably, the government of Israel vocally opposed this transaction, viewing it as inimical to Israel's security. Yet in this instance President Reagan got his way, since by law the president was permitted for reasons of national security to waive the usual thirty-day waiting period for such sales, during which time Congress would have an opportunity to disapprove of the transaction.[38]

In mid-June 1986, the Reagan White House informed Congress that it proposed to transfer ownership to Saudi Arabia of five AWACS aircraft (planes actually purchased by the Saudi government in 1981). The president commended past Saudi efforts to promote peace in the Middle East; he took note of Saudi subsidies to the pro-Western government of Jordan; and he called attention to Riyadh's major role in efforts to aid the Afghan rebels who were resisting Soviet rule. In addition, President Reagan emphasized that American military teams would supervise the security measures required to guarantee that secret AWACS technology would not be compromised. In contrast to the earlier AWACS case, in 1986 the Israeli lobby in the United States did not actively oppose the White House proposal.[39]

Although the Reagan White House gained its immediate objective, executive officials were compelled by their legislative critics to delete Stinger missiles from the Saudi arms package; opponents feared that, in the wrong hands, these missiles could be used against Israeli or even American planes. Legislative opposition also forced the administration to abandon a plan to provide F-15 fighter aircraft, along with the new M-1 tanks, to Saudi Arabia. In the end, the Saudi arms deal was reduced to approximately one-third of its original size.

During this same period also, the State Department informed Congress that it was postponing indefinitely a proposal to sell modern arms, valued at between $1.5 and $2 billion, to the government of Jordan, long regarded as one of the most pro-Western, or "moderate," regimes in the Middle East. Faced with widespread congressional opposition to this step—along with anticipated objections by the government of Israel—executive officials conceded that the proposal had no chance of obtaining legislative approval. Secretary of State Shultz was outspoken in blaming opposition in Congress to the sale of arms to Jordan for Amman's failure to play a more active role in peace negotiations with Israel.

As in 1981, the Reagan White House had won an extremely narrow victory over legislative opponents on the Saudi arms deal. Once again, an intensive lobbying campaign by the president and his supporters was required before victory was achieved. Proponents of the arms sale contended that the ability of the White House to conduct foreign affairs successfully was at stake in the willingness of Congress to support the president's diplomatic efforts in the Middle East.[40]

Arms for Riyadh: The Continuing Issue

The issue of arms sales to Saudi Arabia arose again in the years that followed. In June 1987, for example, the Reagan White House proposed a new arms package for Riyadh. Immediate and massive opposition on Capitol Hill, however, compelled the administration to drop the measure, at least temporarily.[41]

Then late in September, the Reagan administration tried again. It asked Congress to approve a $1.4 billion arms sale package for Saudi Arabia, including American F-15 fighter planes and some 1,600 Maverick antitank missiles, along with electronic equipment, tanks, and other materiel. As in the past, the proposal encountered formidable opposition from pro-Israeli forces within and outside Washington. In time, the president and his advisers were forced to accept a compromise whereby the Maverick air-to-ground missiles were deleted from the package.

With this concession, Congress finally approved the president's request.[42]

Again in 1988, the issue of arms sales to Saudi Arabia and other Persian Gulf nations evoked controversy between the White House and Congress. The Reagan administration proposed to sell weapons and military equipment valued at some $825 million to Saudi Arabia. The news that Riyadh had recently purchased medium-range missiles from China (in part because of legislative restrictions upon their acquisition from the United States) strengthened doubts in the minds of many legislators about the proposed arms sale to the Saudi government. An announcement by Saudi officials, however, that Riyadh would sign the international nuclear nonproliferation agreement went far toward blunting the force of opposition to the transaction on Capitol Hill.

The Reagan White House provided the required formal notice of the proposed Saudi arms deal to Congress late in April. The package included equipment and maintenance services for AWACS aircraft, armored troop carriers, other weapons, ammunition, and spare parts. As in the past, the White House received letters from senators and representatives who opposed the sale, expressing the fear that Saudi Arabia might now join Syria and Iraq in building up a potent military arsenal, perhaps containing chemical or nuclear weapons capable of jeopardizing Israeli security. Yet much of this congressional opposition appeared to be pro forma, or for the political record. State Department officials declared themselves to be satisfied with Saudi assurances that the weapons would be used only defensively and would not be adapted to employ chemical or nuclear warheads.

After considerable give-and-take between executive and legislative officials—as well as concessions to accommodate differing House and Senate viewpoints—in the end, Congress granted the Reagan White House substantially what it had requested in the arms sale package for Saudi Arabia.[43]

During this same period, even more controversy in Washington was engendered by President Reagan's request for legislative approval to sell 40 F-18 aircraft (valued at almost $2 billion), along with advanced missiles and other munitions, to Kuwait. Predictably, friends of Israel on Capitol Hill and throughout the nation objected to this transaction for reasons that were now familiar: the actual or potential danger posed to the security of Israel by the planned arms deal. For many critics, the most objectionable feature was the inclusion of Maverick air-to-ground missiles in the package. (The F-18 aircraft could not reach Israel from Kuwait without much larger and specially adapted fuel tanks.)

In an understanding worked out between executive and legislative policy makers, the Maverick missiles were eliminated from the arms proposal; instead, Kuwait was to receive a larger number of antiship missiles viewed as posing no danger to Israel. Executive officials also promised Congress that Kuwait would not transfer these American weapons to other countries without Washington's prior approval.

In the Senate, however, despite the compromise the Kuwaiti arms package still faced widespread opposition from Israel's support- ers. Yet critics of the proposal appeared to be reluctant to block it completely, while executive officials clearly wanted to salvage some kind of arms deal for the government of Kuwait. As a result, executive and legislative policy makers, together with representatives of the pro- Israel lobby in Washington, arrived at an acceptable understanding. In the end—after the Senate had adopted a resolution calling upon the White House to seek to curb the sale of advanced weapons to nations in the Middle East—a compromise was reached that gained wide support. Congress approved the provision of arms to Kuwait substan- tially upon the terms contained in the House version of the legis- lation.[44]

In contrast to the preceding years, 1989 witnessed no prolonged contest between executive and legislative officials over arms sales to Saudi Arabia. The new Bush administration appeared to be more concerned with finding additional funds to strengthen King Hussein's military establishment in Jordan. The goal was finally achieved in September, when Congress responded to an unusual "personal request" by President Bush and granted Jordan an additional $20 million in military assistance.[45]

As had been true for several years, the preponderance of U.S. economic and military aid in the Middle East went to two recipients: Israel ($3 billion) and Egypt (slightly over $2 billion). Toward most Arab states, legislators wanted to be assured that American-supplied weapons would not be used against Israel or would not fall into the hands of terrorist groups. In Saudi Arabia's case, some members of the House and Senate remained fearful that American-made missiles and other weapons might be converted into stockpiles of chemical or nuclear armaments. For many Americans, Riyadh also lost credibility when it was revealed that (in violation of the letter and spirit of existing American law) money obtained from Saudi Arabia had been used secretly by officials within the Reagan White House to finance the activities of the contras (the leading anti-Communist group) in Central America.

As we shall see, the issue of U.S. military assistance to Saudi Arabia came into sharp relief a few months later, in the Persian Gulf crisis. A high priority of the Bush administration was to preserve the security of Saudi Arabia, particularly in the face of an ominous Iraqi threat.

The Bush Administration and the Persian Gulf Crisis

The Crisis Erupts

On August 2, 1990, the government of Iraq unleashed a large-scale military attack against its much smaller southern neighbor, Kuwait. Kuwait was quickly overrun; President Saddam Hussein of Iraq announced that Kuwait had been annexed and reunited with its Iraqi "motherland." From their new base, Iraqi military forces posed an ominous threat to the security of Saudi Arabia and neighboring Persian Gulf states. Earlier, in an eight-year war beginning in 1980, Iraq had fought a much larger enemy—the Shi'ite-controlled government of Iran—to a standstill. After what many Arabs viewed as at least an Iraqi moral victory in that contest, Saddam Hussein's regime appeared to be seeking to become the arbiter of the Persian Gulf area.[46]

Baghdad's claim to Kuwait derived from historic titles and old maps purportedly showing that at one stage in history Kuwait formed part of Iraq (or Mesopotamia, as the nation was called before World War I). As Arabs viewed it, the boundaries of most Middle Eastern nations had been drawn by the European powers in a deliberate effort to keep the region weak, politically divided, and subordinate to the West.

Another Iraqi motivation was the memory of historic greatness. In ancient history, Mesopotamia had been the site of powerful and often aggressive empires, such as those of Babylon and Assyria. From around 750 through 1000 A.D., Baghdad was the capital of the Abbasid Caliphate, under which the Islamic Empire reached its cultural and intellectual pinnacle.

Saddam Hussein was also the head of the Ba'ath party of Iraq. Meaning "Arab revival" or "Arab rebirth," the Ba'ath sought to revitalize the subordinate position of the Arabs and to make them once again the masters of their own political destiny. To that end, Ba'athists advocated revolutionary changes in nearly all aspects of Arab society. For many years, Ba'athist spokesmen had identified the government of Kuwait as one of those that was not responsive to the needs of its people or of the Arabs generally.[47]

Yet perhaps Iraq's primary objective in invading Kuwait can be reduced to a single word: *oil*. Tiny Kuwait, barely visible on a map of the Middle East, had a population estimated at less than 2 million people (of whom probably over half were aliens), while Iraq had some 17 million. Kuwait's area was less than 7,000 square miles (somewhat smaller than Massachusetts). Yet within the borders of Kuwait lay one of the largest oil reserves on the globe, estimated at close to 100 billion barrels, or approximately 12 percent of the earth's known oil deposits.

When added to Iraq's own oil holdings after its annexation of Kuwait, Saddam Hussein's regime now controlled some 20 percent of the world's oil supply. The threatened addition of Saudi Arabia's and other oil fields of the region to that total would give Baghdad control over nearly 50 percent of the petroleum reserves of the planet! The strategic, economic, and political implications of this prospect were incalculable.[48]

One final objective motivating Iraqi expansionism may be noted briefly. As we have already observed, from the nineteenth century until the post-World War II era, Great Britain had assumed the responsibility for preserving the peace and stability of the Persian Gulf area. With the dramatic decline of British power, Hussein's regime in Iraq was merely the latest to seek primacy in the Persian Gulf area.

The Bush Administration Responds

The response of the Bush administration to the Iraqi invasion of Kuwait was immediate and took place on several diverse fronts. During the weeks preceding Baghdad's attack, some intelligence experts had warned the president and his aides about a steady Iraqi military buildup and possible expansionist moves. Yet the prospect of an overt Iraqi military thrust into Kuwait was discounted by the State Department and, it appeared, by President Bush and most of his advisers. During preceding months, both executive and legislative officials in Washington had attempted to preserve at least minimally cordial relations with Saddam Hussein's government, as illustrated by Washington's evident tilt toward Baghdad during the Iraqi-Iranian war. Yet for that matter, several Arab governments were no less dubious about the likelihood of a full-scale Iraqi thrust into Kuwait.

After Iraq's attack, President Bush and his aides stated repeatedly that Baghdad's aggression was a palpable violation of international law, the UN Charter, and the norms of international conduct. Iraq's annexation of Kuwait, President Bush stated more than once, "would not stand." The deposed government of Kuwait, President Bush promised publicly, would in time be restored as the governing authority of the country. As time passed, Baghdad's behavior was condemned by most members of the United Nations, including the Soviet Union (which in recent years had served as Baghdad's chief supplier of weapons and other military equipment).

The president and his advisers were fully aware, of course, that mere verbal condemnations and UN resolutions alone would not restore Kuwaiti sovereignty or preserve the security of other endangered nations. Iraqi officials exhibited little more than contempt for "world opinion" or the reaction of the West. Iraq's absorption of Kuwait continued, and the danger of new Iraqi expansionism remained imminent. Confronted with this reality, President Bush ordered units of the U.S. army, air force, and navy (including the marines) to converge on the Persian Gulf. Within a matter of weeks, Operation Desert Shield, as it was called, involved the largest concentration of U.S. forces—in time, totaling more than 400,000 troops—witnessed since the Vietnam War. During the weeks that followed, American military might was augmented by the armed forces of the NATO allies, Argentina, Egypt, Syria, and other members of the Arab League. Altogether, some forty nations participated in the coalition assembled to defend the Persian Gulf area.

Late in August, President Bush also activated the military reserves—a move that not only strengthened the nation's military power but also communicated forcefully the gravity with which the Bush White House viewed developments in the Persian Gulf region. By order of the president—later authorized under international law by the UN Security Council—pressure against Hussein's regime was also exerted by a blockade imposed upon commerce to and from Iraq. Another presidential directive blocked Baghdad's access to assets in the United States. In addition, President Bush pointedly warned Baghdad against harming Americans who were being held hostage in Kuwait and Iraq. On the diplomatic front, President Bush and his advisers elicited broad international support for resistance to Iraqi expansionism, especially within the United Nations. Owing in large part to American leadership, and greatly aided by the more positive nature of Soviet-American relations, it appeared that the Persian Gulf crisis had revived the prospect that the UN might yet in time become an effective peacekeeping body.[49]

By contrast, from the beginning of the Persian Gulf crisis, the Bush administration deliberately refrained from seeking overt Israeli participation in the multinational defense force. This decision went far toward refuting Baghdad's claim that the conflict was merely the latest chapter in the Arab-Israeli controversy; the presence of several Arab states in the multinational defense force also discredited Iraqi propaganda.[50]

Recalling how the Johnson administration had steadily lost public and congressional support during the latter years of the Vietnam War, President Bush and his aides were active in seeking public understanding and support for their moves in the Persian Gulf region. On numerous occasions, the president and his advisers relied upon radio, television, and other channels to explain the administration's actions in the Middle East. These efforts no doubt played a key role in accounting for President Bush's high level of public approval—which was usually in the 60 to 80 percent range, but sometimes reached an unprecedented level of close to 90 percent (a degree of public approbation normally reserved for the Founders). Especially in light of President Johnson's Vietnam War difficulties, the Bush administration's effort to gain and hold public support could only be judged remarkably successful.[51]

Since the role of Congress in the Persian Gulf crisis is discussed in detail in Chapter 5, the subject will receive only brief attention here. By the time the White House had sorted out the facts about what was happening in the Persian Gulf area, Congress was in recess—which is one reason why there is no evidence that President Bush consulted legislators in the early stage of the crisis. Yet on September 11, the president did address a joint session of Congress; at that time he explained his goals in the region. Before and after the address, executive officials met with committees of Congress and groups of legislators to defend their strategy in the Middle East and to elicit legislative support for it. Throughout the crisis, it was remarkable that the House and Senate appeared to deliberately *avoid* invoking the provisions of the War Powers Resolution, although a massive buildup of American and allied forces had begun almost immediately after Iraqi troops entered Kuwait. This result could be partially explained by the fact that executive officials assured Congress that U.S. forces were not in danger of "imminent hostilities" in the Persian Gulf region—a condition that changed as diplomacy, economic sanctions, and other methods failed to achieve a withdrawal of Iraqi forces from Kuwait. Indeed, as even some legislators acknowledged, after the Persian Gulf crisis it would not be unwarranted to say that the resolution had little relevance to the conduct of the nation's external policy.[52]

The climax of the legislative role in the Persian Gulf episode came early in January 1991, when the House and Senate formally debated President Bush's request for authority to use military force in the region. (In reality, of course, as already noted, by this stage an impressive buildup of military force by the United States and its allies in the Persian Gulf region was well under way.) The ensuing debate on Capitol Hill was intense, sometimes divisive, and in some cases traumatic for individual legislators. The outcome was also momentous for the American foreign policy process. In the end, on January 16—by a vote of 52 to 47 in the Senate and 250 to 183 in the House—Congress voted to give President Bush the authorization he requested.[53] While the vote may have been closer than the White House had hoped, nevertheless the Bush administration had won an impressive victory on Capitol Hill. Supported by a congressional majority (however slim) and by overwhelming public approval, the Bush White House proceeded to undertake "Operation Desert Storm" to liberate Kuwait and protect the security of other Persian Gulf states from the Iraqi danger. As events proved, it was one of the most impressive victories in the annals of warfare.

Postwar Challenges to U.S. Policy

War always leaves major political problems in its wake, and the Persian Gulf conflict was no exception. After achieving an overwhelming military victory, the American people and their leaders needed to be reminded of Winston Churchill's verdict (said before the Vietnam War) that "the United States has never lost a war or won a peace"! A number of developments following the end of the "100-hour war" in the Middle East confirmed the cogency of Churchill's observation.

In the remainder of the chapter, attention will be devoted to four major challenges to U.S. foreign policy in the Middle East in the aftermath of the Persian Gulf conflict. In nearly every case, there are significant implications for relations between executive and legislative policy makers.

The Future Government and Stability of Iraq. Time and again during the conflict in the Persian Gulf, President Bush and his advisers emphasized two major points concerning the political future of Iraq. One was that they looked forward to the ouster of Hussein's aggressive and ruthless regime; Washington emphasized that this change was essential to a long-range improvement in Iraqi-American relations. The other idea was that the United States did not seek to impair Iraq's integrity or cohesion as an independent nation. In a word, the Bush administration did not want to contribute to the "Lebanonization" of the Iraqi state.

In the period following hostilities, serious obstacles arose to the achievement of these objectives. During its years in power, Hussein's Ba'athist regime had systematically eliminated nearly all actual or potential political rivals. The one group that Washington obviously hoped and expected would oust the dictator was the Iraqi military. But there was no assurance that any new leader arising from this group, controlled by the Ba'ath party, would pursue policies capable of unifying the country or gaining the confidence of nations outside Iraq.

The ago-old problem of Iraq's cohesion as a nation came to the forefront dramatically after the war, when two of the nation's principal minorities—the Shi'ites in the south and the Kurds in the north—rebelled against rule by the country's Sunni Arab minority. (In fact, most students of Middle Eastern affairs are convinced that the Shi'ites now constitute a majority of Iraq's population.) Shi'ite insurgents were active, for example, around the southern city of Basra. Tensions between them and the Iraqi government erupted anew into a series of violent encounters—with first the insurgents and then government forces gaining the upper hand. For years, Iraq's Shi'ites had suffered oppression and neglect from the Sunni-dominated government in Baghdad.

To the north, Iraq's Kurds (around 15 percent of the society) seized the opportunity to do what they always did when authorities in Baghdad faced a crisis: they rose or rebelled, again demanding the creation of an independent Kurdish nation (a "Kurdistan," presumably to be formed from ethnically Kurdish parts of Iraq, Iran, Syria, Turkey, and the Soviet Union). Confronted with the latest Kurdish insurgency— and no doubt motivated in part by a desire for vengeance against his enemies—Hussein directed much of his remaining military power against the Kurdish people, who were subjected to indescribable human suffering and physical damage.[54]

After considerable hesitation about the proper course to take, in time the Bush White House demanded that Baghdad cease its retribution against the Kurds. Acting in concert with its allies, Washington also established "security zones" in which the Kurds would be safe from attack; food, housing, medicines, and other needed supplies were provided to thousands of Kurdish refugees.

Yet the challenge to American foreign policy posed by developments within Iraq would likely continue for many years and would involve difficult choices for the American people and their leaders. How was it possible to reconcile the somewhat contradictory goals of both preserving Iraq's cohesion as a nation and providing support to Kurdish and/or Shi'ite insurgents against Baghdad's authority? What would Washington do if, by chance, *both* of the insurgent movements succeeded in achieving their goals? (From the available evidence, for example, it seemed extremely doubtful that *any* new Iraqi regime would meet the standards of Western democracy.) How long were the United States and other nations prepared to guarantee that Hussein's regime or its successors would not again use force against political dissidents or insurgent movements? And how long would other countries (specifically, Iran and Turkey, which also had substantial Kurdish minorities) give active or passive support to the U.S. policy of assisting or encouraging insurgencies within Iraq? Such difficult issues are likely to face executive and legislative policy makers in Washington for several years to come.

A Revitalized OPEC. Another problem confronting the United States and other members of the global community in the aftermath of the Persian Gulf conflict is a new or revitalized regime for controlling the production, sale, and price of Middle East oil. A contributing factor leading to the Persian Gulf war, for example, was the failure of the existing mechanism—the Organization of Petroleum Exporting Countries (OPEC)—to achieve these goals. For example, it was an open secret that Kuwait (along with certain other members of OPEC) had been cheating by extracting and selling oil in excess of its OPEC quota, thereby depressing oil prices on the world market.

Although the United States is not a member of OPEC, it has a clear interest in the organization's ability to achieve its objectives. The United States remains a large importer of petroleum (some 40 percent of its total consumption by the late 1980s); most projections agreed that U.S. reliance upon foreign oil supplies in the years ahead would almost certainly increase.

Washington also had an interest in a number of related political aspects of the problem. The oil-producing states of the Middle East customarily derived from 50 to 90 percent of their governmental revenues from the sale of oil products. After the war, such income would be crucial for financing the urgent task of postwar reconstruction. According to some reports, oil-rich Kuwait would likely be forced to borrow money for an extended period in the future to repair wartime damage. (Even Iraq's ability to pay a large-scale indemnity to Kuwait and other nations damaged by the war depended upon the rapid rehabilitation of the Iraqi oil industry and Baghdad's ability to sell its output in the world market at a reasonable price.) In addition, the ability of such nations as Kuwait and Saudi Arabia to preserve political stability, and to carry out what officials in Washington hoped would be long overdue political reforms, were contingent in no small measure upon the maintenance of economic and financial stability in the oil-producing nations.

The Persian Gulf crisis and its aftermath once more called attention to a long-neglected need within the United States: *an effective national energy policy.* By the 1990s, the challenge facing the White House and Congress on this front seemed more urgent than ever.[55]

Preserving Persian Gulf Security. In wars in which they have been engaged, Americans have tended to personalize the enemy. In World War I, it was the Kaiser; in World War II, it was Hitler and Tojo; in the Vietnam War, it was Ho Chi Minh; in the Persian Gulf War, it was Saddam Hussein. The inevitable—and nearly always misleading—implication is that once a particular enemy has been defeated, the threat to American security has been eliminated permanently. Yet post-World War II experience in Western Europe cautions against such a conclusion.

In the Middle East, a continuing problem facing Americans will be remembering that the vital interests of the United States *are endangered by any threat to the security of the Persian Gulf region, irrespective of its source.* The most recent threat was posed by Saddam Hussein's expansionism. The elimination of this threat, however, does not necessarily mean that new dangers to America's security and diplomatic interests in the region will not arise. Nor does it signify, as millions of Americans doubtless hope, that now that the war is over the United States can withdraw its military power from this vital zone.

For the indefinite future, the United States is likely to be militarily involved in the Middle East. For example, in the early weeks of the Persian Gulf War, American civilian and military officials carried out an extraordinarily successful propaganda coup, effectively concealing from the Iraqi government the extent of American military *weakness* within the region. That gambit was unquestionably a key element in the ensuing allied victory against Iraqi forces. Yet it is reasonable to conclude that, in any future military engagement, a similar propaganda ploy is unlikely to work again. And this reality in turn means that, if the United States is serious about preserving the security of the region, American forces, equipment, and materiel will have to be pre-positioned in and around the Persian Gulf area, ready for use by the armed forces when needed.

There also remains the problem of the arsenal of chemical and nuclear weapons within Iraq, and more broadly within the region. While Baghdad consented to dispose of its stockpile of these deadly weapons as part of the cease-fire agreement, there is the continuing challenge of *enforcing* the agreement in the months and years ahead. (For many years, for example, Israel and the Arab states have had cease-fire agreements, which seemed to do little to limit military encounters between them!)

Then there is the larger problem of the arms buildup—including the existence of actual or potential nuclear arsenals—broadly throughout the region. Other nations within and adjacent to the Middle East, for example, have (or are acquiring) nuclear arsenals. Israel and Pakistan are widely publicized examples. As the Persian Gulf conflict convincingly demonstrated, today even conventional (or nonnuclear) weapons are capable of inflicting unprecedented destruction.

Throughout the Middle East, and within the Third World generally, in recent years the arms traffic has been brisk. It has been pointed out, for example, that in its military buildup preceding the Persian Gulf War, Saddam Hussein's government acquired most of its weapons from the five permanent members of the UN Security Council (the Soviet Union, the United States, Great Britain, France, and China). This disturbing reality underscores the urgency, both in the Middle East and globally, of arriving at and successfully implementing effective arms control agreements (as discussed more fully in Chapter 3).

In turn, limiting the acquisition of ever more destructive weapons within the Middle East will require international agreement upon and operation of some kind of enforcement mechanism. Any such arrangements will almost certainly necessitate significant American support and commitment if they are to be effective. Another vital element in such mechanisms will, of course, be continued—and quite possibly even expanded—Soviet-American cooperation in behalf of common goals within the Middle East.

A New Start on the Arab-Israeli Question. In the aftermath of the Persian Gulf War, there remains the issue that many commentators would identify as the most intractable problem in the Middle East: the Arab-Israeli conflict. If the beginning of the conflict can be dated from the period of World War I, it has by now been going on more than seventy years. In other words, the Arab-Israeli dispute is well on the way to becoming modern history's Hundred Years' War!

After the Persian Gulf conflict, two viewpoints concerning this deep-seated controversy could be identified. These might be described as the optimistic/rational and the pessimistic/irrational perspectives on the issue. Considerable evidence supports the former viewpoint. A leading member of the Rejectionist Front against Israel—Saddam Hussein's regime in Iraq—suffered a humiliating military defeat. Another member, the Ba'athist government of Syria, had cooperated with the United States in the allied coalition formed against Iraq. The evidence also indicated that Damascus was seeking to improve its relations with the United States and other Western nations. Except perhaps among members of the Palestine Liberation Organization (PLO), Saddam Hussein's effort to gain broad Arab support for his expansionism—and to have it accepted as primarily an attempt to defeat Israel and its American ally—failed. In the light of such developments, now perhaps other Arab leaders would finally engage in the kind of rational policy calculations exhibited earlier by President Sadat of Egypt. After the 1973 war, Sadat concluded that Egypt had no choice except to resolve its differences with Israel and to live in peace with it.

Yet there was quite clearly another side to the coin—as Secretary of State James Baker discovered in his efforts to achieve a breakthrough in peace negotiations between Israel and the Arab states following the Persian Gulf conflict. After hostilities ended, Baker devoted a great deal of time and effort to discovering a new basis for the peaceful resolution of Arab-Israeli differences. By the summer of 1991, he had achieved agreement among the parties to attend a peace conference to be sponsored jointly by the United States and the Soviet Union.[56]

Arab spokesmen repeatedly pointed out that Washington had resorted to a massive military effort to enforce United Nations resolutions against Iraq, but it had never remotely considered doing so when the Israeli government had time and again violated resolutions designed to protect Arab rights. Similarly, the cause of defending the independence of oil-rich Kuwait and Saudi Arabia was not one that evoked widespread sympathy among Arab masses.

While the war had no doubt enhanced the credibility of the U.S. government, for many Arabs Washington's ability or willingness to influence the views and actions of the government of Israel appeared to be minimal. In continued defiance of American wishes and objections, for example, the right-wing Israeli government continued to dispossess Arabs of their lands, to deal harshly with Palestinian dissidents within Israeli-occupied territories, and to expel outspoken Arab leaders from the country. In brief, many Arabs—especially the Palestinians—emerged from the war with a deepened sense of frustration and angst. This was hardly the kind of climate in which a reasonable and lasting solution of the Arab-Israeli conflict was likely to be reached.

For their part, Israelis could widely conclude that, as a result of the Persian Gulf conflict, there was less need than ever to make concessions in behalf of peace with the Arabs. Iraq's behavior appeared to vindicate Israeli viewpoints: a substantial number of Arabs remained dedicated to Israel's destruction. Although it had deliberately refrained from participating directly in the coalition against Iraq, Israel had sustained considerable damage from indiscriminate Iraqi Scud missile attacks, directly mainly against civilian targets. Israel had emerged with its formidable military machine intact, although (as Israeli officials were quick to remind the Bush administration) the financial costs of its defense effort had escalated. Moreover, the war had unquestionably improved Israel's image within the American society. Americans widely admired the courage and fortitude of Israelis in enduring Iraqi missile attacks while their leaders withheld their own military power.

Most crucially, perhaps, the Israeli people and their leaders had been guided by Washington's expressed desires. Israel had refrained from becoming directly involved in the conflict, thereby allowing the allied coalition to remain unified and to refute Baghdad's claim that the war was merely the latest round in the Arab-Israeli contest. Consequently, in the Israeli view, the United States was more indebted to Israel than before. Gratitude was expected to take tangible form—both in solid diplomatic support and in substantially increased economic and military aid to Israel in the years ahead. (Several Arab and other states participating in the coalition against Iraq—and a leading example was the government of Egypt—also doubtless expected favorable treatment from Washington after the war.)

The war in the Persian Gulf area had been accompanied by great expectations, to borrow a phrase from Dickens. Yet it was clear that the

Arab-Israeli conflict would remain high on the American diplomatic agenda for many years to come.

Notes

1. Background on the evolution of American diplomacy in the Middle East is available in William R. Polk, *The United States and the Arab World* (Cambridge, Mass.: Harvard University Press, 1965); John S. Badeau, *The American Approach to the Arab World* (New York: Harper and Row, 1968); Georgiana Stevens, ed., *The United States and the Middle East* (Englewood Cliffs, N.J.: Prentice-Hall, 1964); and George Lenczowski, *American Presidents and the Middle East* (Durham, N.C.: Duke University Press, 1989).

2. The establishment, growth, and goals of the Zionist movement are discussed more fully in Soloman Grayzel, *A History of the Jews,* rev. ed. (New York: New American Library, 1968); Arthur Hertzberg, *The Zionist Idea* (Garden City, N.Y.: Doubleday, 1959); and Oscar I. Janowsky, ed., *Foundations of Israel* (Princeton, N.J.: D. Van Nostrand, 1959).

3. The background and text of the Balfour Declaration may be found in Polk, *The United States and the Arab World,* 108-112.

4. See Janowsky, *Foundations of Israel,* 81-88, 157-173; and Grayzel, *A History of the Jews,* 669-727.

5. Dean Acheson, *Present at the Creation: My Years in the State Department* (New York: W. W. Norton, 1969), 169.

6. Harry S. Truman, *Years of Trial and Hope,* vol. 2 of *Memoirs* (Garden City, N.Y.: Doubleday, 1956), 158.

7. Recent treatments of Israel are Bernard Reich and Gershon R. Kieval, eds., *Israel Faces the Future* (New York: Praeger, 1986); Eric Silver, *Begin: The Haunted Prophet* (New York: Random House, 1984); Peter Grose, *A Changing Israel* (New York: Vintage Books, 1985); Ilan Peleg, *Begin's Foreign Policy, 1977-1983* (Westport, Conn.: Greenwood Press, 1987); and Yoram Ben-Porath, *The Israeli Economy: Maturing through Crisis* (Cambridge, Mass.: Harvard University Press, 1986).

8. Comprehensive information on the contemporary Middle East is available in *The Middle East,* 6th ed. (Washington, D.C.: Congressional Quarterly, 1986); William Spencer, ed., *The Middle East* (Guilford, Conn.: Dushkin, 1986); and Tareq Y. Ismael, *International Relations of the Contemporary Middle East* (Syracuse, N.Y.: Syracuse University Press, 1986).

9. Useful background discussions are Harry S. Allen and Ivan Volgyes, eds., *Israel, the Middle East, and U.S. Interests* (New York: Praeger, 1983); Bernard Reich, *The United States and Israel: Influence in the Special Relationship* (New York: Praeger, 1984); and Stephen L. Spiegel, *The Other Arab-Israeli Conflict: Making America's Middle East Policy from Truman to Reagan* (Chicago: University of Chicago Press, 1985).

10. Quoted in Stephen D. Isaacs, *Jews and American Politics* (Garden City, N.Y.: Doubleday, 1974), 264-265.

11. Marquis Childs, "Stirrings against Carter," *Washington Post,* March 13, 1979.

12. For historical background, see Haim Shaked and Itamar Rabinovic, eds., *The Middle East and the United States* (New Brunswick, N.J.: Transaction Books, 1980). More detailed discussion of recent U.S. policy toward the

Middle East is available in Emile A. Nakhleh, *The Persian Gulf and American Policy* (New York: Praeger, 1982); Robert E. Hunter, "The Reagan Administration and the Middle East," *Current History* 86 (February 1987): 49-53; Nimrod Novik, *Encounter with Reality: Reagan and the Middle East* (Boulder, Colo.: Westview, 1986); Marvin G. Weinbaum, *Egypt and the Politics of U.S. Economic Aid* (Boulder, Colo.: Westview, 1986); and Robert G. Darius, John W. Amos II, and Ralph H. Magnus, *Gulf Security into the 1980s* (Stanford, Calif.: Hoover Institution Press, 1984).

13. The 1948 war in Palestine and the resulting refugee problem are analyzed more fully in Fred J. Khouri, *The Arab-Israeli Dilemma* (Syracuse, N.Y.: Syracuse University Press, 1968), 68-102; and *Toward Arab-Israeli Peace* (Washington, D.C.: Brookings Institution, 1988).

14. The origins, developments, and principal consequences of the Suez Crisis of 1956 are examined in Dwight D. Eisenhower, *Waging Peace* (Garden City, N.Y.: Doubleday, 1965), 20-58; Anthony Eden, *The Suez Crisis of 1956* (Boston: Beacon, 1960); and Peter Calvocoressi, ed., *Suez: Ten Years Later* (New York: Random House, 1967).

15. Informative treatments of the Six-Day War are Khouri, *The Arab-Israeli Dilemma,* 242-292; Trevor N. Dupuy, *Elusive Victory: The Arab-Israeli Wars, 1947-1974* (New York: Harper and Row, 1978), 221-343; and Stephen J. Roth, ed., *The Impact of the Six-Day War: A Twenty-Year Assessment* (New York: St. Martin's, 1988).

16. For more detailed discussion of the PLO, see Kemal Kirisci, *The PLO and World Politics: A Study of the Mobilization of Support for the Palestinian Cause* (New York: St. Martin's, 1987); and Helena Cobban, *The Palestinian Liberation Organization: People, Power and Politics* (New York: Cambridge University Press, 1984).

17. Congressional Quarterly, *The Middle East,* 140-142; and see the more extended discussion in Nadav Safran, *From War to War: The Arab-Israeli Confrontation, 1948-1967* (New York: Pegasus, 1969), 317-417.

18. Moscow's role in the Middle East after the 1967 war is analyzed more fully in R. D. McLaurin, *The Middle East in Soviet Diplomacy* (Lexington, Mass.: D. C. Heath, 1975); Robert O. Freedman, *Soviet Policy Toward the Middle East since 1970* (New York: Praeger, 1975); and Alvin Z. Rubinstein, *Red Star on the Nile* (Princeton, N.J.: Princeton University Press, 1977).

19. The outbreak of the 1973 war, its principal stages, and its consequences are examined in Congressional Quarterly, *The Middle East,* 20-26; Dupuy, *Elusive Victory,* 387-603; and Nadav Safran, "The War and the Future of the Arab-Israeli Conflict," *Foreign Affairs* 52 (January 1974): 215-237.

20. The concept of oil power and its implications for U.S. policy in the Middle East are appraised in Dankwart A. Rustow, "Who Won the Yom Kippur and Oil Wars?" *Foreign Policy* 17 (Winter 1974-1975): 166-176; the symposium on OPEC in *Foreign Policy* 13 (Winter 1973-1974): 123-139; James Akins, "The Oil Crisis: This Time the Wolf Is Here," *Foreign Affairs* 51 (April 1973): 462-491; and G. John Ikenberry, *Reasons of State: Oil Politics and the Capacities of the American Government* (Ithaca, N.Y.: Cornell University Press, 1988).

21. See, for example, the views of President Carter in his *Keeping Faith: Memoirs of a President* (New York: Bantam Books, 1982), and his more extensive views on Middle Eastern questions in *The Blood of Abraham* (Boston: Houghton Mifflin, 1985). See also Juliana S. Peck, *The Reagan Administration and the Palestinian Question: The First Thousand Days*

(Washington, D.C.: Institute for Palestinian Studies, 1984); Ian S. Lustick, "Israeli Politics and American Foreign Policy," *Foreign Affairs* 61 (Winter 1982-83); 379-399; Paul Findley, *They Dare to Speak Out: People and Institutions Confront Israel's Lobby* (Westport, Conn.: Lawrence Hill, 1985); George W. Ball, *Error and Betrayal in Lebanon* (Washington, D.C.: Foundation for Middle East Peace, 1984); James L. Ray, *The Future of American-Israeli Relations: A Parting of the Ways?* (Lexington: University of Kentucky Press, 1985); Eytan Gilboa, *American Public Opinion toward Israel and the Arab-Israeli Conflict* (Lexington, Mass.: D. C. Heath, 1986); and Elia Zureik and Fouad Moughrabi, eds., *Public Opinion and the Palestine Question* (New York: St. Martin's, 1987).

22. The Camp David peace negotiations are described at length in Carter, *Keeping Faith*, and in William B. Quandt, *Camp David: Peacemaking and Politics* (Washington, D.C.: Brookings Institution, 1986). For an Arab perspective, see Ismail Fahmy, *Negotiating for Peace in the Middle East* (Baltimore: Johns Hopkins University Press, 1983).

23. Arab attitudes toward the Camp David accords are conveyed in Mohammed Heikal, *Autumn of Fury: The Assassination of Sadat* (New York: Random House, 1983); and for an American view of the obstacles to peace, see Jimmy Carter, *The Blood of Abraham: Insights into the Middle East* (Boston: Houghton Mifflin, 1985).

24. Studies of Iran since the revolution of 1979 are R. K. Ramazani, *Revolutionary Iran: Challenge and Response in the Middle East* (Baltimore: Johns Hopkins University Press, 1987); Nikki R. Keddie and Eric Hooglund, eds., *The Iranian Revolution and the Islamic Republic* (Syracuse, N.Y.: Syracuse University Press, 1986); Martin Wright, ed., *Iran: The Khomeini Revolution* (Harlow, England: Longman, 1989); Nikki R. Keddie and Eric Hooglund, eds., *The Iranian Revolution and the Islamic Republic* (Syracuse, N.Y.: Syracuse University Press, 1989); and R. K. Ramazani, ed., *Iran's Revolution: The Search for Consensus* (Bloomington: Indiana University Press, 1989).

25. For an analysis of the origins, meaning, and implications of the Carter Doctrine, see Cecil V. Crabb, Jr., *The Doctrines of American Foreign Policy: Their Meaning, Role, and Future* (Baton Rouge: Louisiana State University Press, 1982), 325-371.

26. Historical background and Saudi Arabia's development in the modern era are discussed in R. Bayly Winder, *Saudi Arabia in the Nineteenth Century* (New York: St. Martin's, 1965); Fred Halliday, *Arabia without Sultans: A Survey of Political Instability in the Arab World* (New York: Random House, 1975); and Christine Helms, *The Cohesion of Saudi Arabia* (Baltimore: Johns Hopkins University Press, 1981).

27. For more detailed discussion of Saudi Arabia's role as a member of OPEC, see William B. Quandt, "Riyadh between the Superpowers," *Foreign Policy* 44 (Fall 1981): 37-57; and Ian Skeet, *OPEC: 25 Years of Prices and Politics* (New York: Methuen, 1988).

28. More extended treatment of Saudi Arabia's domestic and foreign policies is available in Nadav Safran, *Saudi Arabia: The Ceaseless Quest for Security* (Cambridge, Mass.: Belknap Press, 1985); Christine M. Helms, *The Cohesion of Saudi Arabia* (Baltimore: Johns Hopkins University Press, 1981); and Sandra Mackey, *The Saudis* (Boston: Houghton Mifflin, 1987).

29. Congressional Quarterly, *The Middle East*, 61. American assistance in helping the government of Saudi Arabia strengthen its air defense system

had initially been extended late in 1973. In the months that followed, Riyadh purchased 115 fighter planes; subsequently, Washington sold Hawk missiles to Jordan and transport aircraft to Egypt as well. Early in 1978, the Carter administration proposed a "package" aircraft sale to Egypt, Saudi Arabia, and Israel. Early in 1980, Saudi officials asked Washington for AWACS aircraft and other modern equipment. See the dispatch by Charles Mohr, *New York Times*, November 1, 1981.

30. President Reagan's letter is reproduced in *Department of State Bulletin* 81 (October 1981): 52.

31. Testimony to the Senate Foreign Relations Committee, in *Department of State Bulletin* 81 (November 1981): 60-67.

32. *Congressional Quarterly Weekly Report*, April 11, 1981, 632; Congressional Quarterly, *The Middle East*, 61-62; and dispatch by Charles Mohr, *New York Times*, November 1, 1981.

33. Congressional Quarterly, *The Middle East*, 61-63.

34. Fuller discussion of the emergence, organization, and techniques utilized by the Arab lobby may be found in ibid., 63-70, and *Congressional Quarterly Weekly Report*, April 22, 1981, 1523-1530.

35. See *Congressional Quarterly Weekly Report*, October 10, 1981, 1942, and December 26, 1981, 2573.

36. The Reagan administration's lobbying activities in behalf of the AWACS proposal are described in *Congressional Quarterly Weekly Report*, April 11, 1981, 632; September 26, 1981, 1868; October 10, 1981, 1942; October 31, 1981, 2095; and December 26, 1981, 2577-2578; and in a dispatch by Phil Gailey, *New York Times*, October 1, 1981.

37. See *Congressional Quarterly Weekly Report*, September 26, 1981, 1868; October 31, 1981, 2095; and December 19, 1981, 2514; and *Newsweek*, November 9, 1981, 30-33.

38. Dispatch by Leslie H. Gelb, *New York Times*, May 29, 1984; and *Congressional Quarterly Almanac, 1984*, 117.

39. *Congressional Quarterly Almanac, 1986*, 376.

40. *Congressional Quarterly Almanac, 1986*, 373-377; and dispatches by Steven V. Roberts, *New York Times*, April 18, 1986, May 7, 1986, and May 22, 1986. See also *U.S. News & World Report*, May 19, 1986, 14.

41. See the Associated Press dispatch in the *Baton Rouge Morning Advocate*, October 9, 1987.

42. *Congressional Quarterly Almanac, 1987*, 18, 169-170, 474.

43. *Congressional Quarterly Almanac, 1988*, 508-509.

44. Legislative action on the White House proposal to sell modern weapons to Kuwait is examined more fully in ibid., 505-507.

45. *Congressional Quarterly Almanac, 1989*, 556, 614, 775-776, 782.

46. Useful background on Iraq's move against Kuwait is provided in Samir al-Khalil, *Republic of Fear: The Politics of Modern Iraq* (Berkeley: University of California Press, 1989); Axelgard, Frederick W., *A New Iraq: The Gulf War and Implications for U.S. Policy* (New York: Praeger, 1988); Christine M. Helms, *Iraq: Eastern Flank of the Arab World* (Washington, D.C.: Brookings Institution, 1984); the discussion of Iraqi foreign policy in Bahgat Korany and Ali E. Dessouki, *The Foreign Policies of the Arab States* (Washington, D.C.: Washington Institute Press, 1991); and Abdul-Reda Assiri, *Kuwait's Foreign Policy: City-State in World Politics* (Boulder, Colo.: Westview, 1990).

47. Deeper insight into the extremely complex Iraqi political environment

is provided in Helms, *Iraq;* Axelgard, *A New Iraq;* al-Khalil, *Republic of Fear;* and Pheobe Marr, *The Modern History of Iraq* (Boulder, Colo.: Westview, 1984).

48. The Persian Gulf as an arena of regional and global rivalry is analyzed in Paul Jabber, ed., *Great Power Interests in the Persian Gulf* (New York: Council on Foreign Relations, 1989); Charles A. Kupchan, *The Persian Gulf and the West: The Dilemma of Security* (Boston: Allen Unwin, 1987); Amitav Acharya, *U.S. Military Strategy in the Gulf: Origins and Evolution under the Carter and Reagan Administrations* (New York: Routledge, Chapman & Hall, 1989); and T. G. Fraser, *The USA and the Middle East since World War 2* (New York: St. Martin's, 1989).

49. America's goals in the Persian Gulf and the reasons for U.S. intervention are explained in President Bush's speech on August 20, 1990, "America's Stand against Aggression," in the Department of State's *Current Policy* series, no. 1294, 1-2; in the remarks by President Bush to members of the news media, in *Weekly Compilation of Presidential Documents*, September 10, 1990, 1315-1319, and September 17, 1990, 1344-1353; and the text of Bush's message to a joint session of Congress on September 11, 1990, as reproduced in *Weekly Compilation of Presidential Documents*, September 17, 1990, 1349-1363.

50. Israel's policy—strongly supported by Washington—of avoiding direct involvement in the Persian Gulf crisis is explained more fully in dispatches by Thomas L. Friedman, *New York Times*, October 11 and October 15, 1990, and in *Congressional Quarterly Weekly Report*, September 15, 1990, 2931.

51. See the results, for example, of several different polls in *Newsweek*, October 22, 1990, 22-24; dispatch by Flora Lewis, *New York Times*, October 17, 1990; *Congressional Quarterly Weekly Report*, August 18, 1990, 2673-2674; the Gallup poll reprinted in the *Baton Rouge Morning Advocate*, August 23, 1990; *USA Today*, August 9, 1990; and *U.S. News & World Report*, August 13, 1990, 20-21.

52. During the early weeks of the conflict, the prevailing view on Capitol Hill toward President Bush's strategy in the Persian Gulf crisis was exemplified by the remarks of New York representative Solarz, who said that Bush could count on congressional support "for whatever steps are deemed essential to liquidate the consequences of this aggression" (quoted in *Congressional Quarterly Weekly Report*, September 8, 1990, 2839). Other tangible evidence that the president's moves were widely approved by legislators lay in the passage of resolutions by both chambers overwhelmingly supporting White House actions in resisting aggression in the Persian Gulf region. At the same time, some legislators were also critical about the lack of consultation between the White House and Congress in formulating the nation's response to Iraqi aggression. See *Congressional Quarterly Weekly Report*, September 22, 1990, 3029-3031; September 29, 1990, 3141; and October 13, 1990, 3440-3441. For the text of the resolution adopted by Congress authorizing the president's use of force in the Persian Gulf crisis, see the *New York Times*, January 14, 1991.

53. See, for example, President Bush's address to the nation on January 16, 1991, announcing the beginning of the allied offensive against Iraq, in *Weekly Compilation of Presidential Documents*, January 27, 1991, 50-52.

54. Continuing sources of political instability and violence in Iraq are examined in Middle East Watch, *Human Rights in Iraq* (New Haven, Conn.: Yale

University Press, 1990); Phoebe Marr, "Iraq's Uncertain Future," *Current History* 90 (January 1991): 1-6; and C. Pelletiere, *The Kurds: An Unstable Element in the Gulf* (Boulder, Colo.: Westview, 1984).

55. Tendencies and major problems facing OPEC are discussed in Edward L. Morse, "The Coming Oil Revolution," *Foreign Affairs* 69 (Winter 1990-91): 36-57; Benjamin Schwadran, *Middle East Oil Crises since 1973* (Boulder, Colo.: Westview, 1986); *The Middle East*, 7th ed. (Washington, D.C.: Congressional Quarterly, 1990), 101-123; and Shukrim Ghanem, *OPEC: The Rise and Fall of an Exclusive Club* (New York: Methuen, 1986).

56. Secretary of State Baker's trip to the Middle East to find a new basis for peace in the region is discussed in a dispatch by Joel Brinkley, *New York Times*, March 8, 1991; and two dispatches by Thomas L. Friedman, *New York Times*, March 17, 1991. Informative background treatments are Lenczowski, *American Presidents and the Middle East;* and Fred J. Khouri, *The Arab-Israeli Dilemma*, 3d ed. (Syracuse, N.Y.: Syracuse University Press, 1985).For Soviet-U.S. agreement on the peace conference, see *Congressional Quarterly Weekly Report*, August 3, 1991, 2193-2194.

The Armed Forces

Nowhere is the Constitution's invitation to struggle more explicit than in the provisions that give Congress the power to declare war but make the president commander in chief of the armed forces. The struggle has generally been an unequal one, especially if the score is kept according to the number of times Congress has declared war versus the number of times a president has sent troops into combat without such a declaration. The issues are not only murky as matters of law; they are also highly charged emotionally, involving as they do questions of life and death.

Underlying the war power is the greatest congressional power of all—the power of the purse, stemming from Article I, Section 9, of the Constitution: "No money shall be drawn from the Treasury, but in Consequence of Appropriations made by Law. ..." Although Congress has generally been indulgent of presidents, it has on occasion aroused itself to use these powers in combination with devastating effect on a president's policies and political future. In this chapter, we look at some case studies of executive-legislative clashes over war powers in the period since World War II.

Congress is pragmatic about troop deployments and even engagement in combat. If Congress agrees with the president's policy, Congress gives the president the benefit of the constitutional doubt. If Congress disagrees with the policy, Congress summons the Constitution as an ally in its struggle to overturn the policy. And from time to time, Congress changes its mind, or—as in the Persian Gulf—events change the nature of the presidential-congressional relationship.

As we review these case studies, we will also note a trend within the executive branch toward assertion of greater presidential power.

Korea

In 1950, Congress was content to let President Truman act on his own authority in sending troops into combat in Korea. In 1977, Congress insisted on having a voice in opposing President Carter's policy to bring some of them home. In 1989 and 1990, Congress was itself divided, but important elements wanted to bring some troops home in opposition to President Bush's policy to leave them there.

Getting In

Korea emerged from World War II a divided country. A Communist regime (the Democratic People's Republic of Korea, or North Korea), installed by the Soviet Union, governed north of the thirty-eighth parallel. Below that line, the Republic of Korea (or South Korea) developed close ties with the United States. Growing tension characterized relations between the two Koreas.

On Sunday, June 25, 1950, North Korean troops crossed the thirty-eighth parallel in an evident attempt to overrun South Korea. In the week of frantic American decision making that followed, Congress played no significant role, nor did it give much indication of wanting to do so.

The Truman administration generally linked its actions during this crucial week more to the United Nations than to Congress. In an emergency meeting on Sunday, the UN Security Council, with the Soviet Union absent, ordered North Korea to cease the invasion and withdraw. Two days later, this resolution having been ignored, the council met again and called on all members of the United Nations to give assistance to the Republic of Korea. Citing these resolutions as authority, the Truman administration during the week incrementally raised the level of American involvement and commitment until on Friday, June 30, Truman gave Gen. Douglas MacArthur, the U.S. commander in the Far East, authority to use the ground forces under his command. That was when, for practical purposes, the United States entered the Korean War.

Meanwhile, there had been some contacts with Congress. On Monday, Truman himself talked to the chairman of the Senate Foreign Relations Committee, Tom Connally, D-Texas. The president inquired whether the senator thought a declaration of war would be necessary "if I decide to send American forces into Korea." Connally warned against a long debate in Congress, "which would tie your hands completely." He

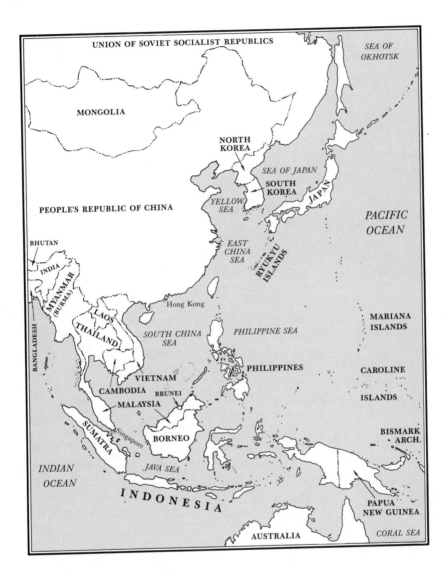

Far East and Southeast Asia

told the president: "You have the right to do it as commander in chief and under the U.N. Charter." [1]

On Tuesday the twenty-seventh, the president met with a bipartisan group of fourteen members of Congress from both houses. Truman later reported in his memoirs that they "approved of my action." [2] According to Secretary of State Dean Acheson, "Senator [Alexander] Wiley [R-Wis.] seemed to express the consensus by saying that it was enough for him to know that we were in there with force and that the President thought the force adequate." [3] (It was not.) Connally recalled that he and others stressed the importance of the UN action and that "a few wondered if Congress should approve." [4]

This question recurred at a second White House meeting, on Friday the thirtieth, when Truman reported to the legislators the orders he had issued about ground troops. There was, says Acheson, "a general chorus of approval," [5] but Senate Republican leader Kenneth Wherry of Nebraska questioned the president's legal authority and Sen. H. Alexander Smith, R-N.J., suggested a resolution approving the action. Truman asked Acheson to prepare a recommendation about this.

As might have been expected, Acheson's recommendation, delivered at a meeting July 3, was in the negative. Congress, incredibly, had recessed for the week of the Fourth of July, and Senate Majority Leader Scott Lucas, D-Ill., was the only member present. He agreed with Acheson, arguing that a minority in Congress could debate and delay a resolution enough to dilute much of its public effect. [6]

Sen. Robert A. Taft, R-Ohio, who had not been included in the White House meetings, raised a lonely voice in dissent. In a speech in the Senate on Wednesday, June 28, Taft noted, "There has been no pretense of consulting the Congress." There was, he said, no legal authority for what the president had done, yet he added that "if a joint resolution were introduced asking for approval of the use of our Armed Forces already sent to Korea and full support of them in their present venture, I would vote for it." [7]

Getting In Deeper

What finally led Congress to involve itself in Korean War policy was a major national controversy which erupted in the spring of 1951, when Truman fired MacArthur as the top American and UN commander. The proximate cause of the uproar was the president's repudiation of an almost mythic American military hero. The deeper issue was over American global strategy.

In the months following the Communist attack in June 1950, the fortunes of war shifted from side to side. Initial Communist successes were followed by UN successes, so many that by October the UN General Assembly approved a radical expansion in war aims. What had started as an operation to defend South Korea now became a campaign to unify North and South, and UN forces invaded the North. But in late November the tide of war turned again. As UN troops neared North Korea's border with China at the Yalu River, massive Chinese forces intervened to drive the UN (mainly American) troops back down the Korean peninsula in a bitter winter of retreat.

Vigorous internal debate took place within the executive branch over how to meet this crisis. Generally, the president, the Joint Chiefs of Staff, and the State Department were arrayed against MacArthur; and when the general's opposition became publicly strident, Truman relieved him of all his commands. The fundamental difference was over whether the United States should pursue a defensive or an offensive global strategy. Should the United States simply attempt to contain the Communist world, or should the U.S. put unrelenting pressure on communism at all available points?

In the context of the Korean War, the debate over this broader issue took the form of a series of narrow, essentially tactical questions, such as whether to bomb Chinese territory north of the Yalu River, as MacArthur advocated. The resolution of such questions obviously affected the broader strategy: a defensive policy to protect the South implied one kind of war; an offensive policy to unify North and South implied a quite different kind of war; and a policy to carry the war to China would require yet another approach to military operations. The converse was also true, though in a more subtle way: the manner in which the war was conducted could gradually, perhaps imperceptibly, lead to a policy different from the one with which the country started. Aggressive tactics, repeated over time, can change a defensive policy into an offensive policy and vice versa.

These questions are so intertwined that they blur the distinction between the *conduct* of the war, which is the prerogative of the president as commander in chief, and the *policy* of the war, in which Congress shares the stage. The questions recurred in connection with Indochina in the Nixon administration, Lebanon in the Reagan administration, and the Persian Gulf in the Bush administration. In each case, Congress played a different role.

In the case of Korea, the public outcry over MacArthur was so immense that Congress felt it had to do something. What Congress did was to invite the general to address a joint session, where he received an emotional ovation. But then Congress proceeded to have what seemed like endless hearings of inquiry which eventually defused the controversy by talking it to death. The Senate Armed Services and Foreign Relations committees jointly held forty-three days of hearings, covering 3,691 printed pages, between May 3 and June 27, 1951. No report was issued. The hearings accomplished the purpose of the Democratic leaders of the Senate—that is, leaving the conduct of the Korean War in the hands of the president.

The policy reverted to the defense of South Korea. Following lengthy negotiations an armistice was signed July 27, 1953, providing for a demilitarized zone approximately along the thirty-eighth parallel— where the boundary had been to begin with.

Getting Out

A quarter of a century later, President Carter moved to withdraw some of the 41,000 U.S. troops that remained in Korea in 1977. But now Congress, which had been indifferent to its prerogatives in sending the troops in 1950, asserted its opposition to bringing them home. At the instigation of Sen. George McGovern, D-S.D., the Foreign Relations Committee added a policy statement to the bill authorizing appropriations for the State Department: "The United States should seek to accomplish, in accord with the President's announced intention, a complete withdrawal of United States ground forces from the Korean peninsula within four or five years." [8]

This encountered such formidable opposition in the Senate that it had to be watered down, not only to avoid repudiation of the president's policy, but more particularly to blunt an effort to enact some kind of prohibition on troop withdrawal. As it passed the Senate, the new language—the handiwork of the majority leader, Sen. Robert C. Byrd, D-W.Va.—said that "U.S. policy toward Korea should continue to be arrived at by joint decision of the President and the Congress" and that "any implementation of the foregoing policy should be done in regular consultation with the Congress." [9]

In 1973, as will be discussed, Congress had passed, over President Nixon's veto, the War Powers Resolution, which sought to circumscribe presidential authority to send troops abroad. Nixon had argued that the resolution was unconstitutional interference with the president's powers as commander in chief. Now Congress was going further and attempting to limit presidential authority to bring troops home. It argued in part from the precedent of the War Powers Resolution.

"I do not think this is strictly an executive branch decision," said Senator Nunn, a prominent member, and later chairman, of the Armed Services Committee. "Under the War Powers Act [sic], we talked a long time about the commitment of troops abroad. I should think that, by implication, we would have some control over the withdrawal of forces that are in a dangerous spot in the world. . . . If it works one way, it works the other." [10]

Congress returned to the subject in 1978. Various proposals to put firm limits on withdrawal were rejected, but the military assistance bill stated that further withdrawal "may seriously risk upsetting the military balance in that region and requires full advance consultation with Congress." [11]

In January 1979, new intelligence estimates showed North Korean military strength to be greater than had previously been thought, and in July the White House announced that further implementation of Carter's plan was being postponed.

The issue was again revived in 1990. By this time, North Korea, which had hitherto insisted on implacable isolation and hostility, was having tentative discussions with Japan and even with South Korea. Economic progress in South Korea had been remarkable, and American manufacturers were feeling South Korean competition. Deployments to the Persian Gulf (discussed later in this chapter) were stretching American military manpower, and important elements in Congress were demanding that U.S. allies shoulder more of the burden. In these circumstances, Rep. Robert J. Mrazek, D-N.Y., offered an amendment to the defense authorization bill for fiscal 1991 to reduce troops in Korea from 43,000 to 30,000 by the end of fiscal 1993. It was rejected, 157 to 265, but the administration had already announced plans for a reduction to 36,000 anyway.

Europe

Getting In

On September 9, 1950, less than three months after U.S. troops had been committed to combat in Korea with little objection from Congress, President Truman announced his approval of a "substantial increase" in U.S. forces in Europe over the two divisions already in Germany. On December 19, the president said the increase would be carried out as soon as possible. Later, it was announced that the increase would be four divisions.

This was part of a U.S. policy to strengthen the North Atlantic Treaty Organization (NATO), which had been established in 1949 to defend western Europe, but it provoked a great debate in the Senate. A major speech by Sen. Robert A. Taft, R-Ohio, on January 5, 1951, foreshadowed arguments that would be heard fifteen years later with respect to Vietnam and forty years later with respect to the Persian Gulf:

> As I see it, members of Congress, and particularly members of the Senate, have a constitutional obligation to reexamine constantly and discuss the foreign policy of the United States. If we permit appeals to unity to bring an end to that criticism, we endanger not only the constitutional liberties of the country, but even its future existence. . . .
>
> [The president] has no power to agree to send American troops to fight in Europe between members of the Atlantic Pact and Soviet Russia. Without authority, he involved us in the Korean war. Without authority, he apparently is now attempting to adopt a similar policy in Europe.[12]

Three days later, Senate Republican leader Kenneth Wherry introduced a resolution asserting Congress's right to make the policy. No troops should be sent, the resolution said, "pending the formulation of a policy with respect thereto by the Congress." [13] This became the focus of prolonged hearings by the Foreign Relations and Armed Services committees and of the Senate debate which followed.

As had happened in the MacArthur controversy, there was a mixing of the issues of the substantive policy and of the proper role of Congress. Senators who favored Truman's policy in Europe tended to take a broad view of the president's power to act on his own. Senators who opposed the policy tended to take a narrow view. The president's supporters really wanted to avoid any action on the part of Congress. They feared that, even if Congress approved the policy, the action might set a precedent that Congress had the right to do so. Much later, this same attitude inhibited the Reagan and Bush administrations in their consultations with Congress about Lebanon and the Persian Gulf.

In the case of sending troops to Europe, the end result of the Senate's debate was ambiguous and not wholly satisfactory to either side, though less so to those who supported a broad concept of presidential powers. The most important element in this result was an amendment by Sen. John McClellan, D-Ark., that no more than four divisions should be sent without the Senate's approval. The McClellan amendment was first rejected by 44 to 46, but it was then reconsidered and agreed to, 49 to 43. It was part of a concurrent resolution that was not acted on by the House and that therefore had no legal force, but it was an assertion of Senate prerogatives that distressed the Truman administration.

Getting Out

Thereafter, discussion of the issue in Congress died out for a time. Over a period of years, the number of U.S. troops in Europe increased to approximately 300,000; the troops were accompanied by 225,000 dependents, most of them in Germany. By 1966, there began to be agitation to bring some of them home. In a sense, this was a spillover of the nascent Senate disillusionment with Vietnam. More directly, it was a consequence of the French withdrawal from the military side of NATO in 1966 and of a generalized feeling that the U.S. contribution to NATO was more than its fair share.

The chief advocate of a reduction in U.S. troops in Europe in the 1960s and early 1970s was Senate Majority Leader Mike Mansfield, D-Mont. Almost annually, he offered amendments to defense authorization and appropriation bills calling for varying cuts in U.S. troop strength in Germany. They were all rejected, sometimes by odd coalitions of senators who thought they cut too much and senators who thought they did not cut enough. If all of the senators who voted for some reduction had been able to get together on a single amendment, they would have prevailed over the strenuous opposition of the Johnson and Nixon administrations, respectively.

After 1971, Congress let the issue drop as the Mutual Balanced Force Reduction (MBFR) talks got under way in Vienna and the administration could argue that the troops ought to be left in Europe as bargaining chips. Ten years later, the MBFR talks were still going on, without measurable progress, and Congress became more restive. Congressional committee reports on defense legislation during the 1980s are sprinkled with stern warnings about the limits of congressional patience. By 1984, Sam Nunn had succeeded Mansfield as the Senate's leading exponent of troop withdrawal. Nunn was actually more interested in using the threat of troop withdrawal to force improvements in NATO forces and changes in NATO strategy. But he had no more success than Mansfield, losing a 1984 vote of 55 to 41.

By 1990, the MBFR talks had been transformed into CFE (Conventional Forces in Europe) talks, and to the astonishment of many a jaded arms-control negotiator, they bore fruit in the form of a long and complicated treaty which was signed in Paris in November. So far as members of NATO were concerned, the treaty dealt only with weapons and equipment, not troops; but the times clearly pointed to a reduction of troops as well.

Ironically, the first major reduction in American troops in Europe came in November 1990, when the Bush administration ordered 50,000 of them redeployed to the Persian Gulf. Significant opinion in Congress had opposed sending them (or their fathers!) to Europe in the first place, certainly without prior congressional approval, but could not prevail against President Truman. Significant opinion had favored bringing them home from Europe long since, but could not prevail against Presidents Johnson, Nixon, and Reagan. Growing opinion in Congress was questioning President Bush's policy in the Gulf. At no time had a majority of Congress been opposed to the European policy of any of the post-World War II presidents, but many members of Congress had been opposed to the level of American military deployment in Europe.

Vietnam

When the French tried to reestablish themselves in their former colony of Vietnam after World War II, they met resistance from Vietnamese who were seeking independence and who were also supported by the Soviet Union and Communist China. The United States supported the French, at least partly because it wanted French support for American policy in Europe.

Matters did not go well for the French, and by 1954 a large part of their forces were besieged in the strong point of Dien Bien Phu. The question arose in Washington whether the United States should intervene with air strikes in support of the French. President Eisenhower was reluctant to act without congressional support; upon being consulted, leaders of Congress (including then Senate Majority Leader Lyndon B. Johnson, D-Texas) were opposed, especially without international support. As a consequence, there was no U.S. military intervention on behalf of the French.[14]

The French position became untenable. An international conference at Geneva later in 1954 created two independent Vietnams—Communist in the north, non-Communist in the south—separated by the sixteenth parallel. France withdrew, and the United States assumed the role of trying to help the South Vietnamese create a viable state.

The congressional role in preventing U.S. intervention in Vietnam in 1954 was important, possibly crucial, but informal. No law was passed; no votes were taken. Consultation worked like Congress thinks it is supposed to—quietly, with a real exchange of opinions. Publicly, speeches were made in the Senate opposing intervention—by Sen. John F. Kennedy, D-Mass., and Majority Leader Johnson, among others.

Getting In

Thereafter, Congress paid little attention as American involvement increased incrementally for ten years under Presidents Eisenhower, Kennedy, and Johnson. To its later regret, Congress did not even pay much attention in 1964 when it acceded to President Johnson's request and provided a statutory basis for the war in the Gulf of Tonkin Resolution. The resolution was occasioned by a reported attack August 2, 1964, on the U.S. destroyer *Maddox* while it was on what was described as a routine patrol in international waters in the Gulf of Tonkin off the North Vietnamese coast. On August 4, there were further attacks reported on the *Maddox* and the *C. Turner Joy,* which had joined it. The destroyers were not damaged, but President Johnson ordered air strikes against North Vietnamese torpedo boat bases. The next day, he asked Congress for a joint resolution. In part, it read:

> The Congress approves and supports the determination of the President, as Commander-in-Chief, to take all necessary measures to repel any armed attack against the forces of the United States and to prevent further aggression.
>   ... the United States is ... prepared, as the President determines, to take all necessary steps, including the use of armed force, to assist any member or protocol state of the Southeast Asia Collective Defense Treaty requesting assistance in defense of its freedom.[15]

This resolution passed Congress August 7—two days after Johnson requested it—by votes of 416 to 0 in the House and 88 to 2 in the Senate. Later, Johnson was fond of carrying a tattered copy of it in his pocket and of showing it to anyone who questioned his authority, especially members of Congress who had voted for it. He and other executive officials considered the resolution the "functional equivalent" of a declaration of war. (The phrase is that of Under Secretary of State and former attorney general Nicholas deB. Katzenbach in testimony before the Senate Foreign Relations Committee August 17, 1967. This statement, along with the rest of Katzenbach's testimony that day along the same lines, inspired Senator McCarthy to run for president in 1968. And McCarthy's campaign was one of the factors in President Johnson's decision not to seek reelection.[16])

One reason Congress passed the resolution so promptly and overwhelmingly was that the immediate military response to the incidents of August 2-4 had been limited. This made Johnson look moderate, especially when compared with Sen. Barry Goldwater of Arizona, his Republican opponent in the 1964 presidential election. Later, however, a serious question developed whether the resolution had passed Congress under false pretenses. A review of navy documents by the Senate Foreign Relations Committee revealed that the *Maddox* had not been on a routine patrol at all, but rather on a sensitive and provocative intelligence mission. There was even some doubt whether one of the reported attacks actually occurred. Congress repealed the Gulf of Tonkin Resolution in 1971.

The Gulf of Tonkin affair is generally considered to be the watershed of U.S. involvement in Vietnam, but the crucial change in the American role—from advising to participating—came in 1965. In February, Johnson ordered the bombing of North Vietnam in retaliation for an attack on an American barracks housing military advisers in South Vietnam. In July, he ordered an additional 50,000 troops to Vietnam, and the United States was in another war.

Getting Out

Once the U.S. role in Vietnam expanded, so did U.S. involvement, reaching a peak of more than 500,000 troops by 1968. Opposition to the involvement grew commensurately. One high official of the Johnson administration, speaking not for attribution after he was out of office, described the evolution of his thinking as growing from a doubt to an opinion to a conviction to an obsession. Similarly, opinion in Congress, as in the public, progressed from acquiescence to opposition by a minority to opposition by a large majority.

Because congressional opponents of the war were in a minority until the 1970s, they could hope to change the policy only through persuasion, not through legislative edict. Argument was ineffective and to some extent was counterproductive. The Johnson administration argued that public dissent from the war simply strengthened the will of the North Vietnamese. (The same argument was to be made by the Bush administration twenty years later with respect to debate about policy in the Persian Gulf.) And many members of Congress who had private doubts about the wisdom of the war felt compelled to support it because American troops were already engaged in large numbers.

Over time, as American casualties grew, willingness to support the war eroded, opposition swelled, and Congress turned to its ultimate power—the power of the purse. Between 1970 and 1974, Congress enacted at least eight prohibitions on the use of funds for military operations in Indochina. Typical of these restrictions was the language of the State Department Authorization Act of 1973:

> Notwithstanding any other provision of law, on or after August 15, 1973, no funds heretofore or hereafter appropriated may be obligated or expended to finance the involvement of United States military forces in hostilities in or over or from off the shores of North Vietnam, South Vietnam, Laos, or Cambodia, unless specifically authorized hereafter by the Congress.[17]

By that time, partly in response to congressional pressure, U.S. involvement was winding down, and disengagement might have occurred anyway. The congressional grip on the purse strings may have prevented a reinvolvement in the hectic days of the final withdrawal in 1975. As the South Vietnamese position was collapsing in April of that year, President Ford asked Congress for additional military assistance for South Vietnam. Congress refused. The Senate Foreign Relations Committee went further. It met privately with Ford in the White House and strongly urged evacuation of the American Embassy in Saigon (later renamed Ho Chi Minh City). Otherwise, members of the committee feared, the administration would send troops back to Saigon under the pretext of protecting the embassy.[18]

The War Powers Resolution

One of the legislative consequences of the Vietnam War was the War Powers Resolution (P.L. 93-148, November 7, 1973), a complicated law in which a number of disparate strands of congressional thought were woven together. Some saw the resolution as a restatement of what the Founders had intended, an intent that in this view had been distorted through congressional abdication. It was not only a way of putting a further check on the president; it was also a way of forcing Congress to share the responsibility for sending Americans into combat, or in the phrase of one of the principal sponsors of the resolution, Sen. Jacob K. Javits, R-N.Y., to give Congress "the responsibility for putting blood on our hands, too." [19] Others viewed the resolution as a way to delineate the powers of the president as commander in chief. Some ended by opposing the resolution because they thought it expanded those powers. Prominent in this group was Sen. Thomas Eagleton, D-Mo., one of the original sponsors. Still others—including Javits—viewed it as providing the basis for a compact between the president and Congress on how their combined powers would be exercised. This concept was shattered when President Nixon vetoed the resolution.

After attempting to catalog the situations in which the president is permitted to involve the armed forces, the resolution prescribes a complicated procedure whereby Congress may bring about the withdrawal of the forces. The initial inspiration for the War Powers Resolution was provided when President Nixon ordered U.S. troops into Cambodia May 1, 1970. The Senate Foreign Relations Committee felt doubly affronted because it had held a secret meeting on Indochina with Secretary of State William P. Rogers April 27 and Rogers had given no hint of the forthcoming action. Several members of Congress—notably Javits and Eagleton in the Senate, Dante B. Fascell, D-Fla., and Clement J. Zablocki, D-Wis., in the House—drafted various proposals. Three years later, after much consideration, the War Powers Resolution emerged and passed Congress in October 1973.

Nixon vetoed it October 24, calling it "unconstitutional and dangerous to the best interests of our Nation." [20] Nixon's objections were directed primarily at what he saw as infringement of the president's powers as commander in chief. Both houses voted to override the veto on November 7, the House by 284 to 135, the Senate by 75 to 18.

Eleven members who were in the Senate for the vote on sending troops to Europe in 1951 were still there in 1973 for the vote on Nixon's veto of the War Powers Resolution. A consistent view of the powers of the president and Congress would have required the same vote on the McClellan amendment asserting congressional authority with respect to sending troops to Europe and on the War Powers Resolution. Those consistently favoring a restriction of the president's power would have voted yea both times, and those opposing a restriction would have voted nay. Only two senators, McClellan himself and Milton Young, R-N.D., voted the same way both times, yea in each case. Nine others changed from a less to a more restrictive view of the president's powers. These included Hubert Humphrey, who served as Johnson's vice president and then returned to the Senate, and J. W. Fulbright, D-Ark., who as chairman of the Foreign Relations Committee in the Johnson and Nixon administrations played a leading role in the reassertion of congressional powers.

Johnson and Nixon were themselves senators in 1951. Johnson, consistent with his later actions as president, voted against the McClellan amendment. Nixon voted for it, then later vetoed the War Powers Resolution.

Alone among the presidents who have served since the resolution was passed, Jimmy Carter did not contest its constitutionality. Notwithstanding, on twenty-three occasions in the fifteen years between 1975 and 1990, these presidents sent Congress the reports required by the resolution whenever American forces are involved in hostilities or "imminent hostilities." With two exceptions, the incidents were of short duration, ranging from a few hours to a few weeks. Members of Congress sometimes complained about lack of consultation, but the question of withdrawing troops did not arise.

The two exceptions—Lebanon and the Persian Gulf—deserve more extended treatment. Each of these cases provoked serious congressional debate, but Congress showed little stomach for invoking the War Powers Resolution.

Lebanon

Following the attainment of independence from France in 1946, Lebanon maintained a precarious balance between its Christian and Moslem populations, each of which was subdivided into disputatious factions. A violent military coup in Iraq in July 1958 prompted President Eisenhower to send marines to Lebanon. Their numbers reached 14,300 in August, but the crisis passed, and the last marines were withdrawn in October.

Internal tensions in Lebanon increased as the population balance (but not political influence) shifted from Christian to Moslem. When King Hussein ejected the Palestine Liberation Organization (PLO) from Jordan in 1970, many PLO fighters came to Lebanon. A bitter and destructive civil war broke out in 1975. Syrian intervention on behalf of the Arab League imposed a tenuous peace in 1976. Israel subsidized a Christian militia to keep the PLO away from northern Israel, but sporadic guerrilla attacks on Israeli settlements continued.

Their patience exhausted, the Israelis invaded Lebanon in the summer of 1982, driving as far as Beirut. In August, agreement was reached, with the crucial diplomatic assistance of the United States, for PLO withdrawal. A part of the agreement was that the evacuation would be observed by an international force of eight hundred Americans, eight hundred French, and four hundred Italians. U.S. marines began arriving August 25, the day after President Reagan reported to

Congress that they were going. The evacuation was carried out successfully (though subsequently, elements of the PLO began to infiltrate
back), and the marines left Lebanon September 10.

They returned September 29, this time numbering twelve hundred
(later increased to seventeen hundred), and again in company with the
French and Italians, later joined by a small British contingent. Their
new mission was to interpose themselves between the various parties to
the conflict—Israelis, Syrians, Lebanese government forces, and the
numerous armed factions. Reagan reported this movement to Congress
September 29.

The marines' presence stretched into 1983, and controversy grew,
not only over the presence but also over whether the situation was one
of "imminent" hostilities. If it was, then under the War Powers
Resolution the marines could stay no more than sixty days—in exceptional circumstances ninety days—unless Congress declared war or
passed a specific statutory authorization. Congress dealt with the
problem tangentially in the Lebanese Emergency Assistance Act of 1983
(P.L. 98-43, approved June 27, 1983, approximately 270 days after the
marines arrived). This law provided, among other things, that the
"President shall obtain statutory authorization . . . with respect to any
substantial expansion in the number or role in Lebanon of United
States Armed Forces." This was a way of saying that Congress accepted,
perhaps even approved, the policy thus far but was uneasy over where it
might lead.

The uneasiness increased after August 29, when the marines had
their first casualties—two killed and fourteen wounded, the consequence of fighting between the Lebanese armed forces and various
factions. The president reported these casualties to Congress August 30.
Two more marines were killed September 6; the French also suffered
casualties. On September 13, the White House announced that U.S. air
power and artillery might be used to defend positions of the Lebanese
armed forces important to the defense of the marines. On September 17,
there was U.S. naval fire against guns in Syrian-held territory that were
shelling the Lebanese defense ministry and the U.S. ambassador's
residence. On September 19, the navy opened fire to prevent the
Lebanese army's loss of a strategic town in the mountains.

Thus, in the space of three weeks there occurred an expansion of
the U.S. role from providing a buffer to taking sides in a civil war. The
change was analogous to the shift in Korea from defense to offense and
in Vietnam from advice to participation.

The president still resisted describing the U.S. forces as being
engaged in hostilities; but the administration did enter into negotiations
about the applicability of the War Powers Resolution with congressional
leaders, principally House Speaker Thomas P. O'Neill, Jr., D-Mass. Out

of these talks emerged a compromise of sorts. It passed the House
September 28 by a vote of 270 to 161 and the Senate September 29 by a
vote of 54 to 46. Reagan signed it October 12. Its key provisions were the
following:

> United States Armed Forces ... in Lebanon are now in hostilities
> requiring authorization of their continued presence under the War
> Powers Resolution. ... The requirements of section 4(a)(1) of the War
> Powers Resolution became operative on August 29, 1983. [This is the
> section applying to actual or imminent hostilities.] ... The Congress
> intends this joint resolution to constitute the necessary specific statu-
> tory authorization under the War Powers Resolution for continued
> participation by United States Armed Forces in the Multinational
> Force in Lebanon. ... Such protective measures as may be necessary to
> secure the safety of the Multinational Force in Lebanon [are not
> precluded].[21]

The authorization was good for eighteen months, meaning that it
would expire April 12, 1985. In signing the resolution, Reagan said:

> I do not and cannot cede any of the authority vested in me under the
> Constitution as President and as Commander-in-Chief of the United
> States Armed Forces. Nor should my signing be viewed as any
> acknowledgement that the President's constitutional authority can be
> impermissibly infringed by statute, that congressional authorization
> would be required if and when the period specified in ... the War
> Powers Resolution might be deemed to have been triggered and the
> period had expired, or that [the eighteen-month authorization] may be
> interpreted to revise the President's constitutional authority to deploy
> United States Armed Forces.

Thus, Congress invoked the War Powers Resolution; and Reagan
signed the measure invoking it, but at the same time said in effect that
he did not recognize it. Further, Congress gave the president authority
to operate under the resolution for eighteen months. The president had
made it plain he would not accept a shorter time, but even so, the House
Appropriations Committee voted 20 to 16 to cut off funds after sixty
days unless the president himself invoked the resolution. The committee backed down under pressure from the Speaker. A proposal in the
Senate to hold strictly to the sixty-day limitation was rejected on a
party line vote of 45 Democrats to 55 Republicans. The eighteen-month
period at least had the advantage in the eyes of some of carrying the
matter past the 1984 election.

Many members were also uneasy over the authority provided for
"such protective measures as may be necessary to ensure the safety of
the Multinational Force in Lebanon." Even before this chilling re-
minder of the Gulf of Tonkin Resolution, members had been comparing
Lebanon to Vietnam. Senate Majority Leader Byrd said the provision

was "a hole that you can run Amtrak through." [22] Rep. Toby Roth, R-Wis., said "If we keep the Marines in Lebanon, we're just waiting for a tragedy to happen." [23]

It happened October 23, when a suicidal terrorist crashed a truck laden with explosives into the lobby of the marine headquarters building at the Beirut airport and blew it up, killing 241. A nearly simultaneous bombing of French paratroop quarters killed 47.

The incident produced a new outcry in Congress, but no action. On November 2, by a vote of 153 to 274, the House defeated an amendment to the defense appropriations bill to cut off funding for keeping the marines in Lebanon after March 1984. In the Senate, Republican parliamentary maneuvers avoided a vote in the Foreign Relations Committee on a proposal to reduce the authorization for the marines to remain in Lebanon from eighteen months to three.

On February 7, Reagan ordered the marines withdrawn (his term was "redeployed") to ships offshore. (The previous week, he had said that withdrawal would have "a pretty disastrous result" for U.S. foreign policy; and as late as February 5, Secretary of State Shultz had criticized Congress for even tolerating discussions about withdrawal.)[24] Total U.S. casualties had been 264 killed and 134 wounded.

The Persian Gulf

In a period of less than four years—from the spring of 1987 to the winter of 1991—United States armed forces were involved twice in the Persian Gulf: the first time in a manner helpful to Iraq in the latter days of the Iran-Iraq war; the second time in a war with Iraq involving hundreds of thousands of troops. The direct beneficiary both times was the small emirate of Kuwait.

Following the Soviet invasion of Afghanistan in December 1979, President Carter enunciated what came to be known as the Carter Doctrine in his State of the Union message to Congress in January 1980: "An attempt by any outside force to gain control of the Persian Gulf region will be regarded as an assault on the vital interests of the United States of America, and such an assault will be repelled by any means necessary, including military force." [25]

Kuwaiti Tankers

Later in 1980, Iraqi forces attacked Iran over a boundary dispute, and a long and costly war ensued. In the spring of 1987, the Reagan administration acceded to a Kuwaiti request to protect Kuwaiti tankers in the gulf from participants in the Iran-Iraq war. The tankers would be registered in the United States so that they could fly the American flag

The Persian Gulf, with Key Oil Fields and Pipelines

and thereby come under the protection of the U.S. Navy. Ironically, in view of later events, Kuwait was technically neutral in the war, but did not conceal its pro-Iraq sympathies; the threat to its shipping came from Iran.

Congress spent a good part of the summer and fall of 1987 discussing the applicability of the War Powers Resolution to the situation in the gulf, but took no action. The administration refused even to consider the matter, because, in its view, the resolution was unconstitutional. But even if it were not, officials said, the level of hostilities was too low for the resolution to apply.[26] Nevertheless, the Pentagon authorized "imminent danger" pay bonuses of $110 a month for personnel on ships operating in the gulf; U.S. forces attacked and seized an Iranian landing craft that was laying mines, and they destroyed an Iranian oil platform in the gulf that had a radar station on it. Reagan reported these actions to Congress. He said the platform had been used as a base for attacks against U.S. helicopters.[27]

In July, before the paperwork for reflagging had been completed, the House rejected, 126 to 283, a proposal by Rep. Charles E. Bennett, D-Fla., to forbid it. The House then agreed to a proposal by Rep. Mike Lowry, D-Wash., 222 to 184, to delay it for three months. A similar proposal in the Senate fell victim to a Republican filibuster. The closest it came to passing was when it received 47 votes on a motion to end the filibuster (60 votes were needed).

Later, Senators Byrd and Nunn devised an amendment to the defense authorization bill that did not mention the War Powers Resolution at all but that in effect would have applied its terms to the Persian Gulf. The Byrd-Nunn amendment would have allowed Kuwaiti tankers to fly the U.S. flag, but only under the time limits of the War Powers Resolution. This amendment was also the target of a filibuster. A cloture motion failed, 54 to 45. Byrd and Nunn then declared that the majority support amounted to a symbolic victory, and they withdrew the amendment.

But the matter was not dead. In October, Sens. Lowell P. Weicker, Jr., R-Conn., and Mark O. Hatfield, R-Ore., introduced a joint resolution to start the sixty-day clock of the War Powers Resolution. Senators Byrd and John W. Warner, R-Va., the ranking Republican on the Armed Services Committee, offered a substitute to require the president to report within thirty days on the policy of reflagging and escorting the Kuwaiti ships. Thirty days after the report, the Senate would act on the policy under special rules precluding a filibuster. The substitute supported a U.S. "presence" in the gulf but expressed "reservations" over the policy of reflagging and escorting. This time the Senate voted cloture, 67 to 28, and then passed the substitute, 54 to 44. But the bill died in the House. It was too strong for those who supported the administration and too weak for those who wanted to apply the War Powers Resolution.

After a lull over the winter, the scope of U.S. involvement was enlarged in April 1988 when the president ordered the navy to assist, in certain circumstances, neutral shipping as well as U.S.-flag vessels. The action was taken in response to an increasing number of attacks on neutral shipping by both belligerents, sometimes in sight of U.S. naval ships, which under their prior rules of engagement could do nothing. Thus, just as the marines' mission in Lebanon had expanded, so, too, did the navy's mission in the Persian Gulf.

But this phase was shortly to end. On July 18, 1988, Iran accepted a year-old UN Security Council resolution calling for a cease-fire and withdrawal to internationally recognized borders. After negotiations, a cease-fire went into effect August 20. Talks looking toward a permanent peace settlement stalled over Iraq's insistence that it be given control over the Shatt-al-Arab waterway leading into the Persian Gulf at the mouth of the Tigris-Euphrates river system, but the cease-fire held.

Iraqi Invasion of Kuwait

Two years later, there was another war. On August 2, 1990, Iraq invaded, and shortly overran, Kuwait. Access to the sea was one Iraqi objective. The Iraqis also accused Kuwait of taking more than its share from the Rumailia oil field which underlies the Iraqi-Kuwaiti border. Finally, Iraq asserted a historic claim to Kuwait (Chapter 4).

The Iraqi forces established themselves in such strength on the Kuwaiti border with Saudi Arabia that the Saudis felt threatened and appealed to the United States for help. (Saudi Arabia has a population of only 16 million, roughly the same as greater Los Angeles, in an area of 865,000 square miles, more than three times the size of Texas.) President Bush responded August 6 by ordering substantial forces to Saudi Arabia and the Persian Gulf. He reported this to Congress "consistent with the War Powers Resolution" August 9. The forces were increased incrementally until by the end of October they numbered approximately 220,000.

On August 2, the day of the Iraqi invasion, the UN Security Council condemned the invasion, demanded Iraq's unconditional, immediate withdrawal, and called on both countries to begin negotiations (Resolution 660). The vote was 14 to 0, with Yemen not participating. Significantly, the fourteen included both the Soviet Union and the People's Republic of China, as clear an indication as one could imagine of a new day in international politics. On August 6, the Council voted 13 to 0 (Cuba and Yemen abstaining) to impose a trade and financial embargo against Iraq and occupied Kuwait (Resolution 661). And on August 25, again by a vote of 13 to 0, with Cuba and Yemen again abstaining, the council called on UN members with ships in the region to enforce the sanctions by inspecting and verifying cargoes and destinations (Resolution 665).

Besides the United States, other countries also sent troops, notably Egypt, Syria, Britain, and France. Naval vessels enforcing the blockade included ships from Australia, Britain and France, among other countries, as well as from the United States. By the end of the year, twenty-seven countries had forces in the area, some of them tiny.

Congress was in adjournment for its summer recess from August 3 to September 5. Defense Secretary Cheney, himself a former member of the House, later called this an "advantage." "We could spend August doing what needed to be done rather than explaining it," he said.[28] (One of the characteristics that distinguishes the United States from many other countries, including Iraq, Kuwait, and Saudi Arabia, is the principle of public accountability—that is, the obligation of the government to explain what it is doing.)

When Congress did come back, Bush addressed a joint session. He appealed for bipartisan support and listed four U.S. objectives: complete, immediate, and unconditional Iraqi withdrawal from Kuwait; restoration of Kuwait's "legitimate government," which had fled into exile; assurance of security and stability in the Persian Gulf; and protection of American citizens abroad.[29]

The feeling grew in Congress that Congress ought to do something, but there were difficulties in deciding what to do. A strict application of the War Powers Resolution depended on whether hostilities were "imminent." The administration insisted they were not. But given the numbers of unfriendly troops facing each other, if hostilities were not imminent, the situation was at least fraught with danger.

Even so, the administration, while welcoming congressional support, refused to endorse any action based on the War Powers Resolution, which it adamantly held to be an unconstitutional infringement of the president's powers. This, in turn, complicated the situation in Congress, because it fueled a suspicion that the president might be inclined to take further, more far-reaching action on his own. Despite the president's repeated assurances of consultation, many members of Congress were not satisfied with the consultative process.

Nor could members of Congress easily agree among themselves on what a congressional resolution about the Persian Gulf ought to say. Most members supported what the administration had done in August and September; the problem came in what, if anything, to say about the future. There was extreme sensitivity about avoiding the precedent of the Gulf of Tonkin Resolution. But the White House would not accept any delineation that seemed to limit the powers of the president.

Out of these multiple dilemmas, the House and the Senate produced separate resolutions—a joint resolution in the case of the House and a concurrent resolution in the case of the Senate. The House passed its resolution October 1 by a vote of 380 to 29; the Senate acted October 2 by a vote of 96 to 3. In both cases, the resolutions were considered under procedures that precluded amendments. This avoided certain confusion and possible embarrassment, but it also discouraged wide-ranging debate with full discussion of the policy involved. Neither house considered the resolution which had passed the other house, and therefore both resolutions died.

The House resolution, which was worked out by the Foreign Affairs Committee, had the following operative provisions:

- It "affirmed" U.S. policy in the Persian Gulf to include not only the four objectives stated by the president in his address to Congress September 11 but also "the fostering of a new world order, freer from the threat of terror, stronger in the pursuit of justice, and more secure in the quest for peace"—a considerable expansion beyond earlier statements.
- It supported the deployment of forces to the Persian Gulf region, and it declared congressional support for them "as they perform their vital role in the achievement of United States objectives."
- It called for a continuation of efforts to achieve a diplomatic solution to the crisis in the Gulf.[30]

The Senate resolution was a product of the leadership and was considered without reference to a committee. Much shorter than the House resolution, it approved the actions of the president in support of the goals stated in the UN Security Council resolutions. It also supported continued action by the president in accordance with Security Council decisions and "in accordance with United States constitutional and statutory processes, including the authorization and appropriation of funds by the Congress, to deter Iraqi aggression and to protect American lives and vital interests in the region."[31]

The Senate's procedure in considering the resolution was revealing of Senate folkways. At 11:45 a.m., Friday, September 28, Majority Leader Mitchell obtained unanimous consent to consider the resolution without amendments or motions to refer to a committee under a limitation of thirty minutes of debate. When Senator Hatfield protested the short debate, the reason emerged. Since it was Friday, senators had planes to catch to their home states beginning in midafternoon. Hatfield was mollified when the agreement was changed to impose no time limitation on debate Friday and to postpone the vote until Monday when senators would have returned to Washington. Actually, the vote came Tuesday.

In any event, the debate both in the Senate and the House, such as it was, revealed congressional unhappiness over the resolutions and over the congressional role in the Persian Gulf, even among those members who formed the lopsided majorities. Senator Hatfield called the Senate resolution a "toothless piece of legislative craftsmanship." He continued, "We, the Congress, have found it most convenient and certainly we have almost developed a skill of letting foreign policy move along, independent and with no finger prints from the Congress, until things may go sour."[32] Sen. Edward M. Kennedy, D-Mass., one of three to vote against the resolution, called it a "blank check ... a Tonkin Gulf resolution for the Persian Gulf." [33] On the other hand, Minority Leader Dole, while agreeing that some day Congress would have to have a showdown about war powers, argued that "a debate right now, which could be misinterpreted or misreported as evidence of an erosion of support for the president's stance, would serve no one's interest—except Saddam Hussein's." [34]

War with Iraq

Congress adjourned for the year on October 28. On November 8, two days after the congressional elections, President Bush announced an approximate doubling—to about 400,000—of the troops in Saudi Arabia. It was reported he had made the decision to do so October 31 but directed that it be kept secret until after the election. The reinforcement was in response to recommendations from military commanders about what it would take to "guaran-damn-tee," as one of them put it, that the United States would prevail. The commanders, in turn, were responding to an injunction from Bush not to produce another Vietnam, where the incremental application of force had contributed to the ruin of the Johnson presidency. [35]

Leading Democratic members of Congress reacted adversely. Sen. Claiborne Pell, D-R.I., chairman of the Foreign Relations Committee, criticized the president for not having consulted with Congress. Senator Nunn, chairman of the Armed Services Committee, said the augmentation enlarged the U.S. mission from deterring Iraqi aggression against Saudi Arabia to preparing for the liberation of Kuwait. Rep. Lee H. Hamilton, R-Ind., chairman of the Foreign Affairs Subcommittee on the Middle East, said the president had failed clearly to explain the American national interest involved. Senate Majority Leader Mitchell and House Armed Services Committee Chairman Les Aspin, D-Wis., reminded the president of the necessity for congressional approval of going to war. [36]

On November 29, the UN Security Council voted 12 to 2 (Cuba and Yemen opposed, China abstaining) to authorize member states "to use all necessary means" to compel Iraq to comply with the council's earlier resolutions if Iraq had not done so by January 15, 1991. [37] Thus did the drafters of the resolution manage to authorize military action without saying so.

Hearings

The Armed Services, Foreign Relations, and Foreign Affairs committees of Congress held a series of hearings in December. Some argued that Bush's decision in November to send more troops increased the pressure on Iraq to comply with the UN resolutions. Others pointed out that if Iraq did not do so, then the increased pressure was on the United

States to choose the military option because of the difficulty of maintaining such a large number of troops so far from home. This further narrowed the range of maneuver for Congress and contributed to congressional nervousness. "If we knew he [the president] would only use force as a last resort, some of the voices . . . would pull back," said Rep. Howard L. Berman, D-Calif., a supporter of the president's policy.[38]

The reinforcement also raised the question of whether, as had been the case in Korea, in Vietnam, and in Lebanon, there had been an enlargement of U.S. objectives. Appearing before the Senate Armed Services Committee, retired Air Force general David Jones, a former chairman of the Joint Chiefs of Staff, specifically warned against such an enlargement. It would, he said, strain the international coalition which was supporting U.S. and UN policy in the gulf and would also strengthen Saddam Hussein's determination to hold out. Jones called the situation "potentially the most dangerous crisis yet in the Middle East." At the same hearing, retired admiral William J. Crowe, Jr., another former chairman of the Joint Chiefs of Staff, also advised caution. "Posturing ourselves to promote stability for the long term is our primary national interest in the Middle East," he said. "It is not obvious to me that we are currently looking at the crisis in that light."[39]

Former secretary of defense Robert S. McNamara, who had been instrumental in persuading the Senate Foreign Relations Committee to approve the Gulf of Tonkin Resolution, now counseled patience to the same committee. He recommended continuing to rely on sanctions for perhaps as long as eighteen months, and said, "I do not believe the president should, and I do not believe he will, initiate action without the approval of the American people expressed by the approval of Congress."[40] Former secretary of state Cyrus Vance advised further pursuing a policy of sanctions and diplomacy. On the other hand, former secretary of state Henry Kissinger specifically called for broadening American objectives so as "to restore the balance of offensive capabilities in the area." [41]

Former national security affairs adviser Zbigniew Brzezinski warned the Foreign Relations Committee about possible side effects of a war: Iranian domination in the Persian Gulf, Syrian leadership of the Arab world, the overthrow of Arab governments friendly to the United States, military involvement of the United States in the area for decades, and the temptation for Israel to use its military force more freely.[42]

On December 4, the House Democratic caucus voted 177 to 37 that no offensive military action should be taken without the formal approval of Congress unless American lives were in immediate danger.

Defense Secretary Cheney told the Senate Armed Services Committee that the United States did not have "an indefinite period of time to wait for sanctions to produce the desired result" and that military action was the only sure way of getting Iraqi troops out of Kuwait.[43] Further, Cheney said, "I do not believe the president requires any additional authority from the Congress." [44] Secretary of State Baker specifically refused to give assurances that the administration would not take military action against Iraq without first seeking a declaration of war or other congressional approval.[45] Assistant Attorney General Stuart M. Gerson argued in court that the power to declare war is optional: it allows Congress to take the initiative to start a war if it chooses, but it does not bind a president. Nor, he went on, does the Constitution say when war has to be declared; the declaration does not have to be in advance, but could be after the fact.[46]

Debate

As January 15 neared, feeling grew in Congress that Congress had to act one way or the other. On January 8, President Bush sent a letter to Congress in which he said:

> It would greatly enhance the chance for peace if Congress were now to go on record supporting the position adopted by the UN Security Council on twelve separate occasions. Such an action ... would help dispel any belief that may exist in the minds of Iraq's leaders that the United States lacks the necessary unity to act decisively in response to Iraq's continued aggression against Kuwait. ... Anything less would only encourage Iraqi intransigence. ... I am determined to do whatever is necessary to protect America's security and I ask Congress to join with me in this task.[47]

The administration's position was embodied in a resolution which was sponsored in the Senate by Senator Dole, the minority leader, and Senator Warner, the ranking Republican on the Armed Services Committee. The House sponsors were Representative Michel, the minority leader, and Representative Solarz, a member of the Foreign Affairs Committee. (This resolution was also supported by Foreign Affairs Chairman Fascell.) The resolution authorized the use of force against Iraq pursuant to the Security Council resolution of November 29. It required that, before using force, the president should report to Congress his determination that all appropriate diplomatic and other peaceful means had not been, and would not be, successful in obtaining Iraqi compliance with the UN resolutions. The Dole-Warner-Michel-Solarz congressional resolution also declared that it constituted the specific statutory authorization contemplated by the War Powers Resolution for sending American armed forces into hostilities.[48]

As an alternative, the Democratic leadership introduced a joint resolution calling for continued international sanctions and diplomatic efforts. This resolution was sponsored in the Senate by Senator Mitchell, the majority leader, and Senator Nunn, chairman of the Armed Services Committee. In the House, a similar resolution was sponsored by Representative Gephardt, the majority leader, and Representative Hamilton, chairman of the Foreign Affairs Subcommittee on Europe and the Middle East. The resolution authorized the use of the armed forces to enforce the economic embargo against Iraq, to defend Saudi Arabia from direct Iraqi attack, and to protect American forces in the region. It pointedly noted that the "Constitution . . . vests all power to declare war in the Congress," and promised that "Congress will expeditiously consider" any presidential request for such a declaration. Complicated provisions were included to prevent a filibuster.[49]

For three days, Thursday through Saturday, January 10-12, 1991, the House and Senate simultaneously but separately debated these different approaches. The debates were carried live and in full by the two C-SPAN television networks. The Public Broadcasting System also broadcast the debates live, switching back and forth between the House and Senate.

These were among the most dramatic congressional debates of the last half-century, their impact heightened by the fact that they were occurring simultaneously in both houses and by the imminence of the January 15 deadline. Most members of both bodies spoke during the long sessions (one night until two thirty in the Senate and until four o'clock in the House). Many said the forthcoming votes were the most important they would cast during their congressional service. Many had secluded themselves in their offices to write their speeches themselves (truly unusual in the 1990s) and had proved themselves better at it than the hired speechwriters on their staffs (who rarely, however, get to write about such a momentous issue). Many referred, sometimes emotionally, to their own experience in war—World War II, or Korea, or Vietnam. In 1991, with respect to the Persian Gulf, these combat veterans were on both sides of the issue. Sen. Daniel K. Inouye, D-Hawaii, who lost an arm in World War II, and Senator Dole, who had an arm crippled, had first met in an army medical rehabilitation center in Battle Creek, Michigan, in the 1940s. Forty-five years later, Inouye voted against another war; Dole voted for it.

In summary, members who favored the Dole-Warner or Michel-Solarz resolutions argued that Congress ought to support the president for the sake of U.S. credibility in the world, if for no other reason, and that sanctions would not be effective, or in any case would take too long. Members who favored the Mitchell-Nunn or Gephardt-Hamilton resolutions argued that sanctions had not been given a chance and dwelt on the November reinforcement decision as a turning point. In general, administration supporters decried the efficacy of sanctions; their opponents focused on the consequences of war, not only in terms of casualties but in terms of economic and international political repercussions. Speaker Foley made one of his rare speeches in the House to argue for the Gephardt-Hamilton resolution.

On the afternoon of Saturday, January 12, the Senate voted first. It defeated the Mitchell-Nunn resolution (S.J. Res. 1) by a vote of 46 to 53. It then agreed to the Dole-Warner resolution (S.J. Res. 2) by a vote of 52 to 47. Senator Hatfield voted against both resolutions. Even the Mitchell-Nunn resolution, he said, authorized the use of force for the economic embargo, for the defense of Saudi Arabia, and for the protection of American forces. And, he added, the Iraqi invasion of Kuwait was not a sufficiently grave threat to the national security of the United States to justify war.[50] The only senator who did not vote was Alan Cranston, D-Calif., who was in his home state undergoing treatment for cancer.

In the House, a short time later, the Gephardt-Hamilton resolution was defeated 183 to 250, and then the Michel-Solarz resolution (H.J. Res. 77) was passed 250 to 183. This was the resolution that went to the president for his signature.

In all cases, the votes went along party lines, but Republicans were more united than Democrats, substantial numbers of whom broke with their leadership to support the administration, especially in the House. In the Senate, Sen. Charles E. Grassley of Iowa was the only Republican to vote for the Mitchell-Nunn resolution on sanctions, while ten Democrats voted against it. The same ten voted for the Dole-Warner use-of-force resolution while Grassley was joined by Hatfield in opposition. In the House, only three Republicans (Silvio Conte of Massachusetts, Constance Morella of Maryland, and Frank Riggs of California) voted for sanctions and against force, while eighty-six Democrats lined up with the administration.

The war started with air attacks against Iraq during the night of January 16-17. It ended, with the UN coalition totally victorious, February 27 when President Bush declared a unilateral cease-fire.

Conclusion

In the five decades since World War II, there have been five major debates in the United States over the war powers of the president and the Congress. During this time, the relevant provisions of the Constitution have not changed, but the interpretation given to the powers of the president by occupants of the office has expanded considerably. Congress, on the other hand, has tended toward a narrower view.

In the case of Korea, Truman relied on the United Nations for his authority to fight a major war. There were those in Congress (notably

Senator Taft of Ohio) who challenged this from the beginning, but they were neither numerous nor insistent. Indeed, Korea did not precipitate much of a debate at all until the war started going badly, and then the debate was more about the conduct of the war than about the war itself, more about the president's wisdom than his powers. Truman won that debate in Congress, but it contributed to the defeat of the Democratic party in the 1952 election.

Truman's decision to send American troops to Europe provoked a major debate, especially in the Senate, before the troops went. The outcome in Congress was ambiguous, but Truman won the political battle when he made the popular Eisenhower the first supreme commander of NATO.

It is perhaps significant that Eisenhower, the first general to occupy the White House since U.S. Grant, was also the most diffident of all the post-World War II presidents in asserting his powers as commander in chief.

The adjective *diffident* has never been applied to Lyndon Johnson, and it was during the Johnson presidency that the constitutional struggle between the president and Congress reached epic proportions. Congress felt it had been tricked into passing the Gulf of Tonkin Resolution with its "functional equivalent" of a declaration of war. This made Congress furious, and its fury contributed to its further reaction.

Testifying before the Senate Judiciary Committee almost thirty years later, Nicholas deB. Katzenbach (who as under secretary of state had coined the "functional equivalent" phrase) denied the trickery. In fact, he put the responsibility on Congress for not insisting "then or later, that the president lay out fairly and frankly the choices, the risks, and the possible consequences of massive intervention."[51]

The Vietnam War led to the fourth major debate, this one over the War Powers Resolution. The resolution was passed over Nixon's veto, and every subsequent president except Carter has denounced it as unconstitutional. (Carter simply said he "accepted" it.) Congress has invoked the resolution twice, once with respect to Lebanon and once with respect to the Persian Gulf. In the Lebanese case, President Reagan as much as said he would ignore the resolution if that suited his purposes.

In the Persian Gulf case, the fifth major debate, there was no doubt that Congress passed another functional equivalent of a declaration of war, and there was no doubt that Congress knew what it was doing. Yet in this case, too, the result was ambiguous. Bush did not ask Congress for authority; he asked for support. He and his secretaries of state and defense maintained that he had the authority anyway. Bush was reported to have refused to assure the congressional leadership that he would not start the war before Congress had a chance to vote.[52] At least some members of Congress voted for the war-making resolution out of fear of the constitutional crisis that would result if Congress disapproved the authority and Bush went to war anyway.

Throughout the Persian Gulf crisis and war, Bush strengthened his position vis-à-vis Congress by skillful use of the United Nations (where he had once served as American ambassador). From beginning to end, the policies of the United States and the United Nations were so closely aligned that one could scarcely say whether the United States was supporting the United Nations or vice versa. This situation created additional pressure on Congress to support the president, because to do otherwise would be seen as weakening the U.S. position in the UN and possibly even reneging on U.S. commitments under the UN Charter.

As it was, the country's legal requirements were met, whatever one's view of them. But the Lebanese and Persian Gulf cases, taken together, raised the question of how much real choice Congress has in these situations. If presidents assert the power to act on their own authority, Congress can either go along, resort to the power of the purse (which means cutting off support to American troops engaged—or about to be engaged—in combat), or pursue impeachment.

There was a paradox, and much irony, about the way the United States went to war in the Persian Gulf in 1991. President Bush sought evidence of congressional support. What he got was a squeaky vote of 52 to 47 in the Senate (the previous closest vote on a declaration of war had been 19 to 12 against England in 1812). But the war was such a resounding, quick, low-casualty triumph that Bush came out of it with record-high approval ratings of 90 percent or more in the opinion polls.

The legislative-executive confrontation over Vietnam had pitted a Democratic Congress against a Democratic president. This removed the partisan aspects and emphasized the institutional nature of the struggle. In the case of the Persian Gulf, there was a Democratic Congress and a Republican president. This submerged the institutional, and highlighted the partisan, aspects. The outcome left the Democrats in disarray and the president hugely popular.

As Johnson left office in 1969, one battle-scarred Senate participant in the executive-legislative struggle remarked that it would take till the end of the century to get the powers of the presidency back where Johnson found them. After the Persian Gulf War, it could perhaps be said that George Bush had beaten that prediction by almost a decade.

Notes

1. Tom Connally, as told to Alfred Steinberg, *My Name Is Tom Connally* (New York: Thomas Y. Crowell, 1954), 346.

2. Harry S. Truman, *Years of Trial and Hope*, vol. 2 of *Memoirs* (Garden City, N.Y.: Doubleday, 1956), 338.
3. Dean Acheson, *Present at the Creation: My Years in the State Department* (New York: W. W. Norton, 1969), 409.
4. Connally, *My Name Is Tom Connally*, 347-348.
5. Acheson, *Present at the Creation*, 113.
6. Ibid., 414.
7. *Congressional Record*, 81st Cong., 2d sess., June 28, 1950, 9319-9323.
8. H. R. 6689, 95th Cong., 1st sess., 1977, as reported in the Senate; see also S. Rept. 95-194, 26-27.
9. *Congressional Record*, 95th Cong., 1st sess., 1977, 19442-19443. The final version of the amendment as it emerged from the House-Senate conference and was passed is found in P. L. 95-105, Sec. 512.
10. *Congressional Record*, 95th Cong., 1st sess., 1977, 19444, 19447.
11. P. L. 95-384, Sec. 23(d).
12. *Congressional Record*, 82d Cong., 1st sess., January 5, 1951, 55, 59.
13. S. Res. 8, 82d Cong., 1st sess., 1951. A Senate resolution is not voted on by the House or signed by the president. It has no force of law, but carries weight as an expression of senatorial opinion.
14. This is treated in exhaustive detail in Senate Foreign Relations Committee, *The U.S. Government and the Vietnam War: Executive and Legislative Roles and Relationships, Part I, 1945-1961*. Senate print 98-185, pt. 1, 98th Cong., 2d sess., 1984, 174-228.
15. P. L. 88-408, August 10, 1964. In 1964, the members of the Southeast Asia Collective Defense Treaty were Australia, France, New Zealand, Pakistan, the Philippines, Thailand, the United Kingdom, and the United States. The protocol states were Cambodia, Laos, and South Vietnam. It was the protocol states that were relevant to the Gulf of Tonkin Resolution.
16. Anthony Austin, *The President's War* (Philadelphia: Lippincott, 1971), 1-8.
17. P. L. 93-126, October 18, 1973, Sec. 13.
18. The evacuation of Saigon is recounted in more detail in Pat M. Holt, *The War Powers Resolution: The Role of Congress in U.S. Armed Intervention* (Washington, D.C.: American Enterprise Institute, 1978), 13-16.
19. Senate Foreign Relations Committee, *War Powers Resolution*, Hearings, 95th Congress, 1977, 182.
20. H. Doc. 93-171, 93d Cong., 1st sess., 1973.
21. Text in *Congressional Quarterly Weekly Report*, October 8, 1983, 2102. Text of Reagan statement on signature is in *Congressional Quarterly Weekly Report*, October 15, 1983, 2142.
22. Quoted in dispatch by T. R. Reid and Helen Dewar, *Washington Post*, September 22, 1983.
23. *Congressional Quarterly Weekly Report*, September 24, 1983, 1964.
24. Reagan's remarks are quoted in *Wall Street Journal*, February 8, 1984; for Shultz's criticisms of Congress, see *New York Times*, February 6, 1984.
25. *Congressional Record*, 96th Cong., 2d sess., 1980, 381.
26. Dispatch by Molly Moore, *Washington Post*, September 28, 1987.
27. *Weekly Compilation of Presidential Documents*, October 19, 1987, 1159-1160, and October 26, 1987, 1206.
28. *Congressional Quarterly Weekly Report*, October 13, 1990, 3441.
29. Text in *Congressional Record*, daily ed., 101st Cong., 2d sess., September 11, 1990, H7414-H7417.

30. H. J. Res. 658, 101st Congress. Text is in *Congressional Record*, daily ed., October 1, 1990, H8441-H8442.
31. S. Con. Res. 147, 101st Congress. Text in *Congressional Record*, daily ed., September 28, 1990, S14221.
32. *Congressional Record*, daily ed., September 28, 1990, S14196.
33. Ibid., October 1, 1990, S14293.
34. Ibid., October 2, 1990, S14330.
35. For a detailed account of this decision, see Rick Atkinson and Bob Woodward, "Prolonged Buildup Reflects Doctrine of Invincible Force," *Washington Post*, December 2, 1990.
36. Michael Weisskopf, "Democrats Criticize Gulf Policy," *Washington Post*, November 12, 1990.
37. United Nations, Security Council Resolution 678 (1990). Text in *Washington Post*, November 30, 1990.
38. *Congressional Quarterly Weekly Report*, December 4, 1990, 4082.
39. Senate Armed Services Committee, unpublished transcript, November 28, 1990.
40. Susan F. Rasky, "House Democrats Caution Bush on War," *New York Times*, December 5, 1990.
41. Ibid. See also Walter Pincus and Ann Devroy, "Ex-Joint Chiefs Chairmen Urge Reliance on Sanctions," *Washington Post*, November 29, 1990.
42. R. W. Apple, Jr., "The Collapse of a Coalition," *New York Times*, December 6, 1990.
43. Michael S. Gordon, "Cheney Sees Need to Act Militarily against the Iraqis," *New York Times*, December 4, 1990.
44. Rick Atkinson and R. Jeffrey Smith, "Cheney: Iraq Likely to Outlast Embargo," *Washington Post*, December 4, 1990.
45. John M. Goshko, "Iraq Must Reap No 'Reward' If It Quits Kuwait, Soviet Says," *Washington Post*, October 19, 1990.
46. Rasky, "House Democrats Caution Bush."
47. *Congressional Quarterly Weekly Report*, January 12, 1991, 70.
48. S. J. Res. 2, 102d Congress. Text in *Congressional Record*, daily ed., January 12, 1991, S403-S404.
49. S. J. Res. 1, 102d Congress. Text is in *Congressional Record*, daily ed., January 10, 1991, S163-S164.
50. Remarks of Senator Hatfield are in *Congressional Record*, daily ed., January 12, 1991, S374-S376.
51. Senate Judiciary Committee, *The Constitutional Roles of Congress and the President in Declaring and Waging War*, Hearings, January 8, 1991 (unpublished transcript), 43.
52. Elizabeth Drew, "Letter from Washington," *New Yorker*, February 4, 1991, 87.

CHAPTER 6

The Intelligence Community

In theory, the relationship of Congress to the intelligence community is, or should be, no different from its relationship to other parts of the executive branch. The role of Congress is to provide basic legislative authority and to oversee how that authority is used. Legislative oversight is a duty that Congress has imposed on itself. The law (2 U.S.C. 190d[a]) requires each standing committee of the House and Senate to "review and study, on a continuing basis, the application, administration, and execution of those laws, or parts of laws, the subject matter of which is within the jurisdiction of that committee."

But several factors make Congress's relationship to the intelligence community unique. One is the necessity for secrecy in an otherwise open government. Another is the failure of Congress to provide basic comprehensive legislation on intelligence activities. A third is the failure of Congress, until 1976 in the Senate and 1977 in the House, to exercise any true oversight. All of these factors combined to create both in the intelligence community and in Congress mental attitudes that made it a traumatic experience for both parties when Congress finally began to assert itself. The intelligence community had been conditioned by more than a quarter-century of experience not to tell Congress what it was doing. And Congress had been conditioned not to ask.

For more than twenty-five years following the passage of the National Security Act, which created the Central Intelligence Agency in 1947, Congress largely ignored the intelligence community. It allowed the National Security Agency and the Defense Intelligence Agency to be created by executive order. It voted for untold billions of dollars in hidden appropriations for intelligence activities with very few, if any, of its members knowing either the amounts or the purposes of the funds. Members of Congress who were actively concerned about the activities of the intelligence community were rebuffed by large majorities on the few occasions when they tried to ask questions or to establish procedures for doing so.

During this period, Congress interested itself in the intelligence community only when something went so horribly wrong that it came to public view, as when the U-2 reconnaissance plane was shot down over the Soviet Union in 1960 or when the Bay of Pigs invasion of Cuba failed in 1961. These crises contributed to what was then still a minority view that Congress ought to do something to keep such things from happening. The emphasis in this view was on preventing mistakes.

Further momentum developed in Congress in the early and mid-1970s with the revelations of CIA activities in Chile and of abuses by the CIA and the FBI of constitutional rights of U.S. citizens. The first serious, broad-scale congressional investigation of the intelligence community, by the Church committee in the Senate in 1975-1976, was directed almost wholly to the question of "illegal, improper or unethical activities." [1] This investigation and a later, more raucous one in the House laid the groundwork for the creation (in 1976 in the Senate and in 1977 in the House) of the permanent intelligence committees. These committees were given legislative jurisdiction as well as broad powers of oversight. In this chapter, we review and assess their efforts.

Scope and Functions

The names and responsibilities of the agencies that comprise the intelligence community were given in Chapter 1. The total intelligence budget remains secret despite various recommendations from congressional committees that an overall figure be made public. The total varies from year to year, sometimes widely, depending on the level of paramilitary action and the cost of complicated new technology. For fiscal 1991, the total has been estimated at $30 billion in the intelligence authorization bill.[2] Almost all of this is hidden in Defense Department appropriations, and Defense carries out most intelligence programs. In 1989, 97 percent of the appropriations were in the Defense Department bill, and Defense carried out 80 percent of the programs.[3] In 1991, the proportion of intelligence funds spent by the Defense Department was more than 85 percent.[4]

The intelligence community performs four main functions: collection, analysis, counterintelligence, and covert action.

Collection: the gathering of information. This can be done in such mundane ways as reading a newspaper or in such exotic ways as taking a picture from space or planting a listening device in an official's office, or by bribery or blackmail. One reason the Defense Department spends such a large percentage of the total intelligence budget is that it operates the high-tech collection systems.

Analysis: making sense out of the information. The flow of information into the intelligence community is immense but nevertheless incomplete and sometimes conflicting. The analyst's task is to distinguish between the trivial and the significant, as well as between the true and the false and then to send to policy makers judgments as to the meaning of the information. This task is frequently akin to doing a jigsaw puzzle with some of the pieces missing or describing an iceberg when only its tip can be seen. Furthermore, even with complete information, political or economic forecasting is an inexact art.

Counterintelligence: protecting one country's secrets from another country's spies—that is, keeping the other fellow from doing to us what we are trying to do to him. Counterintelligence in the United States is in the domain of the FBI. The CIA and military intelligence agencies are responsible for it abroad.

Covert action: sub-rosa and theoretically untraceable efforts to influence (sometimes to subvert or overthrow) foreign governments, groups, or economies. These efforts may include the surreptitious dissemination of information, either true or false, but any collection of information is incidental.

Whatever technique is used, covert action is done secretly because public identification of the U.S. government with the particular activity would be either counterproductive or embarrassing or both. Some examples of covert action that have become public are the secret subsidies of anticommunist labor unions in Western Europe in the late 1940s and early 1950s, the overthrow of the Mossadegh regime and the restoration to power of the Shah in Iran in 1953, the overthrow of the Arbenz government in Guatemala in 1954, the abortive Bay of Pigs invasion of Cuba in 1961, the attempts to destabilize the Allende government in Chile in 1970-1973, support of rebel forces in Afghanistan, Angola, and Cambodia in the 1970s and 1980s, and, most dramatically, the operations against Nicaragua that culminated in the Iran-contra scandal.

Problems of Oversight and Control

Over the course of its history, the United States has developed ways of ensuring that the components of its government are responsive to the public will. If the National Park Service, for example, mismanages the national parks, this shortly becomes apparent to large numbers of people, complaints are made, and changes ensue. The process is sometimes slow and cumbersome and may be diverted by arguments over who is at fault, but it usually works. Government agencies are regularly called on to give a public accounting of themselves, and people know from personal experience whether programs are going well or poorly.

Not so with the intelligence community. The time-tested procedures that work for agencies such as the National Park Service are inappropriate for the CIA. This is an anomaly in a country like the United States, where policy is public. Progress has been made in dealing with this problem, but as of the early 1990s, although it is better understood, one cannot say that it has been solved. Nor is it a problem only for Congress; it has haunted such different presidents as John F. Kennedy and Ronald Reagan. President Bush arrived in the White House with the experience of having served as director of central intelligence in 1976 under President Ford, but this did not advance the search for consensus between the White House and Capitol Hill. On the contrary, some on Capitol Hill found Bush more cooperative as director of the CIA than as president.

Intelligence is an indispensable aid to policy makers; one can scarcely imagine trying to make foreign policy in the dark. But the proper role of the intelligence community stops with its presentation of data and analysis. Some directors of central intelligence—for example, Richard Helms, William Colby, and William Webster—have been very emphatic about this; others, such as William Casey, have actively sought and on occasion played a policy-making role as well.

All of the intelligence functions listed above involve serious problems of oversight and control. What do the nation's policy makers need to know? What intelligence should be collected, with what priorities? How does one balance the risks of hazardous collection methods against the value of the intelligence to be collected? (This was at the heart of the problem of the U-2, as will be discussed.)

With respect to analysis, how does one guard against a bias, conscious or not, on the part of the analyst toward a particular interpretation? How does one guard against the temptation, conscious or not, to shape the analysis to fit the bias of the policy maker who is to receive it?

With respect to counterintelligence, how does one balance efforts against espionage with respect for the constitutional rights of Americans and the international law rights of foreign diplomats?

Covert action presents the most nettlesome problem by far of oversight and control. Collection and analysis are part of the policy-making process, but covert action is a tool of policy implementation. As Rep. Anthony C. Beilenson, D-Calif., chairman of the House Intelligence Committee, said during debate on the 1991 intelligence authorization bill: "We spend far too much time debating whether a policy should be pursued in secret and far too little considering whether it should be pursued at all." [5]

The attractiveness of covert action is that it offers a means to do in secret what could not be done in public, or could be done in public only at a high political price. It raises in an acute form the old question of whether the end justifies the means. It frequently (although not always) involves actions that are illegal in another country and perhaps in the United States as well—the kinds of actions that have come to be known as dirty tricks. Covert action offers presidents of the United States a way to avoid public debate over controversial policies. Several postwar presidents have found it impossible to resist this temptation, sometimes to their later regret—Kennedy in Cuba, Nixon in Chile, Reagan in Nicaragua. Through covert action, presidents can pursue one policy in secret while proclaiming another in public. This is truly subversive of the democratic process in the most profound sense. No better argument could be made for a system of checks and balances.

But covert action has another side, and this is one of the reasons it is such a troubling issue. Some covert actions, perhaps most, are in pursuit of objectives that are generally supported by the American public and that are generally seen to be in the national interest. The question remains: Are such secret activities appropriate, especially in a post-cold war world environment? Who decides? And on the basis of what criteria?

In the remainder of this chapter, we examine how Congress has attempted to answer these questions.

The Era of Congressional Neglect

The National Security Act

The CIA was created by the National Security Act of 1947 (50 U.S.C. 403). Of the agencies whose sole concerns are intelligence and covert action, it is the only one created by legislation (and, even at that, the principal purpose of the National Security Act was to establish the Department of Defense). The act made the CIA responsible to the president but put it under the general supervision of the National Security Council. (The NSC, as noted in Chapter 1, is the highest level executive agency for advising the president on national security problems.)

The rationale of the act was that the NSC, which included the secretaries of state and defense, would see to it that the CIA was responsive to stated public policy. Subsequent developments have revealed three flaws in this rationale. First, the NSC is the creature of the president; his is the only vote on the council that matters. The NSC may supervise the CIA, but it cannot supervise the president. Second, beginning with the service of Henry Kissinger as national security affairs adviser in the Nixon administration, the NSC staff has assumed a far larger role than anyone had anticipated in 1947, to the point that it frequently overshadows the council that it presumably serves. Finally, the drafters of the National Security Act did not contemplate a large role for covert action. After President Truman left the White House, he expressed regret that the CIA had even been created: "I think it was a mistake. And if I had known what was going to happen, I never would have done it." [6]

Beginning with Eisenhower, presidents have sought independent outside advice about the intelligence community's activities. The entities supplying this advice have been variously named. During the Reagan and Bush administrations, there were two: the President's Foreign Intelligence Advisory Board and the President's Intelligence Oversight Board. Both have part-time members and meet irregularly.

Because the act establishing the Department of Defense was also used as the legislative vehicle for creating the CIA, an anomaly was created. Jurisdiction over the CIA in Congress, as to both legislation and oversight, was lodged in the armed services committees. The way the CIA does its job has at least as many political ramifications in the field of foreign policy as military ramifications in the field of defense, yet the foreign policy committees in Congress were effectively excluded from contact with the CIA for many years.

Following the passage of the National Security Act of 1947, subcommittees on the CIA, or on intelligence (they were variously named), were created in the armed services committees of both houses. The meetings of these subcommittees were not announced, and they were infrequent. A subcommittee sometimes went a whole year without meeting. Similar subcommittees were created in the two appropriations committees to provide funds for the intelligence agencies.

CIA officials have maintained that all of the agency's significant actions were reported to these oversight committees. The members of the committees, however, were clearly not prepared to ask questions and usually accepted whatever they were told about intelligence operations. Leverett Saltonstall, R-Mass., one of the senators concerned with intelligence activities for many years, once said flatly that there were some things about these activities that he did not want to know. Most legislators agreed with Saltonstall or, at the very least, were content to accept existing arrangements. So was the CIA, which operated only under the restraints imposed by the National Security Council; in the 1950s, even the nature of these restraints was a tightly held secret.

Some members of Congress, however, were uncomfortable about this situation. Their unease stemmed from a feeling that the CIA was inadequately supervised, that Congress was shirking its responsibilities, and that sooner or later this state of affairs would cause trouble for the United States abroad.

One of those most deeply concerned about this possibility was Senator Mansfield, who later became majority leader and later still ambassador to Japan, in which position he had the responsibility of overseeing intelligence operations in that country. For a number of years after he came to the Senate in 1953, Mansfield introduced resolutions to create a CIA oversight committee. The only time he was ever able to get a Senate vote on his resolution was in 1956, when it was rejected 27 to 59. Ten years later, the Senate effectively killed a somewhat different resolution with the same purpose by voting 61 to 28 to refer it to the Armed Services Committee. On the face of it, things had not changed very much in a decade.

An important factor at work throughout this period was trenchantly described in 1971 by Francis Wilcox, former chief of staff of the Senate Foreign Relations Committee and a former assistant secretary of state:

> What is basically involved is something it pains the Senate to talk about—personality differences and bureaucratic jealousies. To be blunt about it, and perhaps to overstate it, neither the CIA nor the people who now watch over it fully trust the people who want to watch over it; and the people who want to watch over it do not fully trust either the agency or its present watchers.[7]

Although the votes in 1956 and 1966 were almost identical, the underlying concerns in the Senate had changed. By 1966, evidence had accumulated that either intelligence operations or covert actions could have adverse foreign policy repercussions. Two particularly sensitive situations deserve special mention.

The U-2 and the Bay of Pigs

In May 1960, on the eve of a scheduled summit conference between President Eisenhower and Soviet Premier Khrushchev, the Soviet Union shot down a U-2 spy plane and captured the pilot. The U-2 had been developed during the 1950s and had given the United States what for that time was a remarkable aerial reconnaissance capability. It flew above the reach of Soviet antiaircraft weapons; but on that day in May, a mechanical problem forced it to descend to a level where it could be hit. After an initial period of confusion and contradiction, Eisenhower admitted that the plane's purpose was espionage, and Khrushchev angrily canceled the summit. Some observers think this cost the Republicans the 1960 election.

At any rate, the incident marked the first time a congressional committee (in this case, Senate Foreign Relations) held extensive hearings on an intelligence operation. A censored version was published at the time, and most of the rest some years later.[8] Eisenhower had approved a program of several flights over a period of months, but this particular flight had been scheduled on technical grounds of the weather, without regard to political considerations. Administration witnesses refused to say what the plane was looking for (the crucial factor in balancing the value of the intelligence to be obtained against the risk of obtaining it). Most important, a precedent was established for congressional inquiry into intelligence operations.

The precedent was carried further the following year after the failure of the CIA-sponsored invasion of Cuba at the Bay of Pigs. Again the Foreign Relations Committee held closed hearings, which have since been published.[9] The principal result of the hearings was to increase senatorial skepticism of the intelligence community and of the methods by which it was supervised. (The Bay of Pigs also increased Kennedy's skepticism; he shortly moved to improve White House control.)

Quite apart from the hearings, the Bay of Pigs is revealing of the way the U.S. government makes foreign policy and of executive attitudes toward congressional participation in that process. Because of a combination of circumstances—the most important being their personal relationship—the president asked Senator Fulbright, who was chairman of the Foreign Relations Committee, to join him in a meeting with his advisers to consider whether to go ahead with the projected invasion. Fulbright was the only person present to speak against the plan. Others present, all from the executive branch, were puzzled—almost upset, even—by Fulbright's presence. Years later, William P. Bundy, then a deputy assistant secretary of defense, recalled feeling that Fulbright's presence made it improper for the executive branch officials to be frank, that they were honor bound to stand with the president. Paul Nitze, Bundy's boss, thought Kennedy "merely wanted to be polite to Fulbright." [10] When Kennedy insisted that his advisers take clear-cut yes-or-no positions, several suppressed complicated views to vote yes. Thus, two rules of good government were violated in the same meeting: a president is better served by advisers who say no than by those who say yes. (There are always people willing, even eager, to say yes. Even if the nay-sayers are wrong, they may cause a more searching examination of the issue.) And executive-congressional relations are smoother (and produce better results) when Congress is a partner, not an intruder or a guest.

One other incident is also worth mentioning as an indication of congressional inconsistency in approaching oversight. The Foreign Relations Committee, as noted, spent weeks rehashing the failure of the Bay of Pigs mission. After the success of U.S. policy in the Cuban missile crisis the following year, Secretary of State Dean Rusk all but begged the committee to investigate the performance of the intelligence community and of the administration in crisis management. The committee declined. The point is that Congress as a general rule tends to be more interested in investigating failures than successes.

The Beginning of Real Oversight

What finally prodded Congress out of its lethargy about overseeing the intelligence community was a series of events in the early and middle 1970s, all of them involving something that had gone wrong.

Chile

The first of these involved Chile and the Chilean election of 1970. It was not publicly known until much later, but the CIA had successfully intervened in the Chilean election of 1964 to bring about the election as president of Eduardo Frei, the leader of the Christian Democratic party. As president, Frei received massive overt economic and political support from the United States, but under the Chilean constitution he could not be reelected. The leader in the popular balloting in 1970 was Salvador Allende, leader of the Socialist party; but he fell short of a majority and in those circumstances, the constitution threw the election into the Chilean congress, which had traditionally chosen the front runner in the popular votes. It did so in 1970 as well. Allende himself was not a Communist; but on the spectrum of Chilean politics in the 1960s and 1970s, some factions of the Socialist party stood well to the left of the Communist party.

In 1972, columnist Jack Anderson published internal documents of the International Telephone and Telegraph Company indicating that ITT had tried to persuade the CIA to prevent the Chilean congress from electing Allende. The Senate Foreign Relations Committee responded by creating the Subcommittee on Multinational Corporations to investigate Anderson's report and also to conduct an in-depth study of multinational corporations in general.

A year later, in March 1973, the subcommittee held lengthy hearings, which revealed that ITT had even offered to furnish as much as $1 million for the expenses of clandestine intervention but had found no takers. Past and present CIA officials testified that the agency had a policy of not accepting contributions from private businesses. John McCone, a director of ITT and a former director of the CIA, was one of the officials who testified to this effect. (In 1980, Congress passed legislation specifically authorizing the director of central intelligence to accept gifts, bequests, and property on behalf of the CIA.)

Notwithstanding ITT's efforts, Allende had taken office. In September 1973, six months after the ITT hearings, he was overthrown in a bloody coup d'état. This led to further congressional inquiries in closed session, by the Subcommittee on Western Hemisphere Affairs of the Senate Foreign Relations Committee that fall and by the CIA subcommittee of the House Armed Services Committee the following spring. These hearings developed the information that the CIA had been covertly subsidizing certain Chilean newspapers, political parties, and other groups opposed to Allende in the hope of keeping an opposition alive until the next regularly scheduled election in 1976. The substance of the House hearing leaked to the press in September 1974, and this stirred demands for yet more investigations. The brutality of the Chilean regime that succeeded Allende added impetus to these demands (see Chapter 8).

The Hughes-Ryan Amendment

Partly inspired by the Chile affair, Congress used the 1974 foreign aid bill as a vehicle to require that covert actions (as distinguished from operations aimed entirely at intelligence collection) conducted "by or on behalf of" the CIA be reported to "the appropriate committees of the Congress." The amendment by which this was accomplished was the handiwork of Sen. Harold E. Hughes, D-Iowa (a member of the Armed Services Committee), and Rep. Leo J. Ryan, D-Calif., and was known by their names.

The Hughes-Ryan amendment designated the Senate Foreign Relations and the House Foreign Affairs committees as two of the committees to receive the reports; the other "appropriate committees" were not specified. By general agreement, they were defined to be the Appropriations and Armed Services committees in each house and later—after they were established in 1976 and 1977—the two intelligence committees as well. In 1980, Congress provided that only the intelligence committees would receive the reports, and in especially sensitive cases only the chairmen and the ranking minority members, along with the Speaker and minority leader of the House and the majority and minority leaders of the Senate.

The significance of the Hughes-Ryan amendment is that it was the first legal requirement that anything relating to intelligence be reported to Congress. Further, one of the reports Congress received under the amendment led to a legal prohibition against a covert action program in Angola—the first time Congress had ever prohibited a specific intelligence activity.

Domestic Abuses

In December 1974, the *New York Times* published a long story reporting extensive activities by the CIA in the United States, most of which were forbidden by the National Security Act of 1947 and some of which would have been illegal anyway.[11] Intelligence files were maintained on at least 10,000 Americans, it was reported.

The reason for much of this activity had been to look for foreign inspiration in American protests against the Vietnam War. No such inspiration was found. The story also reported other domestic activities, not specifically targeted against Americans, dating back to the 1950s and including break-ins, wiretapping, and the surreptitious inspection of mail.

This story, taken together with similar but less detailed reports, caused such commotion that even the putative oversight subcommittees of the Senate Appropriations and Armed Services committees felt stirred to action. A joint hearing was held January 15, 1975, and the subcommittees released the statement made at that time by CIA director William E. Colby. The statement conceded some improprieties, but maintained that they were "few and far between" and had been corrected.[12]

Meanwhile, President Ford had launched an independent investigation within the executive branch, this one headed by Vice President Nelson Rockefeller. The Rockefeller Commission report, released in May 1975, essentially reached the same conclusion as Colby's testimony to two Senate subcommittees in January. But by that time, momentum on Capitol Hill had outrun the Ford administration's efforts to calm the waters by admitting mistakes but asserting that they had been corrected.

Congressional Investigations

Senate. In January 1975, by a vote of 82 to 4, the Senate established the Select Committee to Study Governmental Operations with Respect to Intelligence Activities (a name that the resolution creating it said was given "for convenience of expression"!)[13] People found it more convenient to call it the Church committee after its chairman, Frank Church, D-Idaho, who had presided over the investigation of CIA-ITT activities in Chile. The committee's vice chairman was John Tower, R-Texas, who later became chairman of the Armed Services Committee and later still chairman of the President's Foreign Intelligence Advisory Board. Other members included Walter F. Mondale, D-Minn., a future vice president; Howard Baker, R-Tenn., a future Senate majority leader; and Barry Goldwater, R-Ariz., a future chairman of both Armed Services and the permanent Intelligence Committee.

It was not until after the Church committee had completed its work that the facts about CIA involvement in Chile came out—and even then no one could be sure it was the full story. The State Department, the American embassy in Santiago, and eventually Congress knew about CIA subsidies for Allende's opponents; but until the Church committee's investigation, they did not know that President Nixon had directly instructed CIA Director Helms to "destabilize" the situation in Chile so much that Allende could not continue in office. For denying the existence of these activities before the Foreign Relations Committee, Helms was subsequently fined $2,000 when he pleaded nolo contendere to charges of failing to testify "fully . . . and accurately." What emerged from the Church investigation was that, although in a technical sense the CIA might not have been involved in the coup that overthrew Allende, its whole course of action in Chile for three years had been designed to create a situation in which such a coup would occur.

The Church committee's work had two principal results: the creation of a standing committee on intelligence, oriented more to continuing oversight than to investigations of past misdeeds; and a recommendation for legislative charters for all intelligence agencies, spelling out permissible and impermissible behavior. Drafting these charters has proven to be more difficult than it once appeared. By 1991, they had still not been written, and the effort to do so had been all but abandoned in favor of an ad hoc approach.

House.   Meanwhile, the House was proceeding with a parallel but much more contentious investigation. The House created the Select Committee on Intelligence in February 1975, with Rep. Lucien Nedzi, D-Mich., as chairman, but its members quarreled among themselves so much that in July the House took the unusual step of abolishing the committee and creating another one with the same name and the same terms of reference but without some of the more quarrelsome members. The new committee was headed by Rep. Otis Pike, D-N.Y. It spent the fall of 1975 wrangling with the administration over access to classified documents.

On January 23, 1976, the Pike committee voted 9 to 4 to release its final report, despite administration objections that it contained material that should remain classified. On January 29, the House took the extraordinary action of voting 246 to 124 to prohibit the committee from releasing a report until it had been "certified by the President as not containing information which would adversely affect the intelligence activities of the Central Intelligence Agency" or other agencies.[14] Then, on February 11, the *Village Voice* in New York published a twenty-four-page supplement containing lengthy excerpts from the report. Two days later, CBS correspondent Daniel Schorr confirmed that it was he who had given a copy of the report to the *Voice*. Schorr's refusal to say where he got the copy set off yet another acrimonious investigation. The House Committee on Standards of Official Conduct tried, and predictably failed, to determine Schorr's source.

The Pike committee's recommendations included the following:

- that the House create a permanent intelligence committee;
- that the president put an overall figure for the intelligence community in his budget;
- that transfers and reprogramming of intelligence funds be subject to the approval of the intelligence and other committees;
- that the General Accounting Office be empowered to investigate and audit intelligence agencies on the same basis as other agencies;
- that a Foreign Operations Subcommittee be created by statute in the National Security Council to deal with covert action and hazardous collection of intelligence;
- that the intelligence community be reorganized to separate the director of central intelligence from the CIA and the National Security Agency from the Defense Department, as well as to abolish the Defense Intelligence Agency;
- that there be no recruitment by the intelligence community of American citizens associated with religious, educational, or communications organizations.

Oversight at Work

The Permanent Committees

In accordance with the recommendations of the Church and Pike committees, the Senate created the Select Committee on Intelligence in 1976, and the House established the Permanent Select Committee on Intelligence in 1977. In both cases, there are overlapping memberships with the Appropriations, Armed Services, Foreign Relations (Foreign Affairs in the House), and Judiciary committees, the last being included because of its jurisdiction over the FBI. In both House and Senate, the majority and minority leaders of the full chambers are ex officio members without votes.

Continuous service of a member is limited on both committees—to eight years in the Senate, to six years in the House. This limitation is designed as a safeguard against co-option, the subtle process by which the overseen persuade their overseers to become their handmaidens. Co-option is particularly noticeable among the regulatory agencies of the government, and it has existed, at one time or another and to one degree or another, in the relations between most other congressional committees and the executive agencies for whose legislation they are responsible. Prior to 1975, it certainly existed with respect to the Appropriations and Armed Services committees, on the one hand, and the CIA on the other.

In 1981, when Senator Goldwater became chairman of the Senate Intelligence Committee, there were signs that it, too, had been co-opted. Goldwater said in an interview that he did not believe the committee should exist, and stated in the Senate that he would have preferred that there be no congressional oversight of intelligence agencies. "The Russians have a very fine system. . . . No part of their government has any idea of what is going on [in the KGB, the Soviet secret service]. That is the way . . . I wish it were here in our country, but it is not." [15] Goldwater brought in as staff director John Blake, who had previously worked for the CIA for thirty-two years, holding positions as high as acting deputy director. Blake was succeeded by Robert R. Simmons, who had worked for the CIA for ten years before moving to Capitol Hill to become legislative assistant to Sen. John H. Chafee, R-R.I. Conversely, the committee's senior budget officer left in 1982 to become comptroller of the CIA. (This sort of staff movement back and forth does not *necessarily* mean co-option or even an undesirably close relationship. There are many examples of committee staff members drawn from executive agencies who are extremely valuable because they know what questions to ask and where to look in the bureaucratic maze. In the case of both intelligence committees, however, even a former CIA director, Stansfield Turner, concluded that "the Congress is now co-opted.")[16]

The six-year limit on service brought substantial change to the membership of the House Intelligence Committee when the 102d Congress convened in 1991. The chairman, Anthony C. Beilenson, D-Calif., and the ranking minority member, Henry J. Hyde, R-Ill., both lost their seats. They were honored at a ceremony at CIA headquarters in Langley, Virginia, when they were given medals for their "sustained outstanding support to the agency." [17] This event again raised the question of co-option.

That question seemed to be put to rest, at least for the time being, by Beilenson's successor as chairman, Dave McCurdy, D-Okla. McCurdy told an interviewer, "The committee has not been aggressive enough." He fired the staff director, a former CIA official (who he said had "done a very positive job") and brought in a retired army colonel with a Ph.D. in Russian studies.[18] McCurdy told another interviewer: "I've already chewed out more people in two weeks as acting chairman than have been chewed out up there in the last seven years. I've got a vision of where I want to go and an agenda. And I don't want to wait around to get there." [19]

Besides McCurdy, other new Democrats joining the committee in 1991 were Ronald V. Dellums of California, who had been a member of the original Pike committee; David E. Bonior of Michigan; Martin Olav Sabo of Minnesota; Wayne Owens of Utah; and Norman D. Dicks of Washington. Collectively they were seen as liberal enough to give the White House "deep concern." [20]

The Levers of Oversight

Money. The intelligence committees of both the House and the Senate get their real power from their jurisdiction over authorizations for appropriations for the intelligence agencies and from congressional rules that prohibit appropriating funds that have not first been authorized. This means that the committees not only have access to information about the secret intelligence budget, but they also can approve or disapprove the budget in whole or in part.

The intelligence authorization bill is unique in that it says "funds are hereby authorized to be appropriated" but does not contain any figures. These are contained in a classified schedule of authorizations made available to the Appropriations and Armed Services committees and to the executive branch. The only figures in the published portions of the bill are for the intelligence community staff, for the CIA retirement and disability fund, and sometimes for some of the counterterrorism and counterintelligence functions of the FBI.

Because of this secrecy, an outsider cannot be sure of how rigorously the intelligence committees scrutinize the community's budgets, but one can be fairly sure that the scrutiny is more rigorous than what went on before. The question arises: If the intelligence committees provide a check on the community, who provides a check on the committees? Ways exist for Congress to do so. Any member is privileged to examine the classified schedules. Any member who finds something he or she does not like can precipitate a classified debate in a closed session. If this member can persuade a majority of other members, the matter will be changed. Except for the fact that the process is conducted in secret, it is the same as the process by which Congress provides a check on the committees that do all their work in public. The fact that the process is available does not mean that it is used, but it is there if any enterprising member wants to use it.

Information. Information is perhaps the most powerful weapon in the ongoing struggle between Congress and the president, especially in connection with intelligence, which is under the control of the president. Congress has passed a law (50 U.S.C. 413) requiring the executive branch to furnish any information requested by the intelligence committees and to keep the committees "fully and currently informed of all intelligence activities." But the law has a loophole—"to the extent consistent with all applicable authorities and duties, including those conferred by the Constitution ... and to the extent consistent with due regard for the protection from unauthorized disclosure of classified information and information relating to intelligence sources and methods. ...."

The loophole has apparently not been used, and in most respects the committees are generally satisfied with the information they have been receiving. Two problem areas have developed, both stemming from the Iran-contra affair.

One of these has to do with an independent inspector general for the CIA and especially with congressional access to his reports. Over the objections of the agency, Congress provided for such an official in 1989. He is to be appointed by the president and confirmed by the Senate. His reports are to be available to the intelligence committees. The director of CIA has authority to prohibit specific investigations, but such cases must be reported to the committees. The inspector general is given broad powers to get information within the agency.[21]

The second problem concerns the reporting of covert actions, in particular, when the report should be made and what it should contain. Since the original Hughes-Ryan amendment in 1974, the law has required that the reports be made "in timely fashion." This phrase was generally interpreted to mean in advance or very shortly after the beginning of an action. However, when President Reagan signed one covert action authorization in connection with the Iran-contra affair, he explicitly directed that it *not* be reported to Congress. Later, the Office of Legal Counsel of the Justice Department held that the president had "virtually unfettered discretion" to decide what "timely fashion" meant.[22]

This assertion became a sticking point in executive-legislative relations. Congress was unwilling to accept what struck many members as a grossly inflated interpretation of presidential powers, and the president was unwilling to give it up. Some members held White House lawyers more at fault than the president. "Basically," said Sen. William S. Cohen, R-Maine, ranking Republican on the Intelligence Committee, "it is a situation in which the Justice Department, having committed an error, is very reluctant to admit it." [23]

Bush vetoed the 1991 intelligence authorization bill because of its requirements concerning the contents of covert action reports. The provision to which the president objected most strongly required that he specify whether any third party not otherwise connected to the U.S. government would be involved in the action. This could, he said, "deter foreign governments from discussing certain topics with the United States at all." [24]

The veto came in November after the 101st Congress had adjourned; so the 102d Congress had to face the issue afresh when it convened in January 1991. The matter was not resolved until July, when agreement was finally reached on a new bill which contained several changes in legal provisions regarding covert action. Congress continued to recognize, reluctantly, presidential discretion with respect to the timing of covert action reports. But the agreement required, among other things, that presidential findings authorizing covert action be in writing; that they not be retroactive; that they identify all government agencies involved; and that they indicate whether any third party will take part.

Issues of Oversight

Collection. Beginning in 1985, primarily on the initiative of the Senate Intelligence Committee, the intelligence community has developed the concept of a national intelligence strategy. This is a management tool, both for the director of central intelligence and for Congress in dealing with the intelligence budget. It is a way of relating intelligence programs to each other in terms of their priorities. It is also a way of fixing the priorities of collection targets.

This became much more important later in the 1980s and continuing into the 1990s with the end of the cold war and the collapse of Communist power. Much of the intelligence collected by the community at great effort in 1980 was no longer relevant, or was less relevant, in 1990. New targets appeared—drugs and terrorism, to mention two—but some critics argued that the intelligence bureaucracy was engaging in the self-justification exercise of creating new targets to replace old ones.

In the Senate, there was particular dissatisfaction with the Defense Department, in which intelligence functions were held to be fragmented, repetitive, disorganized, and unnecessarily expensive. Congress authorized a new position of assistant secretary of defense for intelligence, but Secretary Cheney declined to use it, preferring instead to appoint an assistant in the secretary's office. The Senate Armed Services Committee voted for a 25 percent cut in Defense Department intelligence-related activities beginning October 1, 1992.

In 1991, both Senate and House Intelligence committees embarked on major studies with the purpose of reorganizing the intelligence community.

Analysis. The principal analytical product of the intelligence community is a national intelligence estimate (NIE)—the community's consensus about the situation in a given country. Differences within the intelligence bureaucracy frequently make it difficult to arrive at this consensus. Sometimes these differences are submerged so that an NIE becomes the lowest common denominator of agency views. Sometimes the differences are expressed in footnotes.

Another problem has to do with the interaction between analysts and policy makers, between the producers and consumers of intelligence. Sometimes the product does not fit the preconceived notions, or biases, of the consumers (the principal consumer, of course, being the president of the United States). Since ancient times, kings have been displeased, and have sometimes dealt harshly, with messengers who have brought bad news. It is so in the U.S. government.

During the cold war, there was particular contention over estimates of Soviet military strength and strategic programs. One of the early activities of the Senate Intelligence Committee was to undertake a review of one aspect of this controversy.[25] In 1975, the President's Foreign Intelligence Advisory Board became concerned that recent NIEs on the Soviet Union were underestimating Soviet progress in developing strategic weapons. The board proposed what it called a "competitive analysis" by a group of independent outsiders. This was produced. The regular NIE estimators were known as the A team; the outsiders, as the B team.

The process was inconclusive and controversy continued, with charges of ideological bias on both sides. The committee's investigation produced three sets of separate views from senators. The committee's principal conclusions came down to a call for estimates to "openly express differences of judgment and clearly indicate the assumptions, the evidence, and the reasoning which produce alternative readings." The committee also cautioned policy makers to "define the questions, not the answers." [26]

One of the members of the Intelligence Committee active in that investigation was Sen. Daniel Patrick Moynihan, D-N.Y. In 1990, Moynihan, no longer a member of Intelligence, pursued the matter afresh from his position on the Foreign Relations Committee. The hypothesis Moynihan put forth was that for more than thirty years American intelligence had overestimated the size of the Soviet economy (which by 1990 was in a state of virtual collapse for all to see) and therefore had overestimated the military establishment which that economy could support. The inquiry went to the heart of many of the problems of the collection of data in an economy addicted to secrecy and of analysis based on that data.

The problem of analysis has been equally difficult in the third world. The House Intelligence Committee has looked into the performance in the specific cases of Iran and Central America. In both instances, the mindset of both producers and consumers shut out some of the relevant facts.

In the case of Iran, President Carter himself felt that he had been ill served by intelligence that left him surprised when the shah was overthrown in 1979. (That event was still reverberating on American foreign policy in 1991. An uprising coordinated by the CIA had removed a populist threat to the shah's power in 1953, and from then until his overthrow in 1979 he was regarded as a staunch American ally and a key figure in American strategic planning for the Persian Gulf.) The House Intelligence Committee found that "long-standing U.S. attitudes toward the Shah inhibited intelligence collection, dampened policymakers' appetite for analysis of the Shah's position, and deafened policymakers to the warning implicit in available current intelligence. More profoundly, the committee concluded that "the mechanics of NIE production tend to discourage a sound intellectual process," and "mired key personnel in a frustrating search for superficial consensus." [27]

The House committee also reviewed intelligence performance in Central America and found symptoms of trying to please the boss. Or, as the committee put it:

> The environment in which analytic thought and production decisions occur is under pressure to reinforce policy—or perhaps to oppose it— rather than to inform it. Such pressure would not consist of deliberate efforts to suppress or distort evidence; rather, it would lie mostly in the natural incentives that cause time and talent to be devoted to providing welcome intelligence rather than to tackling questions that, although policy-relevant, seem thankless.[28]

Counterintelligence. As we saw earlier, abuse of the constitutional rights of American citizens was one of the things that led to the establishment of the congressional intelligence committees. This abuse mainly took the form of violation of the Fourth Amendment to the Constitution, which guarantees "the right of the people to be secure in their persons, houses, papers, and effects, against unreasonable searches and seizures." The violations were largely directed against opponents of the Vietnam War and consisted of wiretaps and surreptitious searches.

In the Foreign Intelligence Surveillance Act of 1978 (P.L. 95-511, October 25, 1978) Congress required warrants for wiretaps. It required that burglaries in national security cases be approved on a case-by-case basis by the attorney general and that they be reported to Congress twice a year. Notwithstanding, it was revealed in the 1980s that the FBI had penetrated and otherwise harassed the Committee in Solidarity with the People of El Salvador (CISPES), a group opposed to U.S. policy in Central America. The Senate Intelligence Committee investigated and concluded that the case "was a serious failure in FBI management, resulting in the investigation of domestic political activities that should not have come under governmental scrutiny." [29] Yet in 1991 a U.S. magistrate in Chicago found that the FBI had continued the investigation after the Justice Department had ordered it closed.[30]

The 1980s also saw a serious breakdown of American counterintelligence as one episode followed another in which Americans were arrested and convicted on espionage charges. John A. Walker, Jr., headed a spy ring, which included his son and which sold navy codes to the Soviet Union. Jonathan Jay Pollard, a navy intelligence analyst, sold secrets to Israel; Larry Wu-Tai Chin of the CIA sold secrets to China. There were others.

These cases led the Senate Intelligence Committee to convene a panel headed by businessman Eli Jacobs to consider legislative remedies. Other members included former director of the National Security Agency Bobby Inman, former CIA chief Richard Helms, former White House counsels Lloyd Cutler and A. B. Culvahouse, former deputy secretary of state Warren Christopher, and former ambassador to the Organization of American States Sol Linowitz. Its report in May 1990 was the subject of hearings in July, but no action was taken.

The report recommended, among other things, giving the FBI access to the financial and telephone records of persons with top secret clearances, tightening controls on the handling of top secret documents, and outlawing the possession of certain espionage devices. One recommendation found its way into the 1991 intelligence authorization bill, which was subsequently vetoed on other grounds. This was what the Jacobs commission called "after-care for NSA problem employees." It would authorize assistance in finding subsequent employment, in obtaining medical or psychological treatment, or even in providing financial support. The objective would be to reduce the temptation to sell what the former employee had learned while working for NSA.

The problem of protecting the nation's secrets would clearly remain on the intelligence agenda.

Covert Action

For the reasons alluded to earlier, covert action is the most troublesome and controversial aspect of intelligence, and the most troublesome and controversial kind of covert action is paramilitary. Because of their scope, paramilitary activities are difficult, if not impossible, to keep covert. Other activities are more easily concealed and may very well have goals that most people might applaud, or at least not take strong exception to. Sometimes an organization has received modest support with no objective other than to keep it in being because it adds something worthwhile to a country's public life. Sometimes covert action remains covert, though less innocent—rigging a foreign election, bribing a foreign official, subverting foreign press or television coverage. The types of covert action run a broad spectrum from unexceptional to scandalous.

We concern ourselves here with paramilitary or other assistance that had been intended to remain covert, usually without success. In the Reagan and Bush administrations, there were four major instances that came to public attention: in Afghanistan, Angola, Cambodia, and Nicaragua. Of these, Nicaragua was by far the most important; but each of the four illustrates a different balance in executive-legislative relations.

Afghanistan, Angola, and Cambodia

Afghanistan. The Soviet Union's invasion of Afghanistan in December 1979 set off a guerrilla war. Refugees poured across the borders into Iran and Pakistan. The United States spent hundreds of millions of dollars covertly helping the refugees in Pakistan, as well as the guerrillas in Afghanistan, with arms and also with such nonmilitary items as food, clothing, and medicine. Although the Reagan administration was not at all reluctant to engage in these activities, Congress pressed it to do even more and sometimes appropriated more money than had been requested.

In 1988, under the auspices of the United Nations, the United States, Soviet Union, Pakistan, and Afghanistan signed an agreement under which Soviet troops would be withdrawn from Afghanistan and the parties generally would not interfere in each other's internal affairs. The troop withdrawal was completed in January 1989, but fighting in Afghanistan continued and so did U.S. aid to the Afghan rebels.

Angola. In Angola, there was a Marxist government struggling against insurgencies; but in this case Congress flatly prohibited assistance for any military or paramilitary operation. That was in 1976. In 1985, Congress repealed this prohibition and then got in an argument over whether aid should be overt or covert. When Congress did nothing, President Reagan ordered the CIA to use its contingency fund to start a program. The House Intelligence Committee tried to end this program by barring aid unless the matter had been publicly debated and approved by Congress, but the committee was overridden in the House. The nub of the problem, the Intelligence Committee said in its report on the 1987 intelligence authorization bill, was that the president "cannot expect sustained support for foreign policy initiatives, including covert action operations, that are generally unpopular or where a covert action mechanism can be viewed as having been chosen to avoid public debate or a congressional vote on the matter." [31]

The aid continued, channeled through a group known by its Portuguese acronym as UNITA and headed by Jonas Savimbi. Savimbi retained a prominent Washington public relations firm to lobby for covert assistance (!) and occasionally came to Washington himself to make the rounds on Capitol Hill. An uneasy peace came to Angola after an agreement in December 1990 for a cease-fire, elections, and an end to outside arms shipments.

Cambodia. Following U.S. withdrawal from Cambodia at the end of the Vietnam War in 1975, the country fell under the control of the Khmer Rouge, an extremist Communist group that governed with such singleminded orthodoxy and brutality that perhaps as many as three million people died in the ensuing four years (out of a total population of seven million). The Khmer Rouge were overthrown by the Vietnamese, a different kind of Communist, in 1979, and there followed a prolonged period of rampant political confusion.

By the early 1990s, four groups were identifiable: (1) the government, headed by Hun Sen, that had been installed by the Vietnamese before they withdrew; (2) what remained of the Khmer Rouge (about 45,000 troops who were receiving aid from China through Thailand); (3) the forces led by Prince Sihanouk, who had headed Cambodian governments before the Vietnam War and who was receiving aid from such disparate sources as China, the United States, North Korea, and the Association of Southeast Asian Nations (ASEAN); and (4) a group called the National Liberation Armed Forces (about 10,000 troops) led by Son Samm, who was receiving aid from the same groups as Sihanouk.

The American aid was partly covert, funded through intelligence appropriations, and partly overt, funded through the foreign aid program. It was officially designated as aid for the Cambodian resistance, but both the executive branch and Congress had difficulty identifying the resistance in a way certain to rule out all the groups (first of all, the Khmer Rouge) that nobody wanted to help. Support for the program could best be described as tentative. For fiscal 1992, aid to Cambodia was carried in the foreign assistance appropriation bill at a level of $25 million.

Nicaragua

The roots of the Nicaraguan problem run deep into the history of that country and of its relations with the United States, but for our purposes we may begin with the revolution that culminated in the overthrow of the dictatorial regime of Anastasio Somoza in the summer of 1979. Significantly, the principal faction in the ultimately successful revolutionary movement took its name after César Augusto Sandino, who was the leader of a rebel group against the U.S. marine occupation of Nicaragua in the 1920s and early 1930s.

As the revolution gathered momentum in 1978 and 1979, the United States distanced itself from Somoza and sought, with only partial success, to encourage the broadening of the revolutionary leadership so as to dilute radical Sandinista influence. With the triumph of the revolution, the Carter administration adopted a policy of cooperative, friendly relations and of trying to help, in a modest way, in the recovery of the war-damaged Nicaraguan economy. Congress, on the other hand, delayed for nine months before passing a $75 million aid bill and then hedged it with restrictions. Many members were apprehensive of growing Cuban influence in Nicaragua (the fall of Somoza was followed by an influx of Cuban teachers, doctors, and technicians), and the leftist rhetoric of the Sandinistas caused some nervousness on Capitol Hill. U.S.-Nicaraguan relations began a long slide downhill.

The slide picked up momentum in January 1981 with the advent of the Reagan administration, which was less inclined than its predecessor to be cooperative; with growing evidence of Nicaraguan support for a leftist rebel movement in El Salvador; and with the continued drift of the Sandinistas to the left. As early as March 1981, CIA Director Casey reported to the Intelligence committees on a covert action aimed at protecting Nicaragua's neighbors, Honduras and Costa Rica, against the spread of revolution; more specifically, the action was intended to stop the flow of arms from Nicaragua through Honduras to the guerrilla movement in El Salvador.[32] By December, Casey's plan had evolved into a $19 million program to train and support a force of five hundred anti-Sandinista Nicaraguans—the so-called contras—based in Honduras, with the objective of disrupting the flow of Cuban support through Nicaragua to the Salvadoran guerrillas.

By early 1982, some of this began to leak to the press. The House Intelligence Committee became concerned enough to put a secret amendment in the fiscal 1983 intelligence authorization bill. It prohibited support for military activities "to any group or individual, not part of a country's armed forces, for the purpose of overthrowing the government of Nicaragua or provoking a military exchange between Nicaragua and Honduras." The same language was added to the Defense Department appropriation bill that year.[33] In all, between 1982 and 1989, Congress passed ten versions of this amendment, which took its name from Chairman Edward P. Boland, D-Mass., of the House Intelligence Committee. In some of these years, Congress did accede to the Reagan administration's pleas for some military assistance, but it kept the amounts relatively small.

Meanwhile, the Reagan administration's early anti-Sandinista bent had become an obsession. At first, the administration said U.S.

policy was limited to interdicting supplies to El Salvador, even though the Nicaraguan rebels themselves made no bones about their own intention to overthrow the government. Later, Reagan said aid to the contras would stop when the Sandinistas "keep their promise and restore the democratic rule and have elections," and that "the United States does not seek to destabilize or overthrow the government of Nicaragua; nor to impose or compel any particular form of government there." [34] But these statements were made in the context of a flow of strident rhetoric about the danger that Nicaragua represented as a Western Hemisphere outpost of Soviet communism. At a news conference in February 1985, when Reagan was asked if U.S. policy was to remove the Sandinista government, he replied, "Well, remove it in the sense of its present structure, in which it is a communist, totalitarian state." He added that the United States would ease the pressure "if they'd say: 'Uncle,' or 'All right and come on back into the revolutionary government and let's straighten this out.' " [35] Thus, as had occurred in Korea, in Vietnam, and in Lebanon (see Chapter 5), as the American commitment expanded, so did the objectives that American policy sought to achieve.

It was the singleminded fixation on this broader objective, combined with contempt for established procedures, that led to the Iran-contra scandal. But while this scandal was unfolding, the war in Nicaragua was winding down.

In August 1987, President Reagan and House Speaker Jim Wright, D-Texas, joined in proposing a peace plan featuring a cease-fire, the institution of political freedoms in Nicaragua, and cessation of foreign aid to the contras by the United States and to the Sandinistas by the Soviet Union. Shortly afterward, however, President Oscar Arias of Costa Rica proposed a regional peace plan (for which he was subsequently awarded the Nobel Peace Prize) that was agreed to by the five Central American countries at a conference in Guatemala. This plan provided for, among other things, a cease-fire, civil and political rights, amnesty for political prisoners, reconciliation, and democratization, all to be carried out according to a specific timetable.

Wright immediately endorsed the plan; the Reagan administration did not. The Organization of American States met in Washington in November. President Daniel Ortega of Nicaragua attended, as did several contra leaders and Miguel Cardinal Obando y Bravo, who had been trying to mediate between the contras and the Sandinistas. Wright saw them all, in a flurry of diplomatic activity that was unprecedented for a Speaker of the House and that caused unhappiness in the Reagan administration.

Congress remained reluctant to provide significant funds, but it relented in March 1988 and appropriated $47.9 million after the contras and Sandinistas agreed to a cease-fire as well as a framework for continuing negotiations and for democratization in Nicaragua.

Further negotiations between the Sandinistas and the contras broke down in June 1988, but the cease-fire held, more or less. Soon after the Bush inauguration in January 1989, discussions about Nicaraguan policy were initiated between the president and the congressional leadership of both parties. These resulted in an agreement in March.

The agreement stated three goals of U.S. policy toward Nicaragua: democratization, an end to Nicaraguan subversion and destabilization of neighboring countries, and an end to Soviet bloc military ties "that threaten U.S. and regional security." [36] (By this time, the Soviet Union had made it clear that it was no longer interested in maintaining such ties, let alone paying for them.) The agreement also provided for continuation of humanitarian aid to the contras at the then current level of $4.5 million a month through February 1990.

At that time, elections were held in Nicaragua and were won decisively by the principal opposition candidate, Violeta Chamorro, the widow of the newspaper editor whose murder in 1978 had added fuel to the anti-Somoza revolution. In March, Bush lifted the economic sanctions that had been imposed on Nicaragua in 1985 and asked Congress for $300 million in emergency aid. Congress appropriated the money in May. Meanwhile, under UN supervision (which included 800 troops from Venezuela), the contras were being disarmed. By June, 14,000 out of 16,000 had turned in their weapons. At the same time, the Nicaraguan armed forces were being reduced—from 97,000 in January 1990 to 28,000 in April 1991. In September 1990, the Chamorro government began privatizing industries that the Sandinistas had nationalized. The economy was severely depressed (though scarcely worse than under the Sandinistas), but the politics had made a U-turn.

The Iran-Contra Affair

Over the course of several months beginning in October 1986, a series of theretofore secret activities related to the Nicaraguan rebels emerged into public view. These activities—which, together with their aftermath, came to be known as the Iran-contra affair—were essentially of three kinds. First, as public funds for the contras were exhausted, the administration turned to private donors and even to foreign governments for contributions. Second, in conjunction with the government of Israel, arms (mainly antiaircraft and antitank missiles) were secretly sold to Iran by U.S. officials or persons acting on their behalf, at a time when such sales were prohibited by the United States. The immediate objective of this action was to secure the release of U.S. hostages being held by pro-Iranian groups in Lebanon. A longer-range objective was to establish a relationship with putative moderates in the Iranian government. Third, some of the proceeds of the arms sales were diverted to the contras through secret Swiss bank accounts.

The initial revelations set off a number of investigations. The first, by Attorney General Edwin Meese III, was conducted hurriedly over a weekend; it uncovered the first evidence of the contra diversion. President Reagan then appointed a Special Review Board, headed by former senator Tower; the other members were former senator and former secretary of state Edmund Muskie, and Brent Scowcroft, who had been President Ford's national security affairs adviser and later held the same position under President Bush. The Senate Intelligence Committee also conducted an investigation. The House and Senate both created special committees: in the House, the Select Committee to Investigate Covert Arms Transactions with Iran, and in the Senate, the Select Committee on Secret Military Assistance to Iran and the Nicaraguan Opposition. The committees were headed, respectively, by Representative Hamilton and Sen. Daniel K. Inouye, D-Hawaii. Finally, an independent counsel was appointed under the Ethics in Government Act to investigate whether any crimes had been committed.

The activities of the Iran-contra affair were managed and directed by the staff of the National Security Council (see Chapter 1), principally Vice Adm. John M. Poindexter, who was national security adviser during most of this time, and Marine Lt. Col. Oliver L. North, an NSC staff member. North worked largely through private individuals recruited for that purpose. Various officials of the State Department and the CIA played a subordinate role. Participation by the Defense Department was minimal.

The report of the congressional committees that investigated the affair said it "was characterized by pervasive dishonesty and inordinate secrecy." [37] All the established processes of the government had been ignored or bypassed. The regular procedure for considering covert action in the NSC had not been followed. The affair had gone forward despite the strongly stated opposition of the secretaries of state and defense. The Tower Commission found that "on one or more occasions Secretary Shultz may have been actively misled by VADM Poindexter." [38]

Poindexter maintained that Congress had no right to legislate restrictions that applied to the president or his staff, strongly implying that the president was above the law. He readily admitted that he withheld information from Congress and directed others to do the same: "Our objective here all along was to withhold information." [39] His reason was simply that if Congress had known, it might have objected and interfered with the policy. North went further and held Congress responsible for making the whole operation necessary in the first place:

"The Congress is to blame because of the fickle, vacillating, unpredictable, on-again-off-again policy toward the ... contras."[40] In other words, if Congress had given the president what he wanted to begin with, the president's staff would not have had to controvert the will of Congress. That attitude would relegate Congress to a role of appropriating money on request, without asking questions.

Even when the NSC staff encountered objections from the secretaries of state and defense, it went ahead anyway. Although some of the CIA bureaucracy raised objections, North said Casey was excited by the idea of a permanent "off-the-shelf" covert-action capability that would be so secret it could be controlled only by those who had access to the secret numbers of Swiss bank accounts. (Casey himself could not be questioned. He underwent brain surgery in December 1986 and died in May 1987.) The staff took special pains to deceive Congress. Poindexter kept the contra diversion even from the president himself. Or so it seemed to the investigators at the time. Later, Tower suggested in his memoirs that Reagan might have been part of a "deliberate effort" to cover up the involvement of White House Chief of Staff Donald T. Regan.[41]

The congressional committees produced a report that was subscribed to by all the Democrats and two of the four Senate Republicans, William S. Cohen of Maine and Paul S. Trible, Jr., of Virginia. The other Republicans issued a dissenting minority report. There were also thirteen sets of additional views issued by individual members or groups of members.

The principal conclusion of the majority report was as follows:

Covert actions should be consistent with publicly defined U.S. foreign policy goals. Because covert operations are secret by definition, they are of course not openly debated or publicly approved. So long as the policies which they further are known, and so long as they are conducted in accordance with law, covert operations are acceptable. Here, however, the Contra covert operation was carried out in violation of the country's public policy as expressed in the Boland Amendment: and the Iran covert operation was carried out in violation of the country's stated policy against selling arms to Iran or making concessions to terrorists. These were not covert actions, they were covert policies: and covert policies are incompatible with democracy.[42]

Members of the committees generally took the view that they had asked appropriate questions before the Iran-contra affair came to light (for example, was the Boland amendment being complied with?) but had received dishonest answers. This represented a breakdown of the system, for which Congress was not responsible. The remedy was to fix the system. This was the approach taken by the Framers of the Constitution in providing for checks and balances.

Other people with intelligence oversight experience on Capitol Hill were not willing to let Congress off so easily. In their view, the intelligence committees might have been asking appropriate questions, but they were not asking enough people. The affair was closely held in the NSC staff, but there were people in the CIA, and even in the State Department, who knew at least something about it but who were not asked. One knowledgeable source has stated that the affair was known to sixteen people at the State Department and fifty-five at the CIA.

In the summer of 1991, Lawrence E. Walsh, the independent counsel who had been appointed to investigate the possibility of criminal actions in the affair, was still at work. He had obtained convictions or guilty pleas in the cases of nine defendants, including Admiral Poindexter (obstruction of inquiries, false statements, destruction of documents, and obstruction of Congress); Colonel North (altering documents, accepting an illegal gratuity, aiding and abetting in the obstruction of Congress); and Robert McFarlane, North's predecessor as national security affairs adviser (withholding information from Congress). An appeals court reversed North's conviction on the grounds that insufficient steps had been taken during his trial to protect him from the use of testimony which he had earlier given to the congressional Iran-contra committees under a grant of immunity. In addition, a four-count indictment against CIA officer Joseph Fernandez was dismissed after Attorney General Dick Thornburgh blocked the disclosure of classified information ruled relevant to his defense.

The Iran-contra affair continued to reverberate. In July 1991, Alan D. Fiers, Jr., who had been head of the CIA Central America Task Force, pleaded guilty to two misdemeanor counts of unlawfully withholding information from Congress. And in September, Clair E. George, former CIA deputy director for operations, was indicted on ten counts of perjury and of obstructing investigation of the affair.

Conclusion

After the end of the initial period of congressional neglect, establishment of the House and Senate intelligence committees in the 1970s opened the way to effective oversight of the intelligence community. As we have seen in this chapter, much progress was made, though it was not without problems. But in the 1980s, the predilections of a more activist director of central intelligence (William Casey) and a more ideological president (Ronald Reagan) showed that the existence of the committees was not enough to prevent possibly the worst scandal in the history of the American government. (There is no guarantee that congressional oversight is effective with respect to nonsecret activities, either. The collapse of the savings and loan industry is only one of the more flagrant examples among many that could be cited.)

However, intelligence does present a special problem, and it is one that neither Congress nor the White House had solved in the early 1990s. The lesson of the 1980s for Congress is that it should be unremitting in the questions it asks. If more questions had been asked of more people, the Iran-contra scandal might have been prevented, or at least stopped before it reached its ultimate dimensions.

Going down this road leads to a form of micromanagement—an excessive congressional concern with details, which the executive branch feels impinges on its administrative prerogatives and which in any case diverts Congress from larger concerns. Congress might, for example, be moved to pass more—and more detailed—Boland-type amendments. Micromanagement is a sore point in executive-legislative relations, but it is one way in which Congress responds when the executive appears to ignore legislative intent or flout statutory prohibitions.

These concerns are most acute in the case of covert action, but they apply to intelligence activities across the board. The intelligence community has become a large, sprawling, unwieldy bureaucracy. The intention of the National Security Act of 1947 was that the director of the CIA, wearing his other hat as director of central intelligence, would bring order out of this bureaucratic chaos. The feasibility of that approach is increasingly subject to question.

What alternative arrangements would work better? How does the intelligence community preposition itself to deal with changing world politics and problems? In the end, we come back to how to deal with the basic contradiction of secret activities in an open society. This was well defined by Representative Beilenson, chairman of the House Intelligence Committee, as "how policies originally pursued in secret can be brought into the open in ways that will allow for a debate on their secrets without ending their utility." [43] Or, as Representative Hamilton, a former chairman of the committee, put it: "Secret policies are prone to error and lack the kind of accountability that ensures they will be consistent with United States interests. An open process produces policies that are better and more likely to receive sustained public support." [44]

Notes

1. S. Res. 21, 94th Cong., 1st sess., 1975, establishing the Select Committee to Study Governmental Operations with Respect to Intelligence Activities, which was chaired by Senator Church.
2. George Lardner, Jr., "Amid Defense Cuts, Intelligence Funding Allocations May Shift," *Washington Post,* October 9, 1990.
3. House Armed Services Committee, *Intelligence Authorization Act for Fiscal Year 1989,* H. Rept. 100-591, pt. 2, Dissenting Views.

4. *Congressional Record,* daily ed., 101st Cong., 2d sess., August 3, 1990, S12300. Remarks of Senator Cohen.

5. *Congressional Record,* daily ed., 101st Cong., 2d sess., October 17, 1990, H10021.

6. Merle Miller, *Plain Speaking: An Oral Biography of Harry S Truman* (New York: G.P. Putnam's Sons, 1973), 391.

7. Francis O. Wilcox, *Congress, the Executive, and Foreign Policy* (New York: Harper and Row, 1971), 86.

8. *Executive Sessions of the Foreign Relations Committee* (Historical Series), 86th Cong., 2d sess., 1960, vol. 12, 251-404 (released November 1982).

9. These hearings have since been published. See *Executive Sessions of the Senate Foreign Relations Committee* (Historical Series), 87th Cong., 1st sess., 1961, vol. 13, pt. 1 (released April 1984).

10. Peter Wyden, *Bay of Pigs: The Untold Story* (New York: Simon and Schuster, 1979), 149 (also 122-123, 146-151). Other good accounts of this meeting are in Arthur M. Schlesinger, Jr., *A Thousand Days: John F. Kennedy in the White House* (Boston: Houghton Mifflin, 1965), 251-252; and in J. William Fulbright with Seth P. Tillman, *The Price of Empire* (New York: Pantheon, 1989), 164-166.

11. Seymour M. Hersh, "Huge CIA Operation Reported in U.S. against Antiwar Forces, Other Dissidents in Nixon Years," *New York Times,* December 22, 1974.

12. For text, see *New York Times,* January 16, 1975.

13. S. Res. 21, 94th Cong., 1st sess., 1975.

14. H. Res. 982, 94th Cong., 2d sess., 1976.

15. *Congressional Record,* daily ed., 96th Cong., 2d sess., June 3, 1980, S6147.

16. Dispatch by George Lardner, Jr., *Washington Post,* December 9, 1981.

17. Ann Devroy and George Lardner, Jr., "CIA Honors Supporters," *Washington Post,* March 7, 1991.

18. George Lardner, Jr., "McCurdy: No 'Shrinking Violet,' " *Washington Post,* February 7, 1991.

19. *Congressional Quarterly Weekly Report,* February 9, 1991, 383.

20. Ann Devroy, "Liberals on Intelligence Panel Worry White House," *Washington Post,* February 8, 1991.

21. See Title VIII of the Intelligence Authorization Act for Fiscal Year 1990 (50 U.S.C. 403q).

22. *Congressional Quarterly Almanac, 1989,* 548.

23. Ibid., 549.

24. Memorandum of Disapproval for the Intelligence Authorization Act, Fiscal Year 1991, November 30, 1990. *Weekly Compilation of Presidential Documents,* vol. 26, no. 48, December 3, 1990, 1958-1959.

25. Senate Select Committee on Intelligence, *The National Intelligence Estimates A-B Team Episode Concerning Soviet Strategic Capability and Objectives* (Committee Print, 95th Cong., 2d sess., 1978).

26. Ibid., 5-6.

27. House Permanent Select Committee on Intelligence, *Iran: Evaluation of U.S. Intelligence Performance Prior to November 1978* (Committee Print, January 1979), 5-7.

28. House Permanent Select Committee on Intelligence, *U.S. Intelligence Performance on Central America: Achievements and Selected Instances of Concern* (Committee Print, 97th Cong., 2d sess., 1982), 1.

29. *Report of the Select Committee on Intelligence, United States Senate, January 1, 1987 to December 31, 1988*, S. Rept. 101-219, 101st Cong., 1st sess., 1989, 15.

30. Sharon LaFraniere, "FBI Violated Order, Magistrate Says," *Washington Post*, February 7, 1991.

31. House Permanent Select Committee on Intelligence, *Intelligence Authorization Act, Fiscal 1987*, H. Rept. 99-690, pt. 1, 99th Cong., 2d sess., 1986, 7.

32. A good account of the development of the covert action program against Nicaragua is given in a dispatch by Don Oberdorfer and Patrick E. Tyler, *Washington Post*, May 8, 1983. See also House Permanent Select Committee on Intelligence, *Amendments to the Intelligence Authorization Act for Fiscal Year 1983*, H. Rept. 98-122, pt. 1, 98th Cong., 1st sess., 1983.

33. *Congressional Record*, 97th Cong., 2d sess., December 8, 1982, 29457.

34. As quoted in *New York Times*, March 29, 1984, and April 5, 1984.

35. Text of news conference in *New York Times*, February 22, 1985.

36. *Weekly Compilation of Presidential Documents*, March 27, 1989, 420.

37. House Select Committee to Investigate Covert Arms Transactions with Iran and Senate Select Committee on Secret Military Assistance to Iran and the Nicaraguan Opposition, *Iran-Contra Affair*, H. Rept. 100-433, S. Rept. 100-216, 100th Cong., 1st sess., 1987, 13.

38. *The Tower Commission Report: The Full Text of the President's Special Review Board* (New York: Bantam Books and Times Books, 1987), 81.

39. House Select Committee, *Iran-Contra Affair*, Report, 123, 142, 387.

40. Ibid., Hearings, 100-107, pt. 1, 191.

41. Associated Press, "Tower Book Accuses Reagan of Coverup," *Washington Post*, November 30, 1990.

42. House Select Committee, *Iran-Contra Affair*, Report, 17.

43. *Congressional Record*, daily ed., October 17, 1990, H10022.

44. Ibid., H10040.

CHAPTER 7

Trade Policy

The growing importance of economics in foreign policy has been a principal reason for the increase in congressional assertiveness. It is in connection with economic issues that foreign policy and domestic policy become inextricably mixed. Nowhere is this more evident than with respect to trade. This chapter examines congressional action on foreign trade as a case study of an area of foreign policy that has direct and immediate domestic effects.

The Constitution gives Congress two foundations for involving itself in foreign trade policy. First, Congress is given the power "to lay and collect Taxes, Duties, Imposts and Excises . . ." (Art. I, Sec. 8). All bills for raising revenue must originate in the House of Representatives (Art. I, Sec. 7), and a great deal of foreign trade policy is concerned with duties, or tariffs, on imports, so this provision involves the House in foreign policy in a most important way. (The Senate can amend a revenue bill, but only after it has first passed the House.) Second, the Constitution gives Congress the power to "regulate Commerce with foreign Nations . . ." (Art. I, Sec. 8). Thus, Congress has power over foreign trade even apart from its taxing power.

The last sixty years have seen sweeping changes in Congress's approach to using these powers. In 1934, Congress gave up much of its power over trade by delegating it to the president. In 1974, Congress began to take this power back. By 1991, Congress faced the dilemma that had led it to delegate power in the first place: whether to micromanage trade policy by acting on individual items or simply to reserve to itself the last word on approving or disapproving trade agreements.

A serious problem that heightened congressional interest in foreign trade beginning in the second term of the Reagan administration was the enormous excess of imports into the United States over exports out of the United States. It was generally recognized that this problem could not be resolved without also dealing with the government's budget deficit, the dollar's position in international markets, and even the U.S. economy's efficiency. Thus, the foreign and domestic questions were so interrelated that none could be considered in isolation from the others.

It is with respect to such questions that members of Congress most keenly feel conflicting pressures from their constituents and from larger interest groups. One group wants to be protected from imports of a particular product; another group wants to be able to buy the same product at the lowest possible price. Trade issues tend to bring out the parochialism in Congress.

The late 1980s and early 1990s also brought a reconsideration of the fundamental U.S. approach to trade: Should the United States continue to pursue an open multilateral trading system, as had been its policy since the 1940s, or should the United States work through bilateral agreements and the creation of trading blocs, as exemplified by the U.S.-Canadian Free Trade Agreement and the proposed similar agreement with Mexico? Related to this was the issue of whether the United States should move toward an industrial policy in which a closer partnership between government and business would manage trade.

Background

The tariff is one of the oldest issues in U.S. politics. In the beginning, when the government had far fewer sources of revenue than it has today (there was no income tax, for example), the question was whether tariffs should be levied for revenue only or whether they should be used to protect industry against foreign competition. In general, agricultural interests, whose power base was the great southern plantations, wanted low tariffs. Farmers exported what they produced and relied on imports for many of the things they used; they did not want the prices of these imports increased by tariffs. On the other hand, manufacturing interests, centered in the North, wanted protection from the competition of European goods, and tariffs provided that protection precisely by raising the prices of imports. Over time, the Democratic party became identified with low tariffs or free trade, and the Republican party became identified with high tariffs or protectionism.

The first revenue act passed by the first Congress in 1789 relied mainly on tariffs, and they remained the principal source of the federal government's revenue for more than a century. But that first act also declared in favor of protection as a principle. President George Washington had said that U.S. industries should be promoted and that the country should be "independent of others for essential, particularly for military, supplies." [1]

The strongest statement of the case for a protective tariff came from Alexander Hamilton, the first secretary of the treasury, in his famous *Report on Manufactures* in 1791. Among other things, he argued that tariffs would protect "infant industries" from competitors who were already established abroad. He also made the point that an expansion of industry would permit the employment of more women and children, thereby making them "more useful." [2] In the twentieth century, this argument has been taken up by many of the industrializing countries of the Third World, while voices have been raised in Congress to keep out the products allegedly made by child labor in Third World sweatshops.

As the U.S. economy became more complex during the nineteenth and twentieth centuries, so did congressional consideration of tariff bills. So fierce were the conflicting pressures that, following the deliberations on one such bill, Sen. Arthur Vandenberg, R-Mich., a member of the Finance Committee, expressed to a staff member the hope that "the Lord will take me before I have to deal with another tariff bill."

Protectionism reached its height with passage of the Smoot-Hawley Act of 1930, an omnibus trade measure named after its principal sponsors, the chairmen of the Senate Finance and House Ways and Means committees, respectively. Smoot-Hawley almost doubled tariffs, raising them from an average of 26 percent to an average of 50 percent. This provoked retaliation against U.S. goods by other countries, and world trade plummeted, intensifying the Great Depression.

Congress Yields Power

The Roosevelt administration, coming to office in 1933, adopted a new approach to trade, which was embodied in the Reciprocal Trade Act of 1934. This act authorized the president to negotiate reciprocal tariff reductions of up to 50 percent with other countries. Further, under what was known as the *most-favored-nation principle,* concessions granted to one country would automatically be extended to all others (though certain kinds of exceptions were allowed).

Thus, Congress would no longer write tariffs into law item by item. Instead, within limits set by Congress, tariffs would be negotiated with the nation's trading partners by the president or his representatives. This represented a considerable shift of power from the legislative to the executive branch, and that was one of the issues during congressional consideration of the 1934 act. Finally, and especially since the institution of the income tax in 1913, the tariff had become a minor source of revenue. It was now purely a question of trade policy.

By 1945, much of the tariff-cutting authority of the 1934 act had been used. But since the cuts were measured from the high levels enacted in Smoot-Hawley, the 50 percent reduction did no more than return tariffs to their pre-1930 level. Hence, early in 1945, President Franklin D. Roosevelt asked for, and Congress gave him, authority to negotiate cuts of 50 percent in the existing rates. Later, the president was authorized to cut 15 percent from the 1955 level and in 1958 to cut 20 percent from that level. By 1961, 39 percent of U.S. imports were entering free of duty, and tariffs on the remainder averaged only 12 percent. The three decades from 1930 to 1960 had seen a major change in U.S. trade policy, almost all of it produced by presidents using authority delegated by Congress.

The General Agreement on Tariffs and Trade.   World War II seriously disrupted international trade. Efforts to restore it in the immediate postwar period brought another major change in trade policy, not only for the United States but for its principal trading partners as well. In 1947, twenty-three major trading countries, including the United States, drew up the General Agreement on Tariffs and Trade (GATT). This provided the ground rules by which international trade has been conducted and trade agreements negotiated ever since. It came into force on January 1, 1948. By 1991, 107 countries had adhered to it.

President Harry S. Truman did not submit GATT to Congress. Instead, he committed the United States to it under the authority of the Trade Agreements Act of 1945. Many members of Congress complained that this was stretching the authority of that act, but Congress did not seriously challenge U.S. membership in GATT. Congress did, however, refuse to approve U.S. membership in the International Trade Organization (1948) and the Organization for Trade Cooperation (1955), both of which were intended as administrative bodies for GATT. Neither came into being, mainly because of U.S. nonparticipation. These were two of the few times between 1934 and 1974 that Congress asserted its trade powers in a major way.

The Reciprocal Trade Act of 1934 had moved trade policy from unilateral U.S. determination to bilateral negotiation. GATT made the negotiating forum multilateral. GATT's basic principle is nondiscrimination. Most-favored-nation treatment is fundamental to it; a trade concession extended to one nation must be extended to all nations. Thus, the phrase "most favored nation" becomes something of a misnomer. A nation receiving this treatment is really not favored above most other nations; it is the nation *not* receiving it that is discriminated *against*.

The thrust of GATT is trade liberalization, and there have been a number of multilateral negotiations under its auspices. By its fortieth anniversary on January 1, 1988, GATT had brought average tariffs down from 40 percent to 5 percent. Partly for this reason, there had been an increase in nontariff barriers and "voluntary" restraint agreements, and these new devices assumed greater importance in debates over trade policy.

Trade Expansion Act of 1962.   During the 1930s, 1940s, and 1950s, the Reciprocal Trade Act of 1934 was extended eleven times. By itself, this fact indicated a degree of reluctance in Congress to delegate its authority to the president; the successive delegations were always for short periods. The eleventh extension expired in 1962. President Kennedy decided to let it expire and sought to replace it with a new bill, embodying a new trade policy.

The impetus for this change was the formation in 1958 of the European Common Market, whose original members were West Germany, France, Italy, Belgium, the Netherlands, and Luxembourg. (It was expected that Great Britain would eventually join as well, as indeed it did.) The Common Market, which has since evolved into the larger European Economic Community (EC), created a single economic entity comparable to the United States, one that presented major opportunities and challenges to U.S. trade. The chief opportunity was access to the enormous and growing market in Europe, which opened prospects for substantial increases in U.S. trade. The challenge was to ensure that this market would remain open to the United States. There was a fear in Washington that the Common Market might become closed to outsiders, for it was big enough that such a step would not be wildly impractical. It was felt that the United States had to be forthcoming itself if it was to maintain its access to Europe.

Kennedy asked Congress for five-year authority to cut tariffs by 50 percent and to remove them completely on products traded predominantly between the United States and the Common Market. The president included in the bill he sent to Congress a provision for adjustment assistance to workers and companies hurt by imports. According to his counsel, Theodore C. Sorensen, Kennedy put this provision in the bill both for bargaining purposes and in order to make it easier for organized labor to support the bill. Even at that, Kennedy did not expect it to pass.[3] But it did pass, and it has since become a fixed part of U.S. trade policy.

The Trade Expansion Act of 1962 also created the position of special representative for trade negotiations. This official was to be responsible directly to the president and was to be in charge of all trade negotiations. This represented a major shift of power within the

executive branch. In the Reciprocal Trade Act of 1934 and its successors, Congress had delegated much of its power over tariffs to the
president, but the president had exercised this power mainly through
the State Department. In the 1962 act, Congress transferred the power
to this new official and at the same time reduced the president's
flexibility in organizing the executive branch. The moving force behind
this change was Rep. Wilbur D. Mills, D-Ark., then chairman of the
House Ways and Means Committee. By 1962, along with many others in
Congress, Mills had lost confidence that the State Department would
put U.S. trade interests ahead of diplomatic objectives. Creating the
position of special representative for trade negotiations directly under
the president not only removed negotiations from State but avoided
putting them in the Commerce Department, where they would probably
have been even more exposed to special interest pressures and jealousies.

Congress Reclaims Its Power

The negotiating authority provided by the 1962 act expired in 1967,
and Congress did not act on President Johnson's request for an
extension to 1970. For the first time since 1934, the president had no
authority to negotiate trade agreements. This was the first hint that the
congressional mood was changing. It was possibly related to a general
deterioration in executive-legislative relations during the late 1960s.

When President Nixon came to office in 1969, he asked that this
presidential authority be restored, though by that time there were few
tariffs left to cut. However, Congress was then in a different mood,
disposed toward restricting imports by means of nontariff barriers
(NTBs). Thus, the House response to Nixon's request was a trade bill
that placed quotas on imports of shoes and textiles and provided for
quotas on other products whenever imports reached specified shares of
the U.S. market. The bill also wrote into law the oil-import quotas that
President Eisenhower had established by proclamation in 1959. The bill
was killed by a filibuster in the Senate, but it revealed the strongest
protectionist sentiment in Congress since the days of Smoot-Hawley.
Congress was moving to assert itself again in trade policy, and in a way
that President Nixon and his successors did not like.

In 1973, the other members of GATT were ready to engage in
another round of trade negotiations, the so-called Tokyo Round. But
the government of the world's biggest trading nation, the United States,
found itself without authority to participate. GATT marked time while
Congress considered another trade bill. It took two years.

The main reason for the delay was tangential to trade: It had to do
with Jewish emigration from the Soviet Union (see Chapter 8).

The bill that emerged, the Trade Act of 1974, was noteworthy in other respects for the emphasis it put on NTBs—a reflection of the fact that most tariffs had been negotiated away—and for the steps it took to reclaim some of the authority that Congress had previously delegated. The president was authorized for five years to negotiate further tariff reductions: the elimination of tariffs of 5 percent or less and reductions of up to 60 percent in higher duties. The president was also authorized to increase tariffs by between 20 and 50 percent.

But Congress reserved to itself the power to review most of the other actions the president was permitted to take under the act. Agreements dealing with NTBs, amendments to GATT substantial enough to require changes in U.S. law, and bilateral trade agreements with Communist countries all had to come back to Congress for specific approval. Special so-called *fast-track* rules were provided for congressional consideration of these matters so as to preclude filibusters or other delaying tactics. An important feature of the fast-track procedure was that amendments were prohibited. An agreement had to be approved or rejected as submitted by the president, and within ninety days. Congress thereby gave up its right to pick an agreement apart or to load it down with special interest amendments; but it retained the last word. Congress could, if it wished, reject an agreement in toto and tell the president, in effect, to try again.

Another noteworthy provision of the 1974 act was that it authorized the president to meet the longstanding desire of less developed countries for nonreciprocal tariff preferences. This had been one of the GATT membership's declared objectives for the Tokyo Round. The outcome was the Generalized System of Preferences, whereby industrial nations give favorable treatment to the products of less developed countries without expecting reciprocal treatment. This nonreciprocal feature was a significant departure for GATT from its firm adherence to most-favored-nation treatment. It was a kind of twentieth-century reverse application of the protection for infant industries that Hamilton had urged, and it contributed to such explosive growth in Hong Kong, Singapore, Taiwan, and South Korea that they became known as the "four tigers" of international trade. By 1987, the U.S. trade deficit with the four tigers exceeded its deficit with all of Western Europe, $32.6 billion to $25.1 billion. U.S. electronics companies were making components in Asia and importing them duty free for assembly. Japanese companies were moving production facilities from Japan to the four and exporting from there to the United States. In January 1988, the Reagan administration withdrew the generalized preferences from the four, on the ground that the preferences had served, or more than served, their purpose.

The Reagan Years

The decade of the 1980s brought profound changes to the international economic position of the United States, along with changes in the way world trade, world business, and world finance were organized and carried on. The most dramatic of these changes were the following:

- At the beginning of the decade, the United States was the world's biggest creditor nation. By the end of the decade, it had become the biggest debtor.
- In 1980, the United States had a surplus of $1.9 billion in its international balance of payments. In 1990, it had a deficit of $99 billion.[4]
- In 1980, the deficit in the federal budget was $74 billion. In 1990, it was $220 billion. (The federal budget last showed a surplus—$3.2 billion—in 1969.)
- A change that had long been building in world trading patterns became starkly clear: some less developed countries were no longer less developed. Prominent in this group were Brazil, Mexico, South Korea, Taiwan, and Singapore.
- The multinational corporation, largely a post-World War II phenomenon, came to dominate world business as never before, and it became more truly multinational, with Japanese firms joining American and European companies.
- The world's money and securities markets never closed. The end of the business day in New York was the beginning of the business day in Tokyo, and modern telecommunications tied all the markets together instantaneously.

Each of these changes affected each of the others, and all of them taken together affected the problems with which trade policy had to deal and the environment in which it was made. Some of these interrelationships are imperfectly understood even by experts, but the effects on the day-to-day lives of Americans and the consequent impact on Congress are no less real. Let us examine each in turn.

The Foreign Debt

A country's foreign debt is measured by what economists call its *net international investment position*—that is, its total investments of all kinds abroad minus the total investments of foreigners in the country in question. *Investment* in this context means what is sometimes called an IOU but what economists call a *claim on resources*. It includes bank deposits, notes, bonds, stocks, land, and shares of ownership in factories and other businesses. When Americans have these investments abroad, they are considered assets of the United States; when foreigners have them in the United States, they are considered liabilities. At the end of 1981, the United States had a positive net of $141 billion in international investment. At the end of 1988, it had a negative position of $532.5 billion—a change of $673.5 billion in seven years.

There is nothing good or bad per se about a country's having a foreign debt. The United States had one through most of its history. Much of the industrial and other growth that occurred after the Civil War was financed by foreign money. The United States did not become a creditor until World War I, when it lent large sums to its European allies. What was striking about the change in the U.S. position in the 1980s was its scale and the suddenness with which it occurred.

The foreign debt of the United States is related to its deficits in foreign trade and in the federal budget. The deficit in foreign trade means that the United States has been importing more than it has been exporting. It has therefore been sending more dollars abroad than it has been earning in foreign currency. In order for this to happen, and to continue happening, foreigners had to be willing to hold dollars— that is, to invest them in the United States. Foreigners were willing to do this, and the cumulative effect was to increase foreign investment in the United States and thus to increase the foreign claims on U.S. resources.

The deficit in the federal budget likewise had to be made up with borrowed money, and a great deal of this came from foreigners. (The deficit could have been financed through higher taxes, but that encountered great political resistance.)

The United States has serviced its foreign debt—that is, paid interest on it—by borrowing more, but in the long run the debt can be serviced only by developing a continuing surplus in the balance of payments. Hence, there has been pressure to increase exports and to decrease imports. However, a U.S. trade surplus would not be universally welcome in the rest of the world. A U.S. surplus is some other country's deficit. Many nations depend on exports, including exports to the United States, to provide jobs, economic growth, even political stability. If the United States is selling more than it is buying, at least some other countries will be buying more than they are selling. The rich countries (Japan, Germany) can afford this; the poor, or even the not-so-poor, countries (Brazil, Mexico, India, Korea) cannot.

There is another complication. The Third World has an international debt of its own, amounting to approximately $1 trillion, much of it owed to U.S. banks. If this debt is ever to be repaid, the Third World has to have a trade surplus.

The Trade Deficit

A country with a large surplus in its receipts from foreign investment needs to have a deficit in its balance of trade. Otherwise, its debtors will not earn enough to be able to pay the interest on their loans. Great Britain was such a country in the fifty years before World War I. The United States was such a country in the forty years after World War II. U.S. net earnings from foreign investment peaked at $31 billion in 1981 and thereafter declined until they turned negative by $913 million in 1989.

Conversely, a country with a deficit in its receipts from foreign investment needs to have a surplus in its balance of trade. Otherwise, it will not earn enough to be able to pay the claims of its foreign investors. But in 1990, the United States had a trade deficit of $109 billion, and that was only the latest in an unbroken series going back to 1976. The cumulative balance of trade deficit, 1976 through 1989, was $1,040 billion. The offsetting net investment balance for the same period was $257 billion. This large and persistent trade deficit generated a great deal of political pressure to reduce it, pressure to curtail imports and to increase exports.

The effort to reduce imports has been made mainly through nontariff barriers, especially quotas—that is, quantitative limits on imports of particular products. There was remarkably little talk about the traditional method of raising tariffs, though that is the method preferred in orthodox economics. The pressure for quotas came from the industries that were experiencing the greatest competition from imports. Notable among these were textiles, shoes, automobiles, and certain kinds of steel.

To meet the needs of these industries and to blunt their opposition, the Reagan administration and its immediate predecessors negotiated a number of "voluntary restraint" agreements with the principal exporting nations. In the case of textiles, for example, there was the multinational Multi-Fiber Agreement. Foreign exporters were willing to accept these voluntary restraints in order to avoid more rigorous restrictions. In some cases, the exporters adapted to the numerical limits in the agreements by shipping their more expensive and more profitable models instead of cheaper models. Japanese automobiles are an example. The effect was a double reduction in competitive pressure on the U.S. automobile industry: less overall competition (that is, fewer units imported), and less pressure to produce the smaller, cheaper models that the Japanese had been so successful with. Textile quotas had the effect of increasing clothing prices.

The focus of efforts to improve market accessibility was Japan. It was with Japan that the U.S. trade deficit was the largest—as much as

$50 billion to $60 billion a year in the late 1980s. Part of this was accounted for by the large numbers of Japanese automobiles, television sets, and other products that entered the United States, but Japan also has what many Americans believe are bizarre and discriminatory import requirements. For example, Japanese have defended barriers to the import of skis with the argument that Japanese snow is different from snow in the rest of the world. Rice is not only a staple of the Japanese diet; it is so important in the Japanese culture that it has become a symbol of near-religious significance. Rice growers are also important supporters of the ruling Liberal Democratic party. The import of rice is totally banned. So strongly do the Japanese feel about this that in March 1991 the organizers of an American trade fair were threatened with arrest unless they removed sealed packages of American-grown rice from a display.

Japan has tried to block implementation of a GATT finding that its restrictions on farm imports violated GATT rules. Little by little, restrictions have been eased. A 1988 agreement liberalized import rules on beef and citrus fruits. U.S. beef exports rose from $500 million in 1986 to an annual level of $1 billion in 1991. Exports of telecommunications equipment, medical equipment, and pharmaceuticals also increased. By 1990, the U.S. trade deficit with Japan had decreased to $40 billion.

For their part, the Japanese have complained about the United States. In 1991, when Lee Iacocca of Chrysler asked for more restrictions on Japanese automobile exports to the United States, Japanese pointed out that Chrysler itself imports Japanese engines. "It's very hard to say what is an American company and what isn't an American company," said Shinichi Tanaka of Honda. He added that 54 percent of the Hondas sold in the United States are made there.[5]

It should also be pointed out that Japan is by no means the only country to apply peculiar requirements to imports. The European Community has sought to exclude American beef because of a widely used growth hormone which some European environmentalists find unacceptable. Further, as noted, the United States also enforces nontariff barriers against perhaps 25 percent of its imports.

The drive to increase competitiveness emphasized increasing the productivity, that is, the efficiency, of U.S. industry. As used in economics, *productivity* is the value of what is produced divided by the cost of producing it. Productivity is affected by many variables—among others, the extent of mechanization, the level of investment and taxation, the level of wages and fringe benefits, the skill of the labor force, the cost of raw materials, the cost of energy, even the cost of transportation (hauling raw materials to a plant and finished products away from it). Some of these factors are determined, or significantly

influenced, by a company's management (and the efficiency of management is itself an important element in productivity). Some are determined by collective bargaining between management and labor. Some
are determined by Congress when it makes broad domestic policies,
frequently with little consideration of the impact on foreign trade. Some
(for example, the cost of petroleum) are determined by factors external
to the United States and largely beyond American control.

During the 1980s, as foreign competition intensified, U.S. efforts to
increase productivity likewise intensified and began to show results. By
.the middle of the decade, productivity began to rise after a long period
of stagnation or even decline. But then other, sometimes contradictory,
considerations came into play.

One of these had to do with the environment. Measures to protect
the environment (for example, to control air and water pollution)
frequently raise the cost of production and therefore reduce productivity. This presents a stark trade-off in public policy. Do Americans want
a cleaner environment or more productive industry?

Another consideration had to do with social policy. The cost of
labor is not simply what workers take home in their pay envelopes each
week. It is also the cost of other benefits they receive as a part of their
employment. Some of these are required by law; some are the result of
collective bargaining; some are company policy. Taken together, they
may cost an employer as much as, or even more than, direct wages.
Examples are contributions to Social Security and perhaps other
retirement plans, paid holidays and vacations, paid sick leave and
health insurance, day-care centers for employees' children, subsidized
lunchrooms, transportation, and uniforms. Here is another trade-off:
How much of this are Americans willing to give up for more international competitiveness? (Political pressure runs more to increasing these
benefits than to reducing them. And the argument is made that some of
them, through reducing absenteeism, increase productivity.)

Finally, there is the consideration of national security. Some of the
country's most competitive industries rely on advanced technology, and
the Department of Defense has been reluctant to approve export
licenses for fear that the technology would find its way into unfriendly
hands. A study by the National Academy of Sciences concluded that
what it saw as unnecessary controls on high-technology exports cost $9
billion in sales and 188,000 jobs in 1985.[6]

In 1990, in extending the Export Administration Act, Congress
enacted liberalized criteria for issuing export licenses. However, President Bush vetoed the bill on unrelated grounds after Congress had
adjourned. At the same time, the president issued an executive order
which put into effect many of the new export license criteria. In
February 1991, the Senate passed a similar bill for the second time.

Finally, the United States took a number of steps to reduce the value of the dollar relative to other currencies. When the dollar has a high value, goods made in the United States are relatively costly to foreign buyers and goods made abroad are relatively cheap to U.S. consumers. That situation makes it harder for U.S. companies to sell their products abroad and at the same time encourages people in the United States to buy foreign-made goods, thereby increasing the trade deficit. During the first half of the 1980s, the dollar had an exceptionally high value: one dollar was worth as much as 3 German marks and almost 250 Japanese yen.

The reasons for these exchange rates were complex. One was that, during this period, interest rates in the United States were higher than in the rest of the industrialized world. This provided an incentive for foreigners to invest in the United States and created a demand for dollars, which in turn drove the price of dollars up. On the one hand, the United States benefited from this inflow of foreign money, for it made it possible to finance the budget deficit and service the growing foreign debt. On the other hand, it contributed significantly to the trade deficit. And it also increased the foreign debt and therefore the future requirements for servicing it.

Beginning in 1985, in part because of an agreement on exchange rates among the principal industrial powers, the dollar started to lose value against other currencies. By 1988, it had lost about half its value against the yen and almost that much against the mark and other major European currencies. It then began to creep upward again, but in 1991 it was still well below its high of the preceding decade. In any event, the trade deficit began to decline. From a high of $160 billion in 1987, it dropped to $109 billion in 1990, the lowest level since 1983. But the good news is accompanied by bad. The higher price of imports raises the general price level, thus contributing to inflationary pressures. And the lower volume of imports reduces the incentive for U.S. industry to become more competitive.

The Budget Deficit

President Reagan was elected in 1980 on a platform calling for lower taxes and higher defense spending. He moved immediately to put this program into effect. In 1981, Congress passed a bill cutting taxes substantially, and it adopted a budget increasing defense spending. (It reduced spending on some other programs, but on balance total government spending increased.) The theory behind this tax cut was that it would stimulate the economy so much that total tax revenues would actually increase. Sen. Howard Baker, R-Tenn., the majority leader at the time, called it a "riverboat gamble." It did not pay off, and the United States entered an era of twelve-digit budget deficits (that is, $100,000,000,000 and up). In the ten years from 1980 to 1989, the cumulative deficit was $1.6 trillion. The 1990 deficit added $200 billion more.

After the first year, Congress and the president were at loggerheads over the budget and taxes for the remainder of the Reagan administration. The president adamantly refused to consider raising taxes while just as adamantly insisting on maintaining a high, and even a rising, level of defense spending. Congress, for its part, refused to make significant cuts in nondefense spending. There were minor compromises from time to time, but none big enough to affect the deficit substantially.

"No new taxes" was also an integral part of George Bush's winning campaign for the presidency in 1988, but in the first two years of the Bush administration three things happened with significant impact on the federal budget, two of them bad. One was the serious decline of the savings and loan industry as the United States slipped into recession. Deposits in savings and loan institutions were guaranteed by the federal government up to $100,000 for each account, and as large numbers of savings and loans failed, the government had to make good on those guarantees. The end of the cold war, Soviet military withdrawal from Eastern Europe and Afghanistan, and the collapse of the Soviet economy opened the possibility of large savings in U.S. defense expenditures. But these were offset, at least in the short run, by the costs of the military buildup in the Persian Gulf, followed by the war, even after allowance was made for the financial contributions of other countries.

In the summer of 1990, before the crisis over Kuwait, the Bush administration and the bipartisan congressional leadership began prolonged and tortuous negotiations that eventually produced an agreement designed to reduce the budget deficit by $500 billion over five years through a combination of tax increases and spending cuts. But neither the savings and loan bailout nor the cost of the war was included.

World Trade

Economic theory holds that everybody benefits if nations produce the goods that they can make most efficiently and buy from other nations those goods that are most efficiently produced elsewhere. A nation's advantage in production might lie in the availability of raw materials, land, or labor, or in any of a number of other things. This is an important part of the rationale for free trade, and it has been the root cause for the relocation of much of the world's production. Cheaper labor has sent the shoe industry from New England to Asia and to

Brazil. More efficient machinery has given the European steel industry a competitive edge, and cheaper labor has established steel industries in Korea, Brazil, and India.

The production of textiles is another example. In the nineteenth century, textile mills sprang up in New England, where water power was plentiful and cheap. The mills bought cotton from the southern states, where it was grown with the comparative advantage of a favorable climate and cheap labor—until the 1860s, slave labor. The cotton was processed in New England by recently arrived immigrants, who also worked cheaply.

In the twentieth century, the machinery of the New England mills became obsolete and relatively expensive to operate. The workers became unionized and demanded higher wages. As a result, many of the mills moved south, closer to the source of supply and into a nonunion environment. Comparative advantage had shifted.

New England members of Congress reacted by trying to force up the cost of southern labor in order to deprive the South of that element of its comparative advantage. They tried to raise the federal minimum wage and supported changes in federal labor laws that would make it easier for unions to organize, bargain, and strike. The debates in Congress on these subjects, although not always expressed this way, were as much about shifting comparative advantage as about liberal or conservative philosophies of labor-management relations.

After World War II, comparative advantage shifted again, beginning particularly in the decade of the 1960s. This time it moved to the newly industrialized countries around the Asian rim of the Pacific Ocean—South Korea, Taiwan, Hong Kong, Singapore, and the Philippines. These countries had the cheapest labor and the most up-to-date machinery. Again there was a reaction from members of Congress, especially those from South Carolina, which had become the center of the U.S. textile industry. They set up a clamor for protectionist trade legislation, mainly in the form of quotas. Though they did not succeed in their efforts, they did apply enough pressure to force the negotiation of a series of voluntary restraint agreements.

Three times between 1985 and 1990 Congress passed a textile import quota bill, and three times the president vetoed it (Reagan twice, Bush once). All of the vetoes were sustained. The textile lobby's basic problem was that it could muster a majority, but not two-thirds, despite efforts to put together a broader coalition.

When President Reagan vetoed the 1985 bill, the House leadership postponed the vote on overriding until August 6, 1986, which was the day before the Multi-Fiber Agreement was due to expire. Proponents were hopeful that an uncertain future for MFA would win new converts, especially with a national election only three months away. But a new agreement was reached on August 1 with tighter limits on textile imports. The House voted 276 to 149 to override the veto, but that was less than two-thirds.

In the 1985 bill, the Senate had added import restrictions on shoes and copper. After the House passed another textile quota bill in 1987, textile interests in the Senate tried a different tack: preferential quotas were provided on shoes and textiles for countries that increased their purchases of U.S. farm commodities. Congress did not complete action on this bill until September 1988. President Reagan vetoed it again, and again the House failed to override, 272 to 152. Congress passed a similar bill in 1990, President Bush vetoed it, and the House failed to override by almost the same vote, 275 to 152.

Multinational Corporations

The multinational corporations that came into prominence after World War II might be thought of as being American or Japanese or German, for example, depending on their origin and where they have their main offices. In fact, however, they operate largely without regard to national boundaries, taking them into account only when national laws make it advantageous for them to do so. They not only operate across national boundaries; they form joint ventures with each other.

These characteristics sometimes seem to make the traditional approaches of trade policy irrelevant. Trade policy has traditionally been based on the premise that a product has a "national origin." But the products of multinational corporations frequently have no particular national origin, or they may have so many that trying to single out one becomes a meaningless exercise. The "Japanese" television sets that Sony sells in the United States are assembled in Tijuana, Mexico, from parts made in San Diego, California. In 1987, Sanyo announced plans to export color television sets from the United States to Japan. Ford builds Mercury automobiles in a plant in Hermosillo, Mexico, where most of the equipment is Japanese and most of the parts are supplied by Mazda, a Japanese automobile manufacturer. By 1987, Japan was the second largest foreign investor in Mexico, after the United States.

The International Financial Market

When securities and financial markets open in the morning in Tokyo, Hong Kong, and Sydney, it is early evening the day before in New York. Shortly after Tokyo closes, Frankfurt opens. By the time Frankfurt closes, New York is open; and by the time Chicago closes, Tokyo is almost ready to open again. Somewhere a market is always open. Money is transferred among all of these markets literally at the speed of light. Large banks and securities firms maintain branches and offices around the world to serve their customers in this global market.

An international trade in financial services such as banking has existed since the days of the sailing ships, but it is now much larger and is carried on with great rapidity. It developed after the negotiation of GATT, and the absence of rules covering it is one of GATT's glaring omissions. The issue of including financial services in the GATT framework became one of the contentious issues in the Uruguay Round, the latest in the series of GATT negotiations, which was begun in 1986.

Congress Acts on Trade

The 1980s were a decade of mounting concern in Congress over the economy and especially the deficits in the budget and the balance of payments. This period also saw something of a reversal in the roles of the two political parties.

As noted earlier, the manufacturing industries historically had supported tariffs and other forms of trade protection, whereas agriculture had supported free trade or something close to it. After the Civil War, the Republican party came to be identified with industry and protectionism, the Democratic party with agriculture and low tariffs. These identifications were reinforced by the Smoot-Hawley Act, passed by a Republican Congress and signed by a Republican president in 1930, and by the Reciprocal Trade Act, which was one of the proudest achievements of the Democratic administration of Franklin Roosevelt.

As U.S. foreign trade grew, beginning with the Reciprocal Trade Act and even more after World War II, support for tariffs in the industrial sector began to erode. More U.S. businesses were producing for export, a circumstance that led business leaders to favor liberal trade policies and to oppose high tariffs. On the other hand, organized labor, with which the Democratic party became identified especially in the 1930s, had always had protectionist tendencies, viewing tariffs as a way of protecting jobs. Finally, the Reagan administration pressed its ideological views more than most administrations do, and its ideology was firmly rooted in the principle of private enterprise free of governmental intervention, in the form of tariffs or otherwise.

Consequently, during the 1980s the Democrats in Congress tended to take the lead in pushing for trade legislation, while the Reagan administration and congressional Republicans resisted what they saw as protectionism. These lines were not absolute, and the differences were frequently more of degree than of principle. Many Democrats, such as Rep. Sam Gibbons of Florida, chairman of the Trade Subcommittee of the Ways and Means Committee, remained staunch free traders, while many Republicans, especially those from districts feeling pressure from imports, wavered in their opposition to protectionist measures. The two senators from South Carolina, Republican Strom Thurmond and Democrat Ernest F. Hollings, were united in fighting for textile import quotas.

At the same time, some people began to question whether the United States was even debating the right issues. Until the 1930s, the United States had fixed its tariffs unilaterally. Then, under the Reciprocal Trade Act tariffs were negotiated bilaterally and were effectively generalized by the most-favored-nation principle. Beginning in the 1940s, this was given momentum under GATT, which preached, usually with American support, the doctrine of a steadily more liberal, multilateral, nondiscriminatory world trading system. Under the pressures of the 1980s, the question was raised of whether the GATT policy was correct or whether alternative (or supplementary) policies should be considered.

One of these alternative policies was managed trade. The policy would favor a closer identification of government with industry, and vice versa, for a more vigorous promotion of American exports and more vigorous resistance to discriminatory measures by foreign countries. An example frequently cited was the relationship between Japanese industry and the Japanese Government's Ministry of International Trade and Industry (MITI).

Another alternative was reversion to bilateralism, especially in dealing with foreign practices that discriminated against American exports. In the Omnibus Trade and Competitiveness Act of 1988 (102 Stat. 1107, P.L. 100-418), Congress provided what came to be known as the Super 301 procedure (after the section number of the law), in which the trade representative was required to announce the priority countries to be targeted for discriminating against American exports. In 1989, Trade Representative Carla Hills listed Japan (superconductors, communications satellites, and lumber), Brazil (import licenses generally), and India (insurance and foreign investment generally). In 1990, Japan and Brazil were off the list; India remained. The law provided for a range of retaliatory measures, but the Bush administration generally preferred to rely on negotiations. Super 301 was not in effect after 1990.

Finally, there was the alternative of trading blocs. The European Economic Community (EC) was scheduled to achieve economic integration and become the world's biggest market in 1992. A free trade agreement between the United States and Canada became effective January 1, 1989, and negotiations were contemplated to make Mexico a part of a North American Free Trade Area. Looking further ahead, some officials of the Bush administration envisioned expanding the free trade area to other countries of the hemisphere. Ten Asian countries, plus the United States and Canada, formed Asia-Pacific Economic

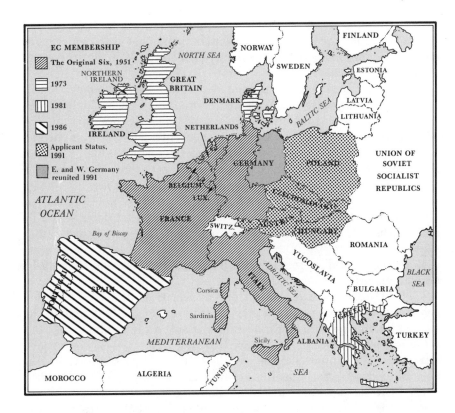

EC MEMBERSHIP

- The Original Six, 1951
- 1973
- 1981
- 1986
- Applicant Status, 1991
- E. and W. Germany reunited 1991

Europe 1991 and the EC Members

Cooperation (APEC) in 1989. Thus, there were in place in 1991 three enormous economic blocs, some more rudimentary than others, but all with potential for growth. The prospect was raised that world trading rules could be made through negotiations among these blocs. That, in turn, raised the question of what would happen to countries that were not a part of any bloc and also the question of whether the blocs would become ingrown and protectionist or outgoing and liberal.

The 1988 trade act had a little of all of these considerations in it. It also had a good deal of economic policy not directly relevant to trade. But by and large, it continued the traditional approach of multilateral negotiation and nondiscriminatory treatment.

The Trade Bill of 1987-1988

The specific need for a new trade bill arose because the president's negotiating authority was scheduled to expire at the end of 1987. An extension was necessary for the United States to participate in the

Uruguay Round of GATT negotiations, so named because of the country in which the negotiations began in September 1986 before being moved to Geneva. The House passed a trade bill in 1986, but there was no action in the Senate.

This 1986 bill was something of a grab bag of policy, but it contained one amendment, sponsored by Rep. Richard A. Gephardt, D-Mo., which was highly controversial and strongly opposed by the administration. The Gephardt amendment prescribed a complicated process by which the president would negotiate agreements for annual 10 percent reductions in the U.S. trade deficit with those countries with which the deficit was largest. Gephardt identified these as Japan, Taiwan, and West Germany. If the negotiations did not have the desired result, tariffs would be raised. If tariffs did not work, quotas would be imposed unless the president determined that this would cause "substantial harm" to the U.S. economy. Gephardt was a Democratic presidential candidate in the early primaries in 1988, and in 1989 he became majority leader of the House.

The Democrats won control of the Senate in the 1986 election, giving them control of both houses of Congress for the first time in the Reagan administration, and immediately made a trade bill one of their top priorities. Gephardt, with more than 180 Democrats as cosponsors, introduced a bill much like the one the House had passed in 1986. But in other respects, the opening of the trade debate obliterated party lines. Fifty-six senators, including both the majority and minority leaders, signed on as cosponsors of a bipartisan bill. More than 150 members of both parties organized the Congressional Caucus on Competitiveness, also with bipartisan leadership in both houses. When the House Ways and Means Committee opened its hearings February 5, 1987, Minority Leader Robert H. Michel, R-Ill., told the committee, "There has been a complete about face in the administration's approach to trade." [7] Chairmen Dan Rostenkowski, D-Ill., of Ways and Means, and Lloyd Bentsen, D-Tex., of Senate Finance, agreed.

The spirit did not last. The administration sent its own bill to Congress, a massive compendium of two thousand pages, which was mainly a wish list and which was not seriously considered on its merits. The bills that had originated in Congress were complicated enough, and congressional procedures for handling them were more so. Ways and Means in the House and Finance in the Senate attended to the fundamental provisions dealing with trade. Separate but somewhat related bills came from thirteen committees in the House and eight in the Senate—another manifestation of the fragmentation and dispersal of power that has characterized Congress since the mid-1970s. The bills were consolidated in the offices of the Speaker of the House and the majority leader of the Senate and were considered in each of the two houses as a single bill. This was called a trade bill, but in fact it was much broader—an economic policy bill.

In the House, the Trade Subcommittee of Ways and Means substantially modified the Gephardt amendment. The subcommittee version required negotiations with countries having "excess trade surpluses" (defined as exports that were 175 percent of imports) if those countries had a pattern of unfair trade practices. Retaliation was required if the negotiations failed, unless it would do "substantial harm" to the national interest. The subcommittee bill also provided for retaliation in a variety of cases involving "unjustifiable" trade practices.

There was a school of thought in the House, especially among Democrats, that the bill's tough tactics would strengthen the administration's negotiating posture. It was reported that some in the administration thought so, too. Nevertheless, in a letter to members of the Ways and Means Committee, Trade Representative Clayton Yeutter wrote, "If the provisions [objectionable] to the administration are not either eliminated or substantially improved, I would find it exceedingly difficult to recommend that the president sign any trade bill including them." [8]

The centerpiece of the House debate was the amendment that Representative Gephardt offered from the floor. Similar to his amendment that had prevailed in 1986, it went beyond the protectionist provisions of the Ways and Means Committee bill, and it split the Democratic leadership. Speaker Jim Wright, D-Texas, supported it; Majority Leader Thomas S. Foley, D-Wash., and Ways and Means chairman Rostenkowski opposed it. It set off feverish lobbying activity by the administration and by business and labor groups.

The AFL-CIO strongly supported the amendment and made it one of the crucial votes on the scorecard that labor keeps on members of Congress. Business was split. The automobile and steel industries and some companies such as Motorola were for the amendment. Chrysler president Lee Iacocca even urged Chrysler suppliers to work for it. Opponents included the National Association of Manufacturers, the Chamber of Commerce of the United States, the Emergency Committee for American Trade (an organization of corporate chief executive officers), and such companies as Hewlett-Packard (a high-tech manufacturer that exports), and K Mart (a retailer that sells low-price imports).

In the end, the Gephardt amendment passed the House by a vote of 218 to 214. The whole bill, as amended, was then sent to the Senate by a vote of 290 to 137.

The Senate debated its own bill, a 1,013-page document that came from Finance and eight other committees. The trade provisions were generally along the lines of the House bill minus the Gephardt amendment, but there were plenty of other things in it that the administration did not like. The administration particularly did not like (and business liked even less) a requirement that companies give workers notice of intended plant closings.

The bill passed the Senate in July by a vote of 71 to 27. This was more than enough to override a veto, but it was not indicative of Senate sentiment on the merits of the bill. Some senators cast yea votes simply to keep the legislative process moving. (That was true also in the House.)

Given the length and complexity of the bills and the number of committees involved, the process was cumbersome at best. It took until October to appoint conferees to resolve differences between the House and Senate bills, and then there were 199 of them—155 from the House and 44 from the Senate. They organized themselves into seventeen subgroups, some of which had sub-subgroups. In the meantime, the principal conferees, those from Ways and Means and Finance, had become preoccupied with the negotiations between Congress and the administration over reducing the budget.

On November 10, Minority Leader Michel moved to instruct the House conferees to recede from the Gephardt amendment. His motion was defeated, 175 to 239, but that was more reflective of House views on procedure than on substance.

Nothing more was done in 1987. By the time the second session of the 100th Congress convened in January 1988, the bill was caught up in the presidential election campaign. The House trade conferees, led by Rostenkowski and Sam Gibbons, D-Fla., wanted to dump the Gephardt amendment. But Gephardt was then an active candidate for the Democratic presidential nomination. He was making trade policy a major issue, and his House colleagues did not want to disavow him in those circumstances. So one of the major issues in the bill was held in abeyance until March, when Gephardt, not having done well in the early primaries, withdrew from the race. At that point, the Gephardt amendment was removed from the bill, and the conference began to move forward.

The final bill was less protectionist than either the House bill or the Senate bill had been and also carried fewer extraneous provisions, but one of these concerned plant closings: companies were required to give sixty days' notification to workers. Labor strongly insisted on this. Business equally strongly resisted it. The administration was also opposed and promised a veto if the provision stayed in the bill. The remaining Democratic presidential candidates—Massachusetts Governor Michael S. Dukakis and the Rev. Jesse Jackson—announced their support.

The House agreed to the conference report, 312 to 107, on April 21, 1988, with the plant-closing notification and without the Gephardt amendment. Gephardt was one of two Democrats who voted against the conference report. The Senate agreed on April 27 by 63 to 36, not enough to override a veto.

In an effort to gain more votes in the Senate, House Democrats then resorted to a highly unusual procedure. They called up and passed, 253 to 159, a resolution instructing House clerks to remove from the official copy of the bill two provisions restricting the export of Alaskan oil. This would be done before the bill was sent to the president. These provisions had been opposed by Alaska's senators, both Republicans, and the Democrats hoped that this conciliatory gesture would win the Alaskans' support. But this ploy was blocked in the Senate by the bill's opponents, and the bill went to the president unchanged.

The expected veto came May 24. The president's veto message cited the Alaskan oil provisions, but it was clear that his principal objection was to the plant-closing notification.[9] The House overrode the veto the same day it was received by a vote of 308 to 113. The Senate sustained the president June 8 by voting 61 to 37 to override.

Congress then took the plant-closing provisions out of the trade bill and passed them separately. President Reagan allowed this separate bill to become law without his signature. Finally, Congress passed the trade bill without the plant-closing or the Alaskan oil provisions, but the bill still had to clear one more hurdle before going to the president. The bill extended to December 31, 1989, the authority for ethanol (alcohol for fuel) processed in certain Caribbean plants to enter the United States duty free even though it did not meet the general standard that 35 percent of the product's value had to consist of Caribbean parts and labor. This upset corn state representatives (whose constituents also produced ethanol). Minority Leader Michel tried to eliminate the provision in the House, but lost, 183 to 237. After the Senate had passed the bill, corn state senators got through a concurrent resolution to eliminate that section before sending the bill to the president. This was the same ploy the House had used to get the Alaskan oil provisions out of the earlier bill, although its effort had been rebuffed in the Senate. Now the situation was reversed, and the Senate's provision fared no better in the House.

The bill went to the president as passed, and he signed it August 23, 1988.

Free Trade Agreements

Canada. While Congress was working on the omnibus trade bill in 1987, the Reagan administration was negotiating a free trade agreement with Canada. The agreement was signed January 2, 1988, by President Reagan and Prime Minister Brian Mulroney. It provided for tariffs to be phased out over a ten-year period, though they were low to begin with: Canadian duties on U.S. goods averaged 9 percent; U.S. duties on Canadian goods averaged 4 percent. The agreement also ended some restrictions on cross-border investments and trade in services and provided that no new restraints would be imposed. It guaranteed the United States access to Canadian oil, gas, and uranium. It did not cover government subsidies or intellectual property.

Despite their preoccupation with the trade bill, the Ways and Means and Finance committees considered the agreement informally before it was submitted to Congress, because the submission would trigger the fast-track procedure. In effect, the committees and the trade representative worked out an agreed bill in advance. This bill passed the House August 9, 1988, by a vote of 366 to 40. It passed the Senate September 19 by a vote of 83 to 9, and President Reagan signed it September 28.

The agreement was much more controversial in Canada, where it forced an election and approval was delayed almost to the deadline. The agreement was approved by the Canadian House of Commons August 31, but the Senate (controlled by the opposition Liberal party) demanded an election. This was held November 21 and resulted in a victory for the governing Progressive Conservative party. The agreement received Canada's final approval December 24 and became effective January 1, 1989.

Mexico.   In a meeting in the White House in June 1990, President Bush and President Carlos Salinas de Gortari of Mexico endorsed the idea of a "comprehensive free trade agreement." [10] In February 1991, it was announced that the negotiations would begin during the forthcoming summer and that they would be broadened to include Canada. A new acronym was born: NAFTA, North American Free Trade Area.

The proposed agreement with Mexico was highly controversial. American labor has complained for years about a provision in the U.S. customs law under which parts can be manufactured in the United States, assembled in Mexico, and brought back to the United States with duty paid only on the value added by the assembly. A counterpart Mexican law provides that parts imported into Mexico for assembly are free of Mexican duties if the assembled products are re-exported. These twin provisions led to the establishment of a number of assembly plants (*maquiladoras* is the Mexican term) on the Mexican side of the border to take advantage of much lower wage rates. The AFL-CIO foresaw an acceleration of this trend as well as the relocation of entire manufacturing plants. Environmentalists warned against a flight of industry seeking to take advantage of looser environmental constraints.

Agriculture and business were split. Growers of protected commodities—sugar, peanuts, some fruits and vegetables—were opposed. Other agricultural groups, including the American Farm Bureau Federation, supported the administration: free trade opened the prospect of larger markets in the growing Mexican population for grains and meat. The textile industry was opposed: Mexico was another place for textile plants to relocate, and it was closer (and on that score, more attractive) than the Pacific rim. But big business was by and large supportive of the free trade idea. Big business had long felt itself hurt by Mexico's protectionist trade policy.

President Salinas was changing that policy. A widely respected economist with a Ph.D. from Harvard, he moved to bring down inflation, reschedule Mexico's large foreign debt, attract foreign investment, and open Mexican industry to competition. He particularly wanted the free trade area for the foreign investment it would attract, and to North Americans he held out the prospect of a reduction in illegal Mexican immigration into the United States. "We want to export goods, not labor," he said.[11]

The Bush administration saw the agreement as a means of supporting President Salinas, whose policies were generally welcomed in Washington. It was admitted that the agreement would precipitate the movement of some businesses from the United States to Mexico, but it was argued that in the long run the agreement would contribute to Mexican economic development and therefore make Mexico a better market for U.S. products.

In effect, this argument revived the old slogan of "trade, not aid," which had figured in the debates over foreign aid a generation earlier. And that was precisely what the AFL-CIO saw as wrong with the free trade agreement. Free trade, the AFL-CIO spokesman told the Senate Finance Committee, will substitute for foreign aid. And, he asked, will the development of Mexico be financed by U.S. taxes or by lost jobs?[12]

The Fast-Track Procedure

The North American Free Trade Area was dependent on the fast-track, ninety-day, no-amendment procedure provided by the trade acts of 1974 and 1988. So was any agreement resulting from the Uruguay Round. But fast track, by its own terms, was scheduled to expire June 1, 1991.

The complicated rules governing the matter provided that fast track could be extended if (1) the president notified Congress of his intention to do so by March 1, 1991, and (2) neither house of Congress disapproved of the extension before June 1. This is substantively the same thing as the legislative veto, which the Supreme Court outlawed in

1983 (see Chapter 2); but it is different technically, because fast track has to do with the rules of the House and Senate. The Constitution gives each house the power to make its own rules, and therefore congressional rules do not involve legislation.

On March 1, 1991, President Bush notified Congress of his intention to extend fast track for two years, or until June 1, 1993. Administration officials made it clear that without fast track, there would be no negotiations with Mexico, with Canada, or in GATT. The reason was less the prospect of delay than the prospect that amendments would peck an agreement to death.

The presidential notification set off a furious lobbying campaign pro and con. Opponents of free trade with Mexico, led by the AFL-CIO, sought to generate support for a resolution disapproving the fast-track extension. Supporters, led by the Bush White House, sought votes to kill such a resolution. The only issue before Congress was the procedure under which it would consider a free trade agreement if and when one was ever negotiated.

Supporters of an agreement sought to calm the opposition with assurances that Congress could reject the whole thing if it were so inclined. The White House went further. On May 1 the administration sent an action plan to Congress in which it tried to meet opposition concerns by spelling out guidelines for an agreement: long transition periods (perhaps ten years or more); provision for temporary restoration of duties or other controls in cases of serious injury; tough rules of origin requiring 50 percent or more Mexican content; protection of labor and environmental standards in Mexico.

The administration got a big boost on May 9 when Representative Gephardt, sponsor of the leading protectionist amendment to the 1988 trade bill, announced his support of fast track. Another boost came May 14, when Gephardt joined Ways and Means Chairman Rostenkowski in fashioning a resolution calling on the president to keep the promises of the May 1 action plan which the resolution endorsed and emphasized. This resolution had the advantage of giving members something to vote for to put them on the side of protecting interests that felt threatened by a free trade agreement but without interfering with the negotiating process.

On May 23, the House rejected a resolution disapproving fast-track extension by a vote of 192 to 231. It then passed the Rostenkowski-Gephardt resolution, 329 to 85. The following day, the Senate rejected a resolution of disapproval, 35 to 59.

The debate and vote over fast-track extension was dominated by the prospect of extending the North American Free Trade Area to include Mexico, but the extension was also of crucial importance to GATT and the Uruguay Round. It had not been possible to conclude those negotiations before expiration of the old fast-track authority; without fast-track extension, they would come to naught.·

The principal stumbling block was agriculture, specifically the European Community's Common Agricultural Policy under which it heavily subsidized agricultural production and then further subsidized the export of the surpluses that resulted from the first group of subsidies. This was not different in principle from what the United States had been doing, but by 1990 the U.S. agriculture program was different in two practical respects: (1) the size and scope were on a downward curve, driven in part by budget pressures, and (2) the United States had put all of its agricultural practices on the bargaining table.

By 1990, a substantial part of the world was arrayed against the EC in demanding a change in agriculture policy: The United States; other major agriculture exporting nations (Argentina, Australia, and Canada); and a number of Third World countries. European farmers, especially in France and Germany, exercised their political influence. The concessions offered by the EC negotiators were deemed insufficient by the other parties, and the negotiations broke up in some bitterness in December 1990.

They were resumed in February 1991 after the EC agreed at least to talk about further concessions, but progress was slow. Two other issues, which were high priorities for the United States, remained unresolved. These were services (transportation, insurance, banking) and intellectual property (patents, copyrights, licenses). These areas have not been covered by GATT, but they are of great importance to American business; in 1989 they accounted for about one-third of total world trade ($1.3 trillion out of nearly $4 trillion).[13]

Conclusion

Just thirty years ago, it was axiomatic on Capitol Hill that members who looked after the particular interests of their state or district could vote as they pleased on foreign policy without fear of political repercussions. That piece of political wisdom seems to be valid no longer. The line between local interests and foreign policy has disappeared. Similarly, it is now impossible to separate trade policy from policies affecting the federal budget, the position of the dollar in international finance, Third World debt, the role of multinational corporations, even the condition of education and the cost of social programs. In short, no one element of economic policy can be isolated from the whole. This was recognized during debates on the trade bill in 1987 and 1988. Indeed, strictly speaking, the trade bill was not even a trade bill; it was an economic policy bill. No one thought that the trade provisions by themselves would close the U.S. trade deficit.

Because of the importance to Congress of local interests, Congress tends to take a more parochial view of trade policy than does the president, who has a broader constituency. Before Congress surrendered most of its tariff-setting powers to the president in 1934, it typically approached trade policy item by item. Congress abandoned this approach after it began to reclaim some of its powers in 1974. Trade legislation of the last two decades has been couched in more general, less product-specific, terms.

It is characteristic of Congress to delegate power, or to acquiesce in the presidential use of power, as long as Congress finds the results satisfactory. It is characteristic of presidents to attempt to retain all the power they have acquired, however it came to them. Congress began to be uncomfortable with the results of U.S. trade policy in the 1970s. By the 1980s, Congress was seriously disturbed. The range of issues in trade policy by then encompassed the whole of the economy. There was no simple mechanism for delegating to the president powers confined to trade. Policy making had become an endless series of trade-offs. If the value of the dollar goes down to discourage imports, there is the danger of inflation. If interest rates go up to attract foreign investment, there is the danger of depression. Finally, the process of making policy amid these precarious circumstances is complicated by cumbersome congressional procedures.

If trade policy could ever have been made on the basis of purely trade considerations, that day had long passed by 1991. When Congress deals with trade, it deals with the whole intricate question of economic policy, an area in which everything is related to everything else, frequently in ways that do not immediately meet the eye. The way in which the world economy operates has changed. The challenge of the 1990s is to find the best way for the American economy to fit into the new world structure and practices.

Notes

1. Quoted in Charles A. Beard and Mary R. Beard, *The Rise of American Civilization* (New York: Macmillan, 1942), 349.
2. Nathan Schachner, *Alexander Hamilton* (New York: D. Appleton-Century, 1946), 276.
3. Theodore C. Sorensen, *Kennedy* (New York: Harper and Row, 1965), 411.
4. U.S. Congress, Joint Economic Committee, *Economic Indicators*, 100th Cong., 2d sess., April 1988, 36. Also, 102d Cong., 1st sess., March 1991, 36.
5. Paul Blustein, "Rice Incident, Iacocca Demand Fuel Japanese Fears," *Washington Post*, March 27, 1991. See also Blustein, "Scrapping Trade Barriers to U.S. Beef," *Washington Post*, March 31, 1991.
6. National Academy of Sciences, *Balancing the National Interest: U.S. National Security Export Controls and Global Economic Competition* (Washington, D.C.: National Academy Press, 1987).

7. *Congressional Quarterly Weekly Report,* February 7, 1987, 238.
8. Ibid., March 21, 1987, 519.
9. *Congressional Record,* daily ed., 100th Cong., 2d sess., May 24, 1988, H3531-H3532.
10. Larry Rohter, "U.S. and Mexicans Cautiously Back Free-Trade Idea," *New York Times,* June 12, 1990.
11. Ibid.
12. *Congressional Quarterly Weekly Report,* February 9, 1991, 362.
13. Stuart Auerbach, "Hills Stumps to Shift Focus to GATT Talks," *Washington Post,* May 3, 1990.

CHAPTER 8

Human Rights and Democracy

Two threads that had been weaving in and out of American foreign policy for two hundred years came together as the country's third century began. One thread was concern for human rights; the other, concern for democracy. Both stemmed from a deeply rooted preoccupation in the American psyche with the relationship between a government and its people. A corollary of this concern is the belief that the United States should be a model for others to follow.

Ronald Reagan, both as a candidate and as president, was fond of citing an early description of America as "a shining city on a hill." (The quotation is from John Winthrop, the first governor of Massachusetts Bay Colony, writing in 1630: "For we must consider that we shall be like a City upon a Hill; the eyes of all people are on us." [1]) The Declaration of Independence in 1776 flowed from "a decent respect to the opinions of mankind," and went on to assert as self-evident certain God-given "unalienable rights," including those to "life, liberty, and the pursuit of happiness."

In a Fourth of July address in 1821, Secretary of State John Quincy Adams drew a distinction between setting an example and forcing that example upon others:

> Wherever the standard of freedom and independence has been or shall be unfurled, there will her [America's] heart, her benedictions and her prayers be. But she goes not abroad, in search of monsters to destroy. She is the well-wisher to the freedom and independence of all. She is the champion and vindicator only of her own. She will commend the general cause by the countenance of her voice, and the benignant sympathy of her example. [2]

In 1849-1850, the Senate debated this question with respect to a specific proposition arising out of the European revolutions of 1848: Should the Foreign Relations Committee inquire into the advisability of suspending diplomatic relations with Austria as a measure of disapproval of its suppression of the revolt in Hungary? The Senate answered this particular question in the negative, but throughout the remainder of the nineteenth century both Congress and the executive branch protested from time to time against the persecution of Jews in Russia and other countries, the massacre of Armenians in Turkey, oppression of the Irish, and mistreatment of prisoners in Siberia.[3]

In his address to Congress seeking a declaration of war against Germany in 1917, President Wilson went beyond the immediate *casus belli* of German unrestricted submarine warfare and said:

> We are glad . . . to fight thus for the ultimate peace of the world and for the liberation of its peoples, the German peoples included: for the rights of nations great and small and the privilege of men everywhere to choose their way of life and of obedience. The world must be made safe for democracy. Its peace must be planted upon the tested foundations of political liberty. . . . We are but one of the champions of the rights of mankind. We shall be satisfied when those rights have been made as secure as the faith and the freedom of nations can make them.[4]

On the eve of U.S. involvement in World War II, President Franklin Roosevelt looked forward to "a world founded upon four essential human freedoms"—freedom of speech, freedom of religion, freedom from want, and freedom from fear.[5]

Congress Gets Involved

Despite these recurring themes in American history—all the way from John Winthrop to Franklin Roosevelt—it remained for Congress to begin, tentatively at first, to bring them into focus as operating foreign policies. At first, congressional concern amounted to no more than uneasiness over the kinds of foreign governments the United States was identified with, particularly in Latin America.

During the late 1950s, Latin American dictators were being ousted and replaced by democratic governments. The United States had long been criticized by liberals, both at home and throughout Latin America, for having supported the dictators. (The degree and nature of support varied; what some of the critics meant was that Washington had not actively aided groups seeking a dictator's overthrow, and this was quite a different matter.)

The criticism reached its most dramatic point in May 1958, when Vice President Richard Nixon, on a tour of South America, was set upon by anti-U.S. rioters in Caracas, Venezuela. Later Nixon set forth what remains the most sensible policy: "A formal handshake for dictators; an *embraso* [he probably intended *abrazo,* meaning embrace] for leaders in freedom." [6]

Congressional involvement in human rights questions was largely rhetorical until the late 1960s. By that time, the wheel of Latin American political history had taken another turn, moving away from democratic governments and back toward the old pattern of dictatorships.

Police Aid

The human rights issue was posed with painful clarity with respect to Brazil in the aftermath of a military takeover of the government in April 1964. The previous government had led Brazil into a chaotic situation, with inflation running 100 percent a year or more. The new government adopted economic policies that started Brazil on the road to what was widely described as a miracle of economic development. Using draconian measures of repression, it also energetically set about a transformation of Brazilian political institutions.

These two policies led to opposite reactions in the United States. The business community and the Johnson administration hailed the sound economic policies and the favorable treatment of foreign investment evident in Brazil under the new regime. Others deplored the disregard for civil liberties and the growing reports of torture by Brazilian authorities. The reaction of the State Department was to downplay the reports of human rights violations and to continue its warm embrace of the new government.

The situation in Brazil focused attention on one of the minor activities of the Agency for International Development (AID)—its public safety program. This program had been started a few years before to help selected developing countries deal with growing problems of public order, ranging all the way from street demonstrations to terrorist activities. The purpose of AID's public safety program was to provide equipment (tear gas and radios were two of the most popular items) and training for foreign police and paramilitary forces in techniques of crowd control and investigative work. One of the countries that received this kind of foreign aid was Brazil.

As reports of police torture in Brazil increased, charges were made that the AID public safety team was somehow involved in these abuses. Given the difficulty during this period of distinguishing between Brazil's police and military, the American military mission in the country was also implicated in these charges. Some of the accusations were quite specific—that torture techniques were part of AID's program of instruction and that torture devices were among the equipment supplied Brazil by the United States.

No reliable evidence was ever found to substantiate these charges. Indeed, the object of AID's public safety program was precisely the opposite: to teach the techniques and to supply the equipment needed for effective law enforcement *without* the use of torture. But the accusations of American complicity in Brazilian violations of human rights persisted. They were made in connection with other countries as well. In Uruguay, for example, an American public safety adviser was kidnapped and murdered by terrorists who accused him of complicity in policy brutality.

By 1971, Senator Church, chairman of the Latin American Subcommittee of the Foreign Relations Committee, was sufficiently exercised about such complaints to hold comprehensive hearings on U.S. policy toward Brazil. These hearings, augmented by subsequent staff reports on Guatemala and the Dominican Republic, demonstrated, at least to the satisfaction of Church and some of his colleagues, that the basic problem of the American public safety program was one of public relations. Police forces in Brazil, Guatemala, and the Dominican Republic were undoubtedly guilty of using excessive force against citizens—to put the most charitable interpretation on the evidence. Through its public safety program, the United States was identified with these excesses.

Because of this unfortunate association, a movement began in the Senate to abolish the public safety program. It eventually succeeded in 1974, after overcoming stiff bureaucratic opposition and some resistance in the House.

Chile

Just as events in Chile brought a turning point in congressional relations with the intelligence community (see Chapter 6), so did they alter Congress's response to the problem of international human rights. The overthrow of President Salvador Allende's regime in September 1973 ushered in a period of mass arrests; prisoners were commonly held incommunicado without charges for long periods. These actions were accompanied by the inevitable allegations of mistreatment and torture. Some of the allegations were impressively documented.

The Nixon administration reacted to the overthrow of Allende and the emergence of the new military government in Chile much as the Johnson administration had reacted to the new government in Brazil in 1964. Although the Nixon embrace was perhaps a trifle less fervent, the administration made no secret of its approval of the downfall of the

Allende government (while deploring the fact that the president had been killed in the process), and it loosened the strings on American loans and grants to Chile.

The initial congressional action (as distinguished from oratory) toward those developments was quite mild. The Foreign Assistance Act of 1973, approved December 17, contained two provisions that did no more than express the sense of Congress. Expressions of the sense of Congress are intended as guidance to the executive branch and do not have the force of law. They are frequently the result of legislative compromise over stronger proposals, which, if cast in mandatory language, would provoke debate and opposition. They are, in short, a means of avoiding a test of strength in Congress while getting some kind of a policy on record. They may also indicate that majority support does not exist in Congress for stronger measures; the administration can usually expect not to be called to account if it does not take the sense of Congress seriously. That was not, however, the case in this instance.

The two human rights provisions in the Foreign Assistance Act of 1973 dealt with the question of political prisoners in general and with the problem of human rights in Chile in particular. With respect to political prisoners in all countries, it was the sense of Congress that the president should deny foreign aid to any government "which practices the internment or imprisonment of that country's citizens for political purposes." [7] With respect to Chile, Congress asked for an investigation by the Inter-American Commission on Human Rights.

After the passage of the Foreign Assistance Act of 1973, Congress became steadily more assertive about Chile and enacted a series of specific limits on aid that could be given that country. In 1974 it placed a limit of $25 million on military assistance. In 1975 it put a ceiling of $90 million on economic assistance, including housing guarantees and sales of surplus agricultural commodities. (During the 1960s American assistance to Chile had sometimes been twice that amount.)

In 1976 Congress prohibited any kind of military assistance, sales, exports, or training; economic assistance was limited to $27.5 million (not including grants of surplus agricultural commodities distributed by charitable organizations). This amount could be increased if Chilean economic performance improved.

In 1981, Congress switched the emphasis. Instead of prohibiting assistance unless the government of Chile was *not* engaging in consistent and gross human rights violations, Congress now would permit assistance if certain positive findings were made. The most important of these were that the government of Chile had made "significant" progress in human rights, that it was not encouraging international terrorism, and that it had cooperated in prosecuting Chileans indicted in connection with the murders of Orlando Letelier and Ronni Moffitt.*

In 1983 the House Foreign Affairs Committee amended the 1984 foreign aid authorization bill to add a further and much tougher precondition: that an elected civilian government be in power. The committee applied this requirement to Argentina as well, and a similar one was applied to Paraguay and Uruguay. However, the bill was not considered by the House, and for the third year foreign aid was financed through stopgap spending authority. In 1986, Congress barred economic aid to Chile and provided that the administration should oppose loans by international financial institutions until Chile ended human rights abuses and took "significant steps" toward restoring democracy. (The same legislation barred aid to any country where the military overthrew an elected government.)

The "significant steps" occurred in 1988-1990. General Augusto Pinochet, who had ruled Chile since the overthrow of Allende in 1973, permitted a referendum in 1988 in which a majority of Chileans voted against his continuance as president. In 1989, Patricio Aylwin, a Christian Democrat, was elected president. He took office in 1990. Although Pinochet remained as commander of the army, Chile was clearly on the road back to democracy, and the congressional strictures enacted during the 1970s and 1980s no longer applied.

A General Human Rights Policy

Congress got in the human rights arena—or briar patch, as some would call it—because of its concern about U.S. identification with the excesses of Latin American dictators. Once involved, Congress globalized the policy and tried three approaches to implementation. First, Congress tried to reshape the foreign aid program to make it an instrument of a general human rights policy. This was largely accomplished by 1980. Second, Congress enacted a host of ad hoc provisions applying to specific countries. Third, since Communist countries do not receive foreign aid, Congress sought to use trade as a lever in those cases.

---

* Letelier was Allende's foreign minister and had earlier been ambassador to the United States. After Allende's overthrow Letelier was imprisoned in Chile for a time and then went into exile in the United States. In September 1976 the car in which he was riding with Moffitt, his research assistant, was blown up on a Washington street by a remote-controlled bomb. An American working for the Chilean intelligence service was convicted of the murders, and three Chilean officials were indicted for their roles in the conspiracy. The Chilean government refused to extradite them.

Foreign Aid

It is one thing to cut off aid to a repressive government for economic infrastructure projects (such as road building or harbor construction) or for balance of payments support; in that case the government is hurt first and most. It is something else to cut off shipments of food; then the people oppressed by the government suffer most.

Congress attempted to deal with this problem by distinguishing between security assistance, on the one hand, and food and development assistance on the other. (In the jargon of foreign aid, *security assistance* is military aid, including military credit sales, military training, and economic assistance directly related to military or political purposes. *Development assistance* is aid directly related to economic progress.)

Security Assistance. The Foreign Assistance Act of 1974 expressed the sense of Congress that

> except in extraordinary circumstances, the President shall substantially reduce or terminate security assistance to any government which engages in a consistent pattern of gross violations of internationally recognized human rights, including torture or cruel, inhuman or degrading treatment or punishment; prolonged detention without charges; or other flagrant denials of the right to life, liberty, and the security of the person.[8]

In cases in which assistance was proposed or furnished to such governments, the president was to inform Congress of the extraordinary circumstances necessitating the assistance. In determining whether a government consistently violated human rights, consideration was to be given to the extent of its cooperation in permitting unimpeded investigations "by appropriate international organizations." This left the president considerable leeway in determining what circumstances were "extraordinary." The requirement for these to be reported to Congress gave Congress the chance to second-guess him and tended to ensure that presidential definitions of *extraordinary* would not be whimsical.

In 1976, Congress rewrote this section of the Foreign Assistance Act of 1974, tightening the standards and procedures. Now, for the first time, Congress did more than withhold aid from human rights violators. It declared that "a principal goal of the foreign policy of the United States shall be to promote the increased observance of internationally recognized human rights by all countries." Security assistance programs generally were to be formulated and conducted "in a manner which will promote and advance human rights and avoid identification of the United States, through such programs, with governments which deny to their people internationally recognized human rights and fundamental freedoms." [9]

Congress tinkered with the law again in the International Security Assistance Act of 1978. For governments consistently and grossly violating human rights, security assistance could not be provided to the police, domestic intelligence agencies, or similar law enforcement agencies, nor could licenses be issued for the export of crime control and detection equipment. Neither could members of the armed forces of such a country receive American military education or training. In each case, exceptions were made if the president certified to Congress that extraordinary circumstances existed. Although Congress had ordered the demise of the AID public safety program in 1974, the 1978 revisions went one step further in preventing the export of crime control and detection equipment (even through commercial channels) to governments with bad human rights records.

In 1979, Congress added the carrot to the stick in its approach to human rights. It directed that in allocating security assistance funds, "the President shall take into account significant improvements in the human rights records of recipient countries, except that such allocations may not contravene any other provision of law." [10] This made explicit what had long been implicit in the legislative requirements for withholding aid from governments that violate human rights. The withholding implied that if human rights performance improved, the aid would be restored. Now Congress as much as said that explicitly. But it left unanswered the weight that should be given to this consideration in the totality of American interests presumably served by security assistance programs.

Finally, in 1980 Congress added the clause "causing the disappearance of persons by the abduction and clandestine detention of those persons" to the acts included as "gross violations of internationally recognized human rights." This was a slap at Argentina, where the military government had been the object of particular complaints over its alleged complicity in the disappearance of some thousands of persons, although the practice is not confined to Argentina.

Development Assistance. In 1974 Congress had attempted to shift the thrust of foreign aid programs from large infrastructure projects (for example, hydroelectric dams) to activities that more directly and immediately affected the lives of the poor (for example, food production, health, education). The following year, when Congress considered the matter of development assistance to governments violating human rights, it faced the problem of how to punish those governments without at the same time punishing the people they were mistreating, among whom needy people were presumably suffering the most. The answer it came up with was to cut off aid to the governments unless the aid was directly benefiting the needy.

This answer at best proved only partially satisfactory. To the degree that the United States helps the needy in a country, it relieves the government of that country of its own obligations to do so. More to the point, it relieves the government of having to face the consequences of not doing so—consequences that are likely to take the form of internal political pressures, social unrest, and possible economic collapse. All of these would be likely to hasten the replacement of the offending government, perhaps by a less oppressive one.

Furthermore, it is next to impossible to operate an aid program, even one limited to helping the needy, without dealing with the country's government. The worse a government's record is with respect to human rights (especially in the Third World), the worse it is also likely to be with respect to honesty and efficiency in public administration.

A case in point is Haiti, which has been chronically misgoverned. During the oppressive regime (1957-1971) of President Francois Duvalier it was impossible for the United States even to carry out free food distribution programs without becoming entangled in red tape and demands for payoffs by government officials. This is why the Kennedy administration stopped trying to operate an aid program in Haiti.

Food. In 1977, Congress amended the Agricultural Trade Development and Assistance Act (P.L. 480, popularly known as Food for Peace) so as to link human rights and the sale of surplus agricultural commodities:

> No agreement may be entered into to finance the sale of agricultural commodities to the government of any country which engages in a consistent pattern of gross violations of internationally recognized human rights ... unless such agreement will directly benefit the needy people in such country.

Congress also produced guidelines as to what would, or would not, benefit the needy:

> An agreement will not directly benefit the needy people unless either the commodities themselves or the proceeds from their sale will be used for specific projects or programs which the President determines would directly benefit the needy people of that country. The agreement shall specify how the projects or programs will be used to benefit the needy people and shall require a report to the President on such use within six months after the commodities are delivered.[11]

These guidelines are lacking in specificity, but they serve to underline the point that regardless of the indirect benefits to governments and others from P.L. 480 sales, the direct benefits must go to the needy. This is perhaps easier to require in legislation than it is to carry out in administrative practice.

Multilateral Aid Programs.   In 1976, Congress ordered the U.S. executive directors of the Inter-American Development Bank and the African Development Fund "to vote against any loan, any extension of financial assistance, or any technical assistance to any country which engages in a consistent pattern of gross violations of internationally recognized human rights . . . unless such assistance will directly benefit the needy people in such country." [12] Limiting aid to what directly benefits the needy is a tougher standard for multilateral lending agencies than for the bilateral aid program. The multilaterals are more likely to finance large capital projects such as port improvements or industrial development programs, in which it is more difficult to show direct benefits to the needy.

In 1977, Congress introduced a positive emphasis on human rights, as distinguished from the approach of denying benefits to countries violating rights. The United States was called upon to use "its voice and vote" in the international financial institutions to advance the cause of human rights, and it was encouraged to channel assistance toward countries other than those with bad human rights records.[13]

This law covered all international financial institutions in which the United States participates except the International Monetary Fund (IMF). With respect to that institution, a 1978 law simply directs the secretary of the treasury to report annually to Congress on the status of human rights in each country that draws on funds made available under the IMF's Supplementary Financing Facility. In 1983, when Congress authorized an increase of $8.4 billion in the American contribution to the IMF, it also required the U.S. executive director of the fund to vote against loans to any country that practices apartheid, or racial segregation. This provision was aimed at South Africa. The law also required a U.S. vote against loans to any country with a Communist dictatorship. Both requirements could be waived if the secretary of the treasury gave Congress thirty days' notice and certified that the loan was in the best interests of a majority of the people of the borrowing nation.

Country-Specific Enactments

At one time or another, Congress has enacted some kind of human rights provisions applying to more than twenty countries singled out by name. A partial list includes Argentina, Armenia, Cambodia (Kampuchea), Chile, El Salvador, Estonia, Guatemala, Haiti, Iraq, Kenya, Korea, Latvia, Lithuania, Mexico, Mozambique, Myanmar

(Burma), Nicaragua, Pakistan, Panama, Paraguay, South Africa, and Uganda. Some of these provisions have been largely hortatory. Most have sought to use foreign aid or investment as levers to bring about improvements in human rights. The most important by far, in terms of the attention Congress has given them, have been those concerning El Salvador and South Africa, and it is to these that we now turn our attention.

El Salvador. El Salvador has traditionally been governed by an alliance of the political elite and the army. The elite consists of the legendary "fourteen families" (actually, somewhat more) whose wealth is based mainly on coffee. The army has had a highly developed esprit de corps stemming from the close relationships that grow among officers during their days at the military academy.

El Salvador was not a one-man dictatorship like Nicaragua (see Chapter 6), but it was governed by a succession of military strong men and juntas which were not above using brutality to suppress their opponents. The Salvadoran record on this score was bad enough that the Carter administration (1977-1981) suspended American foreign aid. Following a coup by younger officers in October 1979, a series of mixed civilian-military juntas tried to implement a program of land reform and other social measures, but with indifferent success.

Violence and discontent, which had been simmering for years, grew into a full-scale civil war and presented the United States with a familiar dilemma. Should it try to persuade a repressive, right-wing government to reform itself and move toward moderation; should it try to moderate a left-wing rebellion; or should it keep hands off? In El Salvador, the United States opted for governmental reform, and the Carter administration reinstated a modest aid program shortly before it left office in January 1981.

President Reagan asked Congress for more aid, and now Congress faced the dilemma. Congress dealt with it by tying continued aid to improved performance with respect not only to human rights but also to political and social reform. The International Security and Development Cooperation Act of 1981 (P.L. 97-113, approved December 29, 1981) made military assistance contingent on a certification to Congress by the president that the government of El Salvador

(1) is making a concerted and significant effort to comply with internationally recognized human rights; (2) is achieving substantial control over all elements of its own armed forces, so as to bring to an end the indiscriminate torture and murder of Salvadoran citizens by these forces; (3) is making continued progress in implementing essential economic and political reforms, including the land reform program; (4) is committed to the holding of free elections at an early date.

In connection with the last point, the Salvadoran government was also required to demonstrate good-faith efforts to reach a political solution of its internal strife which would include a renouncement of further military or paramilitary activity.

The first such certification by the president was required within 30 days of enactment of the act (that is, by January 28, 1982), and others were required at intervals of 180 days thereafter through fiscal years 1982 and 1983 (that is, through September 30, 1983). Each certification was to discuss fully the justifications for each of the four findings required, and the first two certifications could be made only if they included findings that the Salvadoran government had made good-faith efforts to bring to justice those responsible for the murders of six American citizens in December 1980 and January 1981. In the summer of 1983 a separate bill was passed, requiring a report on prosecutions in these cases to be included also in the certification due in July of that year.

President Reagan made each of the four certifications required by this act, and they became increasingly weak in their findings. In January 1983 he said that "the situation is not perfect and the progress was not as great as desired, but it is progress nonetheless." This provoked Sen. Christopher Dodd, D-Conn., to say that certification was "unwarranted" and showed the administration was "going to certify regardless of the circumstances." [14]

The July 1983 certification noted the rise in civilian deaths, the continuing inability of the government to identify and punish those in the military who abuse human rights, and "uneven and disappointing" progress toward solving the murders of four American churchwomen. But it said that those shortcomings were counterbalanced by the establishment of a Peace Commission to persuade all factions to participate in elections, an amnesty program that had resulted in the release of five hundred political prisoners, and extension of land reform. In an accompanying letter, Secretary of State Shultz wrote, "It is evident that the record falls short of the broad and sustained progress which both the Congress and the administration believe is necessary for the evolution of a just and democratic society in El Salvador."

This led Sen. Patrick J. Leahy, D-Vt., to say, "There has been no progress in the nuns' case and civilian deaths have gone up. If we can have certification under these circumstances, I cannot imagine how bad things would have to get before this administration would not certify that the conditions of the law had been met." [15]

Washington's Salvador-watchers were encouraged in May 1984 when Jose Napoleon Duarte, a Christian Democrat, was elected president over the candidate of the right-wing ARENA party allied with the armed forces. (ARENA is the Spanish acronym for National Republican

Alliance.) Duarte was warmly welcomed on two visits to Capitol Hill, where he promised to end human rights abuses, control the military, and investigate right-wing death squads.

Congress dropped the human rights conditions on aid, but not for long. A new certification requirement was included in the urgent supplemental appropriation bill, and on July 12 the State Department certified that the Salvadoran government had in fact made significant progress in curtailing killings of civilians by death squads. Critics agreed.

Throughout the rest of the 1980s and into the 1990s, congressional consideration of El Salvador revolved around what sort of standards to require and how much (and what kind of) aid to withhold pending presidential certification that the standards had been met. Frequently when it seemed that an agreed policy was in place, some new incident would revive the debate. In 1985, four U.S. marines were among a number of people killed in apparently random firing on an outdoor restaurant in San Salvador. Leftists were accused. In 1987, Salvadoran human rights activist Herbert Anaya Sanabria was assassinated. Right-wing death squads were suspected. The same year, the government pardoned two national guardsmen convicted of killing two American agricultural advisers in 1981, and the Salvadoran National Assembly passed a general amnesty for leftist guerrillas, government soldiers accused of atrocities, and right-wing death squad members. The 1980 killers of Archbishop Romero, still unknown, were excepted. In 1989, the Salvadoran attorney general was killed by a car bomb in April and the minister of the presidency was assassinated in June. Leftist rebels were suspected. In October, the headquarters of the antigovernment National Federation of Salvadoran Workers was wrecked by a bomb, with ten killed and thirty-five wounded, including two Americans.

The murders with the widest reverberations occurred in November 1989, when six Jesuit priests, their cook, and her daughter were shot by thirty uniformed men at the University of Central America. This brought a new round of proposals in Congress to tie aid to investigation and prosecution of the case. Both parties in the House appointed task forces, the Democrats under Rep. Joe Moakley, D-Mass., and the Republicans under Rep. Bud Shuster, R-Pa. After an investigation aided by the FBI and Scotland Yard, the Salvadoran government charged Col. Guillermo Alfredo Benavides (the highest ranking officer ever charged in a human rights case) and eight other military personnel. But in a report in May 1990, the Moakley task force said the investigation was at a "virtual standstill" and expressed doubt that those charged would ever be punished. Shuster said he thought the report was generally "fair." [16] Congress voted to withhold half the military aid requested for El Salvador for fiscal 1991 ($42.5 million out of $85 million), pending satisfactory progress in the case. A new and potent factor at work was lobbying by American Jesuits in favor of a tough stand.

In January 1991, the shoe was again on the other foot. Rebels shot down a U.S. helicopter with a crew of three. The pilot was killed in the crash, but the other two crewmen survived and were shot by the rebels, who at first denied and then admitted the killings.

Developments in El Salvador also reopened the debate over aid to police forces, the activity that had first involved Congress in human rights twenty years before. Beginning in 1985, the Reagan administration began asking for waivers to prohibitions on aid for police. Congress provided waivers a step at a time and rather grudgingly. First, Congress said that police aid could be given to democratic countries that did not have standing armies and that did not violate human rights. In Central America, this meant Costa Rica. Then Congress added El Salvador to the approved list and injected a new element—aid directed to improvements in the criminal justice system.

Another new element was stop-and-go negotiations between the government and the rebels. After some false starts in Mexico, negotiations began again under UN auspices in Caracas in May 1990. After the American helicopter crew was killed in January 1991, the Bush administration announced it would release the $42.5 million in military aid which had been withheld because of the Jesuits, but that deliveries would be suspended for sixty days in an effort to encourage the negotiations. Deliveries remained suspended until June, when the administration released $21 million in spare parts, medical supplies, and field rations.

Negotiations between the government and the rebels continued in Venezuela and Mexico. They were said to be making progress, but as of August 1991 there had been no conclusion. One concrete step was agreement to ask the United Nations to monitor human rights. The Security Council responded by establishing the UN Observer Mission in El Salvador, which deployed 110 persons in July, the first such activity undertaken by the United Nations in a member state.

South Africa.   In the space of less than twenty years, Congress did a complete reversal with respect to human rights in the neighboring countries of Zimbabwe and South Africa. As the British colony of Southern Rhodesia, Zimbabwe was the scene of a particularly intractable racial dispute over the political arrangements for the transition to independence. In 1965, the white-dominated colonial government, under Premier Ian Smith, unilaterally declared its independence. Great Britain, backed by the United Nations, refused to recognize this declaration, which it held to be illegal.

The UN Security Council voted trade sanctions against the rebellious Rhodesian government in December 1966, and in January 1967 President Johnson issued an executive order for U.S. compliance. The principal commodity involved was chrome ore, which the United States began to import from the Soviet Union instead of Rhodesia. In 1971, the Senate adopted a convoluted amendment offered by Sen. Harry F. Byrd, Jr., Ind.-Va., to the defense authorization bill which had the effect of requiring the import of chrome from Rhodesia if any was imported from Communist countries. The amendment survived repeated attempts to repeal it, backed up by importunings from Presidents Nixon and Ford.

Finally in 1977, President Carter got authority to waive it, and then withstood attempts to reenact it. The issue became moot in 1979-1980 when the Rhodesia dispute was settled, the nation of Zimbabwe became independent, and white rule gave way to black. The debate over the Byrd amendment was couched in terms of support for the United Nations and protection of supplies of strategic materials, but racial questions were never far below the surface.

By contrast, beginning in 1984 Congress set up a continuing clamor against apartheid (that is, total racial segregation by government decree) in South Africa. The initial congressional activity was directed not against the State Department or the White House but against the South African embassy. Walter E. Fauntroy, the District of Columbia's nonvoting delegate in the House of Representatives, started it with a sit-in in the ambassador's office. As the South Africans learned to be careful about whom they admitted to their building, the protests moved outside. Large numbers of prominent individuals, in and out of Congress, deliberately violated the limits on demonstrations outside embassies so that they could be photographed while being taken away by the police.

In 1985, Congress moved from photo opportunities to serious legislating. It passed a bill prohibiting bank loans to the South African government, as well as most nuclear and computer sales. It also prohibited the import into the United States of the South African gold coins known as Krugerrands. The congressional votes were impressive: 295 to 127 on passage in the House (380 to 48 on the conference report) and 80 to 12 on passage in the Senate. But these majorities disguised the depth and extent of the opposition.

The Reagan administration was opposed to the bill on the grounds that by hurting the South African economy, the bill would hurt most the people (blacks) that its purpose was to help. Yet the numbers on the Hill indicated that a veto was almost certain to be overridden. In these circumstances, after the House had passed the conference report but before the Senate took it up, the president signed an executive order embodying most of the bill's provisions. Thus did he attempt to mollify, at least to some extent, the proponents of sanctions while retaining for himself the ability to waive or repeal them at will. There was a further maneuver in the Senate so extraordinary that it deserves special notice. The Senate leadership simply removed the official copy of the bill from the Senate chamber, thereby preventing the Senate from acting on it.

The issue was kept alive by continuing racial violence in South Africa and by the approach of the 1986 congressional elections in the United States. In June 1986, the House took up a bill which built on, and went beyond, the sanctions that Reagan had decreed by executive order the previous year. It would have banned new investments and loans in South Africa as well as imports of South African coal, steel, and uranium. And it would have clamped down on energy development and computer sales unless the South African government moved to free political prisoners and negotiate with black leaders.

On the House floor, Rep. Ronald V. Dellums, D-Calif., offered an amendment with much broader sanctions. It would suspend virtually all trade with South Africa and require U.S. businesses to leave within six months. Surprisingly, it passed on a voice vote. Whether it would have passed on a roll call is uncertain, but nobody asked for one. Opponents of sanctions were following the strategy that as the bill became more extreme, it would encounter more difficulty in the Senate and perhaps collapse of its own weight.

This strategy turned out to be mistaken. Instead of having the anticipated effect, the Dellums amendment simply shifted the spectrum of the debate: it made what had previously looked like extreme proposals seem moderate, and it made moderate proposals seem weak.

With the bill before the Senate Foreign Relations Committee, President Reagan made a nationally televised speech in which he opposed apartheid but also opposed sanctions and attacked the African National Congress, the principal black opposition group in South Africa. At about the same time the European Community urged changes on the South African government and was rebuffed.

The Foreign Relations Committee's bill was less far reaching than the House bill but still had a good deal in it. It prohibited new U.S. investment in South Africa as well as trade in agricultural products, steel, and nuclear supplies. The Senate passed the bill August 14 by a vote of 84 to 14.

There was more drama over a House-Senate conference to adjust differences between the two bills. Leaders of the House, especially leaders of the Congressional Black Caucus, wanted a conference where they thought they could preserve more of the House bill. The Senate, and especially Foreign Relations Chairman Richard G. Lugar, R-Ind., did not want a conference; Lugar wanted the House to agree to the bill as it passed the Senate. That it had passed the Senate at all without scads of amendments designed to overburden it was a tribute to Lugar's considerable skills as a legislative tactician. A conference might be prolonged to the point that the bill would pass so late in the session that Reagan could pocket veto it after Congress had adjourned. When House leaders were not impressed with this argument, Lugar gave them another one. Conferees, especially in the Senate, are almost always selected by the chairman of the relevant Senate committee. If there were a conference, Lugar said, there would be only three Senate conferees: himself; Sen. Jesse Helms, R-N.C., the next most senior Republican; and Sen. Claiborne Pell, D-R.I., the ranking Democrat. Lugar and Helms would not agree to any change in the Senate bill, and therefore nothing could come out of conference. The House yielded and passed the Senate bill, 308 to 77.

Reagan vetoed the bill September 26 on the grounds that sanctions would hurt blacks instead of the white South African government. Congress was unimpressed. The House overrode the veto September 29 by a vote of 313 to 83, and the Senate overrode October 2 by a vote of 78 to 21.

The act itself stipulated the conditions under which its sanctions could be removed. These were the release from prison of Nelson Mandela, a leader of the African National Congress, and of "all persons persecuted for their political beliefs or detained unduly without trial"; the repeal of the state of emergency; freedom for democratic political parties; repeal of the Group Areas Act and the Population Registration Act; and agreement by the government "to enter into good faith negotiations with truly representative members of the black majority without preconditions." [17]

Congress returned to the issue in 1988. Not much had changed in South Africa. Supporters of sanctions argued that this was because the 1986 law was too weak and had too many loopholes. Opponents argued that it simply proved their point that sanctions were unworkable and were hurting blacks more than whites. The House passed a stronger bill August 11 by a vote of 244 to 132. Among other things, it would have stopped virtually all trade in both directions between the United States and South Africa and would have prohibited American citizens or companies from holding investments in South Africa. The Senate Foreign Relations Committee diluted this bill somewhat, but it was not considered by the Senate before Congress adjourned.

In 1989 a process of change began in South Africa, propelled by a change in government occasioned by the illness of President P. W. Botha. He was replaced by Frederick W. de Klerk. This process coincided with an increase in organized defiance of the restrictions imposed under the state of emergency in effect since 1986. For elections in September, de Klerk and his National party campaigned on a program of moving away from apartheid, but not moving so far as majority rule. The National party lost seats in Parliament but retained control, and de Klerk began to implement his program.

Walter Sisulu, former secretary general of the African National Congress (ANC), and seven other political prisoners were released. This was followed in early 1990 by repeal of the decree that had banned the ANC, the South African Communist party, and the Pan-Africanist Congress. Shortly thereafter, Mandela, who had been in prison since 1962, was released. He toured the country speaking at mass rallies, one of which at Port Elizabeth reportedly attracted 500,000 people. Later in the year, Mandela made a triumphant tour of the United States, where he addressed a joint session of Congress.

During the course of 1990, Great Britain and the European Community lifted their ban on investments in South Africa. The question arose whether the United States should do likewise. The African National Congress rejected its leadership's recommendations for a review of sanctions and voted that they should remain in place.

In March 1991, the South African government introduced in Parliament legislation repealing the Land Acts, which divide farmland between whites and blacks; the Group Areas Act, which segregates residential neighborhoods; and the Population Registration Act, which puts South Africans into one of four categories—white, black, Indian, or mixed-race colored. In July, after the Parliament had approved the legislation, President Bush announced that the conditions of the 1986 act for lifting the sanctions imposed in the act had been met, and he lifted them. Some members of Congress disagreed, but they admitted they could not do anything about the removal. Sen. Paul Simon, D-Ill., chairman of the Foreign Relations subcommittee on Africa, said, "I think the votes are not there to override a veto, and for us to do anything that won't have the force of law would be meaningless." [18]

Communist Countries

Congress found foreign aid to be the most readily available instrument for a human rights policy in the Third World, where most countries received aid. But there were no aid programs in the Communist world. So Congress turned to trade policy. Initially, congressional concern was narrowly focused on the right of emigration.

The Trade Act of 1974.   The main purpose of the Trade Act of 1974 was to provide the president with authority to engage in a new round of international trade negotiations aimed at stimulating world commerce through mutual reductions both in tariffs and in nontariff barriers to trade (see Chapter 7). One of the additional purposes was to authorize the extension of most-favored-nation treatment to Communist countries, most of which had been excluded from it by earlier legislation.

Implementation of a trade agreement negotiated in October 1972 between the United States and the Soviet Union was dependent on the extension to the Soviet Union of most-favored-nation status. An earlier U.S.-Soviet agreement settling the Soviet lend-lease debt from World War II, in turn, was dependent on implementation of the trade agreement.

The trade bill was designed, among other things, to make it possible to put these two agreements into effect. The bill was considered in 1973 and 1974 in the context of a larger debate over the Kissinger policy of détente with the Soviet Union. The issue of human rights was injected into this debate by an argument over linking most-favored-nation treatment with Soviet emigration practices. At issue was the desire of many Soviet Jews to resettle in Israel.

In 1972 the Soviets began levying steep exit taxes on emigrants holding advanced academic degrees, a group that included many Jews. The Soviet rationale was that the taxes would repay the cost of the free education that such persons had received and from which Soviet society would no longer benefit if the persons emigrated. The Soviets also denied exit visas on national security grounds to persons who had had access to classified information. There were other obstacles to emigration, the most common being the de facto one of simple inaction on applications for emigrant visas.

The two issues of détente and emigration came together in a confusing way. Americans opposed to détente were also generally opposed to closer trade relations with the Soviet Union and were skeptical that such relations would result in net economic or political benefits to the United States. This school of thought held that, on the contrary, the trade bill, on balance, would benefit the Soviet Union. Such a benefit, it was further argued, provided leverage to the United States in forcing Soviet concessions on emigration.

The Jackson-Vanik Amendment.   "To assure the continued dedication of the United States to fundamental human rights," Sen. Henry M. Jackson, D-Wash., and Rep. Charles A. Vanik, D-Ohio, offered an amendment to the Trade Act of 1974.[19] After this rhetorical beginning, the Jackson-Vanik amendment proceeds to outline specific provisions. Products from "any nonmarket country" shall not be eligible for most-favored-nation treatment. Nor shall any such country participate in any United States government program "which extends credits or credit guarantees or investment guarantees directly or indirectly."

The amendment also states that the president shall not conclude "any commercial agreement" with any such nonmarket economy country if the president determines that the country: (1) "denies its citizens the right or opportunity to emigrate"; (2) "imposes more than a nominal tax on emigration or on visas or other documents required for emigration, for any purpose or cause whatsoever"; or (3) "imposes more than a nominal tax, levy, fine, fee or other charge on any citizen as a consequence of the desire of such citizen to emigrate to the country of his choice."

Once the president makes the determination that a country engages in the emigration restrictions cited, there are two ways it can be removed from the ban on credits and most-favored-nation treatment. One is a presidential finding and report to Congress that the country is no longer restricting emigration.

The other way is through a presidential waiver of the ban with respect to a particular country. The waiver has to be based on a presidential determination that it will "substantially promote" the objective of free emigration and on assurances that the emigration practices of the country in question "will henceforth lead substantially" to the same objective. The waiver was to be good only for the eighteen-month period immediately following enactment of the act (that is, January 3, 1975, to July 3, 1976). Thereafter, it could be renewed for no more than a year at a time, and each renewal was subject to a legislative veto (which has since been found by the Supreme Court to be unconstitutional).

A separate provision of the Trade Act deals in a similar way with any Communist country that "denies its citizens the right or opportunity to join permanently through emigration, a very close relative in the United States, such as a spouse, parent, child, brother, or sister." [20]

The Jackson-Vanik amendment posed a complex set of issues. There was general sympathy for the plight of Soviet Jews, and members of Congress were reluctant to oppose anything that looked like it would ease that plight. Yet real doubts existed that the amendment, in fact, would do so. As Secretary of State William P. Rogers put it to the Ways and Means Committee in May 1973, the best hope for a satisfactory resolution of Soviet emigration practices "will come not from the confrontation formal legislation would bring about, but from a steady improvement in our over-all relations." [21] This was essentially the same quiet diplomacy argument that Kissinger was to make later with respect to human rights legislation in connection with foreign aid.

Throughout the debate, the Soviet Union repeatedly made it clear that it regarded its emigration practices as an internal matter and not an appropriate subject for international negotiation. Yet once the issue had been raised in Congress, it was taken as a political imperative that some provision on the subject go in the trade bill. The problem for the administration and its supporters thus became one of finding language that would satisfy a majority in Congress without driving the Soviets to scuttle the trade agreement and perhaps to clamp down on emigration even more. The task was complicated by the fact that some members of Congress no doubt wanted to use an emigration amendment as a device to kill most-favored-nation treatment for the Soviets, or at least would not care if that proved to be the result.

During most of 1973 and 1974 two sets of negotiations were in progress: negotiations between Kissinger and the Soviet Union and negotiations between Kissinger and the Jackson-Vanik forces on Capitol Hill. By October 1974 it appeared that an agreement had been reached. It was formalized in an exchange of letters between Secretary Kissinger and Senator Jackson.

"On the basis of discussions that have been conducted with Soviet representatives," Kissinger wrote to Jackson, "I should like on behalf of the Administration to inform you that we have been assured that the following criteria and practices will henceforth govern emigration from the USSR." There followed six understandings, the most important of which were that there would be no discrimination in issuing exit visas, that no punitive measures would be taken against applicants for emigration, and that the exit visa tax that had been suspended would remain suspended.[22]

Jackson went further. He said the agreement assumed that the annual rate of Soviet emigration would rise from the 1973 level of about 35,000 and in the future would correspond to the number of applicants. (The rate in 1974 was about two-thirds that of 1973.) He also said that 60,000 emigrants a year would be the "minimum standard" of compliance in order for the president to certify to Congress that Soviet practices were leading to substantially free emigration. He added that this was based on assurances from Soviet leaders.

In testimony before the Senate Finance Committee on December 3, Kissinger said, in effect, that Jackson was overstating the matter. According to Kissinger, his own letter to Jackson had been based on "clarifications" given to him and President Ford by Soviet officials. No commitments "either in form or substance" had been made by the Soviet Union. Jackson's letter, Kissinger said, contained interpretations and elaborations "which were never stated to us by Soviet officials," and there was no Soviet "commitment as to numbers."[23]

The Senate passed the Jackson amendment by a vote of 88 to 0 on December 13. Five days later, the Soviet Union denied it had given any specific assurance, as Senator Jackson had indicated. To the contrary, Moscow asserted that the number of emigrants was declining. It released the text of an October 26 letter to Kissinger from Foreign

Minister Andrei A. Gromyko, calling the Jackson-Kissinger exchange a "distorted picture of our position as well as what we told the American side on that matter." Gromyko restated the longstanding Soviet position that the emigration issue was a wholly domestic one.[24]

Both houses agreed to the conference report on the trade bill December 20, and President Ford signed it January 3, 1975. On January 14, Kissinger announced that the Soviets had rejected the conditions of the Jackson-Vanik amendment and consequently would not implement the 1972 trade agreement.

The Soviet Union.   For several years after 1974, the Soviet Union turned Jewish emigration on and off according to criteria that were not always clear in the West. After inauguration of the Gorbachev policy of *glasnost,* or openness, in the mid-1980s, there was a noticeable liberalization with respect to emigration as well as in other areas. At the Malta summit in December 1989, President Bush said he was prepared to waive the Jackson-Vanik amendment if the Supreme Soviet passed legislation codifying the liberalized emigration practice. In November alone, Jewish emigration, mainly to Israel, had exceeded 25,000.

On December 12, during a visit to Washington by Soviet Foreign Minister Eduard Shevardnadze, Bush waived Jackson-Vanik as it applied to U.S. government credits, thereby freeing guarantees of $1 billion for the purchase of mainly agricultural commodities. In April 1990, negotiators completed most of a trade agreement, and Bush and Gorbachev signed it at the Washington summit in June. But there was delay in the Supreme Soviet with respect to emigration legislation, and Bush similarly delayed sending the trade agreement to Congress. By the spring of 1991, a further complication had arisen. Economic conditions in the Soviet Union had so deteriorated that some members of the Supreme Soviet were said to fear that liberal emigration laws would result in a mass exodus of non-Jews as well as Jews.

Nor was this all. Separatist tendencies in some parts of the Soviet Union raised a new human rights question. This was particularly acute for the United States in the Baltic republics of Lithuania, Latvia, and Estonia. These countries had been annexed to the Soviet Union pursuant to a secret agreement with Nazi Germany during World War II. This annexation had never been recognized by the United States, which even continued to maintain the fiction of diplomatic relations with the countries in question.

Acting separately beginning in 1988, the Baltic states confronted Moscow with steadily more insistent demands, first of a measure of autonomy and then of independence. Tensions increased. Moscow sent troops, which in January 1991 used force to assert the authority of the central government. This was too much for Congress. On January 23, the House voted 417 to 0 for a resolution condemning violence in the Baltic states and asking the president to work with European allies for a coordinated approach to sanctions if the Soviets continued to use force to suppress the Baltic independence movements.[25] The Senate voted 99 to 0 for a similar resolution the following day.[26]

At the Moscow summit in July, President Bush announced that he was extending most-favored-nation treatment and that the trade agreement that had been negotiated in Washington the year before would be sent to Congress. In August, events in the Soviet Union took another unexpected turn with the failure of an attempted coup d'etat aimed at ousting President Gorbachev. Shortly thereafter, the United States formally recognized the new governments of Estonia, Latvia, and Lithuania.

The People's Republic of China. The overall record of China on human rights was scarcely better than that of the Soviet Union, but the Chinese emigration policy was not a problem for the United States. As part of a broader policy of normalization of relations, the Carter administration signed a trade agreement extending most-favored-nation treatment to China in 1979. During the 1980s, MFN was extended annually through a presidential waiver with congressional approval. Toward the end of the decade, the Chinese government instituted a program of reforms giving more range for free enterprise and local business initiative. These were accompanied, as in the Soviet Union, by modest political reforms in the direction of somewhat more democratization, including limited freedom of speech and the press.

In a series of demonstrations and sit-downs in Beijing's Tiananmen Square, students shortly carried the political reforms beyond what the government had intended and demanded even more. The first week of June 1989, the government cracked down with army troops and hundreds were killed in a violent confrontation, much of which was televised worldwide. This was followed by government moves to round up, try, and imprison student leaders.

President Bush suspended military sales to China as well as high-level contacts between the two governments. The United States also encouraged international financial institutions to postpone consideration of Chinese loan applications.

These steps were not enough for Congress. It passed a bill permitting Chinese who were in the United States on student visas to remain until June 1990 (the argument being that they would be subject to persecution if they returned to China). Bush vetoed the bill on the grounds that it interfered with his flexibility to conduct foreign policy, though he agreed to issue an executive order accomplishing the same result. (The difference was that he could change an executive order at will; he could not change the law.) The Senate sustained the veto by voting 62-37 to override.

Congress then seized on the State Department authorization bill as a convenient vehicle for more sanctions. Government insurance programs for private investment in China were suspended. Exports of a long list of items were prohibited—weapons and other military equipment; instruments and equipment used for crime control or detection; satellites; and nuclear supplies, equipment, and technology. There was provision for presidential waiver. Bush vetoed this bill for unrelated reasons, but that dispute was resolved and a compromise bill with the sanctions was enacted in January 1990.

Anti-Chinese fervor on Capitol Hill was fanned when National Security Adviser Brent Scowcroft and Deputy Secretary of State Lawrence S. Eagleburger arrived in Beijing in December 1989 for meetings with Chinese officials. The criticism was intensified when it was revealed that they had been there secretly in July, only a month after Bush had announced the suspension of high-level government contacts. To cap this off, there were television pictures of Scowcroft toasting his Chinese hosts. Bush said the purpose was to underscore U.S. shock and concern and that he did not want to undermine long-term relations. Senate Majority Leader George J. Mitchell, D-Maine, said Bush, who had been chief of the U.S. Liaison Office in Beijing in 1974-1975, had "kowtowed to the Chinese government." [27]

In late 1989, Bush used his authority to waive some of the sanctions—a sale of airliners, a sale of communications satellites, and some credits of the Export-Import Bank. In May 1990, he announced he would continue MFN for China for another year, and in July the House Ways and Means Committee approved renewal provided that the president certify "significant progress" toward specified human rights objectives. But in October, the House voted 247 to 174 to disapprove the president's waiver of Jackson-Vanik. Then, since that margin was not enough to override a veto, the House passed a second bill as a fallback position. This second bill provided that before Jackson-Vanik could be waived, the president must certify that the Chinese government had accounted for and released the citizens detained following the May-June 1989 demonstrations and that significant progress had been made in meeting other specified human rights goals. This bill passed by a vote of 384 to 30. There was no action in the Senate, so the waiver stood.

A larger battle developed in 1991. The Chinese gave no indication of moderating their repressive policies. In addition, they seemed to be having second thoughts about how much reform they really wanted in their economy. Furthermore, aside from human rights, some of their trade policies were the subject of protests in the United States. It was charged that they were exporting goods made by prison labor (American law prohibits the import of such goods). It seemed well documented that they were using third countries to avoid American quotas on textile goods. And there were recurring complaints about their failure to protect intellectual property (patents, copyrights, computer software).

Bush remained steadfast in his determination to keep MFN for China. His basic argument, in which he was supported by some China scholars, was that China was more likely to improve its human rights performance if it had more contacts with the West than if it had fewer. MFN would encourage such contacts; the denial of MFN would discourage them.

The counterargument, expressed by human rights activists and some congressional Democrats, was that extending MFN in light of China's human rights performance would make a mockery of the law and of the professed U.S. devotion to human rights. If MFN were extended in these circumstances, the Chinese could not be expected to take the United States seriously about human rights or anything else.

On May 29, Bush formally notified Congress that he intended to renew MFN for China for one year. This intensified the lobbying and political battle that had been in the making anyway; in the course of the battle, the issues broadened. They came to include not only the fate of the protesters who had been arrested in Tiananmen Square but also China's general policies with respect to human rights, China's general trade policies, and even American trade policy broadly defined.

MFN was no small matter in U.S.-Chinese trade. With MFN, the average U.S. tariff on imports from China was 8.4 percent; without MFN, it would be 47.5 percent. In 1980, U.S. trade with China was in surplus by $2.7 billion. In 1990, it was in deficit by $10.4 billion, making China the highest deficit country after Japan and Taiwan. Notwithstanding the deficit, China was an important market for American exporters. Wheat sales alone amounted to more than $1 billion a year, and China was also a major market for fertilizer and airplanes. One-third of the toys sold in the United States are made in China, and without MFN the tariff would rise from 6.8 percent to 70 percent. Still, the business community was split. The American Farm Bureau Federation, interested in promoting farm exports, supported extension of MFN. So did the U.S.-China Business Council, but individual corporations did not "want to be seen as condoning the Chinese government," as one of them put it.[28]

Rep. Robert T. Matsui, D-Calif., succinctly captured the foreign policy dilemma when he argued that more trade would bring more democratization. Cutting off MFN, said Matsui, was like telling the Chinese, "You improve your human rights policy or we'll burn our house down." [29]

On June 26, the House Ways and Means Committee approved two bills: one, by Rep. Gerald B. H. Solomon, R-N.Y., would cut off MFN; the other, by Rep. Nancy Pelosi, D-Calif., would extend it for a year but make further extension subject to a long list of conditions, some of wnich were added by the committee. These included an accounting for the Tiananmen Square protesters; the release of those in jail; and "significant overall progress" toward ending gross violations of human rights, religious persecution, restrictions on the media, harassment of Chinese students in the United States, torture and inhumane conditions in prisons, and coercive abortion or sterilization. The bill also demanded an end to Chinese missile sales to the Middle East and export of nuclear technology.

The House passed both bills July 10. The vote on cutting off MFN was 223 to 204. The vote on extension with conditions was 313 to 112. The House rejected, 118 to 308, a proposal by Rep. Bill Archer, R-Texas, to give the president discretion about the conditions.

In the Senate, debate centered on a bill by Majority Leader Mitchell, which, like the Pelosi bill in the House, would extend MFN for a year but condition future extensions on improved human rights performance and trade practices. This bill was passed July 23 by a vote of 54 to 45.

Congress adjourned for its August recess without resolving the House-Senate differences.

Organization of the State Department

Foreign policy is made by Congress and the top officials of the executive branch, but it is implemented by the bureaucracy. Organizational structure has a great deal to do, sometimes in subtle ways, with how a policy is implemented and the enthusiasm with which it is pursued. During the Ford administration, 1974-1977, Congress perceived a lack of enthusiasm for human rights in the upper echelons of the State Department. Congress therefore moved to create a bureaucratic self-interest in the policy.

The Ford administration's foreign policy was dominated by Secretary of State Henry Kissinger, who greeted each new congressional initiative on human rights with resistance that varied in proportion to the specificity and stringency of the initiative. In this, Kissinger was reacting in a typically bureaucratic fashion. Regardless of who has been secretary, the State Department has never liked binding policy directives or limitations from Congress. (There are rare exceptions to this in cases when the department is seeking to bolster its negotiating position with a foreign country and wants to be able to say, in effect, "Look, we understand your position, but Congress has tied our hands." Even in these cases, the department does not like to have its hands tied too tightly.)

In the case of human rights, Kissinger made the usual bureaucratic plea for diplomatic flexibility. He argued that public protests of human rights violations were likely to be counterproductive and that more could be achieved through quiet diplomacy. In the abstract, there is much to be said for this argument. Sovereign governments ordinarily do not respond well to public criticism, let alone preaching, from other governments, particularly when it is directed at something they regard as a domestic matter.

The trouble with the argument in this case was a widespread disbelief that Kissinger was really conducting any quiet diplomacy aimed at improving the human rights of Chileans or anybody else. When Sen. Claiborne Pell, D-R.I., who had been particularly outraged by the Johnson and Nixon administrations' embrace of a repressive government in Greece, asked Kissinger to cite some examples of quiet diplomacy, the secretary demurred that it would be inappropriate to do so in public. Pell accepted that objection and invited the secretary to submit a classified memorandum. It took the State Department eight months to find a handful of examples worldwide.

It must also be remembered that these exchanges took place as the full story of the CIA's maneuvers in Chile was beginning to unfold. If Kissinger had had any credibility left in the human rights area, Congress (or at least the Senate) might well have accepted his argument for quiet diplomacy. But he did not, and Congress took the bit in its teeth on the human rights question. In doing so, it subsequently complicated life for the Carter administration, which ironically had promised to put more emphasis on human rights in American foreign policy. Still later, Congress complicated life even more for the Reagan administration, which did not share the congressional enthusiasm for human rights in the first place.

In 1975 the State Department established by administrative action the position of coordinator for humanitarian affairs (with a total staff of two) in the office of the deputy secretary of state. As one result of the congressional suspicion that Henry Kissinger's quiet diplomacy on human rights was really no diplomacy at all, the new position was provided for by law in 1976 and was made a presidential appointment subject to confirmation by the Senate. The coordinator was to be responsible to the secretary of state for matters pertaining to human rights and humanitarian affairs in the conduct of foreign policy, including those relating to refugees, prisoners of war, and members of the armed services missing in action. Finally, human rights reports to Congress were to be the responsibility of the coordinator.[30]

In 1977, Congress upgraded the position of coordinator to the status of assistant secretary. The expanded duties of the assistant secretary for human rights and humanitarian affairs included:

- Gathering "detailed information regarding humanitarian affairs and the observance of and respect for internationally recognized human rights" in countries affected by foreign assistance requirements
- Preparing the statements and reports to Congress required in connection with security assistance
- Making recommendations to the secretary and to the administrator of AID regarding compliance with human rights requirements of the foreign aid legislation
- Performing "other responsibilities which serve to promote increased observance of internationally recognized human rights by all countries" [31]

The statutory creation of this office and its subsequent upgrading to the level of assistant secretary were acts of more than ordinary bureaucratic significance. Congress spelled out the duties and responsibilities of the office to a greater extent than is normal with respect to assistant secretaries of state. These congressional actions provided a focal point for human rights concerns in the executive branch. Congress gave the new assistant secretary a legislative mandate. More particularly, it created a vested bureaucratic interest in human rights. The assistant secretary for human rights and humanitarian affairs has a constituency in Congress, and members of Congress interested in human rights have a constituency in the assistant secretary's office.

The arrangement centralizes, in terms of organization, concern for human rights in the State Department; it gives the assistant secretary a measure of bureaucratic independence; and it ensures that a voice advocating consideration of human rights is going to be heard in the department's policy-making process. As this worked in practice during the Carter administration, the role of the assistant secretary for human rights and humanitarian affairs in policy decisions was the source of irritation to the State Department's geographic bureaus.

The Reagan administration's first nominee for the position— Ernest W. Lefever—so unfavorably impressed the Senate Foreign Relations Committee that it recommended against his confirmation by a vote of 13 to 4. The nomination was then withdrawn. It is highly unusual for the Senate to refuse to confirm a nomination by a new president in the first six months of his term. In the Lefever case, the

Foreign Relations Committee doubted the nominee's commitment to human rights. It was also troubled by evidence of conflicts of interest involving Lefever as director of the Ethics and Public Policy Center, the center's corporate contributors, and some of its consultants. There was particular difficulty over a contribution by Nestlé to finance a report on infant formula sales in developing countries.

The president next nominated Elliott Abrams, who had been serving as assistant secretary for international organization affairs. Abrams was a Washington lawyer who had worked for Democratic senators from 1975 to 1979; he was confirmed without difficulty. He brought a low-key approach to the job, and the turmoil subsided. But the position remained vacant from Reagan's inauguration January 20 to Abrams's confirmation November 20. Abrams was succeeded in 1985 by Richard Schifter, another Washington lawyer, who continued in the post in the Bush administration.

Most significant organizationally during the Carter, Reagan, and Bush administrations was that human rights became institutionalized in the bureaucratic structure of the State Department. By 1991, every bureau had a human rights officer. Every overseas post had a human rights officer whose responsibilities included compiling the annual human rights reports on that country. By the simple act of requiring such reports, Congress forced the department to focus on human rights. Some geographic bureaus and old-line foreign service officers might not have liked the idea any more in 1991 than they did in 1975, but instead of fighting it, they took it for granted.

National Endowment for Democracy

During the Reagan administration, human rights policy was broadened to include the promotion of democracy and related political rights. This time, it was the president, not Congress, who took the initiative. In an address to the British Parliament in June 1982, President Reagan proposed a "campaign for democracy."

> Since the Exodus from Egypt historians have written of those who sacrificed and struggled for freedom: the stand at Thermopylae, the revolt of Spartans, the storming of the Bastille, the Warsaw uprising of World War II. . . .
> If the rest of this century is to witness the gradual growth of freedom and democratic ideals, we must take action to assist the campaign for democracy. . . . We must be staunch in our conviction that freedom is . . . the inalienable and universal right of all human beings. . . .
> The objective I proposed is quite simple to state: To foster the infrastructure of democracy—the system of a free press, unions, political parties, universities—which allows a people to choose their

own way, to develop their own culture, to reconcile their own differences through peaceful means.[32]

The president went on to say that the chairman of the national Republican and Democratic party organizations were beginning a study "to determine how the United States can best contribute—as a nation—to the global campaign for democracy now gathering force."

The president's budget for fiscal 1984 (sent to Congress in January 1983) contained $85 million over three years for a program called Project Democracy in the United States Information Agency. The purpose was to support a variety of activities ranging from training foreign legislators to helping labor movements. The response in Congress was skeptical. Some members thought the program was too intrusive; others feared it would be used to support conservative parties or otherwise help the administration's friends abroad.

An alternative appeared in April in the form of the National Endowment for Democracy. This proposal emerged from a private group headed by William E. Brock III, Reagan's trade representative and a former Republican senator from Tennessee. A member of the group was Dante Fascell, chairman of the House Foreign Affairs Subcommittee on International Operations and soon to be chairman of the full committee. The endowment was established by Brock and others as a private, nonprofit organization in the District of Columbia. It is financed by the U.S. government, and it makes grants to foundations created by the Republican and Democratic parties, the AFL-CIO, and the Chamber of Commerce. This was the proposal that passed Congress with administration support.

Since 1983, the endowment and the various foundations have been unobtrusively active in many countries. In countries emerging from dictatorship, the National Republican Institute for International Affairs and the National Democratic Institute for International Affairs have helped foreign political parties in the techniques of political organizing. They have frequently collaborated in providing poll watchers and other election observers in such farflung countries as the Philippines, Chile, and Bulgaria. After the anti-Communist revolutions in Eastern Europe in 1989, they provided a good deal of technical assistance on legislative organization and procedures.

Congress contributed to this work as an institution, both through visits by ad hoc congressional delegations and through the more structured work of the Commission on Security and Cooperation in Europe (the Helsinki Commission). This commission was created in 1976 to monitor compliance with the agreements signed at the conclusion in 1975 of the Helsinki Conference on Security and Cooperation in

Europe. It consists of nine members of each house plus representatives of the Departments of Defense, Commerce, and State.

In 1991, the umbrella Conference on Security and Cooperation in Europe (CSCE) acquired an interparliamentary component in which the U.S. Congress participated. CSCE consists of the thirty-four countries that participated in the Helsinki conference and signed the agreement negotiated at that conference. The assembly has 245 members, with 17 each from the United States and the Soviet Union, the biggest members. It meets annually to make recommendations on security questions, economics, and human rights.

Conclusion

The multifaceted practice of diplomacy involves balancing frequently contradictory national interests, such as military security, access to essential raw materials, the protection of American business abroad, the growth of foreign trade—and the protection and promotion of human rights and democracy. The line between standing up for human decency and meddling in another country's internal affairs is exceedingly fine. Violations of human rights can range from the occasional roughing up of a prisoner by police to systematic torture and mass murder. At what point in this spectrum does international concern become appropriate?

And what is a human right anyway? Congressional attention has focused on the right not to be physically abused; but the Jackson-Vanik amendment involves the right to emigrate, and the American government through both the president and the Congress has spoken out on the treatment of Soviet dissidents—an issue that essentially involves free speech.

To much of the Third World, however, human rights encompass what many Americans regard not as rights so much as desirable social or economic goals, such as education, housing, and medical care. A further difficulty comes in avoiding the appearance of self-righteousness or hypocrisy. The record of the United States with respect to human rights, particularly with respect to racial discrimination, is far from flawless. The history of Soviet Jewry is scarcely sadder than the history of American Indians.

Nevertheless, the record is clear that the United States generally enjoys better relations with countries where there is a decent respect for the individual than with those where there is not. The most prominent example, of course, is America's relations with its European allies and with countries like Canada and Australia, but the point applies to other countries as well.

The emphasis that human rights issues began to receive in the 1970s was in part a reaction to the neglect these issues had suffered during the cold war period, when considerations of national security were paramount. But the change entailed more than that. It followed the flowering of the civil rights movement in the 1960s and the national disillusionment over Vietnam.

Exactly how to implement a human rights policy remains a question on which Congress and the White House do not always see eye to eye. Short of military intervention, the options available to the United States (from the less to the more drastic) include:

- Private diplomatic representations
- Public criticism
- Reduction or termination of foreign aid or credits
- Call for action by an international organization (actions ranging from a condemnatory resolution to international sanctions)
- Recall of the American ambassador
- Severance of diplomatic relations
- Embargo of trade

All of these options are available to the executive branch, but only some of them (public criticism, reduction of aid, trade restrictions) are available to Congress. Taking any of these actions on behalf of human rights may mean a sacrifice of some other foreign policy objective. Nor is there any guarantee that the observance of human rights by other countries actually will be improved.

The trade-offs are sometimes agonizing, and it is rarely easy to strike an acceptable balance. The decision to sacrifice one foreign policy objective for another has led to charges of inconsistency or even hypocrisy. The Carter administration, for example, bore down hard on human rights abuses in Argentina, to the consternation of the American business community there, but not in China, where the abuses were equally egregious. Larger reasons of global geopolitics dictated a policy of rapprochement with China; no such considerations prevailed with respect to Argentina. China was an even more painful dilemma in the Bush administration: its brutality in Tiananmen Square was more evident; its support (or at least abstention) in UN Security Council action on Iraq was more crucial. The Reagan administration made a distinction, of which Ambassador Jeane Kirkpatrick was the principal architect, between what were labeled totalitarian and authoritarian governments. The former (for example, Cuba) sought to control every facet of a country's life according to a particular ideology. The latter (for example, South Korea or the Philippines under Marcos) merely ruled with an iron hand, frequently corruptly, but ordinarily ignored actions not perceived as threatening to the regime in question.

The results of administration policies are difficult to assess and impossible to quantify. One of the few certainties is that some political dissidents themselves, notably in Brazil and Uruguay, said they felt less threatened because of Carter administration pressure on their governments. In connection with its policy in Central America, the Reagan administration pressured the government of El Salvador to control the death squads, but the government was unable to do so; nonetheless, the administration continued to support the Salvadoran government. The problem recurred in the Bush administration with respect to brutality by both sides in El Salvador. Such are the dilemmas that confront U.S. policy makers in balancing human rights and foreign policy.

Notes

1. *The Annals of America,* vol. 1 (Chicago: Encyclopedia Britannica, 1968), 115.
2. Walter LaFeber, ed., *John Quincy Adams and American Continental Empire: Letters, Speeches and Papers* (Chicago: Times Books, 1965), 45.
3. See Arthur Schlesinger, Jr., "Human Rights and the American Tradition," *America and the World 1978, Foreign Affairs* 57 (no. 3, 1979): 503-526.
4. Norman A. Graebner, ed., *Ideas and Diplomacy: Readings in the Intellectual Tradition of American Foreign Policy* (New York: Oxford University Press, 1964), 448.
5. Text in *Congressional Record,* 77th Cong., 1st sess., January 6, 1941, 44-47.
6. Richard M. Nixon, *Six Crises* (Garden City, N.Y.: Doubleday, 1962), 192.
7. Foreign Assistance Act of 1973, sec. 32, P.L. 93-189, approved December 17, 1973.
8. Foreign Assistance Act of 1974, sec. 46, P.L. 93-559, approved December 30, 1974.
9. International Security Assistance and Arms Export Control Act of 1976, sec. 301(a). This section in its present form is sec. 502B of the Foreign Assistance Act of 1961, as amended.
10. International Security Assistance Act and Arms Export Control Act of 1979, sec. 4, P.L. 96-92, approved October 29, 1979.
11. Agricultural Trade Development and Assistance Act of 1954, as amended, sec. 112, added by the International Development and Food Assistance Act of 1977.
12. P.L. 94-302, approved May 31, 1976, secs. 103(a) and 211.
13. International Financial Institutions Act, P.L. 95-118, approved October 3, 1977, sec. 701.
14. *Congressional Quarterly Weekly Report,* January 29, 1983, 217-219.
15. Lou Cannon and Charles Fishman, "Reagan to Seek Additional Aid for Region," *Washington Post,* July 21, 1983.
16. *Congressional Quarterly Weekly Report,* May 5, 1990, 1370.
17. Comprehensive Anti-Apartheid Act of 1986, sec. 311(a), P.L. 99-440, 100 Stat. 1086.
18. Ann Devroy and Helen Dewar, "Citing S. Africa's Transformation, Bush Ends Most Sanctions," *Washington Post,* July 11, 1991.
19. Trade Act of 1974, sec. 402, P.L. 93-618, approved January 3, 1975.
20. Ibid., sec. 409.
21. House Ways and Means Committee, *Hearings on H.R. 6767, Trade Reform Act of 1973,* 93d Cong., 1st sess., May 9, 1973, 165.

22. *New York Times,* October 19, 1974, 10.
23. Senate Finance Committee, *Hearing on Emigration Amendment to the Trade Reform Act of 1974,* 93d Cong., 2d sess., December 3, 1974, 53-54.
24. *New York Times,* December 19, 1974, 1, 18.
25. H. Con. Res. 40, 102d Cong. Text in *Congressional Record,* daily ed., January 23, 1991, H623-H624.
26. S. Con. Res. 6, 102d Cong. Text in *Congressional Record,* daily ed., January 24, 1991, S1146.
27. *Congressional Quarterly Almanac, 1989,* 518.
28. Lena H. Sun, "China's Trading Status with U.S. Becomes Issue," *Washington Post,* April 18, 1990; and Rick Gladstone, "China Trade Decision Boon for Toy, Clothes Importers," *Washington Post,* May 25, 1990.
29. *Congressional Quarterly Weekly Report,* August 4, 1990, 2570.
30. International Security Assistance and Arms Export Control Act of 1976, sec. 301(b), P.L. 94-329, approved June 30, 1976.
31. Foreign Assistance Act of 1961, as amended, sec. 624(f)(1), added by the Foreign Relations Authorization Act, Fiscal Year 1978, 91 Stat. 846.
32. Text of speech in *New York Times,* June 9, 1982.

PART III

Conclusion

Part I (Chapters 1 and 2) provided a general discussion of the roles of the executive and legislative branches—focusing upon the powers of the president and of Congress in the foreign policy process. In Part II (Chapters 3-8), six specific issues from recent American diplomatic experience were selected to illustrate the role of Congress in foreign policy since the Vietnam War. These case studies had two common elements: they addressed significant questions confronting the United States in foreign relations, and they identified one or more important prerogatives of Congress and the president in the foreign policy field.

In the final chapter of this study, which comprises Part III, we have two purposes. The first is to identify congressional behavior patterns in the recent era of legislative activism in foreign relations. What approaches has Congress taken to a series of diverse external problems? In what respects has Congress's approach in recent years marked a change from the long preceding period of legislative acquiescence in presidential diplomatic leadership?

Second, what are the noteworthy long-term implications of an active and independent role by Congress in foreign affairs? To answer that question, we must consider the factors that have sustained congressional assertiveness in confronting foreign policy questions. How durable are these factors? Are they likely to provide momentum for forceful legislative initiatives in foreign relations in the years ahead? Or can they be expected to diminish as memories of the Vietnam conflict recede and are replaced by the more positive memories of the Persian Gulf War? On balance, what has been the impact of an assertive Congress upon American diplomacy?

What are the principal implications of congressional activism in foreign affairs for the future? What specific forms does this activism take? How has congressional assertiveness in foreign affairs affected the ability of the United States to respond effectively to diverse challenges abroad? What kind of new balance (or what is called here a de facto division of labor) may be emerging in executive-legislative relations in the years ahead? Such questions are fundamental in any attempt to understand the American foreign policy process today and in the future. Our answers to them must be tentative: they are inescapably conditioned by underlying value judgments, and they cannot anticipate the conditions that will confront the United States in its relations with over 160 independent nations. As the Persian Gulf War indicated, a single event can sometimes have a momentous impact upon the roles of the president, Congress, public opinion, and other actors in the foreign policy process. With due recognition of these uncertainties, Chapter 9 presents an assessment of the overall impact of Congress upon the nation's foreign policy process.

To understand the evolution in Congress's foreign policy role more clearly, in the twentieth century that role may be envisioned in five reasonably distinct stages. First, beginning with the foundation of the American republic and extending until World War II, there was the long *isolationist era*. Some commentators believe that toward the European powers at least, isolationism meant that the United States really had no foreign policy. Accordingly, the influence of Congress was directed principally at keeping the United States out of foreign conflicts, at promoting trade and commerce overseas, and at prohibiting American participation in international organizations. This period formally came to an end with the nation's initiative in establishing, and its subsequent membership in, the United Nations.

There followed the second stage, lasting for approximately a decade after the war. This was the high tide of *bipartisanship* or close executive-legislative cooperation in the foreign policy field. Officials in both branches of the government collaborated to produce the foundationstones of American postwar foreign policy, such as the UN Charter, the Greek-Turkish Aid Program, the Marshall Plan for European reconstruction, the North Atlantic Treaty Organization (NATO), the program of arms-aid to the NATO allies and later to other endangered nations, and the "Point Four" program of economic aid to developing societies. The symbol of this era was Sen. Arthur H. Vandenberg, R-Mich., a former isolationist who came to epitomize bipartisan collaboration in the sphere of external policy. After Vandenberg's death in the early 1950s, it proved extremely difficult to find a replacement for him on Capitol Hill. Despite repeated efforts, since that time the concept of bipartisan cooperation in foreign affairs has never reached the level it attained during the early postwar period.

The third stage was the era of the *imperial presidency*, associated with the Johnson and Nixon administrations during the Vietnam War. (In reality, of course, as explained more fully in Chapter 1, presidents before that time were also sometimes viewed as acting imperially, as in the Lincoln administration and the long presidency of Franklin D. Roosevelt.) During the Vietnam War, it would not be amiss to say that Presidents Johnson and Nixon, with their chief aides, largely dominated the foreign policy process. By contrast, legislative influence upon the course of American foreign policy declined to one of the lowest levels in the nation's history. Not until the closing stage of the Vietnam conflict did Congress begin to assert its powers independently, to publicize the fact that the United States was losing the war, and to impose limits upon the president's power to wage it. More generally, the outcome of the Vietnam War provided a powerful impetus toward legislative activism and independence in dealing with foreign policy issues.

This leads to the fourth stage in the cycle of legislative involvement in American foreign relations: the post-Vietnam War era of *the assertive Congress* during the 1970s. After witnessing what was widely viewed as presidential mismanagement of foreign affairs in Southeast Asia and perhaps other settings—along with the flagrant abuse of presidential power in the Watergate episode, which brought the demise· of the Nixon administration—many legislators were determined to make Congress a more forceful instrument of government, especially in dealing with foreign policy questions. Implicit in this approach was the idea that to the degree that Congress became a full partner with the president in conducting foreign affairs, the nation would avoid another Vietnam or other major reverses abroad. The visible symbol of this state of mind was the War Powers Resolution (1973), discussed in detail in Chapter 5. Other examples were efforts by Congress to prohibit or limit certain kinds of intelligence activities; requirements that executive officials make detailed reports to Congress on progress (or the lack of it) in protecting human rights abroad; restrictions upon the use of American military force in Africa; and congressionally imposed limitations upon trade and commerce with the Soviet Union because of Moscow's treatment of Soviet Jews and other minorities.

The era of congressional activism in external policy lasted until the election of Ronald Reagan. The major developments that brought an end to this period were the Iranian revolution, which resulted in a serious American diplomatic setback in the Persian Gulf area; the Soviet invasion of Afghanistan; the eruption of terroristic attacks directed against Americans abroad; and the overall decline of the nation's power and credibility overseas.

The fifth stage began with the Reagan presidency and extends to the present day. In many respects, it differs significantly from both the earlier period of the imperial presidency and the period of congressional militancy that followed the Vietnam War. In the light of developments during the 1970s and 1980s, many public officials and commentators on the nation's foreign policy concluded that Congress had gone too far in efforts to gain a dominant position in the decision-making process—a viewpoint that was expressed even by those who had earlier called for greater congressional influence in the foreign policy field. Congress, it now appeared, had tied (or had attempted to tie) the president's hands, making it extremely difficult for the White House to promote and safeguard the nation's interests overseas. Meanwhile, for reasons to be explained in Chapter 9, it had also become evident that Congress itself was increasingly incapable of providing the kind of forceful and unified leadership in the foreign policy realm which was required in an unstable and dangerous external environment. From the era of the imperial presidency, it appeared that the nation had moved to the "imperiled presidency," with serious attendant concerns that its interests abroad would be endangered. In some measure, Ronald Reagan's election to the White House was a result of this prevailing sentiment among the American people.

Accordingly, and as the United States continued to face a series of major and minor crises abroad, many of the restrictions placed by Congress upon presidential management of foreign affairs were repealed, substantially modified, or (in the case of the War Powers Resolution) tacitly ignored. During the Persian Gulf crisis in the early 1990s, for example, little or nothing was heard about this resolution. In dealing with this challenge, the transcendent fact about the legislative role was the degree to which Congress supported the steps taken by the Bush administration in the Middle East.

Yet fears of "another Vietnam" remained pervasive on Capitol Hill and throughout the American society at large. During the Persian Gulf crisis, many voices were heard calling upon President Bush to involve Congress more meaningfully and extensively in arriving at key foreign policy decisions, especially those entailing the use of armed force abroad. Early in 1991, Congress did debate at length whether the United States ought to undertake offensive military operations against Iraq, and in the end it gave the Bush White House the authority it requested to do so.

With regard to the pattern of executive-legislative relations during this most recent stage, the period since 1980 might be characterized as an attempt to formulate and apply the familiar principle of "division of labor" to the field of American foreign policy. Events had revealed rather convincingly, for example, that Congress is not equipped to manage or conduct foreign relations—and, in fact, the evidence strongly suggested that in the final analysis, most members of the House and Senate really did not *want* to do so. Conversely, a paramount lesson of the Vietnam War was that every president must make certain that the nation's foreign policy is solidly grounded in legislative and public support, since failure to do so risks almost certain defeat in the sphere of external policy. The discussion that follows will provide other examples of the division-of-labor principle in the foreign policy field.

Expressed differently, among executive and legislative officials alike, awareness exists today that a dominant need is what might be called an "invitation to cooperate." As the American republic enters the third century as an independent nation, it seems incontestable that both the president and Congress make essential contributions in the formulation and administration of American foreign policy. If their respective roles are often quite different, they are nevertheless indispensable. To no insignificant degree, skill in statesmanship will consist in keeping this reality at the forefront of the policy-making process and in discovering new ways in which each branch of the American government can make its distinctive contribution most effectively.

CHAPTER 9

Congressional Assertiveness
and Foreign Affairs:
A Balance Sheet

Late in President Reagan's second term, Secretary of State Shultz publicly decried the "seemingly inexorable encroachment of Congress into the conduct of foreign policy" by the United States. While the executive branch welcomed "a constructive dialogue with the legislative branch" on foreign policy questions, Shultz said, "increasing congressional restrictions" upon the president's diplomatic freedom of action were severely hampering the ability of the United States to achieve its foreign policy objectives. In remarkably blunt language for a secretary of state who had cultivated cooperative executive-legislative relations, Shultz stated, "This is no time for the Congress to be hauling down the American flag around the world." Secretary Shultz's observations supported what a recent British ambassador described as the "extraordinary power of ... Congress over foreign policy" in the United States. In the same period, news reports referred to a congressional mood that was "bold and bitter" in dealing with foreign policy issues. Many legislators believed that they had repeatedly been "misled" by executive officials about world problems. As one member of the House Foreign Affairs Committee expressed the disaffection: "The days of a single-handed foreign policy are over." Former House Speaker O'Neill declared that since the Vietnam War Congress had "asserted itself ... it took back the power that the President had assumed" in the foreign policy field.[1]

Executive policy makers have increasingly acknowledged the crucial role that Congress plays in the foreign relations of the United States. Although before entering government service, Henry Kissinger had been dubious about undue legislative influence in foreign affairs, as secretary of state he called for "a new national partnership" between the president and Congress in dealing with international issues.[2] During the early 1980s, the chairman of the Senate Foreign Relations Committee, Sen. Charles H. Percy, R-Ill., observed that unless there was "a joint approach to U.S. foreign policy, which both branches of government backed by substantial elements of both parties must work to forge," the United States would be unlikely to achieve its foreign policy goals.[3] Early in his administration, President Reagan sought to revive the concept of bipartisanship in foreign affairs that had characterized executive-legislative relations under the Truman and Eisenhower administrations, and he periodically repeated his call for a return to bipartisan collaboration in dealing with foreign policy questions. In the Bush administration, one study found that two of President Bush's top foreign policy assistants—National Security Adviser Brent Scowcroft and Secretary of State James A. Baker—had been chosen in no small measure because of their ability to deal effectively with Congress. Early in his administration, Bush indicated a strong interest in reviving the concept of bipartisanship, and he asked the help of the House and Senate in dealing with difficult foreign policy problems. During the Persian Gulf crisis, Bush asserted that the White House had "been having the darndest consultations with Congress you've ever seen." [4]

Although executive officials and informed students of American foreign policy are becoming increasingly aware of the expanding role of Congress in foreign policy, they are often far from enthusiastic about its implications. Presidents Johnson, Nixon, Ford, Carter, Reagan, and Bush vocally opposed legislative efforts to limit their powers abroad and to exercise powers they believed to be constitutional and historical prerogatives of the executive branch.

From the perspective of the White House, President Ford, himself a representative from Michigan for more than twenty years, lamented that congressional activities not infrequently impeded America's ability to achieve its foreign policy objectives. "The pendulum has swung so far," he once said, "that you could almost say we have moved from an imperial Presidency to an imperiled Presidency. Now we have a Congress that is broadening its powers in foreign relations too greatly." [5]

Similar judgments were expressed by informed students of the American governmental system during the Reagan administration. An experienced State Department official, for example, feared that legislative activism in foreign affairs had brought about a reversal in the traditional contributions of the president and Congress to the foreign policy process—to the detriment of American diplomatic undertakings. Sen. Alan K. Simpson, R-Wyo., complained that Congress was so internally "fragmented" that it was perhaps incapable of providing leadership in foreign and domestic affairs. Another experienced observer of the U.S. political scene asked: "How does a nation live with a Congress that counts more brilliant men than ever before but cannot lead, and will follow no leadership?" Since the Watergate crisis of the Nixon administration, Congress had been "in revolt" against the presidency. Yet Congress itself "can offer no solutions" to urgent internal and external problems.[6]

What have been the principal causes of recent congressional activism in the foreign policy field? What can be identified as the most significant consequences of forceful legislative influence upon American foreign relations? And what will be the future balance between executive and legislative influence in the foreign policy process? These three important and interrelated questions provide the framework for discussion in the concluding chapter of our study.

Congressional Assertiveness: Background and Causes

According to the provisions of the Constitution, as we saw in Part I, Congress possesses a number of prerogatives that allow it to influence foreign relations. Congress must appropriate funds needed for innumerable programs in foreign affairs. It has the power to declare war; and it must raise and support the armed forces. The Senate has two unique constitutional functions not shared with the House of Representatives: the requirement that treaties receive the advice and consent of the Senate, and the provision that most of the president's major appointments be confirmed by the Senate. From the foundation of the American republic, therefore, it was envisioned that Congress would be involved in the solution of diplomatic problems, although in many important respects the exact scope and nature of its involvement was left to be determined by experience.

The powers of the chief executive in foreign relations expanded significantly over the course of time—leading by the mid-1960s to a condition of virtually unchecked presidential authority in diplomacy. The accretion of the president's diplomatic influence became particularly pronounced after the United States emerged as a superpower at the end of World War II. Perhaps the most remarkable fact about this growth in presidential authority in foreign relations was how seldom it was challenged by Congress. In fact, during several eras the enhancement of presidential power could have occurred only with the explicit or tacit concurrence of Congress. The Roosevelt administration's conduct of World War II and the escalation of the Vietnam War under Presidents Kennedy and Johnson are two examples.

Today, the era of congressional passivity or acquiescence in presidential decisions in the foreign policy field has ended. As a former official of the Johnson administration has expressed it: "In the present world situation, far greater congressional and public involvement in formulating our foreign policy seems to me not only right but nearly inevitable." [7] One reason for greater congressional involvement in foreign policy making is the interrelationship between foreign affairs and domestic issues. According to a former member of the House of Representatives, "foreign and domestic policy have merged into a seamless web of interlocking concerns." [8]

Since the New Deal program of the 1930s, American society has also witnessed what might be called a legislative explosion of vast dimensions. Untold thousands of new laws have been enacted by Congress during the past sixty years. An increasing proportion of Congress's time is devoted to adding to this list, to making needed changes in existing legislation, and to overseeing the administration of the laws already enacted. Much of this activity is based upon the premise that the solution to pressing national problems lies in the enactment of legislation. [9]

In America's approach to problems beyond its own borders since World War II, basically the same tendency can be discerned. The Truman administration's adoption of the containment strategy for resisting Communist expansionism in 1947 committed the United States to a new diplomatic role, inescapably enhancing the powers of Congress in foreign affairs. For over a generation thereafter, the continuity of American foreign policy—from ongoing economic and military assistance programs, to the defense of NATO, to the creation and maintenance of an adequate defense establishment—has depended upon favorable action by Congress. Moreover, congressional behavior in confronting closely related domestic issues, such as the level of taxation, overall governmental spending, and the development of natural resources, has directly affected U.S. relations with other countries.

Internal Changes in Congress

A number of identifiable changes that have occurred within Congress in recent years have contributed to legislative activism in foreign affairs. We will examine three of the most important of these changes.

Diffusion of Power. Partly as a result of efforts to reform Congress since World War II, the problem of dispersed power within the House and Senate has become increasingly acute in recent years. As noted in Chapter 2, most congressional committees are involved in some aspect of foreign affairs, and their jurisdictions over foreign policy issues frequently overlap. During the 1970s, for example, when Congress was called upon to respond to the challenge of dealing with a national energy crisis, the leadership of the House of Representatives found that more than eighty committees and subcommittees of the House had some jurisdiction in the field.

Congressional deliberations today seem more disunified than at any other stage in American history. According to an experienced observer of the Washington scene, "Never since the Senate defied Woodrow Wilson on the importance of creating a League of Nations ... has the Congress ... seemed as parochial, personal or divided as it does now." [10]

An examination of the committee structure of Congress during 1989, for example, reveals that almost every major legislative committee claimed some jurisdiction in the foreign policy field. To cite merely a few illustrations of the phenomenon, the Senate's Agriculture, Nutrition and Forestry Committee had a subcommittee dealing with domestic and foreign marketing. The Appropriations Committee had subcommittees on commerce and the State Department, on defense, on energy and water development, and on foreign operations. The Judiciary Committee had a subcommittee on immigration and refugee affairs. The principal committee in the field, Foreign Relations, had seven subcommittees assigned to deal with some aspect of external policy.

The same pattern existed in the House of Representatives. There, the Merchant Marine and Fisheries Committee had six subcommittees that dealt with issues having international dimensions. The Ways and Means Committee had a subcommittee on international trade. The House Armed Services Committee had seven subcommittees whose province was some aspect of the armed forces and military operations. The House Foreign Affairs Committee had eight subcommittees concerned with different regions of the world and major foreign policy issues.

The 1980s provided several examples of the degree to which disunity and fragmentation in Congress seriously impaired its ability to influence the course of American foreign policy. A noteworthy illustration was the foreign aid program. In 1985, Congress finally authorized a new foreign aid bill—which it had been unable to do from 1981 through 1984! Then in the appropriations stage, Congress lumped foreign aid with other expenditures, in an "omnibus" spending bill, making it virtually impossible for legislators and the public to debate the foreign aid program separately. As a result of such legislative confusion and deadlock, in the end it was much easier for the Reagan White House to gain legislative approval of its proposed foreign aid budget. Despite repeated proposals and recommendations designed to achieve it, the "reform" of Congress remains an urgent and seriously neglected problem.

The problem of internal disunity within the legislative branch has not diminished in recent years. Thus, in 1982 one study of how

American legislators themselves perceive Congress found widespread complaints about the lack of effective leadership in the House and Senate, about the independence enjoyed by the principal committees of Congress, and about the degree to which overlapping committee jurisdictions and responsibilities inhibited a unified legislative approach to major policy issues.[11]

Expansion of Staff.   A second change that has affected the ability of Congress to play a more assertive role in foreign policy making is the expansion of legislative staff. In mid-1979, Sen. William Proxmire, D-Wis., confounded his colleagues by conferring his "Golden Fleece Award" for questionable expenditures of taxpayers' money on none other than Congress itself. Proxmire pointed out that the staff of the Senate and House had risen sharply: in 1969 the average number of staff employees per senator was thirty-four; ten years later, it was sixty-eight. The cost of maintaining this legislative bureaucracy had climbed from $150 million to $550 million annually.[12] By 1987, the two houses of Congress had more than eighteen thousand staff members.

Today, members of the House and Senate can no longer legitimately complain about staff shortages on Capitol Hill. One study of Congress has asserted that "Congress ... has developed a virtual counter-State Department composed of predominantly young, experienced and aggressive experts who are out to make their own marks on the foreign policy map." During the Persian Gulf crisis, a White House spokesman complained that on Capitol Hill "every committee up there has got 40 brilliant little staff guys running around drafting resolutions" on what the United States should do in the Middle East.[13]

A greatly expanded staff has had a twofold impact upon Congress's role in foreign affairs. A larger staff provides Congress the means to assert its own independent position vis-à-vis the executive branch with regard to major international questions. It also supplies national legislators with a new incentive to become active in a field where, during an earlier period, they often had neither the interest nor the expertise to become deeply involved.

Staff expansion has also added momentum to centrifugal tendencies within Congress itself. Hardly a committee or individual member of Congress lacks (or is unable to acquire) adequate staff assistance for dealing with international issues. As one commentator has observed, now each member of the House and Senate is better equipped than ever "to go his separate way and establish his own domain of power and prestige." [14]

Increased Participation by the House.   Until the period of the Vietnam War, the House of Representatives usually played a subordinate role in the foreign policy process. Although members of the House sometimes chafed at their inferior position vis-à-vis the Senate in external policy making, they were normally content to accept understandings worked out between executive officials and influential senators and Senate committees with jurisdiction over foreign policy questions.[15] In recent years, however, the era of passivity by the House in foreign relations has ended. For example, members of the House tried to influence the new Panama Canal treaties, negotiated and ratified by the Carter administration. Members of the House objected to being excluded from the treaty-making process. Before the agreements were formally ratified, committees and subcommittees in the House played an active role in efforts to influence their provisions relating, for example, to the nation's defense commitments in the Panama Canal area.

Increased participation by the House in foreign affairs can be explained on several grounds other than mere jealousy of the Senate's constitutional prerogatives. The growing interrelationship between domestic and external problems dictates a more dynamic role by the House in diplomatic decision making. As never before, Congress is called upon to enact legislation and to appropriate funds for implementing foreign policy proposals and programs. Advocates of greater House influence are convinced that the House can make a vital and distinctive contribution in Congress's deliberations on international questions. Since its members must stand for election every two years, the House provides the kind of "recurrent plebiscite on the foreign policy of the United States" that no other institution of the American government can contribute.[16]

External Influences on Congress

Legislative activism in foreign affairs has been influenced not only by changes within Congress, but also by several new forms of external pressure: by the nature and dynamics of American public opinion, by increased lobbying efforts by interest groups and foreign governments, and by lobbying on the part of executive agencies. Let us examine each of these influences.

Public Opinion. Since the Wilsonian era, public opinion has emerged as an influential force affecting the course of American diplomacy. Mounting public opposition to Soviet expansionism, for example, was a potent factor inducing the Truman administration to adopt the policy of containment against the Soviet Union. Conversely, a generation later, growing public disenchantment with the nation's role in Southeast Asia was crucial in the Nixon administration's decision to terminate the war in Vietnam. In the late 1970s and the 1980s congressional opinion and public opinion were significant factors in inducing the Carter and Reagan administrations to stiffen their positions toward Soviet interventionism and to strengthen the American defense establishment. Then during the early 1990s, public opinion within the United States solidly supported the efforts of the Bush administration to liberate Kuwait after it had been overrun by Iraqi forces. Only the future would tell whether such public support was forthcoming for the continuing challenge of achieving long-range peace and stability in the region.

In keeping with the idea that Congress is the most representative branch of the American government, legislators believe that viewpoints expressed in the House and Senate provide the most authoritative expression of public thinking available to the president and his advisers. The House International Relations Committee (now the Foreign Affairs Committee) emphasized this point in a 1976 report on Congress and foreign policy:

> Congressmen, by being in continuous contact with the people and representing their disparate interests and concerns, have served not only to ensure democratic control over the foreign policymaking process, but have also been the conveyors of sometimes ambivalent and occasionally vociferous public opinion.
>
> Recent events have demonstrated that without a genuine public consensus of support, the executive branch cannot legitimately and effectively pursue any foreign policy.[17]

Congress's perception of its relationship to public opinion as it bears upon foreign relations has several specific implications. Many legislators believe it is uniquely incumbent upon Congress to foster public awareness and better understanding of foreign policy issues. As the chairman of the Senate Foreign Relations Committee defined its responsibilities in 1979, the committee had an obligation to "stimulate public debate"; it was the "main forum" for promoting public discussion of external policy questions.[18]

The coin of Congress's role as a barometer of public sentiment has another side. If discontent with the president's policy is evident on Capitol Hill, the White House may be reasonably certain that millions of Americans also have doubts about the nation's external policy. Conversely, when—as during the Persian Gulf crisis of 1990-1991—Congress gives the president support of his actions in the Middle East, this fact in turn testifies to the existence of widespread public approval of the chief executive's approach to the crisis in the region.

Lobbying by Interest Groups and Foreign Governments. While lobbying is not a new phenomenon in the nation's history, some members and former members of Congress believe that legislators have become increasingly responsive to the campaigns of well-funded and highly organized pressure groups. Thus a prominent political commentator observed in 1990 that the political culture of the United States was characterized by a "maelstrom of interest groups generated by omniprovident government. . . ." This condition "makes coherent congressional government impossible; hence presidential ascendancy is necessary." [19] A number of factors have produced a favorable environment for pressure group activity in recent years: the expanding role of government in all spheres of American life; the lack of a public consensus in the United States on foreign policy issues; the decline of party identification by citizens and the weakening of party discipline on Capitol Hill; the emergence of single-issue politics (in which one issue, such as gun control or abortion, can dominate a political campaign); and the growing diffusion of power within the House and Senate. One recent study called attention to the "385 standing committees and subcommittees [of Congress] being pursued by more than 1,300 registered lobby groups." Instead of the traditional two-party system, there now appeared to exist on Capitol Hill "a 385-party system." [20]

Lobbying by foreign governments, whose efforts are frequently supported by internal pressure groups, has also had momentous consequences for recent American foreign policy. In many cases, foreign governments appeal White House decisions in foreign affairs to the more sympathetic legislative branch. Governments abroad now routinely ignore the once firmly established principle that the president is "the sole organ" of the nation in its relations with other countries. [21] This phenomenon is highlighted by the fact that the State of Israel has a minister in Washington who is in charge of "congressional relations."

Many foreign governments today have a direct stake in supporting a more active and independent foreign policy role for Congress. [22] As we saw in Chapter 4, the pro-Israeli lobby has repeatedly mounted intensive campaigns to have Congress block or reverse White House decisions thought inimical to Israel. Early in the 1980s, a report on lobbying by foreign interests referred to "multimillion dollar lobbying campaigns aimed at swaying U.S. policies" abroad. It is estimated that overall spending by lobbyists representing governments and political groups overseas exceeds $100 million annually. Justice Department records show that 701 persons were registered as agents of foreign governments in 1982 (compared with 452 in 1970). Among this group were a number of former senators and representatives. [23]

Lobbying by the Executive Branch. Lobbying activities by executive agencies on behalf of the president's programs and policies can be another crucial factor in determining Congress's role in the foreign policy process. Most executive agencies have one office that is primarily responsible for communicating to Congress the views of the executive branch. For example, within the State Department the legislative liaison function is performed by the Bureau of Congressional Relations. Sometimes executive agencies also form alliances with private citizens' organizations to influence attitudes both within Congress and throughout American society.[24] Efforts by the Bush administration to achieve and maintain a high level of legislative support for its policies in the Persian Gulf area and toward the Soviet Union were for the most part quite successful. Critics of the administration's Persian Gulf policy, for example, were seldom able to change the direction of the president's military and diplomatic moves.

A correlation exists between effective lobbying activities by the executive branch and the level of congressional activism in foreign affairs, as illustrated by the record of the Carter administration. On numerous occasions President Carter and his advisers complained about congressionally imposed restraints upon executive management of foreign affairs. Yet President Carter's aides were inexperienced in legislative relations and, in some instances, their tactics in dealing with legislators generated resentment and irritation on Capitol Hill.[25]

The failure of a president and his subordinates to engage in effective legislative liaison activities produces a condition tailor-made for legislative diplomatic activism. Not only does it ensure that Congress will exert its viewpoints and prerogatives forcefully in the foreign policy process; it also contributes to making congressional efforts episodic, uncoordinated, and inconsistent.

Congressional Assertiveness: Consequences and Implications

What impact has a more assertive and independent diplomatic role by Congress had upon American foreign policy? What have been its consequences—both positive and negative—upon the conduct of foreign relations by the United States? These questions merit more detailed examination in the light of our case studies and of other examples of Congress's recent dynamism in the foreign policy field.

Independent Legislative Initiatives

Until the period of the Vietnam War, it was a clearly established principle that negotiations with foreign governments were an executive prerogative. For example, longstanding precedent supports the view that the president or his designated agent makes or negotiates treaties with other governments. One of the earliest enactments of Congress was the Logan Act, which prohibits unauthorized contacts or negotiations between Americans and foreign officials.[26] Although such contacts today have become commonplace—and no citizen has ever been prosecuted for violating its terms—the Logan Act remains the law of the land.

In the period since World War II, legislators have frequently been involved in the conduct of diplomatic negotiations—but nearly always at the invitation of the president. Today the appointment of legislators as members of American negotiating teams is an accepted technique for creating bipartisan support for the nation's foreign policy. The Carter administration attempted to win widespread congressional support for the proposed SALT II agreements with the Soviet Union by allowing "26 Senators, 14 Republicans and 12 Democrats, including opponents and critics, and 46 members of the House of Representatives, to sit in on the arms negotiations in Geneva" at one time or another.[27] President Reagan utilized legislators as "observers" of national elections in El Salvador in 1982; in 1983, he appointed a former senator, Richard Stone, to serve as his special envoy in an effort to promote political stability in Central America.

The novel feature of Congress's involvement in diplomatic negotiations today is the tendency of legislators to engage in them independently—without White House approval, and sometimes in the face of presidential opposition. In 1979, Senator Helms, a member of the Foreign Relations Committee, sent two staff members to London to observe diplomatic discussions (to which the United States was not even a party) designed to end the longstanding civil conflict in Zimbabwe (formerly Rhodesia). Senator Helms's justification was candid: "I don't trust the State Department on this issue." [28]

Another newsworthy example of Congress's direct intervention in foreign relations occurred after Iranian students seized the American embassy in Tehran on November 4, 1979, and held some fifty Americans hostage. After early White House efforts to gain the release of the hostages failed, Rep. George Hansen, R-Idaho, undertook his own self-appointed peace mission to Iran, where he visited the hostages and sought to obtain their release. Hansen's efforts also failed, and his unauthorized negotiations during the crisis were criticized by executive and legislative officials alike, who feared his initiatives would undermine the president's authority and would provide evidence of disunity within the American government during the crisis.[29]

Earlier, reference was made to House Speaker Wright's involvement in efforts to negotiate a political settlement in Central America. Once again, the White House criticized this legislative intrusion into the sphere of diplomatic negotiations. A few months before the eruption of the Persian Gulf crisis in August 1990, a group of legislators visited Baghdad. One legislator told President Hussein that with regard to his poor image in the West, his main problem seemed to be the distorted

picture that the American news media often projected of his regime!
These examples clearly support the precedent that legislators may now
engage in the negotiating process freely. Perhaps legislators do so on the
theory that, in the absence of overt White House objections, they have
the president's tacit approval. In any case, the practice is bound to raise
questions abroad about who is ultimately in charge of American foreign
policy and about how durable agreements reached with a variety of
American officials are likely to be.

The recognition of other governments is another area—long regarded as an executive province—into which Congress has intruded
during the past decade. Early in 1979 several senators attempted to
make President Carter's decision to recognize the People's Republic of
China (PRC) contingent upon Peking's pledge not to use force in
exerting its longstanding claim to sovereignty over Taiwan. In effect,
these legislators wanted to threaten the PRC with withdrawal of
American recognition if it attempted to seize Taiwan by force. While the
president and his advisers were mindful of congressional concern about
the future of Taiwan, they were unwilling to condition American
recognition upon the PRC's behavior in the matter.

Expansion of Treaty-Making Role

As noted in Chapter 2, the Senate has relied upon its constitutional
prerogatives in the treaty-making process to assert its influence in the
diplomatic field, and the House has sought to use other prerogatives (for
example, its dominant role in the appropriations process) to compensate
for the Senate's constitutionally unique position. Several significant
aspects of Congress's involvement in the negotiation and ratification of
treaties have come to the fore in recent years. In contrast to earlier
years, since World War II the Senate has shown that it is determined to
construe its role in the treaty process actively and to leave its imprint on
major international agreements entered into by the United States.
Three recent examples—the Panama Canal treaties, the SALT II arms
limitation accord, and demands on Capitol Hill that the Reagan
administration negotiate a nuclear freeze with the Soviet Union—are
cases in point.

In the instances of the Panama Canal treaties and SALT II, Senate
deliberations were prolonged, thorough, and in the end extremely
influential. (Mounting Senate opposition to SALT II was one factor
motivating President Carter to withdraw the treaty from further Senate
deliberation.) The issue of the nuclear freeze presented an essentially
different question: Could legislators compel an obviously reluctant chief
executive to undertake negotiations with another government in behalf
of a nuclear freeze or some other goal favored by Congress? Legally and

on the basis of precedents, the answer was not really in doubt: as explained in Chapter 1, under the Constitution the president makes treaties or enters into negotiations with other governments; the Senate considers treaties submitted to it by the executive branch. Yet realistically, President Reagan and other modern chief executives knew that such forceful expressions of legislative sentiment unquestionably reflected deep public concern about the threat of nuclear devastation; and they were no less aware that, even if Congress could not force a president to negotiate a Soviet-American arms freeze, legislators could demonstrate their discontent about American diplomacy in other ways (such as by cutting defense expenditures).[30]

Still another interesting aspect of the treaty power arose during President Reagan's second term, involving the meaning of the ABM treaty between the United States and the Soviet Union in 1972 (as explained in Chapter 3). As interpreted by the Reagan White House, the provisions of this agreement should be construed flexibly, to permit the administration to move ahead with the development of the Strategic Defense Initiative (or "Star Wars") space-based defense system, designed to protect the nation from enemy missiles. When the Senate considered the treaty, officials of the Nixon administration gave assurances that it prohibited what the Reagan administration said it permitted. A number of leading senators, therefore, contended that the president could not unilaterally decide upon the meaning of an international obligation entered into by action of both branches of the government. This latter point of view, needless to say, was unacceptable to the chief executive and other high-ranking executive officials involved in the foreign policy process. While it is difficult to see how legislators could force a certain interpretation of a treaty upon an unwilling president, critics on Capitol Hill could spearhead a movement to deny the White House funds needed to move ahead with the Star Wars scheme or other programs in national defense and foreign affairs.[31]

The Pattern of Overseas Commitments

Since World War II, Congress has been determined to play a more influential role in the assumption and maintenance of the overseas commitments of the United States. Has there been a consistent pattern of legislative activity concerning these overseas obligations? For the most part, the answer is no. Congress has curtailed some of them, it has expanded others, and it has maintained still other international commitments largely intact. Most important, Congress has insisted far more adamantly than ever before that the nation's international obligations be made a matter of public record.

First, let us examine overseas commitments that have been cut or curtailed by Congress since the late 1960s. The Vietnam War was terminated by act of Congress (although in the Nixon administration's view, that process had already begun before Congress ordered it). In the ensuing years, adverse congressional sentiment remained a potent factor in preventing possible consideration of foreign aid to North Vietnam.

By enacting the War Powers Resolution in 1973, Congress imposed several new limitations upon the authority of the chief executive to use the armed forces; yet, as we saw in Chapter 5, congressional insistence upon strict compliance with the terms of the War Powers Resolution has been less than stringent. Toward Angola, Congress denied the White House authority to use military force and to carry on covert intelligence operations (a restriction Congress later lifted). And in several foreign countries with repressive governments that jeopardized the rights of their citizens, Congress has—or has threatened to—cut off American aid and trade.

The limitations imposed by Congress upon the president's management of foreign affairs operate both ways, however. Beginning with the Johnson administration, every chief executive has complained about congressionally imposed restrictions upon presidential freedom of action in foreign relations. President Nixon and his national security adviser, Henry Kissinger, were persuaded that—except for congressional interference in the conduct of the Vietnam War—executive policy makers could have obtained a much more advantageous settlement of the conflict.[32] President Reagan believed that congressionally imposed restrictions upon executive activities in Central America seriously impeded his efforts to contain Communist expansionism in the western hemisphere.

On other occasions, however, executive policy makers have found actual or potential congressional restraints upon their freedom of action diplomatically useful. Former Secretary of State Kissinger has recounted several instances in which the president and his advisers used the threat of a severe congressional reduction in America's overseas commitments as a diplomatic gambit in negotiating with foreign governments. And the Nixon administration repeatedly informed the NATO allies that unless they increased their contribution to the defense of the western alliance, Congress would almost certainly reduce America's troop contribution to the NATO area.[33] A similar situation arose during the early months of the Persian Gulf crisis, when Congress expressed its view forcefully that the nation's friends and allies ought to be making a larger contribution to the joint effort to repel Iraqi aggression. Aimed specifically at prosperous nations like Germany and Japan, this legislative effort was welcomed by executive policy makers.

Since the Vietnam War congressional activism in foreign affairs has not infrequently taken the opposite course: *expansion* of the nation's overseas obligations. Congress has at least tacitly approved most military base agreements negotiated by executive officials with foreign countries. It did not block efforts by the White House to augment American military power in the Indian Ocean. Despite criticisms about failure to consult Congress, legislators did not fundamentally object to the Reagan administration's use of force against Libya or to the more extensive and costly buildup of American military power in the Persian Gulf area. Similarly, legislators widely applauded (sometimes belatedly) efforts by the White House to eliminate dictatorial regimes in the Philippines and Panama. (Yet it could not be said that Congress always recognized an obligation thereafter to assist new governments in these nations to solve the societies' deep-seated and pervasive problems.)

Owing in no small measure to congressional initiatives, contemporary American foreign policy is governed now, more than in any previous era of history, by the Wilsonian principle of "open covenants, openly arrived at." Henry Kissinger's visit to the Chinese mainland in 1971 on behalf of the Nixon administration was remarkable not only because it inaugurated the new era of rapprochement in Sino-American relations, but also because it was a diplomatic initiative by the executive branch that was kept secret for some time from Congress.[34] Time and again since the Vietnam War, the House and Senate have insisted that the White House make public its diplomatic moves and initiatives. As much as any other single factor perhaps, efforts by the Johnson and Nixon administrations earlier to "manipulate" the news media and to conceal their policies led to the characterization "imperial presidency."

To the degree that a better informed Congress and citizenry provide a more secure foundation for effective diplomacy, legislative insistence upon maximum publicity for international commitments has clearly been a gain. The Vietnam War experience demonstrated convincingly that public support is indispensable for military and diplomatic success abroad.

Problems with Congressional Policy Making

Although Congress has adopted a more assertive role in foreign affairs, it may be doubted that the nature of congressional decision making lends itself to effective foreign policy management. A former State Department official has called legislative power in foreign policy a "blunt instrument," which not infrequently has resulted in "a series of uncoordinated actions that annoyed the Secretary of State more than it advanced coherent policy." On some occasions, legislators have threatened to paralyze American foreign policy unless the White House abandoned or changed a proposed course of action.[35] According to one of President Carter's aides, "Congress ties the President's hands on foreign policy, scrutinizing and criticizing every move he makes, sometimes jeopardizing relations with our allies and unpredictable foes." [36]

Even individuals with legislative experience have expressed concern about Congress's intrusion into the foreign policy field. J. William Fulbright, former Senate Foreign Relations Committee chairman, said:

> I confess to increasingly serious misgivings about the ability of the Congress to play a constructive role in our foreign relations. . . . those of us who prodded what seemed to be a hopelessly immobile herd of cattle [Congress] a decade ago, now stand back in awe in the face of a stampede.[37]

Basically the same complaints, as well as others, were expressed about Congress's foreign policy role in the 1980s. Thus, one legislator acknowledged that cabinet members and other officials of the executive branch could justifiably complain about the "repetitive testimony" they were required to give the House and Senate and about the lack of identifiable and effective leadership on Capitol Hill. Another legislator lamented the Senate's apparent inability "to control events," its internal fragmentation, and its growing susceptibility to pressure group campaigns. As legislators were considering such complex issues as the proposed MX missile system and Soviet-American arms-control negotiations, another senator deplored "the incredible lack of knowledge about the Soviet people and Soviet history" that existed on Capitol Hill. After reviewing the consequences of a number of congressionally imposed restrictions upon the president's diplomatic behavior during the 1970s, another experienced legislator called upon Congress to "reexamine its role in the conduct of foreign policy and repeal or amend, as necessary" most of this legislation, since it clearly posed an obstacle to "a unified, coherent and cohesive foreign policy." [38] Repeatedly during the Persian Gulf crisis, President Bush and his advisers stated that a refusal by Congress to support the White House would pose a serious obstacle to the achievement of the nation's foreign policy goals. On some occasions, they said or implied that dissent on Capitol Hill strengthened the determination of the Iraqi adversary to continue the conflict.

In the words of one young, liberal senator, Congress possesses the ability to "foul up foreign policy," and it has done so from time to time in recent years.[39] The congressional response to the discovery in August 1979 of a large contingent of Soviet troops in Cuba, for example, was confusing and ambiguous. One national news journal concluded that the Kremlin was "notoriously loath to let U.S. Senators beat them with sticks" on the Cuban question. Mishandling of the whole affair in Washington, the article concluded, not only casts still more doubt on the leadership of the Carter administration but also raises a longer-term and more disturbing question about whether the Congress—recently so assertive about playing a bigger role in foreign policy—can help solve crises rather than manufacturing and aggravating them.[40]

During the 1970s and 1980s, it might be doubted how much congressional interest in the subject actually advanced the cause of human rights in other countries. It was at least debatable, for example, whether legislative initiatives had in fact advanced the cause of freedom in Iran or Pakistan, although it may have done so in other settings (like Brazil).

Congress often approaches external policy making as an exercise in lawmaking, and that may be one reason why its assertive role in foreign affairs has not always been productive. According to a former State Department official, by the end of the 1970s Congress had imposed "more than 150 statutory limitations on the United States' relations with foreign countries." Commenting on the congressional tendency to envision diplomatic questions in legal terms or as legal contests, he added: "Foreign policy has become almost synonymous with law making. The result is to place a straitjacket of legislation around the manifold complexity of our relations with other nations." [41]

Foreigners have always found unique and bewildering the American system of separation of powers among three coordinate branches of government. But in no previous era has the foreign policy process in the United States perhaps proved so mystifying and frustrating for outsiders. Recent diplomatic experience has shown that agreement with the administration, even when the president's party controls Congress, often counts for little. After arriving at understandings with executive officials, in many cases foreign negotiators then have "to enter into separate external relations with the American Congress, and renegotiate ... the agreement reached." [42]

Most governments endeavor to arrive at a unified foreign policy position before they enter into negotiations with other states, but judging from recent examples, a unified position among policy makers in the United States is often arrived at only *after* understandings have been reached with foreign governments. This led one Soviet spokesman to ask, "With whom in America can we have dealings?" For foreign officials, it was "still not clear who exactly in the U.S. can speak in international relations on behalf of the United States." [43]

Congressional Assertiveness:
Probabilities and Prospects

What is the future of congressional assertiveness in American foreign relations? Has it become a permanent feature of the foreign policy process in the United States, or is it merely a phase that will be followed in time by a new era of executive dominance in external affairs? A number of diverse and contrary factors will determine the answers to these questions in the years ahead.

Factors Favoring an Expanded Role

A persuasive case can be made for the contention that Congress will continue to exercise a powerful—in some instances, a decisive—voice in foreign affairs for the indefinite future. Executive officials, foreign governments, and the public must come to terms with this possibility.

The United States as a Superpower. Transcending all other reasons why the role of Congress in the foreign policy realm has expanded and shows no sign of diminishing perhaps is the fact that *the United States is a superpower.* By the 1990s, in the light of developments in the Soviet Union, a strong case could be made for the contention that it was in fact the only superpower in the international system. At any rate, as was illustrated by the Persian Gulf crisis of the early 1990s, only the United States was in a position to take the lead in preserving the security of the region. Dynamic American leadership would no doubt be required in restoring long-range peace and stability to the Middle East, by such specific steps as resolving the Arab-Israeli conflict and undertaking the reconstruction of the war-devastated area. Meanwhile, on another front, the response of the United States was a crucial element in determining whether President Gorbachev would succeed in solving the severe economic problems confronting the Soviet Union. In brief, Congress would continue to concern itself actively with foreign policy issues because from the Western Hemisphere to East Asia, a broad range of challenges confronted the United States abroad.

Global and Domestic Setting. Among the other forces that engender and sustain an energetic role by Congress in foreign affairs, few are perhaps more important than the changing nature of the global agenda. In the second half of the twentieth century, unique and often extremely difficult issues have come to the forefront of international concern: economic stability, the pressing needs of the less developed societies, the increasingly acute world food shortage, runaway population growth throughout most of the Third World, and worldwide environmental problems. Today the solution to these major international and regional problems requires active participation by Congress, if for no other reason that, in the end, the solutions nearly always require substantial funds for their implementation. In many cases also, they entail treaties or executive agreements between the United States and other nations to deal with such problems on a multinational basis.

In the United States and in most other countries since World War II, the role of government has expanded to meet these challenges. This trend is both exemplified and sustained by the volume of legislation produced by Congress in the postwar era. One way of looking at the diplomatic activism of Congress, therefore, is to observe that the legislative branch is finally taking the same approach in dealing with external affairs that it has taken toward domestic issues since the New Deal: Congress is attempting to solve major public policy questions by enacting legislation and by relying upon other powers incident to lawmaking, such as the oversight function.

Executive Encouragement. As much out of necessity as conviction, perhaps, executive officials today frequently support a more dynamic and meaningful role by Congress in foreign relations. The president, the secretary of state, and other high-ranking executive officials at times have called upon legislative officials to join them in creating a unified approach to foreign policy issues.[44] Moreover, the attitude of executive officials toward congressional activism in foreign affairs is often highly variable and ambivalent. While executive officials routinely complain about congressional restrictions upon the president's authority, in particular instances they have favored forceful legislative intrusion into the diplomatic arena. From time to time, for example, executive policy makers have unquestionably invoked the threat of harsher legislative action, if other countries (such as the NATO allies and Japan) did not cooperate more fully in supporting the president's policy. Toward South Africa, successive administrations have relied upon the threat or prospect of sanctions and other coercive measures by Congress to gain concessions from the nation's white-ruled government. Even if it does not always approve of the action taken (or threatened) by Congress, the White House sometimes finds congressional action a useful tool in dealing with other governments.

Factors Favoring Restraint

A number of short- and long-term factors, however, point to restraint and possibly a reversal in the pattern of legislative activism witnessed since the Vietnam War. Initially, we need to be reminded that a forceful and independent role in foreign affairs by legislative bodies is a distinctive phenomenon among modern governments, confined almost entirely to the American system. In nearly all other countries, the tide has been running strongly in the contrary direction; other national legislatures have steadily lost the power to act independently, especially in the foreign policy field.

In Great Britain, France, Germany, Japan, and other democracies today, the responsibility for managing foreign affairs is vested almost solely with executive officials. In the rare cases when the legislative body does successfully challenge the incumbent government's foreign policy, a political crisis (followed by new national elections) normally ensues. The experience of many countries suggests that the successful conduct of foreign relations inherently militates against a high degree of legislative activism and independence.

Cycles in Diplomatic History.   Moreover, the forceful assertion of Congress's powers in foreign relations has been a cyclical occurrence in the nation's diplomatic experience. The "War Hawks of 1812," who demanded and got another war with Great Britain, had many members on Capitol Hill. Following the end of the Mexican War in 1848, Congress once more asserted its influence dynamically in foreign affairs. And the period before and after World War I marked another era of congressional assertiveness.

The cyclical nature of Congress's diplomatic militancy—and of the ensuing struggle between executive and legislative officials for primacy in foreign affairs—may be explained in various ways. No single existing theory adequately accounts for it. To some extent, congressional assertiveness in foreign relations may be related to the oscillating isolationist and interventionist moods of the American people toward international affairs.[45]

Alternatively, it may be a function of the political balance between the executive and legislative branches and of the shifting political tides within American society. For reasons that are even now difficult to explain satisfactorily, the zenith of bipartisan cooperation in foreign affairs in the postwar era was reached under the Truman and early Eisenhower administrations—when the presidency and Congress were controlled by different political parties. President Truman had much greater success in arriving at a constructive working relationship with a Republican-controlled Congress on foreign policy than President Carter experienced with a House and Senate controlled by his own political party.[46] By contrast, under the Reagan administration the Democratic-controlled House of Representatives was the center of intense congressional activism in dealing with such issues as the national defense budget, the proposed new MX missile system, and political developments in Central America. Although Democratic majorities existed in the House and Senate during the Bush administration, in key areas of foreign policy—such as relations with the Soviet Union and the Persian

Gulf crisis—as a rule Congress supported the diplomatic and military moves of the White House.

Problems with Executive-Legislative Consultation. The nature of consultation between policy makers in the executive and legislative branches of government is a significant factor in determining the outcome of efforts to achieve constructive bipartisan collaboration on major foreign policy issues. As emphasized in Chapter 5, there is the problem of when to consult—before or after the president has decided upon a particular diplomatic course of action? There is the additional question of which members of Congress should be included in such discussions. Who really represents Congress and can arrive at understandings in its name?

Even if the problems of when and whom to consult can be solved, a third serious inhibition upon successful executive-legislative consultation remains. What responsibility do members of Congress incur by participating in consultation on foreign policy issues? Does a policy decision resulting from such consultations become their decision, fully as much as the president's?

More specifically, does concurrence in a particular intelligence mission by selected members of the House and Senate make Congress as a whole responsible for its success or failure? Does a president's consultation with a selected group of legislators make Congress equally responsible with the executive branch when American military forces are used for diplomatic objectives?

If the answer to such questions is yes, how can this fact be reconciled with the idea of an "independent" legislative branch and with the traditional role of Congress as a critic of executive policies, especially when they miscarry? Alternatively, if the answer is no, what inducement does an incumbent president have to consult legislators on particular domestic questions, when they refuse to share with executive officials responsibility for the outcome of a proposed policy?

The success or failure of executive-legislative consultation may also be determined by individual personalities. During the late 1940s Secretary of State Dean Acheson and other executive officials worked harmoniously and effectively with influential legislators such as Senators Arthur H. Vandenberg and Tom Connally to formulate diplomatic undertakings (such as the Marshall Plan) acceptable to the White House and Congress. Although these officials often belonged to different political parties, an atmosphere of mutual trust and respect governed their deliberations. Agreements reached between them nearly always were subsequently supported by majorities in the House and Senate.[47]

By contrast, during the Johnson administration, legislative and executive officials were often far from agreement on foreign policy issues. Senator Fulbright outspokenly criticized White House policies toward Vietnam, the Dominican Republic, and other areas. The personal animosity and distrust ultimately existing between Johnson and the Senate Foreign Relations Committee chairman served as a major deterrent to constructive executive-legislative relations in the foreign policy field.

Public Attitudes toward President and Congress.   "Capacity in government," one informed student of the American system has said, "depends, in the United States as elsewhere, on leadership." [48] By the beginning of the 1980s, the American people's desire for clear and firm White House leadership in meeting the nation's internal and external problems was unmistakable. President Jimmy Carter's inability, for example, to manage Congress—to create and maintain minimal unity on Capitol Hill in behalf of his programs—proved to be a key element in the widespread perception that he was a weak and indecisive chief executive.[49]

Even congressional voices have been heard in the chorus calling upon the chief executive to exhibit forceful and dynamic diplomatic leadership. Sen. Adlai Stevenson III, D-Ill., declared that in recent years Congress had excelled at the game of "kick the President"—perhaps an understandable reaction on Capitol Hill to recent abuses of presidential power. Yet, Stevenson informed his colleagues, Congress's "weaknesses will come back to haunt us. I want a strong executive." [50]

According to one study of contemporary executive-legislative relations:

> Left and right want a strong Presidency, the left in domestic affairs, the right for foreign policy. . . . Americans not only prefer Presidential leadership but the scope of foreign and domestic problems and the recurrent emergencies facing a world power simply demand Presidential power—particularly when Congress' foreign policy decisions are so often governed by domestic policies.[51]

Or as another study of public attitudes expressed it, for most Americans the presidency is "everyone's first resort." Realistically or not, the American people expect the chief executive to be forthright and successful in solving national problems; they complain vocally about the lack of White House leadership when this does not happen.[52]

The celebrated American comedian Will Rogers once told his audiences, "There's good news from Washington. Congress is adjourned." Such humor always strikes a responsive chord with Americans, for whom the denigration of Congress's deeds and misdeeds sometimes seems a national pastime.[53] Today, as in the past, the American people are aware that during some periods Congress's record has been badly tarnished. Influence peddling on Capitol Hill, misuse of campaign contributions, scandalous personal behavior by legislators, recurring disunity within the House and Senate, and obstructionist moves by Congress in dealing with national policy issues have become public knowledge. Legislators often can be energetic and decisive in dealing with executive wrongdoing but dilatory and ineffectual in correcting unethical practices, illegal activities, and organizational problems on Capitol Hill. During the early 1990s, for example, deadlocks, jurisdictional disputes, and fragmentation within Congress made it extremely difficult for executive and legislative officials to solve federal budgetary problems.

Public confidence in Congress's performance has fallen steadily in recent years. In 1974, a poll showed that almost half of the American people approved of the way Congress was doing its job; by mid-1979 this figure had declined to 19 percent. According to another study of public attitudes, twice as many Americans blamed Congress as blamed President Carter for deadlocks between the two branches of the government. Another study, in 1983, found that just over 7 percent of those interviewed believed that Congress was doing a better than adequate job of dealing with urgent internal and external issues; almost half (46.5 percent) thought that Congress's performance was disappointing or poor. According to one experienced observer, Congress still needed to display "more backbone in confronting the president" and to be less concerned with "nitpicking, constituency service, and the thousands of small issues" dominating the activities of legislators. A Gallup Poll in 1982 showed that only 29 percent of the public approved of the way Congress was performing its duties, while 54 percent disapproved. Earlier Gallup Polls showed that public approval of Congress's performance varied from a low of 19 to a high of 38 percent. Aware of such public attitudes, even members of the House and Senate deplored the fact that on some occasions, the behavior of legislators was "demeaning," making Congress the "laughing stock of America." If anything, the public assessment of Congress's performance was even lower in the 1990s. A CBS/*New York Times* poll late in 1990, for example, found that some 76 percent of Republicans and 71 percent of Democrats asked said they "disapproved" of the way legislators were doing their job. According to a study made a few weeks earlier, some 60 percent of those polled said Congress was doing a poor job, and some 67 percent said it was time most members of the House and Senate were replaced. The overall image emerging from this analysis of public sentiment was that of a Congress "driven by special interests and by the lawmakers' own concerns, rather than those of the people" who elected them.[54] The recent movement to limit legislative terms of office was a graphic example of such public discontent.

Public and Congressional Domestic Concerns. Another factor restraining congressional activism in foreign policy is that the American public exhibits a low level of interest in international questions. This has been true of American society historically (it was a major force, for example, sustaining the isolationist approach to foreign relations), and it is not significantly less the case in the contemporary period. Almost invariably, on a list of the dominant concerns of the American people, pollsters have found that citizens give highest priority to internal problems. Some 15 percent or less of the people belong to the "attentive public"—that minority of opinion which is interested in and reasonably well informed about foreign relations.[55] The behavior of Congress is inescapably affected by this public opinion trait.

This leads to another, closely related factor likely to inhibit a dynamic and sustained role by Congress in the diplomatic field. Constituency-related business ranks as a primary claim upon the time and energies of most legislators. Even with greatly enlarged staffs, most legislators today are hard pressed to meet the diverse demands made upon them by their constituents. To cite a different example, during the Persian Gulf crisis early in 1991, one news report found that the issue uppermost in the minds of most legislators was not taxes or the recession or foreign policy. It was legislative redistricting in the light of the latest census findings.[56]

As several of our case studies emphasized, relatively few legislators have the time to acquire expert knowledge of a broad range of complex foreign policy questions. For example, only a minority of legislators has shown any real desire to receive and to assimilate detailed information about the activities of intelligence agencies—although legislators are legally entitled to it. Similarly, few legislators are inclined to read and digest voluminous reports from executive officials regarding human rights problems in more than 160 independent nations.

The high priority accorded to domestic concerns by the American people and their legislative representatives has two specific consequences. First, perhaps even more today than in the past, Congress's approach to foreign affairs is heavily colored by local and domestic considerations vis-à-vis a commitment to the national interest. Several years ago, one of the nation's most knowledgeable reporters characterized the foreign policy process in the United States in such terms as "chaos" and "an international scandal." To a considerable degree, he blamed Congress for this state of affairs: "Seldom in memory has it seemed so divided, so concerned with personal, local or state interests and so indifferent to its own Congressional leadership or the disturbing problems of the 1980s."[57]

Second, Congress's involvement in external affairs is likely to be characterized by a short attention span and to be heavily conditioned by the current newsworthiness of a particular foreign policy issue. As our discussion in Chapter 6 illustrated, members of the House and Senate were actively concerned for a time about various misdeeds of the CIA. After a relatively brief period, however, the attention of most legislators had shifted to other issues, leaving only a handful of senators and representatives to monitor intelligence activities on a continuing basis. Summing up a conversation about attempts by Congress to restore its powers, one senator characteristically exclaimed, "I think we've made substantial headlines—I mean headway." [58] Basically the same point could be made about the Iran-contra affair during President Reagan's second term. For a period of a few brief weeks, this episode dominated the headlines and appeared to monopolize the energy and attention of Congress. Then interest in the affair waned rapidly and other issues (such as the challenge to U.S. diplomatic interests in the Persian Gulf and the prospects for arms-control agreements between the superpowers) were at the forefront of public and legislative concern. As is true of American public opinion generally, it is difficult for Congress to exhibit sustained interest in a particular foreign policy problem or issue for an extended length of time.

Invitation to Struggle

From the time of George Washington's administration until the present day, the president and Congress have vied for control over foreign relations. Although many formal and informal changes have been made in the Constitution since 1789, the basic pattern of divided responsibility and power in foreign affairs remains unaltered. The president still serves as commander in chief of the armed forces; he alone has the power to recognize other governments; and only he and his agents can officially negotiate treaties and agreements with other countries in the name of the United States.

After two centuries, Congress also retains influential prerogatives in national security and foreign affairs. The size and nature of the American military establishment are determined by Congress; funds for current military operations and for the development of new weapons must be provided by the legislative branch. In addition, Congress must authorize and appropriate funds for a host of other programs and governmental activities in the foreign policy field—ranging from the State Department's budget, to foreign military and economic aid programs, to the activities of intelligence agencies. Also implicit in Congress's lawmaking function is its power to investigate the operations of executive agencies and the administration of programs it has authorized and funded—a power the House and Senate have used with telling effect on numerous occasions since World War II.

Continuing Disunity in the Policy Process

Since the Vietnam conflict, the executive and legislative branches of the American government have faced comparable problems with respect to their role in the foreign policy process. Stated negatively, the efforts of both branches have often been seriously weakened by schisms, organizational rivalries, and centrifugal forces that impair their internal cohesion and their ability to arrive at unified positions on major diplomatic issues.

Our discussion in Chapter 1, for example, called attention to the fact that within the executive branch the traditional authority and premier position of the State Department in the diplomatic field have been steadily diluted by the proliferation of executive agencies that play a major or minor role in contemporary American foreign policy. Since the Nixon administration particularly—with the emergence of the president's national security adviser as a rival to the secretary of state— executive efforts in foreign affairs appear to have become increasingly disunified and uncoordinated.[59] Under the Reagan administration, the dramatic resignation of Secretary of State Alexander Haig—and in the years that followed, the Iran-contra affair—raised the question anew: Who really speaks for the administration in foreign affairs?

As our case studies have shown, the role of Congress in contemporary American foreign policy is also beset by comparable difficulties. If the House and Senate have now established—and can be expected to maintain—an influential congressional presence in the foreign policy field, how well equipped are they to continue to play this role? Recent experience indicates that the answer must be: rather poorly and inadequately. To date, in terms of organizational, procedural, and behavioral changes required, few members of Congress have faced up squarely to the necessary implications of their demand for a position of equal partnership with the White House in foreign affairs. By the 1990s, Congress appeared to be more decentralized, fragmented, and resistant to unifying influences than in any previous period of American history. To date Congress has supplied little evidence to show that it is prepared to adapt its own organizational structure and internal procedures to the demands of an active and effective foreign policy role.[60]

Shared Goals

Executive and legislative officials alike, we may safely assume, ultimately seek the same goal: a unified, rational, and successful foreign policy for the United States. Moreover, all participants in foreign policy decision making would no doubt subscribe to the theoretical proposition that continuing discord, disunity, and competing efforts within the

American government—regardless of whether they arise within the executive branch, within Congress, or from conflicts between the executive and legislative branches—nearly always impair the ability of the United States to achieve its diplomatic objectives.

If broad agreement exists in Washington on these propositions, it follows that officials in each branch need to devote greater attention to defining their respective contributions to the foreign policy process more clearly. By virtue of their differing constitutional responsibilities, experiences, and resources, executive and legislative policy makers ought to make different contributions to the common effort, reflecting what each group is uniquely prepared to supply.

Presidential Role. What contributions are the president and his executive advisers singularly qualified to make? The president symbolizes and represents the national interest of the United States both to the American people and to foreign countries. The chief executive alone can speak in behalf of the nation to governments, leaders, and political movements abroad. As commander in chief of the armed forces, only the president is in a position to respond promptly and decisively to external threats.

The president and the executive officials under his jurisdiction also play an indispensable role in policy formulation. Relying upon the State Department's communications system with American embassies overseas and upon the intelligence community's resources for collecting and analyzing data, the White House remains in an unrivaled position to consider available options and to devise diplomatic strategies and programs for which it will later seek legislative support.

Moreover, the president's position as a leader and educator of public opinion remains dominant. As the presidency of the "great communicator," Ronald Reagan, illustrated, the chief executive is in a unique position to inform the American people about major diplomatic issues and to elicit their support in behalf of foreign policies and programs advocated by the White House. In the past (and the presidency of Franklin D. Roosevelt provided a graphic example), this has been a potent instrument of presidential influence in foreign relations. Relying upon press conferences, interviews with members of the news media, and other devices, President Bush and his advisers made a concerted effort to keep the American people informed of significant developments during the Persian Gulf crisis.

The Contributions of Congress. Congress also brings certain distinctive powers and perspectives to bear in foreign policy making. First, there is the legislative power to grant or to withhold funds for foreign policy ventures and programs. Although Congress has possessed this prerogative since 1789, only since the closing stage of the Vietnam War has it relied regularly upon its control over the purse strings to influence the course of American diplomacy.

Second, Congress makes an essential contribution in supplying a base of legitimacy to American foreign policy. For a democracy, this vital element—a pervasive public belief that the nation's diplomatic goals are rational, are attainable at reasonable cost, and are consonant with American society's cherished values—is a prerequisite for diplomatic success. Especially since the Vietnam War, even executive officials have acknowledged this legislative contribution to the foreign policy process. Thus, at the end of the 1970s, one State Department official said that there was "an important need after Vietnam and Watergate to legitimize American foreign policy." [61] During the early 1980s the Reagan administration depended upon this same contribution of Congress to create a foundation of legitimacy under its efforts to counter Communist influence in Central America. Early in 1991, as explained more fully in Chapter 4, President Bush asked Congress for explicit approval of his military moves in the Persian Gulf area. The president was aware that, without such legislative support, his policies risked losing the legitimacy required if they were to be successful.

Third, as our discussion of legislative activities with regard to the intelligence community illustrated (Chapter 6), Congress can make a positive contribution to foreign policy decision making—and to the future of American democracy—by continuously scrutinizing the activities of executive agencies and by imposing more stringent guidelines upon their operations. This contribution of the legislative branch is highlighted by the perennial challenge of imposing effective controls upon the CIA and other members of the intelligence community. On the basis of recent experience, it seems safe to conclude that the American people and their legislative representatives have a decidedly mixed attitude about intelligence operations. The vast majority of citizens believes that the United States is required to engage in intelligence operations to preserve its security in a dangerous world. At the same time, Americans remain apprehensive about such operations—especially about "covert" intelligence activities abroad. In many instances, such covert operations are quickly made "overt" by the news media, thereby often defeating the purpose of such undertakings.

A fourth essential and distinctive contribution of Congress to the foreign policy process was brought into sharp focus by our analysis of Congress's role in the disposition and control of the armed forces (Chapter 5). Diplomatic experience under the Reagan and Bush administrations indicates rather convincingly that legislative restraints upon the president's reliance upon armed force to achieve the nation's foreign policy goals are less than totally effective. As already noted, for example, the impact of the War Powers Resolution upon the conduct of American foreign relations proved to be much more limited than expected—to the point that by the early 1990s, it could be questioned whether this legislation had not become altogether a dead letter. Inevitably perhaps, once the president has committed the armed forces in situations endangering American lives, the tendency is always for Congress to refrain from actions that might undermine White House efforts or place American forces in jeopardy. Nor is the legislative branch really well equipped to determine long-range military strategy or battlefield tactics.

Yet as commander in chief, the president can command only the military establishment that Congress provides. The overall size of the armed forces; the size and composition of the reserves; the disposition of forces among the three service branches; the weapons with which the nation's land, sea, and ground forces are equipped; the supplies available to U.S. forces; the rules and regulations governing the operation of the armed services—these are all matters falling within the constitutional purview of Congress. In brief, it is possible for the United States to possess, and to be able from time to time to use, the kind of military establishment required to achieve its objectives abroad only to the degree that the executive and legislative branches collaborate in behalf of a common goal.

"Invitation to Cooperate."   The basic theme of this study is that America's unique constitutional system creates an "invitation to struggle" between the president and Congress in the foreign policy field. From time to time in the nation's diplomatic experience, that struggle has been intense; and in some instances, it has directly affected the course of American foreign relations. As the American republic enters its third century, there is every reason to expect that in the future, as in the past, this struggle will be a feature of the decision-making process and that sometimes it will significantly influence the nation's behavior abroad.

Yet experience since the 1960s also supports another conclusion. This is that neither the imperial presidency nor the model of a very assertive Congress provides an approach to diplomatic decision making that contributes positively to achieving national objectives overseas. Few informed citizens desire a return to the pattern of presidential behavior associated with the Vietnam War, the Watergate episode, and the Iran-contra affair. While most Americans continue to look to the White House for dynamic and imaginative leadership in meeting challenges at home and abroad, they also expect the president to observe constitutional and legal restraints, to work constructively with Congress, to be receptive to diverse viewpoints among his advisers, and to take account of public opinion and of the nation's traditions in managing foreign affairs. When the first president declined to be addressed or treated as His Majesty, the venerated George Washington established a precedent other chief executives were expected to follow! Difficult as it may be to formulate the differences clearly and logically, most citizens understand and value the distinction between a forceful president and an imperial president; and they want the former, while avoiding the latter. Americans want the presidential model to stay somewhere between the Johnson-Nixon and the Carter styles of presidential management.

By the same token, well-informed citizens and observers also discern a number of problems regarding a very assertive role bv Congress in the foreign policy process. On the one hand, is Congress ʒ role as one of the three coordinate branches of the government. The Revolutionary War motto of "No taxation without representation" underscored the vital role played by the legislative branch in the American democracy. Under the Constitution as it has evolved over more than two hundred years, Congress (in some cases, the Senate alone) is assigned certain powers and responsibilities that crucially affect the nation's foreign relations, such as the requirement that treaties receive the advice and consent of the Senate; that the provision of funds for the armed forces, the State Department, and other operations be provided by act of Congress; and that the House and Senate from time to time investigate diverse aspects of foreign affairs. Above all, as the Vietnam War underscored, no major undertaking by the United States in the foreign policy field is likely to be successful without the continuing support of Congress.

On the other hand, on the basis of the available evidence it seems equally evident that the people are concerned about the implications of unrestrained legislative actions and intrusions into the foreign policy sphere. For example, as an institution Congress nearly always ranks below (and sometimes well below) the presidency in public esteem and confidence. Indeed, as noted earlier, in recent years the credibility of Congress in the eyes of citizens appears to have *declined*.[62]

In foreign affairs specifically, few Americans are reassured by the era of legislative assertiveness that followed the Vietnam War. The 1970s were not widely regarded as a high point of American diplomatic leadership and accomplishment. While Congress's behavior in the foreign policy field was not of course solely responsible for that fact, it was certainly one contributing cause—as even a number of legislators themselves in time conceded. Ultimately, public opinion reacted very negatively against the kind of weakened and indecisive presidency—the president's actions were often restrained by congressionally imposed limitations upon his conduct abroad—witnessed during much of this period. Repeated efforts by the House and Senate to "micromanage" the nation's foreign affairs in some measure contributed to the decline of American power and influence abroad evident by the late 1970s. If for no other reason, the phenomenon frequently raised anew the question of who was really in charge of American foreign policy.

The election of Ronald Reagan to the White House in 1980, for example, could be at least partially explained by the widespread public dissatisfaction with a weakened and indecisive presidency. Significantly also, no public complaint was heard about the effective demise of such restraints upon presidential behavior as the War Powers Resolution. The Vietnam War experience aside, little evidence could be cited to show that the American people really wanted to entrust the management of the nation's foreign affairs to Congress. By the 1990s, for example, it had become obvious that Congress was experiencing real difficulty successfully managing the federal budget and successfully overseeing a variety of domestic programs. Or as an aide to President Bush was heard to remark during the Persian Gulf crisis, the United States could not conduct foreign affairs successfully if "it has 535 secretaries of state"!

Several years ago, a former State Department official advocated a "compact" between the executive and legislative branches in the sphere of external policy.[63] In so many words, every chief executive since Franklin D. Roosevelt has called for a partnership between executive and legislative officials in dealing with major foreign policy issues. During the months before FDR died, and then under the Truman and Eisenhower administrations, the concept of bipartisanship governed relations between the White House and Congress in their approach to major foreign policy problems. Or to employ the term used in the introduction to Part III, ideally the president and Congress need to follow the familiar principle of the division of labor in the formulation and administration of foreign policy. In general terms, this idea means that each branch would make the kind of contribution to the foreign policy decision-making process that each is uniquely qualified and equipped to make.

This idea is made more concrete if we invoke the familiar metaphor of the American ship of state. After more than two centuries of diplomatic history, it seems clear that *the captain of the ship of state is the president*—a reality confirmed by the recent experience of the Persian Gulf crisis. The chief executive and his principal aides are on the bridge. The president commands the crew and, with the assistance of his subordinates, issues orders to it. Similarly, the president instructs the navigator, who plots the course and keeps the ship on it. In longstanding naval tradition, as captain of the ship the president is responsible for its overall operation and for the successful completion of the voyage. No ship in recent memory has been successfully operated by a committee consisting of officers, crew, passengers, and onlookers.

Yet it is also true that the American ship of state was built, and is maintained, by Congress; and its owners are the American people. Legislative authorization and funding are essential for its operation, maintenance, repair, and renovation. The ship's officers are confirmed in their positions by the Senate (although they may be removed by the president alone or, in rare instances, by impeachment). The recruitment, size, composition, and compensation of the crew are directly or indirectly determined by acts of Congress. Similarly, the size, nature, and effectiveness of the ship's armaments are also the result of legislative decisions. Essential support facilities and services—such as supply depots, ports and drydocks, and needed ancillary vessels (defensive ships and aircraft, supply vessels, and hospital facilities)—must also be made available by Congress. Congress serves as the chief quartermaster: all of the ship's supplies and provisions must be acquired with funds provided by the legislative branch. Moreover, the rules and regulations governing the conduct of the ship's personnel are specified by Congress. Periodically, committees of the House and Senate investigate various aspects of the ship's operation, especially if problems are encountered in completing its mission successfully. Congress no less plays an important role in communicating to the president and other members of the crew the desires and concerns of the owners of the vessel—the American people—and in insisting that their views be carefully considered in decisions made by the captain and his subordinates. In extreme cases (comparable perhaps to a court martial), Congress can relieve the captain and other high-ranking officers of their commands and initiate the process whereby an entirely new crew is placed in charge of the ship of state.

Now this is admittedly an idealized conception of the American foreign policy process. It does not allow sufficiently, for example, for longstanding institutional rivalries and jealousies, for personal ambitions and rivalries on both ends of Pennsylvania Avenue, for perceptions and misperceptions by executive and legislative officials, and for other irrational and personal factors that often crucially influence the policy-making process. Yet as is commonplace in natural science, ideal typologies (such as the perfect vacuum or perpetual motion) sometimes enable us to gain greater insight, even if they are not encountered in nature. Such conceptions provide a yardstick or standard for measuring actual behavior or performance.

Experience has shown rather convincingly that the president or Congress cannot do what the other does well. Least of all will the American ship of state be able to make the voyage safely and remain steady on course if it is subjected to continual conflicts and tensions involving the captain and crew, the support services, the owners, the passengers, and perhaps onlookers and members of the news media. The minimum precondition for successful completion of the mission, often upon stormy international seas, is for the president and Congress to make the contribution each is best qualified to make in defining, achieving, and safeguarding the nation's interests in a continually changing and often hostile global environment.

Notes

1. See the statement by Secretary of State George Shultz, "From the Secretary of State," *Foreign Affairs* 66 (Winter 1987-1988): 426-428; the views of former House Speaker Thomas P. O'Neill in the *New York Times,* October 23, 1986; the views of several legislators in the *New York Times,* June 2, 1987; and the views of the former British ambassador to the United States, Peter Jay, as quoted in William D. Rogers, "Who's in Charge of Foreign Policy?" *New York Times Magazine,* September 9, 1979, 49. (The author is a former State Department official, but he is not to be confused with former secretary of state William P. Rogers.)
2. Dispatch by Bernard Gwertzman, *New York Times,* January 25, 1975.
3. Charles H. Percy, "The Partisan Gap," *Foreign Policy* 45 (Winter 1981-1982): 3.
4. Dispatch by Francis X. Clines, *New York Times,* May 16, 1983; and dispatch by R. W. Apple, Jr., *New York Times,* December 19, 1990.
5. Quoted in Marvin Stone, "Presidency: Imperial or Imperiled?" *U.S. News & World Report,* January 15, 1979, 88. See also Gerald R. Ford, *A Time to Heal* (New York: Harper and Row and the Reader's Digest Association, 1979), 138-139, 150.
6. Warren Christopher, "Ceasefire between the Branches: A Compact in Foreign Affairs," *Foreign Affairs* 60 (Summer 1982): 998; dispatch by Steven V. Roberts, *New York Times,* March 21, 1983; and Theodore H. White, "Weinberger on the Ramparts," *New York Times Magazine,* February 6, 1983, 77.
7. Nicholas DeB. Katzenbach, "Foreign Policy, Public Opinion and Secrecy," *Foreign Affairs* 52 (October 1973): 18.
8. For the views of John V. Lindsay, former member of Congress and mayor of New York, see "For a New Policy Balance," *Foreign Affairs* 50 (October 1971): 1; and for a more recent view in the same vein, see Richard G. Lugar, *Letters to the Next President* (New York: Simon & Schuster, 1988), by a former chairman of the Senate Foreign Relations Committee.
9. For a detailed analysis of the "legislative explosion" witnessed since World War II, see James McClellan, "The State of the American Congress," *Modern Age* 21 (Summer 1977): 227-239.
10. Dispatch by James Reston, *New York Times,* September 21, 1979.
11. "What Congress Really Thinks of Itself," *U.S. News & World Report,* March 15, 1982, 22-24. See also the views of Senator Simpson as described in a dispatch by Steven V. Roberts, *New York Times,* March 21, 1983; and Martin Tolchin, "Howard Baker: Trying to Tame an Unruly Senate," *New York Times Magazine,* March 28, 1982.

12. *New York Times,* January 5, 1987; and Marvin Stone, "Proxmire's Well-Placed Jab," *U.S. News & World Report,* September 10, 1979, 84.

13. The study was conducted by Professors Thomas Franck and Edward Weisband, and it is discussed in *New York Times,* November 29, 1976; the views of Marvin Fitzwater are found in *Congressional Quarterly Weekly Report,* December 22, 1990, 4202.

14. McClellan, "State of the American Congress," 237. See also Susan W. Hammond, "Congressional Change and Reform: Staffing the Congress," in Leroy N. Rieselbach, ed., *Legislative Reform: The Policy Impact* (Lexington, Mass.: D. C. Heath, 1978), 183-193. For a recent study on the subject, see Mark Bisnow, *In the Shadow of the Dome: Chronicles of a Capitol Hill Aide* (New York: Morrow, 1990).

15. See Dean Acheson, *Sketches from Life of Men I Have Known* (New York: Harper and Row, 1961), 124-125. For historical background, see Holbert N. Carroll, *The House of Representatives and Foreign Affairs* (Boston: Little, Brown, 1966).

16. See the views of Rep. Paul Findley, as described in the *New York Times,* October 6, 1966.

17. House Committee on International Relations, *Congress and Foreign Policy,* 94th Cong., 2d sess., 1976, 19. See also the dialogue between executive and legislative officials on the role of public opinion in foreign affairs in William O. Chattick, *State Department, Press, and Pressure Groups* (New York: Wiley, 1970), 43-45.

18. Senator Church, quoted in a dispatch by Richard Burt, *New York Times,* January 9, 1979.

19. The extent of lobbying activities by foreign governments in the contemporary period is conveyed by an examination of the voluminous data in *Washington Representatives, 1986* (Washington, D.C.: Columbia Books, 1986). This work contains a list of organizations engaged in such activities that occupies ten closely packed pages (633-643). The numbers range from thirty-three for Taiwan, thirty-seven for France, twenty-three for Israel, and thirty-four for Mexico to ten for the People's Republic of China, four for Cuba, eight for Panama, and eight for the Soviet Union. See also later volumes in the same series.

20. "What Carter's Aides Really Think of Congress," *U.S. News & World Report,* August 14, 1978, 15.

21. For specific examples of lobbying by foreign governments, see F. C. Ogene, *Interest Groups and the Shaping of Foreign Policy: Four Case Studies of United States African Policy* (New York: St. Martin's, 1983); Abdul A. Said, ed., *Ethnicity and U.S. Foreign Policy* (New York: Praeger, 1981); Steven Emerson, *The American House of Saud: The Secret Petrodollar Connection* (New York: Franklin Watts, 1985); *The Washington Lobby,* 5th ed. (Washington, D.C.: Congressional Quarterly, 1987); Jack Holland, *The American Connection: U.S. Guns, Money, and Influence in Northern Ireland* (New York: Penguin Books, 1988); Mathias, "Ethnic Groups and Foreign Affairs"; George W. Shepherd, *Racial Influences on American Foreign Policy* (New York: Basic Books, 1970); "Middle East Lobbying," *Congressional Quarterly Weekly Report,* April 22, 1981, 1523-1530; and Deborah M. Levy, "Advice for Sale," *Foreign Policy* 67 (Summer 1987): 64-87.

22. See *U.S. News & World Report,* November 22, 1976, 30.

23. More detailed examination of pro-Zionist and pro-Arab lobbying in the United States is available in Nimrod Novik, *The United States and Israel:*

Domestic Determinants of a Changing U.S. Commitment (Boulder, Colo.: Westview, 1986); Abraham Ben-Zvi, *Alliance Politics and the Limits of Influence: The Case of the U.S. and Israel, 1975-1984* (Boulder, Colo.: Westview, 1984); "Middle East Lobbying"; Paul Findley, *They Dare to Speak Out: People and Institutions Confront Israel's Lobby* (Westport, Conn.: Lawrence Hill, 1985); Edward W. Said, *Covering Islam* (New York: Pantheon Books, 1981); Elia Zureik and Fouad Moughrabi, *Public Opinion and the Palestine Question* (New York: St. Martin's, 1987); Cheryl A. Rubenberg, *Israel and the American National Interest* (Champaign: University of Illinois Press, 1986); Stephen L. Spiegel, *The Other Arab-Israeli Conflict: Making America's Middle East Policy from Truman to Reagan* (Chicago: University of Chicago Press, 1985); and Peter Grose, *Israel in the Mind of America* (New York: Alfred A. Knopf, 1983).

24. For a detailed study of efforts by the executive branch to influence the deliberations of Congress, see Abraham Holtzman, *Legislative Liaison: Executive Leadership in Congress* (Chicago: Rand McNally, 1970).

25. Alton Frye and William D. Rogers, "Linkage Begins at Home," *Foreign Policy* 35 (Summer 1979): 55-56.

26. 1 U.S. Statutes-at-Large 613 (1799).

27. Dispatch by Hedrick Smith, *New York Times*, August 14, 1979.

28. Dispatch by James Reston, *New York Times*, September 21, 1979.

29. Dispatch by John Kifner, *New York Times*, November 26, 1979, and dispatch by Bernard Gwertzman, November 27, 1979.

30. *U.S. News & World Report*, February 19, 1979, 52-54. See also Alan Platt and Lawrence D. Weiler, *Congress and Arms Control* (Boulder, Colo.: Westview, 1978).

31. For recent discussions of the ABM agreement, its meaning, and its implications, see Raymond L. Garthoff, *Policy versus Law: The Reinterpretation of the ABM Treaty* (Washington, D.C.: Brookings Institution, 1987); William J. Durch, *The ABM Treaty and Western Security* (Cambridge, Mass.: Ballinger, 1987); and dispatch by Fred C. Iklé, *New York Times*, June 8, 1987, and dispatches by Gerard C. Smith and David Riley, and by Jonathan Fuerbringer, *New York Times*, October 2, 1987.

32. For the views of the Nixon-Kissinger White House on the results of congressional action toward the Vietnam War, see Richard Nixon, *The Memoirs of Richard Nixon* (New York: Grosset and Dunlap, 1978), 744, 888-889; and Henry Kissinger, *White House Years* (Boston: Little, Brown, 1979), 1413, 1461.

33. Kissinger, *White House Years*, 400-401.

34. Ibid.

35. George W. Ball, *Diplomacy for a Crowded World: An American Foreign Policy* (Boston: Atlantic/Little, Brown, 1976), 204.

36. "What Carter's Aides Really Think of Congress," 15.

37. J. William Fulbright, "The Legislator as Educator," *Foreign Affairs* 57 (Spring 1979): 719-733.

38. Percy, "The Partisan Gap," 12; dispatch by Steven V. Roberts, *New York Times*, March 21, 1983, quoting Senator Simpson; John Tower, "Congress versus the President: The Formulation and Implementation of American Foreign Policy," *Foreign Affairs* 60 (Winter 1981-1982): 229-247; and dispatch by Steven V. Roberts, *New York Times*, June 4, 1983, quoting then-Senator Dan Quayle, R-Ind.

39. Dispatch by Adam Clymer, *New York Times*, July 3, 1977.

40. See "SALT Debate Is Complicated by Soviet Troops in Cuba," *Congressional Quarterly Weekly Report,* September 8, 1979, 1913; see also an excerpt from the report on SALT II by the Senate Foreign Relations Committee, in *New York Times,* November 20, 1979; and *Time,* October 1, 1979, 100.

41. Rogers, "Who's in Charge of Foreign Policy?" 44, 47, 50. Basically the same criticism is made of Congress's approach to foreign affairs by former secretary of state Henry Kissinger, who contrasts the fields of law and diplomacy. See Kissinger, *White House Years,* 940-941.

42. Genrikh Trofimenko, "Too Many Negotiators," *New York Times,* July 13, 1979.

43. Ibid.

44. For the views of Assistant Secretary of State for Congressional Relations Douglas J. Bennet, Jr., see "Congress: Its Role in Foreign Policy-Making," *Department of State Bulletin* 78 (June 1978): 35-36, and "Congress in Foreign Policy: Who Needs It?" *Foreign Affairs* 57 (Fall 1978): 40-51.

45. The concept of oscillating isolationist and interventionist foreign policy moods by the American people is identified and explained in F. L. Klingberg, "The Historical Alternation of Moods in American Foreign Policy," *World Politics* 4 (January 1952): 239-273.

46. For a detailed discussion of bipartisan collaboration during the Truman administration, see Cecil V. Crabb, Jr., *Bipartisan Foreign Policy: Myth or Reality?* (New York: Harper and Row, 1957), and Arthur H. Vandenberg, Jr., ed., *The Private Papers of Senator Vandenberg* (Boston: Houghton Mifflin, 1952).

47. Acheson, *Sketches from Life of Men I Have Known,* 123-146.

48. James L. Sundquist, "Congress and the President: Enemies or Partners?" in Lawrence C. Dodd and Bruce I. Oppenheimer, eds., *Congress Reconsidered* (New York: Praeger, 1977), 222.

49. *U.S. News & World Report,* August 27, 1979, 20.

50. Elizabeth Drew, "Why Congress Won't Fight," *New York Times Magazine,* September 23, 1973, 83.

51. The findings of the study, conducted by Thomas E. Cronin and Lawrence C. Dodd, are summarized in a dispatch by Tom Wicker, *New York Times,* November 18, 1977.

52. Dispatch by Terence Smith, *New York Times,* October 28, 1979.

53. For detailed analyses of public attitudes toward Congress, see "What Congress Really Thinks of Itself"; Malcolm E. Jewell and Samuel C. Patterson, *The Legislative Process in the United States,* 3d ed. (New York: Random House, 1977), 315-317; and Roger H. Davidson, David M. Kovenock, and Michael K. O'Leary, *Congress in Crisis: Politics and Congressional Reform* (Belmont, Calif.: Wadsworth, 1971), 38-66.

54. See the survey data presented in *Time,* October 1, 1979, 25; *U.S. News & World Report,* July 16, 1979, 21, March 15, 1982, 22-24, and May 23, 1983, 48; dispatch by Steven V. Roberts, *New York Times,* December 26, 1982; *Baton Rouge Morning Advocate,* August 1, 1982; poll data in the dispatch by Robin Toner, *New York Times,* October 12, 1990; dispatch by Michael Oreskes, *New York Times,* November 4, 1990; and the Gallup Poll on public opinion toward the Persian Gulf crisis in the *Baton Rouge Morning Advocate,* January 16, 1991.

55. Ralph B. Levering, *The Public and American Foreign Policy: 1918-1978* (New York: Morrow, 1978), 29.

56. John Bibby and Roger Davidson, *On Capitol Hill: Studies in the Legislative Process* (New York: Holt, Rinehart and Winston, 1967), 111-112. See also McClellan, "The State of the American Congress," 229, 237; and see the discussion of what one analysis calls Congress's "obsession" with redistricting above other issues, in *Newsweek*, January 14, 1991, 20. Another recent study found that the average lawmaker "spends half his time fund raising" for reelection. See *Newsweek*, October 22, 1990, 24-25.
57. Dispatch by James Reston, *New York Times*, September 21, 1979.
58. This unnamed senator is quoted in Drew, "Why Congress Won't Fight," 16.
59. For numerous examples of the decline of the State Department in the foreign policy process during the Nixon administration, see Kissinger, *White House Years*.
60. On the perennial problem of congressional reform, see Roger H. Davidson, David M. Kovenock, and Michael K. O'Leary, *Congress in Crisis: Politics and Congressional Reform* (Belmont, Calif.: Wadsworth, 1966); Thomas E. Mann and Norman Ornstein, *The New Congress* (Washington, D.C.: American Enterprise Institute, 1981); Philip M. Stern, *The Best Congress Money Can Buy* (New York: Pantheon, 1988); and Leroy Rieselbach, *Congressional Reform* (Washington, D.C.: CQ Press, 1986).
61. Assistant Secretary of State for Congressional Relations Brian Atwood, as quoted in a dispatch by Martin Tolchin, *New York Times*, December 24, 1979.
62. See the results of public opinion polls dealing with the people's attitudes toward Congress in dispatch by Robin Toner, *New York Times*, October 12, 1990; dispatch by Michael Oreskes, *New York Times*, November 4, 1990; and the Gallup Poll on the Persian Gulf crisis in the *Baton Rouge Morning Advocate*, January 16, 1991.
63. See Christopher, "Ceasefire between the Branches: A Compact in Foreign Affairs," 989-1006.

SUGGESTED READING

Acheson, Dean. *Present at the Creation: My Years in the State Department.* Garden City, N.Y.: Doubleday, 1956.

Adelman, Kenneth L., and Norman R. Augustine. *The Defense Revolution.* San Francisco: ICS, 1990.

Aho, C. Michael, and Marc Levinson. *After Reagan: Confronting the Changed World Economy.* New York: Council on Foreign Relations, 1988.

Al-Chalabi, Fadhil J. *OPEC at the Crossroads.* New York: Pergamon, 1989.

Antle, John M. *World Agricultural Development and the Future of U.S. Agriculture.* Lanham, Md.: American Enterprise Institute, 1988.

Arian, Asher, and Michael Shamir, eds. *The Elections in Israel: 1988.* Boulder, Colo.: Westview, 1991.

Austin, Anthony. *The President's War: The Story of the Tonkin Gulf Resolution and How the Nation Was Trapped in Vietnam.* Philadelphia: Lippincott, 1971.

Avi-Ran, Reuven. *The Syrian Involvement in Lebanon since 1975.* Boulder, Colo.: Westview, 1991.

Bailey, Harry A., Jr., and Jay M. Shafritz. *The American Presidency: Historical and Contemporary Perspective.* Pacific Grove, Calif.: Brooks/Cole, 1988.

Bailey, Sydney D. *Four Arab-Israeli Wars and the Peace Process.* New York: St. Martin's, 1990.

Barnaby, Frank. *The Invisible Bomb: The Nuclear Arms Race in the Middle East.* New York: St. Martin's, 1990.

Barnhart, Michael A., ed. *Congress and United States Foreign Policy: Controlling the Use of Force in the Nuclear Age.* Albany: State University of New York Press, 1987.

Beichman, Arnold. *The Long Pretense: Soviet Treaty Diplomacy from Lenin to Gorbachev.* New Brunswick, N.J.: Transaction Books, 1990.

Berg, Robert J., and David F. Gordon, eds. *Cooperation for International Development: The United States and the Third World in the 1990s.* Boulder, Colo.: Lynne Rienner, 1989.

Bergsten, C. Fred. *America in the World Economy: A Strategy for the 1990s.* Washington, D.C.: Institute for International Economics, 1988.

Berkowitz, Bruce D., and Allan E. Goodman. *Strategic Intelligence for American National Security.* Princeton, N.J.: Princeton University Press, 1990.

Berry, Jeffrey M. *The Interest Group Society.* Glenview, Ill.: Scott, Foresman, 1989.

Berry, Nicholas O. *Foreign Policy and the Press: An Analysis of the New York Times' Coverage of U.S. Foreign Policy.* Boulder, Colo.: Westview, 1990.

Bialer, Seweryn, and Michael Mandelbaum. *Gorbachev's Russia and American Foreign Policy.* Boulder, Colo.: Westview, 1988.

Bill, James A. *The Eagle and the Lion: The Tragedy of American-Iranian Relations.* New Haven, Conn.: Yale University Press, 1988.

Blaker, James R. *United States Overseas Basing: An Anatomy of the Dilemma.* Boulder, Colo.: Westview, 1990.

Bowles, Nigel. *The White House and Capitol Hill: The Politics of Presidential Persuasion.* New York: Oxford University Press, 1987.

Breckinridge, Scott D. *The CIA and the U.S. Intelligence System.* Boulder, Colo.: Westview, 1986.

Brown, Janet W., ed. *In the U.S. Interest: Resources, Growth, and Security in the Developing World.* Boulder, Colo.: Westview, 1990.

Calleo, David P. *Beyond American Hegemony: The Future of the Western Alliance.* New York: Basic Books, 1989.

Campbell, Colin. *Managing the Presidency: Carter, Reagan, and the Search for Executive Harmony.* Pittsburgh, Pa.: University of Pittsburgh Press, 1986.

Carpenter, Ted G., ed. *NATO at 40: Confronting a Changing World.* Washington, D.C.: CATO Institute, 1990.

Cigler, Allan J., and Burdett A. Loomis. *Interest Group Politics.* 3d ed. Washington, D.C.: CQ Press, 1991.

Cohen, Yoel. *Media Diplomacy: The Foreign Office in the Mass Communications Age.* Savage, Md.: Rowman and Littlefield, 1987.

Coker, Christopher. *Reflections on American Foreign Policy since 1945.* New York: St. Martin's, 1988.

Collier, Ellen. *War Powers Resolution: Fifteen Years of Experience.* Washington, D.C.: Congressional Research Service, 1988.

Cordesman, Anthony H. *The Gulf and the West.* Boulder, Colo.: Westview, 1988.

Corwin, Edward S. *The President: Office and Powers, 1787-1957.* 4th rev. ed. New York: New York University Press, 1957.

Crabb, Cecil V., Jr., and Kevin V. Mulcahy. *Presidents and Foreign Policy Making: From FDR to Reagan.* Baton Rouge: Louisiana State University Press, 1986.

Crovitz, L. Gordon, and Jeremy A. Rabkin, eds. *The Fettered Presidency: Legal Constraints on the Executive Branch.* Washington, D.C.: American Enterprise Institute, 1989.

Davies, Peter, ed. *Human Rights.* Rutledge, N.Y.: Chapman and Hall, 1989.

Deibel, Terry L. *Presidents, Public Opinion, and Power: The Nixon, Carter, and Reagan Years.* New York: Foreign Policy Association, 1987.

Deitchman, S. J. *Beyond the Thaw: A New National Strategy.* Boulder, Colo.: Westview, 1991.

DeMuth, Christopher C., et al. *The Reagan Doctrine and Beyond.* Lanham, Md.: University Press of America, 1988.

Destler, I. M. *American Trade Politics: System under Stress.* Washington, D.C.: Institute for International Economics, 1986.

Donnelly, Jack. *Universal Human Rights in Theory and Practice.* Ithaca, N.Y.: Cornell University Press, 1990.

Eberstadt, Nicholas. *Foreign Aid and American Purpose*. Lanham, Md.: University Press of America, 1989.

Edwards, George C. III, and Wallace E. Walker, eds. *National Security and the U.S. Constitution*. Baltimore: Johns Hopkins University Press, 1988.

Eveland, Wilbur Crane. *Ropes of Sand: America's Failure in the Middle East*. New York: Norton, 1980.

Farouk-Sluglett, Marion, and Peter Farouk-Sluglett. *Iraq since 1958: From Revolution to Dictatorship*. New York: St. Martin's, 1991.

Findlay, Trevor. *Chemical Weapons and Missile Proliferation*. Boulder, Colo.: Lynne Rienner, 1991.

Fisher, Louis. *The Politics of Shared Power*. 2d ed. Washington, D.C.: CQ Press, 1987.

Flynn, Gregory, ed. *The West and the Soviet Union: Politics and Strategy*. New York: St. Martin's, 1990.

Forsythe, David P. *Human Rights and U.S. Foreign Policy: Congress Reconsidered*. Gainesville: University of Florida Press, 1988.

_____. *The Politics of International Law: U.S. Foreign Policy Reconsidered*. Boulder, Colo.: Lynne Rienner, 1990.

Fraser, T. G. *The USA and the Middle East since World War 2*. New York: St. Martin's, 1989.

Freedman, Robert O. *Moscow and the Middle East: Soviet Policy since the Invasion of Afghanistan*. New York: Cambridge University Press, 1991.

Frei, Daniel. *Perceived Images: U.S. and Soviet Assumptions and Perceptions in Disarmament*. Savage, Md.: Rowman and Littlefield, 1986.

Fulbright, J. William, with Seth P. Tillman. *The Price of Empire*. New York: Pantheon Books, 1989.

Garthoff, Raymond L. *Policy versus Law: The Reinterpretation of the ABM Treaty*. Washington, D.C.: Brookings, 1987.

Gerner, Deborah J. *One Land, Two Peoples*. Boulder, Colo.: Westview, 1990.

Geron, Leonard. *Soviet Foreign Economic Policy under Perestroika*. New York: Council on Foreign Relations, 1990.

Gibbon, William Conrad. *The U.S. Government and the Vietnam War: Executive and Legislative Roles and Relationships*, pt. 3. Princeton, N.J.: Princeton University Press, 1986.

Gill, William J. *Trade Wars against America: A History of United States Trade and Monetary Policy*. Boulder, Colo.: Westview, 1990.

Godson, Roy, ed. *Intelligence Requirements for the 1990s*. Lexington, Mass.: Lexington Books, 1988.

Golan, Galia. *Soviet Policies in the Middle East: From World War II to Gorbachev*. New York: Cambridge University Press, 1991.

Gold, Dore. *Arms Control in the Middle East*. Boulder, Colo.: Westview, 1991.

Goldberg, David Howard. *Foreign Policy and Ethnic Interest Groups: American and Canadian Jews Lobby for Israel*. Westport, Conn.: Greenwood, 1990.

Goldscheider, Calvin. *Israel's Changing Society: Population, Ethnicity, and Development*. Boulder, Colo.: Westview, 1991.

Goldwin, Robert A., and Robert A. Licht, eds. *Foreign Policy and The Constitution*. Lanham, Md.: University Press of America, 1990.

Graz, Liesl. *The Turbulent Gulf*. New York: St. Martin's, 1990.

Green, Fitzhugh. *American Propaganda Abroad*. New York: Hippocrene, 1988.

Greene, Fred, ed. *The Philippine Bases: Negotiating for the Future: American and Philippine Perspectives*. Washington, D.C.: Council on Foreign Relations, 1988.

Gwertzman, Bernard. *The Lobby: Jewish Political Power and American Foreign Policy.* New York: Simon and Schuster, 1988.

Halberstam, David. *The Best and the Brightest.* New York: Random House, 1972.

Hallenbeck, Ralph A., and David E. Shaver. *On Disarmament: The Role of Conventional Arms Control in National Security Strategy.* Westport, Conn.: Praeger, 1991.

Hamilton, Edward K., ed. *America's Global Interests: A New Agenda.* New York: Norton, 1989.

Hartmann, Frederick H., and Robert L. Wendzel. *Defending America's Security.* New York: Pergamon, 1988.

Hasegawa, Tsuyoshi, and Alex Pravda, eds. *Perestroika: Soviet Domestic and Foreign Policies.* London: Sage, 1990.

Hendrickson, David C. *Reforming Defense: The State of American Civil-Military Relations.* Baltimore: Johns Hopkins University Press, 1988.

Hill, Dilys M. *Human Rights and Foreign Policy.* New York: St. Martin's, 1989.

Hirschbein, Ron. *Newest Weapons/Oldest Psychology: The Dialectics of American Nuclear Strategy.* New York: Peter Lang, 1989.

Holt, Pat M. *The War Powers Resolution: The Role of Congress in U.S. Armed Intervention.* Washington, D.C.: American Enterprise Institute, 1978.

Holtfrerich, Carl-Ludwig, ed. *Economic and Strategic Issues in U.S. Foreign Policy.* New York: Aldine de Gruyter, 1988.

Hudson, Michael C., ed. *The Palestinians: New Directions.* Washington, D.C.: Center for Contemporary Arab Studies, Georgetown University, 1990.

Hunt, Michael H. *Ideology and U.S. Foreign Policy.* New Haven, Conn.: Yale University Press, 1990.

Hyland, William, ed. *The Reagan Foreign Policy.* New York: New American Library, 1988.

Inderfurth, Karl, and Loch K. Johnson, eds. *Decisions of the Highest Order: Perspectives on the National Security Council.* Pacific Grove, Calif.: Brooks/Cole, 1988.

Jackson, John H. *Restructuring the GATT System.* New York: Council on Foreign Relations, 1990.

Jeffreys-Jones, Rhodri. *The CIA and American Democracy.* New Haven, Conn.: Yale University Press, 1989.

Johnson, Loch K. *America's Secret Power: The CIA in a Democratic Society.* New York: Oxford University Press, 1989.

――. *A Season of Inquiry: Congress and Intelligence.* Pacific Grove, Calif.: Brooks/Cole, 1988.

Jorden, William J. *Panama Odyssey.* Austin: University of Texas Press, 1984.

Karnow, Stanley. *In Our Image: America's Empire in the Philippines.* New York: Random House, 1989.

Karp, Aaron. *The United States and the Soviet Union and the Control of Ballistic Missile Proliferation in the Middle East.* Boulder, Colo.: Westview, 1990.

Kegley, Charles W., Jr., and Kenneth L. Schwab, eds. *After the Cold War: Questioning the Morality of Nuclear Deterrence.* Boulder, Colo.: Westview, 1991.

Kellerman, Barbara. *The Political Presidency: The Practice of Leadership from Kennedy through Reagan.* New York: Oxford University Press, 1986.

Kellerman, Barbara, and Ryan J. Barilleaux. *The President as World Leader.* New York: St. Martin's, 1990.

Kernell, Samuel. *Going Public: New Strategies of Presidential Leadership.* Washington, D.C.: CQ Press, 1986.

Kerry, Richard J. *The Star-Spangled Mirror: America's Image of Itself and the World.* Savage, Md.: Rowman and Littlefield, 1990.

Kienle, Eberhard. *Ba'th v. B'ath: The Conflict between Syria and Iraq 1968-1989.* New York: St. Martin's, 1990.

Kim, Ilpyong J. *Korean Challenges and American Policy.* Washington, D.C.: Washington Institute Press, 1991.

Kipper, Judith, and Harold Saunders, eds. *The Middle East in Global Perspective.* Boulder, Colo.: Westview, 1991.

Kirkpatrick, Jeane J. *The Withering Away of the Totalitarian State ... and Other Surprises.* Washington, D.C.: American Enterprise Institute, 1990.

Kissinger, Henry. *White House Years.* Boston: Little, Brown, 1979.

____. *Years of Upheaval.* Boston: Little, Brown, 1982.

Klingberg, Frank L. *Cyclical Trends in American Foreign Policy Moods: The Unfolding of America's World Role.* Lanham, Md.: University Press of America, 1983.

Korany, Bahgat, and Ali E. Hillal Dessouki. *The Foreign Policies of Arab States.* Washington, D.C.: Washington Institute Press, 1991.

Kornacki, John J., ed. *Leading Congress: New Styles, New Strategies.* Washington, D.C.: CQ Press, 1990.

Kozak, David C., and James M. Keagle, eds. *Bureaucratic Politics and National Security: Theory and Practice.* Boulder, Colo.: Lynne Rienner, 1988.

Krickus, Richard J. *The Superpowers in Crisis: Implications of Domestic Discord.* Elmsford, N.Y.: Pergamon, 1988.

Kull, Steven. *Minds at War: Nuclear Reality and the Inner Conflicts of Defense Policymakers.* New York: Basic Books, 1990.

Kyvig, David E., ed. *Reagan and the World.* Westport, Conn.: Praeger, 1990.

Laird, Robbin R., and Susan L. Clark, eds. *The USSR and the Western Alliance.* Boston: Unwin Hyman, 1990.

Lande, Carl H., ed. *Rebuilding a Nation: Philippine Challenges and American Policy.* Washington, D.C.: Washington Institute Press, 1987.

Lawson, Edward H., ed. *Encyclopedia of Human Rights.* Bristol, Pa.: Taylor and Francis, 1991.

Lenczowksi, George. *American Presidents and the Middle East.* Durham, N.C.: Duke University Press, 1989.

Levine, Robert A. *Still the Arms Debate.* Brookfield, Vt.: Dartmouth, 1990.

Lindeman, Mark. *The United States and the Soviet Union: Choices for the 21st Century.* Guilford, Conn.: Dushkin, 1990.

Long, William J. *U.S. Export Control Policy: Executive vs. Congressional Reform.* New York: Columbia University Press, 1989.

Lowi, Theodore J. *The Personal President: Power Invested, Promise Unfulfilled.* Ithaca, N.Y.: Cornell University Press, 1985.

Lukacs, Yehuda, and Abdalla M. Battah, eds. *The Arab-Israeli Conflict: Two Decades of Change.* Boulder, Colo.: Westview, 1988.

Lustick, Ian. *For the Land and the Lord: Jewish Fundamentalism in Israel.* New York: Council on Foreign Relations, 1988.

McNeil, Francis, and Seizaburo Sato. *The Future of U.S.-Japan Relations: A Conference Report.* New York: Council on Foreign Relations, 1988.

Makin, John H., and Donald C. Hellman, eds. *Sharing World Leadership? A New Era for America and Japan.* Westport, Conn.: Greenwood, 1989.

Makinson, Larry. *Open Secrets: The Dollar Power of PACs in Congress.* Washington, D.C.: CQ Press, 1990.

Mann, Thomas E., ed. *A Question of Balance: The President, the Congress, and Foreign Policy.* Washington, D.C.: Brookings, 1990.

Mansfield, Harvey C., Jr. *Taming the Prince: The Ambivalence of Modern Executive Power.* New York: Free Press, 1989.

Marr, Phoebe. *The Modern History of Iraq.* Boulder, Colo.: Westview, 1985.

Maull, Hanns, and Otto Pick. *The Gulf War.* New York: St. Martin's, 1990.

Mayer, Ann Elizabeth. *Islam and Human Rights.* Boulder, Colo.: Westview, 1991.

Mayers, David. *George Kennan and the Dilemmas of U.S. Foreign Policy.* New York: Oxford University Press, 1988.

Melanson, Richard A. *Reconstructing Consensus: American Foreign Policy since the Vietnam War.* New York: St. Martin's, 1991.

Menashri, David, ed. *The Iranian Revolution and the Muslim World.* Boulder, Colo.: Westview, 1990.

Middle East Watch. *Human Rights in Iraq.* New Haven, Conn.: Yale University Press, 1990.

Milkis, Sidney M., and Michael Nelson. *The American Presidency: Origins and Development, 1776-1990.* Washington, D.C.: CQ Press, 1991.

Miller, Judith, and Laurie Mylroie. *Saddam Hussein and the Crisis in the Gulf.* New York: Random House, 1990.

Miner, William M., and Dale E. Hathaway. *World Agricultural Trade: Building a Consensus.* Washington, D.C.: Institute for International Economics, 1988.

Mintz, Alex. *The Politics of Resource Allocation in the U.S. Department of Defense: International Crises and Domestic Constraints.* Boulder, Colo.: Westview, 1988.

Molineu, Harold. *U.S. Policy toward Latin America: From Regionalism to Globalism.* Boulder, Colo.: Westview, 1990.

Morici, Peter, ed. *Making Free Trade Work: The Canada-U.S. Free Trade Agreement.* New York: Council on Foreign Relations, 1990.

Morley, Morris, ed. *Crisis and Confrontation: Ronald Reagan's Foreign Policy.* Savage, Md.: Rowman and Littlefield, 1988.

Muravchik, Joshua. *The Uncertain Crusade: Jimmy Carter and the Dilemmas of Human Rights Policy.* Lanham, Md.: University Press of America, 1986.

——. *The Senate and National Security: A New Mood.* Lanham, Md.: University Press of America, 1986.

Murphy, Craig N., and Roger Tooze. *The New International Political Economy.* Boulder, Colo.: Lynne Rienner, 1991.

Muskie, Edmund, Kenneth Rush, and Kenneth Thompson, eds. *The President, the Congress, and Foreign Policy.* Lanham, Md.: University Press of America, 1986.

Nassar, Jamal R., and Roger Heacock. *Intifada: Palestine at the Crossroads.* Westport, Conn.: Greenwood, 1991.

Nau, Henry R. *The Myth of America's Decline: Leading the World Economy into the 1990s.* New York: Oxford University Press, 1990.

Nelson, Michael. *Presidents and the Public.* Washington, D.C.: CQ Press, 1990.

Nelson, Michael, ed. *The Presidency and the Political System.* 3d ed. Washington, D.C.: CQ Press, 1991.

Newhouse, John. *War and Peace in the Nuclear Age.* New York: Knopf, 1989.

Newsom, David D. *Diplomacy and the American Democracy.* Bloomington: Indiana University Press, 1988.

Newsom, David D., ed. *The Diplomacy of Human Rights*. Lanham, Md.: University Press of America, 1986.

Nuechterlein, Donald E. *America Recommitted: United States National Interests in a Restructured World*. Lexington: University of Kentucky Press, 1991.

Nye, Joseph S. *Bound to Lead: The Changing Nature of American Power*. New York: Basic Books, 1989.

O'Brien, Lee. *American Jewish Organizations and Israel*. Washington, D.C.: Institute for Palestine Studies, 1986.

Organski, A. F. K. *The $36 Billion Bargain: Strategy and Politics in U.S. Assistance to Israel*. New York: Columbia University Press, 1990.

Packard, David. *Management of America's National Defense*. Lanham, Md.: American Enterprise Institute, 1987.

Patterson, Bradley H., Jr. *The Ring of Power: The White House Staff and Its Expanding Role in Government*. New York: Basic Books, 1990.

Perry, Mark. *Four Stars: The Inside Story of the Forty-Year Battle between the Joint Chiefs of Staff and America's Civilian Leaders*. Boulder, Colo.: Westview, 1989.

Pfiffner, James P. *The Managerial Presidency*. Pacific Grove, Calif.: Brooks/Cole, 1991.

_____. *The Strategic Presidency: Hitting the Ground Running*. Pacific Grove, Calif.: Brooks/Cole, 1988.

Pipes, Daniel, and Adam Garfinkle, eds. *Friendly Tyrants: An American Dilemma*. New York: St. Martin's, 1990.

Pirages, Dennis O. *Global Technopolitics: The International Politics of Technology and Resources*. Pacific Grove, Calif.: Brooks/Cole, 1989.

Porter, Michael E. *The Competitive Advantage of Nations*. New York: Free Press, 1990.

Powaski, Ronald E. *March to Armageddon: The United States and the Nuclear Arms Race, 1939 to the Present*. New York: Oxford University Press, 1987.

Quandt, William B. *The United States and Egypt*. Washington, D.C.: Brookings, 1990.

Quandt, William B., ed. *The Middle East: Ten Years after Camp David*. Washington, D.C.: Brookings, 1988.

Rabie, Mohammed. *The Politics of Foreign Aid: U.S. Foreign Assistance and Aid to Israel*. New York: Praeger, 1988.

Ranelagh, John. *The Agency: The Rise and Decline of the CIA*. New York: Simon and Schuster, 1990.

Reilly, John E., ed. *American Public Opinion and U.S. Foreign Policy, 1987*. Chicago: Chicago Council on Foreign Relations, 1987.

Rezun, Miron. *Iran at the Crossroads: Global Relations in a Turbulent Decade*. Boulder, Colo.: Westview, 1990.

Richelson, Jeffrey T. *The U.S. Intelligence Community*. Cambridge, Mass.: Ballinger, 1985.

Rizopoulos, Nicholas X., ed. *Sea-Changes: American Foreign Policy in a World Transformed*. New York: Council on Foreign Relations, 1990.

Rondinelli, Dennis A. *Development Administration and U.S. Foreign Aid Policy*. Boulder, Colo.: Lynne Rienner, 1987.

Rozell, Mark J. *The Press and the Carter Presidency*. Boulder, Colo.: Westview, 1989.

Sarkesian, Sam C. *U.S. National Security: Policymakers, Processes, and Politics*. Boulder, Colo.: Lynne Rienner, 1989.

Schieffer, Bob, and Gary Paul Gates. *The Acting President*. New York: Penguin, 1990.

Schott, Jeffrey J., ed. *Free Trade Areas and U.S. Policy*. Washington, D.C.: Institute for International Economics, 1989.

Schott, Jeffrey J., and Murray G. Smith, eds. *The Canada-United States Free Trade Agreement: The Global Impact*. Washington, D.C.: Institute for International Economics, 1988.

Schraeder, Peter J., ed. *Intervention in the 1980s: U.S. Foreign Policy in the Third World*. Boulder, Colo.: Lynne Rienner, 1989.

Seabury, Paul, and Angelo Codevilla. *War: Ends and Means*. New York: Basic Books, 1990.

Seligman, Lester G., and Cary R. Covington. *The Coalitional Presidency*. Pacific Grove, Calif.: Brooks/Cole, 1989.

Serfaty, Simon, ed. *The Media and Foreign Policy*. New York: St. Martin's, 1990.

Shalev, Aryeh. *The Intifada*. Boulder, Colo.: Westview, 1991.

Shoemaker, Christopher C. *The NSC Staff: Counseling the Council*. Boulder, Colo.: Westview, 1991.

Sick, Gary. *All Fall Down: America's Tragic Encounter with Iran*. New York: Random House, 1985.

Sicker, Martin. *Israel's Quest for Security*. Westport, Conn.: Greenwood, 1989.

Smith, Carolyn. *Presidential Press Conferences: A Critical Approach*. Boulder, Colo.: Westview, 1990.

Smoller, Fredric T. *The Six O'Clock Presidency: A Theory of Presidential Press Relations in the Age of Television*. Boulder, Colo.: Westview, 1990.

Smyrl, Marc E. *Conflict or Codetermination? Congress, the President, and the Power to Make War*. Cambridge, Mass.: Ballinger, 1988.

Snow, Donald M. *National Security: Enduring Problems in a Changing Defense Environment*. 2d ed. New York: St. Martin's, 1991.

——. *Soviet-American Security Relations in the 1990s*. Lexington, Mass.: Lexington Books, 1989.

Sonn, Tamara. *Between Qur'an and Crown*. Boulder, Colo.: Westview, 1990.

Spector, Leonard S. *The Undeclared Bomb: The Spread of Nuclear Weapons, 1987-88*. Hagerstown, Md.: Ballinger, 1988.

Spero, Joan E. *The Politics of International Economic Relations*. 4th ed. New York: St. Martin's, 1991.

Springborg, Robert. *Mubarak's Egypt*. Boulder, Colo.: Westview, 1989.

Starr, Richard F. *United States-East European Relations in the 1990s*. New York: Crane Russak, 1989.

Stein, Herbert. *Presidential Economics: The Making of Economic Policy from Roosevelt to Reagan and Beyond*. Westport, Conn.: Greenwood, 1988.

Steinbruner, John D., ed. *Restructuring American Foreign Policy*. Washington, D.C.: Brookings, 1988.

Stock, Ernest. *Partners & Pursestrings: A History of the United Israel Appeal*. Lanham, Md.: University Press of America, 1987.

Strong, Robert J. *Bureaucracy and Statesmanship: Henry Kissinger and the Making of American Foreign Policy*. Lanham, Md.: University Press of America, 1986.

Tanter, Raymond. *Who's at the Helm? Lessons of Lebanon*. Boulder, Colo.: Westview, 1990.

Tarr, David W. *Nuclear Deterrence and International Security*. New York: Longman, 1991.

Taylor, Alan R. *The Islamic Question in Middle East Politics*. Boulder, Colo.: Westview, 1988.

Thompson, Kenneth W., ed. *Sam Nunn on Arms Control*. Lanham, Md.: University Press of America, 1988.

Thornton, Richard C. *The Carter Years: Toward a New Global Order*. Washington, D.C.: Washington Institute Press, 1991.

Thurber, James A. *Divided Democracy: Presidents and Congress in Cooperation and Conflict*. Washington, D.C.: CQ Press, 1991.

Tillema, Herbert K., *International Armed Conflict since 1945*. Boulder, Colo.: Westview, 1991.

Tomasevski, Katarina. *Development Aid and Human Rights*. New York: St. Martin's, 1989.

Tow, William T., ed. *Building Sino-American Relations: An Analysis for the 1990s*. Washington, D.C.: Washington Institute Press, 1991.

Treverton, Gregory F. *Covert Action: The Limits of Intervention in the Post-War World*. New York: Basic Books, 1989.

Treverton, Gregory F., ed. *Europe and America beyond 2000*. Washington, D.C.: Council on Foreign Relations, 1989.

Truman, Harry S. *Memoirs: Year of Decisions*. Garden City, N.Y.: Doubleday, 1955.

_____. *Memoirs: Years of Trial and Hope*. Garden City, N.Y.: Doubleday, 1956.

Tuch, Hans N. *Communicating with the World: U.S. Public Diplomacy Overseas*. New York: St. Martin's, 1991.

Vernon, Raymond, ed. *The Promise of Privatization: A Challenge for American Foreign Policy*. Washington, D.C.: Council on Foreign Relations, 1990.

Vernon, Raymond, and Debora Spar. *Beyond Globalism: Remaking American Foreign Economic Policy*. New York: Free Press, 1988.

Vincent, R. J., ed. *Foreign Policy and Human Rights*. New York: Cambridge University Press, 1986.

Vogelgesang, Sandy. *American Dream, Global Nightmare: The Dilemma of U.S. Human Rights Policy*. New York: Norton, 1980.

Warburg, Gerald Felix. *Conflict and Consensus: The Struggle between Congress and the President over Foreign Policymaking*. New York: Harper and Row, 1989.

Warner, Edward L. III, and David A. Ochmanek. *Next Moves: An Arms Control Agenda for the 1990s*. New York: Council on Foreign Relations, 1988.

The Washington Lobby. 5th ed. Washington, D.C.: Congressional Quarterly, 1987.

Webber, Philip. *New Defense Strategies for the 1990s*. New York: St. Martin's, 1991.

Weinberg, Alvin M., and Jack N. Barkenbus. *Strategic Defenses and Arms Control*. Washington, D.C.: Washington Institute Press, 1988.

West, Darrell M. *Congress and Economic Policymaking*. Pittsburgh, Pa.: University of Pittsburgh Press, 1987.

Weston, Burns H., ed. *Alternative Security: Living without Nuclear Deterrence*. Boulder, Colo.: Westview, 1990.

Whalen, Charles W., Jr. *The House and Foreign Policy: The Irony of Congressional Reform*. Chapel Hill: University of North Carolina Press, 1982.

Wiarda, Howard J. *Foreign Policy without Illusion*. Glenview, Ill.: Scott, Foresman, 1990.

_____. *On the Agenda: Current Issues and Conflicts in U.S. Foreign Policy*. Glenview, Ill.: Scott, Foresman, 1990.

Williams, Phil. *The Senate and U.S. Troops in Europe.* New York: St. Martin's, 1985.

Woodward, Bob. *VEIL: The Secret Wars of the CIA: 1981-1987.* New York: Simon and Schuster, 1987.

Wormuth, Francis D., and Edwin B. Firmage. *To Chain the Dog of War: The War Power of Congress in History and Law.* 2d ed. Champaign: University of Illinois Press, 1989.

Wyden, Peter. *Bay of Pigs: The Untold Story.* New York: Simon and Schuster, 1979.

INDEX